LITERATURE OF THE EARLY REPUBLIC

LITERATURE

OF THE

EARLY REPUBLIC

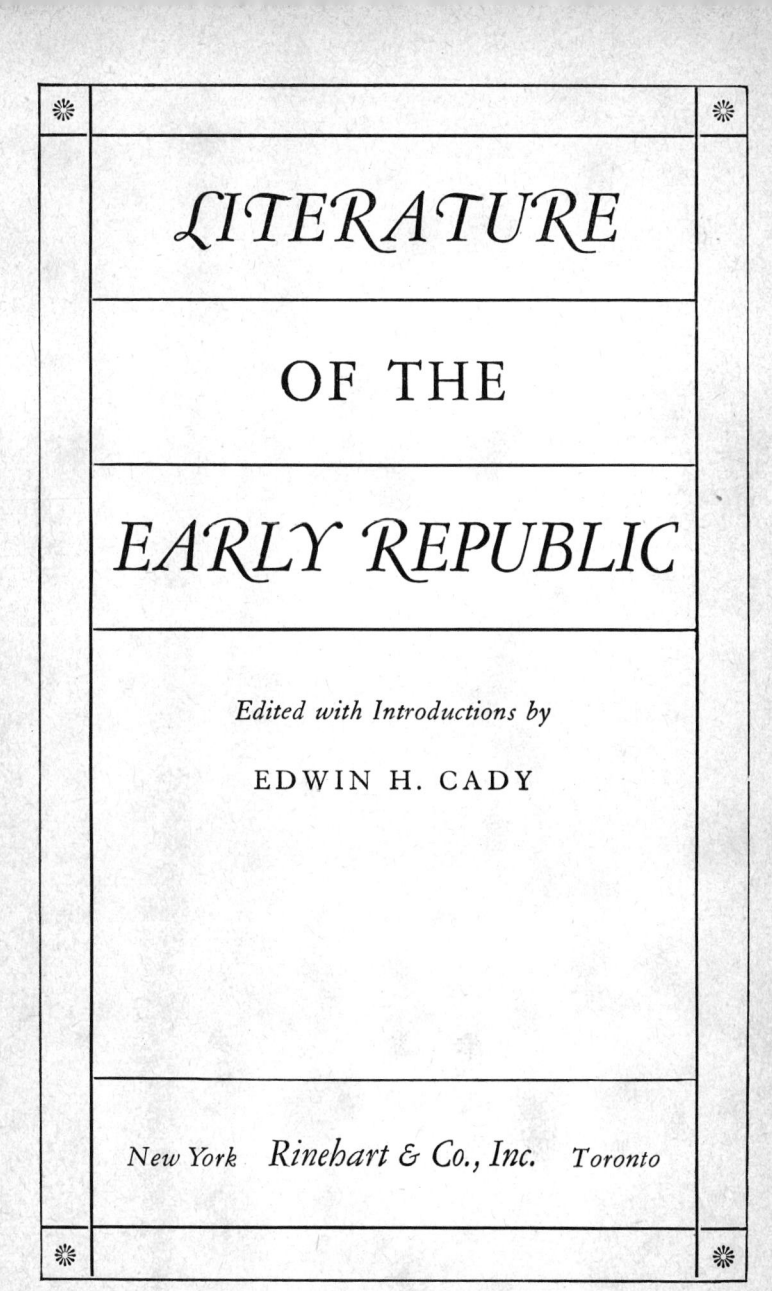

Edited with Introductions by

EDWIN H. CADY

New York *Rinehart & Co., Inc.* Toronto

Third Printing, April 1960

Introduction *copyright, 1950, by Edwin H. Cady*
Typography and Cover Design by Stefan Salter
Printed in the United States of America

INTRODUCTION

The contents of this book represent American literature in the period roughly from 1763 until 1815. These are the years, between the expulsion of the French imperial power and American survival of the War of 1812, of what may be called the period of the early republic. The most important feature of that period was the shaping of America—its laws, institutions, manners, ideas, and art—its character and culture. In simple but useful terms one may define literature as writing which aims at and achieves some emotional-imaginative, some artistic goal beyond mere direct sign-communication. In these terms, the core of this book is the literature of the shaping of American character and culture. The contents, therefore, were selected to represent the major minds, the major genres, the dominant conventions, ideas, and themes of the day. For the purposes of this collection, however, these features were considered more for their importance to the greater future of American writing than for vogue or prestige limited to the period. As in its companion volume, *Colonial American Writing,* the emphasis is on origins and sources which, out of this gestative period, develop into the later flowering of American literature and culture.

The book is divided into three sections. Section I gathers the literature of persuasion which particularly had to do with the making of the republic, from the early intimations of independence in John Dickinson to the vibrant reminiscences of Jefferson and Adams. Section II gathers writing which reflects important patterns of life and thought in the period. Section III is concerned with the effort of the day to create an American literature both genuinely national and genuinely artistic. Each section and each selection has its own brief introduction. In these an effort has been made to provide interesting background and peripheral materials but to avoid coming between reader and text, or between student and teacher. The suggested readings throughout have been rigorously screened for importance and general availability.

Edwin H. Cady

SUGGESTED READINGS

The three major studies of the period are Moses Coit Tyler, *The Literary History of the American Revolution, 1763-1783* (New York: 1897; reprinted Cornell University Press: 1949); Vernon L. Parrington, *Main Currents in American Thought* (New York: 1930); and the multi-edited *Literary History of the United States* (New York: 1948) vol. I, and especially the bibliographies in vol. III. Other useful general sources are: Merle Curti, *The Growth of American Thought* (New York: 1943); Herbert L. Schneider, *A History of American Philosophy* (New York: 1946); Oliver Larkin, *Art and Life in America* (New York: 1949); Dixon Wecter, *The Saga of American Society* (New York: 1937); Edwin H. Cady, *The Gentleman in America* (Syracuse: 1949); William Charvat, *The Origins of American Critical Thought, 1810-1835* (Philadelphia: 1936); Joseph Dorfman, *The Economic Mind in American Civilization,* I (New York: 1946); G. A. Koch, *Republican Religion* (New York: 1933); Lyon Richardson, *A History of Early American Magazines, 1741-1789* (New York: 1931); Leon Howard, *The Connecticut Wits* (Chicago: 1943); and two extraordinarily suggestive articles by H. H. Clark: "Factors to be Investigated in American Literary History from 1787 to 1800," *The English Journal,* Vol. XXIII, June, 1934; and "Influence of Science on American Ideas, from 1775 to 1809," *Trans. Wisconsin Academy of Science, Art, Letters,* Vol. XXXV, 1944.

GENERAL INTRODUCTION

CONTENTS

GENERAL INTRODUCTION — v

SECTION I
THE MAKING OF THE REPUBLIC

INTRODUCTION — 1
1. John Dickinson: from *Letters from a Farmer in Pennsylvania*, Letter XII — 4
2. Thomas Jefferson: *Declaration of Independence* — 13
3. Thomas Paine: — 19
    from *The Crisis*, no. I — 20
    from *The Rights of Man*, Part II — 28
    from *The Age of Reason* Credo — 55
4. Mercy Warren: from *History of the American Revolution*, Chapter XXX — 57
5. George Washington: *Circular to the States* — 64
6. Alexander Hamilton and James Madison: from *The Federalist*, I, X, XXIII — 75
7. Philip Freneau: from *Letters on Various ... Subjects*, Introduction, XIX, XX — 94
8. Fisher Ames: from *The Dangers of American Liberty* — 108
9. John Adams and Thomas Jefferson: from Correspondence, 1813-1826 — 117

SECTION II
PATTERNS OF LIFE AND THOUGHT IN AMERICA

INTRODUCTION — 149
1. John Trumbull: from *The Progress of Dulness* — 151
2. Hugh Henry Brackenridge: from *Modern Chivalry* — 182
3. Timothy Dwight: from *Greenfield Hill* — 214
4. Lorenzo Dow: from *Exemplified Experience* — 221
5. Benjamin Rush: *The Influence of Physical Causes Upon the Moral Faculty* — 241

6. John Taylor of Caroline: from *Arator,* nos. 59, 60	262
7. Two French Views of America:	
Moreau de St. Méry: from *The American Journey*	271
Hector St. John de Crèvecoeur: from *Letters from an American Farmer,* II, III	284

SECTION III

A NATIONAL LITERARY CULTURE

INTRODUCTION	299
1. Benjamin Franklin:	
To Mrs. Abiah Franklin, April 12, 1750	302
The Way to Wealth	303
To Miss Mary Stevenson, June 11, 1760	313
To Peter Collinson, October 19, 1752	315
To Joseph Priestley, February 8, 1780	316
An Edict by the King of Prussia	317
The Sale of the Hessians	321
The Ephemera	323
The Whistle	325
Articles of Belief and Acts of Religion	328
A Parable Against Persecution	335
A Parable on Brotherly Love	336
2. Philip Freneau	
"To an Author"	338
from *Pictures of Columbus,* XIV-XVII	340
The House of Night	347
The Beauties of Santa Cruz	357
"The Hurricane"	373
"To the Memory of the Brave Americans"	375
"The Wild Honey Suckle"	376
"The Indian Burying Ground"	377
"The Vanity of Existence"	378
from *Political Biography*	379
"A Political Litany"	379
"Epigram"	381

"Lines [on Rivington]"	381
"To a Noisy Politician"	382
"Stanzas [on Thomas Paine]"	383
"Ode [God Save the Rights of Man]"	384
"Reflections"	386
"On the Universality and Other Attributes of the God of Nature"	388
"On the Uniformity and Perfection of Nature"	389
"On the Religion of Nature"	390
3. Royall Tyler: *The Contrast*	392
4. Literary Criticism	
I Hugh Henry Brackenridge: from *Modern Chivalry*	452
II Timothy Dwight: from *The Friend*, no. IV	461
III Noah Webster: "To the Authors of the London Review"	467
IV Joseph Dennie: On Gothicism	474
On Franklin	477
"Freneau's Poems"	481

LITERATURE OF THE EARLY REPUBLIC

THE MAKING OF THE REPUBLIC

The men and women who made the American republic produced a body of writings as enduringly important as their historic actions. These writings belong to a minor but significant form of literature, a form practiced at its height in times of historic crisis. The form may be called the literature of persuasion, and the Founding Fathers commanded it with greatness. In the highest sincerity they created propaganda which was effective in its own day and which sometimes transcended its immediate and transient aim to reach the stature of permanent thought. To succeed so well this writing had to be well conceived. But its writers also had to use all the arts of persuasion. They had to master the forms of those arts—oratory, pamphleteering, satire, irony, the manifesto. They had to control the strategies of logic, imagery, rhetoric, and rhythmic force. They did all these things with a virtuosity which makes modern politicians and patriots often seem pale by contrast.

Any reader or student of these writings will profit from being alert to spot the themes in them which were decisive in shaping the future of large portions of American life and letters. Many of them have remained alive as issues or problems until our own day. Though such enduring themes are interlocked and inseparable in their real, living forms, they may be separately named for convenience. One rapidly developing theme, running from the writings of John Dickinson to those of the aged Jefferson and Adams, is the question of American identity. It begins as an assertion that America *is* a separate entity and Americans a family of men, different from their European ancestors and cousins, entitled to justice and relief from Tory tyranny and exploitation. Then came the declaration of American independence, and after the war the reality of independence. But when America becomes an independent nation, the question arises: what is its destiny to be? Is this not a special experiment, conceived in liberty? And with affirmative answers to that question comes the assertion of the American Dream. America is to be the "last, best hope of earth," a nation where humanity, freed of the centuries of inherited guilt and crime on ancient soils, can spring up to new heights of perfection, freedom, security, and self-fulfillment.

Two other major themes are equally fateful: the opposed but mutually supporting issues of liberty and security. The theme of liberty stems from a wide-flung net of cultural configuration involving philosophy, religion, economics, geography, and social patterns. It gains expression in the drives for independence, representative government, the relaxation of restrictions upon the individual in all areas of life, and eventually in the creation of the ideal of democracy as a way of life resting upon a special set of values. The theme of security, of responsibility, efficiency, and unity, begins partly in recoil from the possibilities of chaos following on revolutionary action, and partly in creative response to the demands and potentialities of the new situation. Its patterns are equally wide and in the main overlaid upon the democratic patterns. But it is concerned with structure and function, with making society and its institutions work well. Stressing statesmanship and responsibility, it tends to restrain the democratic rush toward newness. It reverts, even, toward the tradition of government by gentry, toward the patterns and values of patricianism. Except in the midst of political warfare, almost every good mind responds to both themes. But Jefferson, Freneau, and Mercy Warren tend toward the democratic; Dickinson, Washington, Adams and Hamilton toward the patrician. Paine is on the far, democratic left; Ames on the reactionary right; Madison apparently firmly in the center.

The selections have also been arranged to help give some historical context to what the writers have to say. By moving from Dickinson through Paine and Jefferson into Mercy Warren's summary, one can get a broad view of the American Revolution. In Washington, Hamilton, and Madison he can find the issues summarized which led to the Constitution. In Freneau and Ames he can find typical statements from the Federalist-Jeffersonian controversy which continues still to reverberate in American politics and thought. And in Adams and Jefferson there is a long, mellow, uniquely well-informed view of the entire scene.

JOHN DICKINSON
(*1732-1808*)

So long as the debate between the Colonies and England was confined to issues short of revolution, John Dickinson was the ideal American spokesman. His legalism, Latinity, and moderation were welcome to his fellows among the gentry. His proclamation of American identity and American rights and his defiance of Tory machinations in London had popular appeal. *The Letters from a Farmer in Pennsylvania* (1768) were widely reprinted in colonial newspapers. They won reputation in Great Britain and even recognition on the Continent.

Dickinson lost much of his reputation and influence as soon as the American situation became revolutionary. One of the few members of the Congress actually in the field as a soldier, he was nevertheless lastingly stigmatized by his refusal to join the famous Fourth of July acceptance of the Declaration of Independence. Eventually he served as a distinguished member of the Constitutional Convention, moderation having come into fashion again. Just as the American Revolution is a classic among revolutions, so John Dickinson—the man, the style, the works—is a classic example of the moderate, his function and his fate, in the developing course of a revolution.

Bibliography: Charles J. Stillé: *The Life and Times of John Dickinson,* 1732-1808, Philadelphia, 1891; Tyler, I, 234-241; II, 21-34; Parrington, I, 219-232.

Text: *The Writings of John Dickinson:* Vol. I, *Political Writings, 1764-1774,* Philadelphia, 1895.

from LETTERS FROM A FARMER IN PENNSYLVANIA

LETTER XII

My Dear COUNTRYMEN,

Some states have lost their liberty by *particular accidents:* But this calamity is generally owing to the *decay of virtue.* A *people* is travelling fast to destruction, when *individuals* consider *their* interests as distinct from *those of the public.* Such notions are fatal to their country, and to themselves. Yet how many are there, so *weak* and *sordid* as to *think* they perform *all the offices of life,* if they earnestly endeavor to encrease their own *wealth, power,* and *credit,* without the least regard for the society, under the protection of which they live; who, if they can make an *immediate profit to themselves,* by lending their assistance to those, whose projects plainly tend to the injury of their country, rejoice in their *dexterity,* and believe themselves entitled to the character of *able politicians.* Miserable men! Of whom it is hard to say, whether they ought to be most the objects of *pity* or *contempt:* But whose opinions are certainly as *detestable,* as their practices are *destructive.*

Tho' I always reflect, with a high pleasure, on the integrity and understanding of my countrymen, which, joined with a pure and humble devotion to the great and gracious author of every blessing they enjoy, will, I hope, ensure to them, and their posterity, all temporal and eternal happiness; yet when I consider, that in every age and country there have been bad men, my heart, at this threatening period, is so full of apprehension, as not to permit me to believe, but that there may be some on this continent, *against whom you ought to be upon your guard*—Men, who either[1] hold, or expect to hold certain advantages, by

---

[1] It is not intended by these words, to throw any reflection upon gentlemen, because they are possessed of offices: For many of them are certainly men of virtue, and lovers of their country. But supposed obligations of *gratitude,* and *honor,* may induce them to be silent. Whether these obligations *ought to be* regarded or not, is not so much to be considered by others, in the judgment they form of these gentlemen, as whether *they think* they ought to be regarded. Perhaps, therefore, we shall act in the properest manner towards them, if we neither *reproach* nor *imitate* them. The persons meant in this letter, are the *base-spirited wretches,* who may endeavour to *distinguish themselves,* by their sordid zeal in defending and promoting measures, which *they know beyond all question,* to be *destructive* to the *just rights* and *true interests* of their country. It is scarcely possible to speak of *these men* with any degree of *patience*—It is scarcely possible to speak of them with any degree of *propriety*—For no words can truly describe their *guilt* and *meanness* —But every honest bosom, on their being mentioned, will *feel* what cannot be *expressed.*

If their wickedness did not blind them, they might perceive along the coast of these colonies, many men, remarkable instances of wrecked ambition, who after *distinguishing themselves* in the support of the *Stamp-Act,* by a courageous contempt of their country, and of justice, have been left to linger out their miserable existence, without a government, collectorship, secretaryship, or any other commission, to console them *as well as it could,* for loss of virtue and reputation—while numberless offices have been bestowed in these colonies on people from *Great-*

setting examples of servility to their countrymen. Men, who trained to the employment, or self taught by a natural versatility of genius, serve as decoys for drawing the innocent and unaware into snares. It is not to be doubted but that such men will diligently bestir themselves on this and every like occasion, to spread the infection of their meanness as far as they can. On the plans *they* have adopted, this is *their* course. *This* is the method to recommend themselves to their *patrons*.

From *them* we shall learn, how *pleasant* and *profitable* a thing it is, to be for our SUBMISSIVE behavior *well spoken of* at *St. James* or *St. Stephen's;* at *Guildhall,* or the *Royal Exchange*. Specious fallacies will be drest up with all the arts of delusion, to persuade one colony *to distinguish herself from another,* by unbecoming condescensions, *which will serve the ambitious purposes of great men* at home, and therefore will be thought by them *to entitle their assistants in obtaining them* to considerable rewards.

Our fears will be excited. Our hopes will be awakened. It will be insinuated to us, with a plausible affection of *wisdom* and *concern,* how *prudent* it is to please the *powerful*—how *danger-*

Britain, and new ones are continually invented, to be thus bestowed. As a *few great prizes* are put into a lottery to TEMPT *multitudes to lose,* so *here* and *there* an *American* has been raised to a good post.—"*Apparent* rari nantes *in gurgite vasto.*" [A few swimmers appear in a mighty flood.] Mr. *Greenville,* indeed, in order to recommend the *Stamp-Act,* had the *unequalled* generosity, to pour down a golden shower of offices upon *Americans;* and yet these *ungrateful* colonies did not thank Mr. *Greenville* for shewing his kindness to their countrymen, nor *them* for accepting it. How must that great statesman have been surprised, to find, that the unpolished colonies could not be reconciled to *infamy* by *treachery?* Such a *bountiful* disposition toward us never appeared in any minister before him, and probably never will appear again: For it is *evident,* that *such a system* of policy is to be established on this continent, as, in a short time, is to render it utterly unnecessary to use the least *art* in order to *conciliate* our approbation of any measures. Some of our countrymen may be employed to *fix* chains upon us, but *they* will never be permitted to *hold* them afterwards. So that the utmost, that any of them can expect, is only a *temporary provision,* that *may* expire in their own time; but which they may *be assured,* will preclude their children from having any consideration paid to *them.* NATIVES of *America* must sink into total NEGLECT and CONTEMPT, the moment that THEIR COUNTRY loses the constitutional power she now possesses.—*Dickinson.*

ous to provoke them—and then comes in the perpetual incantation that freezes up every generous purpose of the soul in cold, inactive expectation—"that if there is any request to be made, compliance will obtain a favorable attention."

Our *vigilance* and our *union* are *success* and *safety*. Our *negligence* and our *division* are *distress* and *death*. They are *worse*—they are *shame* and *slavery*. Let us equally shun the benumbing stillness of *overweening sloath,* and the feverish activity of that *ill informed zeal,* which busies itself in maintaining *little, mean,* and *narrow* opinions. Let us, with a truly wise *generosity* and *charity,* banish and discourage all *illiberal distinctions,* which may arise from differences in *situation,* forms of *government,* or modes of *religion.* Let us consider ourselves as MEN—FREEMEN—CRHISTIAN FREEMEN—*separate from the rest of the world,* and *firmly bound together* by the *same rights, interests* and *dangers.* Let *these* keep our attention inflexibly fixed on the GREAT OBJECTS, which we must CONTINUALLY REGARD, in order to *preserve those rights,* to *promote those interests,* and to *avert those dangers.*

Let these *truths* be indelibly impressed on our minds—*that we cannot be* HAPPY, *without being* FREE—that we cannot be free, *without being secure in our property*—that *we* cannot be secure in our property, *if, without our consent, others may, as by right, take it away*—that *taxes imposed on us by parliament,* do thus take it away—that *duties laid for the sole purpose of raising money,* are taxes—that *attempts* to lay such duties *should be instantly and firmly opposed*—that this opposition can never be effectual, *unless it is the united effort of these provinces*—that therefore BENEVOLENCE *of temper towards each other,* and UNANIMITY *of councils,* are essential to the welfare of the whole—and lastly, that for this reason, every man amongst us, who in any manner would encourage either *dissension, diffidence,* or *indifference,* between these colonies, is an enemy to *himself,* and to *his country.*

The belief of these truths, I verily think, my countrymen, is indispensably necessary to your happiness. I beseech you, therefore,[2] "teach them diligently unto your children, and talk of them when you sit in your houses, and when you walk by the way, and when you lie down, and when you rise up." What have these colonies to *ask*, while they continue free? Or what have they to *dread*, but insidious attempts to subvert their freedom? *Their prosperity* does not depend on *ministerial favors doled* out to *particular* provinces. *They* form *one* political body, of which *each colony* is a *member*. *Their happiness* is founded on *their constitution;* and is to be promoted, by preserving that constitution in unabated vigor, *throughout every part.* A spot, a speck of decay, however small the limb on which it appears, and however remote it may seem from the vitals, should be alarming. We have *all the rights* requisite for our prosperity. The *legal authority* of *Great-Britain* may indeed lay hard restrictions upon us; but, like the spear of *Telephus,* it will cure as well as wound. Her unkindness will instruct and compel us, after some time, to discover, in our *industry* or *frugality,* surprising remedies—*if our rights continue unviolated:* For as long as the *products* of our *labor,* and the *rewards* of our *care,* can properly be called *our own,* so long it will be worth our while to be *industrious* and *frugal.* But if when we plow—sow—reap—gather —and thresh—we find that we plow—sow—reap—gather—and thresh *for others,* whose PLEASURE is to be the SOLE LIMITATION *how much* they shall *take,* and *how much* they shall *leave,* WHY should we repeat the unprofitable toil? *Horses* and *oxen* are content with *that portion of the fruits of their work,* which their *owners* assign them, in order to keep them strong enough to raise successive crops; but even *these beasts* will not submit to draw for their *masters,* until they are *subdued* by *whips* and *goads.*

Let us take care of our *rights,* and we *therein* take care of *our prosperity.* "SLAVERY IS EVER PRECEDED BY SLEEP."[3] *Individuals* may be *dependent* on ministers, if they please. STATES SHOULD SCORN IT;—and if *you* are not wanting *to yourselves,* you

---
[2] Deuteron, vi. 7.—*Dickinson.*
[3] *Montesquieu's* Spirits of Laws, Book 14, Chap. 13.—*Dickinson.*

will have a *proper regard* paid *you* by *those,* to whom if you are not *respectable,* you will be *contemptible.* But—if *we have already forgot* the *reasons* that urged us, with unexampled unanimity, to exert ourselves two years ago—if *our zeal* for the public good is *worn out* before the *homespun cloaths,* which it has caused us to have made—if *our resolutions* are *so faint,* as by our present conduct to *condemn* our own late *successful* example—if *we are not affected* by any reverence for the memory of our ancestors, who transmitted to us that freedom in which they had been blest—if *we are not animated* by any regard for posterity, to whom, by the most sacred obligations, we are bound to deliver down the invaluable inheritance—THEN, indeed, any *minister*—or any *tool* of a minister—or any *creature* of a tool of a minister—or *any lower[4] instrument of[5] administration,* if lower there be, is a *personage* whom it may be dangerous to offend.

---

[4] "Instrumenta regni." *Tacitus's* Ann. *Book* 12, § 66.—*Dickinson.*

[5] If any person shall imagine that he discovers, in these letters, the least dislike of the dependence of these colonies on *Great-Britain,* I beg that such persons will not form any judgment on *particular expressions,* but will consider the *tenor of all the letters taken together.* In that case, I flatter myself, that every unprejudiced reader will be *convinced,* that the true interests of *Great-Britain* are as dear to me, as they ought to be to every good subject.

If I am an *Enthusiast* in any thing, it is in my zeal for the *perpetual dependence* of these colonies on their mother country.—A dependence founded on *mutual benefits,* the continuance of which can be secured only by *mutual affections.* Therefore it is, that with extreme apprehension I view the smallest seeds of discontent, which are unwarily scattered abroad. *Fifty* or *Sixty* years will make astonishing alterations in these colonies; and this consideration should render it the business of *Great-Britain* more and more to cultivate our good dispositions toward her: But the misfortune is, that those *great men,* who are wrestling for power at home, think themselves very slightly interested in the prosperity of their country *Fifty* or *Sixty* years hence, but are deeply concerned in blowing up a popular clamour for supposed *immediate advantage.*

For my part, I regard *Great-Britain* as a Bulwark, happily fixed between these colonies and the powerful nations of *Europe.* That kingdom remaining safe, we, under its protection, enjoying peace, may diffuse the blessings of religion, science, and liberty, thro' remote wildernesses. It is therefore incontestably our *duty,* and our *interest,* to support the strength of *Great-Britain.* When confiding in that strength, she begins to forget from whence it arose, it will be an easy thing to shew the source. She may readily be reminded of the loud alarm spread among her merchants and tradesmen, by the universal associations of these colonies, at the time of the *Stamp-Act,* not to import any of her MANUFACTURES.

I shall be extremely sorry, if any man mistakes my meaning in anything I have said. Officers employed by the crown, are, while according to the laws they conduct themselves, entitled to legal obedience, and sincere respect. These it is a duty to render them; and these no good or prudent person will withhold. But when these officers, thro' rashness or design, desire to enlarge their authority beyond its due limits, and expect improper concessions to be made to them, from regard for the employments they bear, their attempts should be considered as equal injuries to the crown and people, and should be courageously and constantly opposed. To suffer our ideas to be confounded by *names* on such occasions, would certainly be an *inexcusable weakness,* and probably an *irremediable error*.

We have reason to believe, that several of his Majesty's present ministers are good men, and friends to our country; and it seems not unlikely, that by a particular concurrence of events, we have been treated a little more severely than they wished we should be. *They* might not think it prudent to stem a torrent. But what is the difference to *us*, whether arbitrary acts take their rise from ministers, or are permitted by them? Ought any point to be allowed to[6] a good minister, that should be denied to a bad one?

In the year 1718, the *Russians* and *Swedes* entered into an agreement, not to suffer *Great-Britain* to export any NAVAL STORES from their dominions but in *Russian* or *Swedish* ships, and at their own prices. *Great-Britain* was distressed. *Pitch* and *tar* rose to *Three pounds* a barrel. At length she thought of getting these articles from the colonies; and the attempt succeeding, they fell down to *Fifteen shillings*. In the year 1756, *Great-Britain* was threatened with an invasion. An easterly wind blowing for six weeks, she could not MAN her fleet, and the whole nation was thrown into the utmost consternation. The wind changed. The *American* ships arrived. The fleet sailed in ten or fifteen days. There are some other reflections on this subject, worthy of the most deliberate attention of the *British* parliament; but they are of such a nature, that I do not chuse to mention them publicly. I thought it my duty, in the year 1765, while the *Stamp-Act* was in suspence, to write my sentiments to a gentleman of great influence at home, who afterwards distinguished himself, by espousing our cause, in the debates concerning the repeal of that act.—*Dickinson*.

[6] Ubi imperium ad ignaros aut minus bonos pervenit; *novum illud exemplum,* a dignis, & idoneis, ad indignos & non idoneos *transfertur.*—*Sall*. Bell. Cat. § 50. —*Dickinson*. [Where power belongs to the ignorant or the bad, the new model, from the worthy and fit, becomes the unworthy and unfit.]

The mortality of ministers, is a very frail mortality. A ——— may succeed a *Shelburne*—A ——— may succeed a *Cornway*.

We find a new kind of minister lately spoken of at home—"THE MINISTER OF THE HOUSE OF COMMONS." The term seems to have peculiar propriety when referred to these colonies, *with a different meaning annexed to it,* from that in which it is taken there. By the word "minister" we may understand not only a *servant of the crown,* but a *man of influence* among the commons, who regard themselves as having a share in the *sovereignty* over us. The "minister OF the house" may, in a point respecting the colonies, be so strong, that the minister of the crown *in* the house, if he is a distinct person, may not choose, even where his sentiments are favorable to us, to come to a pitched battle upon our account. For tho' I have the highest opinion of the deference of the house for the King's minister, yet he may be so good natured, as not to put it to the test, except it be for the mere and immediate profit of his master or himself.

But whatever kind of *minister* he is, that attempts to innovate *a single iota* in the privileges of these colonies, him I hope you will *undauntedly oppose;* and that you will never suffer yourselves to be either *cheated* or *frightened* into any *unworthy obsequiousness.* On such emergencies you may surely, without presumption, believe, that ALMIGHTY GOD himself will look down upon your righteous contest with gracious approbation. You will be a *"band of brothers,"* cemented by the dearest ties,—and strengthened with inconceivable supplies of force and constancy, by that sympathetic ardor, which animates good men, confederated in a good cause. Your *honor* and *welfare* will be, as they now are, most intimately concerned; and besides—*you are assigned by divine providence,* in the appointed order of things, the *protectors of unborn ages,* whose *fate* depends upon your *virtue.* Whether *they* shall arise the *generous* and *indisputable heirs* of the noblest patrimonies, or the *dastardly* and *hereditary drudges* of imperious task-masters, YOU MUST DETERMINE.

To discharge this double duty to *yourselves,* and to your *posterity,* you have nothing to do, but to call forth into use the *good sense* and *spirit* of which you are possessed. You have nothing to do, but to conduct your affairs *peaceably—prudently—firmly—jointly*. By *these means* you will support the character of *freemen*, without losing that of *faithful subjects*—a good character in any government—one of the best under a *British* government —You will *prove,* that *Americans* have that true *magnanimity* of soul, that can resent injuries, without falling into rage; and that tho' your devotion to *Great-Britain* is the most affectionate, yet you can make PROPER DISTINCTIONS, and know what you owe *to yourselves,* as well as to her—You will, at the same time that you advance your *interests,* advance your *reputation*—You will convince the world of the *justice of your demands,* and the *purity of your intentions.*—While all mankind must, with unceasing applauses, confess, that YOU indeed DESERVE *liberty,* who so *well understand* it, so *passionately love* it, so *temperately enjoy* it, and so *wisely, bravely,* and *virtuously assert, maintain,* and *defend* it.

"*Certe ego libertatem, quæ mihi a parente meo tradita est, experiar: Verum id frustra an ob rem faciam, in vestra manu situm est, quirites.*" [7]

For my part I am resolved to contend for the liberty delivered down to me by my ancestors; but whether I shall do it effectually or not, depends on you, my countrymen.

"How little soever one is able to write, yet when the liberties of one's country are threatened, it is still more difficult to be silent."

A FARMER.

Is there not the strongest probability, that if the universal sense of these colonies is immediately expressed by RESOLVES of the assemblies, in support of their rights, by INSTRUCTIONS to their agents on the subject, and by PETITIONS to the crown and parliament for redress, these measures will have the same success now, that they had in the time of the *Stamp-Act.*   D.

---

[7] "Indeed, I shall possess liberty, which was transmitted to me by my father: but, citizens, whether I shall do that in vain or profitably is placed in your hands."

THOMAS JEFFERSON
(*1743-1826*)

When it was decided on June 10, 1776, to appoint a committee to draft a declaration of the independence from Britain of the new American States, Thomas Jefferson, John Adams, and Benjamin Franklin were named. As Jefferson makes clear in his *Autobiography,* there was no real question by then whether independence would be declared. Delay was necessary only to get some of the state delegations free from obsolete pledges not to act. It was understood that Jefferson, with his particularly graceful and forceful style, would do the writing. Franklin and Adams were on the committee presumably to represent the Middle and New England States and for the immense combined prestige of their names.

While it has been customary to acknowledge that Adams was right in pointing out later on that there was nothing new or original in the ideas Jefferson put into the Declaration, it has not always been appreciated that Jefferson did exactly the right thing in appealing to what everybody thought. Nothing could be clearer from the document itself than the fact that it is a magnificent work of propaganda. It starts from decorum in its assertion of the duty to "declare the causes" of separation. It proceeds through affirmations of principles and then statements of grievances, and it climaxes with an echoing one sentence of declaration. From the cool opening to the solemn plighting of faith at the end, Jefferson's style, surprisingly little corrected or amended by his colleagues, blends the whole into a literary document equal to its historic function.

Bibliography: Carl Becker, *The Declaration of Independence: A Study in the History of Political Ideas,* New York, 1922; Julian P. Boyd, *The Declaration of Independence: The Evolution of the Text* . . . , Princeton, 1945; Adrienne Koch, *The Philosophy of Thomas Jefferson,* New York, 1943.

Text: *The Declaration of Independence* . . . , ed., James Brown Scott, New York, 1917.

THE DECLARATION OF INDEPENDENCE—1776

IN CONGRESS, JULY 4, 1776

THE UNANIMOUS DECLARATION OF THE THIRTEEN UNITED STATES OF AMERICA

When in the Course of human events, it becomes necessary for one people to dissolve the political bands which have connected them with another, and to assume among the Powers of the earth, the separate and equal station to which the Laws of Nature and of Nature's God entitle them, a decent respect to the opinions of mankind requires that they should declare the causes which impel them to the separation.

We hold these truths to be self-evident, that all men are created equal, that they are endowed by their Creator with certain unalienable Rights, that among these are Life, Liberty and the pursuit of Happiness. That to secure these rights, Governments are instituted among Men, deriving their just powers from the consent of the governed. That whenever any Form of Government becomes destructive of these ends, it is the Right of the People to alter or to abolish it, and to institute a new Government, laying its foundation on such principles and organizing its powers in such form, as to them shall seem most likely to effect their Safety and Happiness. Prudence, indeed, will dictate that Governments long established should not be changed for light and transient causes; and accordingly all experience hath shown, that mankind are more disposed to suffer, while evils are sufferable, than to right themselves by abolishing the forms to which they are accustomed. But when a long train of abuses and usurpations, pursuing invariably the same Object evinces a design to reduce them under absolute Despotism, it is their right, it is their duty, to throw off such Government, and to provide new Guards for their future security.—Such has been the patient sufferance of these Colonies; and such is now the necessity which constrains them to alter their former Systems of Government.

The history of the present King of Great Britain is a history of repeated injuries and usurpations, all having in direct object the establishment of an absolute Tyranny over these States. To prove this, let Facts be submitted to a candid world.

He has refused his Assent to Laws, the most wholesome and necessary for the public good.

He has forbidden his Governors to pass Laws of immediate and pressing importance, unless suspended in their operation till his Assent should be obtained; and when so suspended, he has utterly neglected to attend to them.

He has refused to pass other Laws for the accommodation of large districts of people, unless those people would relinquish the right of Representation in the Legislature, a right inestimable to them and formidable to tyrants only.

He has called together legislative bodies at places unusual, uncomfortable, and distant from the depository of their Public Records, for the sole purpose of fatiguing them into compliance with his measures.

He has dissolved Representative Houses repeatedly, for opposing with manly firmness his invasions on the rights of the people.

He has refused for a long time, after such dissolutions, to cause others to be elected; whereby the Legislative Powers, incapable of Annihilation, have returned to the People at large for their exercise; the State remaining in the mean time exposed to all the dangers of invasion from without, and convulsions within.

He has endeavoured to prevent the population of these States; for that purpose obstructing the Laws for Naturalization of Foreigners; refusing to pass others to encourage their migration hither, and raising the conditions of new Appropriations of Lands.

He has obstructed the Administration of Justice, by refusing his Assent to Laws for establishing Judiciary Powers.

He has made Judges dependent on his Will alone, for the tenure of their offices, and the amount and payment of their salaries.

He has erected a multitude of New Offices, and sent hither swarms of Officers to harass our People, and eat out their substance.

He has kept among us, in times of peace, Standing Armies without the Consent of our legislature.

He has affected to render the Military independent of and superior to the Civil Power.

He has combined with others to subject us to a jurisdiction foreign to our constitution, and unacknowledged by our laws; giving his Assent to their acts of pretended Legislation:

For quartering large bodies of armed troops among us:

For protecting them, by a mock Trial, from Punishment for any Murders which they should commit on the Inhabitants of these States:

For cutting off our Trade with all parts of the world:

For imposing taxes on us without our Consent:

For depriving us in many cases, of the benefits of Trial by Jury:

For transporting us beyond Seas to be tried for pretended offences:

For abolishing the free System of English Laws in a neighbouring Province, establishing therein an Arbitrary government, and enlarging its Boundaries so as to render it at once an example and fit instrument for introducing the same absolute rule into these Colonies:

For taking away our Charters, abolishing our most valuable Laws, and altering fundamentally the Forms of our Governments:

For suspending our own Legislatures, and declaring themselves invested with Power to legislate for us in all cases whatsoever.

He has abdicated Government here, by declaring us out of his Protection and waging War against us.

He has plundered our seas, ravaged our Coasts, burnt our towns, and destroyed the lives of our people.

He is at this time transporting large armies of foreign mercenaries to compleat the works of death, desolation and tyranny, already begun with circumstances of Cruelty & perfidy scarcely paralleled in the most barbarous ages, and totally unworthy the Head of a civilized nation.

He has constrained our fellow Citizens taken Captive on the High Seas to bear Arms against their Country, to become the executioners of their friends and Brethren, or to fall themselves by their Hands.

He has excited domestic insurrections amongst us, and has endeavoured to bring on the inhabitants of our frontiers, the merciless Indian Savages, whose Known rule of warfare, is an undistinguished destruction of all ages, sexes and conditions.

In every stage of these Oppressions We have Petitioned for Redress in the most humble terms: Our repeated Petitions have been answered only by repeated injury. A Prince, whose character is thus marked by every act which may define a Tyrant, is unfit to be the ruler of a free People.

Nor have We been wanting in attention to our British brethren. We have warned them from time to time of attempts by their legislature to extend an unwarrantable jurisdiction over us. We have reminded them of the circumstances of our emigration and settlement here. We have appealed to their native justice and magnanimity, and we have conjured them by the ties of our common kindred to disavow these usurpations, which, would inevitably interrupt our connections and correspondence. They too have been deaf to the voice of justice and of consanguinity. We must, therefore, acquiesce in the necessity, which denounces our Separation, and hold them, as we hold the rest of mankind, Enemies in War, in Peace Friends.

We, therefore, the Representatives of the united States of America, in General Congress, Assembled, appealing to the Supreme Judge of the world for the rectitude of our intentions, do, in the Name, and by Authority of the good People of these Colonies, solemnly publish and declare, That these United Colonies are, and of Right ought to be Free and Independent States, that they are Absolved from all Allegiance to the British

Crown, and that all political connection between them and the State of Great Britain, is and ought to be totally dissolved; and that as Free and Independent States, they have full Power to levy War, conclude Peace, contract Alliances, establish Commerce, and to do all other Acts and Things which Independent States may of right do. And for the support of this Declaration, with a firm reliance on the Protection of Divine Providence, we mutually pledge to each other our Lives, our Fortunes and our sacred Honor.

THOMAS PAINE
(1737-1809)

One of the best practitioners of the art of propaganda, Thomas Paine repeatedly established in his works classic examples of the techniques of the literature of persuasion. Seizing on the logic of events with perfect timing, Paine shattered Dickinson's moderation program with *Common Sense* at the beginning of 1776, thus hastening Congressional commitment to independence. Then in the influential series of *Crisis* papers, he became the official propagandist of the American cause and one of the true Founding Fathers of the nation.

If Paine had been content to retire as a national hero at the end of the war, his own happiness and the integrity of his reputation would have been more secure. But his real significance, and the historical stature he has been granted in the present century would have been smaller. He became an international firebrand, apostle of democracy to Tory England, and the one member of the revolutionary French National Assembly with courage enough to vote against the execution of Louis XVI. As in America, however, his real importance was not as an actor in historical roles but as a propagandist of ideas. In *The Rights of Man,* and in *The Age of Reason,* Paine laid out for popular consumption, and with the lucidity and verve peculiar to his pen, the configuration of democratic-deistic ideas of the eighteenth-century Enlightenment. Paine had not invented or even seriously modified these ideas, but he had understood them and helped put them to work. And his extraordinarily vivid powers of expression and presentation made his books almost scriptures of the linked movements toward democracy and humanitarianism in society and toward rationalism and humanism in religion.

Reaction in politics and camp-meeting evangelicism in religion eventually inverted his reputation. Rejected and systematically slandered in the countries whose common people he had sought to serve, deprived of most of his American pensions and even barred from voting in New Rochelle, N. Y., Paine died in poverty and disgrace. Only in the present century have the slander and disgrace worn away to reveal Thomas Paine's true stature as one of the great figures of the early years of American democracy.

Bibliography: Harry Hayden Clark, *Thomas Paine,* New York, 1944; Moncure D. Conway, *The Life of Thomas Paine,* New York, 1892; Philip S. Foner, ed., *The Complete Writings of Thomas Paine,*

New York, 1945; Dixon Wecter, "Hero in Reverse," *Virginia Quarterly Review,* XVIII (1942), 243-259.

Text: Moncure D. Conway, ed., *The Writings of Thomas Paine,* New York, 1894-1896.

from THE CRISIS

NUMBER I

These are the times that try men's souls. The summer soldier and the sunshine patriot will, in this crisis, shrink from the service of his country; but he that stands it *now,* deserves the love and thanks of man and woman. Tyranny, like hell, is not easily conquered; yet we have this consolation with us, that the harder the conflict, the more glorious the triumph. What we obtain too cheap, we esteem too lightly: it is dearness only that gives everything its value. Heaven knows how to put a proper price upon its goods; and it would be strange indeed if so celestial an article as FREEDOM should not be highly rated. Britain, with an army to enforce her tyranny, has declared that she has a right (*not only to* TAX) but "TO BIND *us in* ALL CASES WHATSOEVER"; and if being *bound in that manner* is not slavery, then is there not such a thing as slavery upon earth. Even the expression is impious; for so unlimited a power can belong only to God.

Whether the independence of the continent was declared too soon, or delayed too long, I will not now enter into as an argument; my own simple opinion is, that had it been eight months earlier it would have been much better. We did not make a proper use of last winter; neither could we, while we were in a dependent state. However, the fault, if it were one, was all our own; we have none to blame but ourselves. But no great deal is lost yet. All that Howe has been doing for this month past is rather a ravage than a conquest, which the spirit of the Jerseys a year ago would have quickly repulsed, and which time and a little resolution will soon recover.

I have as little superstition in me as any man living; but my secret opinion has ever been, and still is, that God Almighty will not give up a people to military destruction, or leave them unsupportedly to perish, who have so earnestly and so repeatedly sought to avoid the calamities of war, by every decent method which wisdom could invent. Neither have I so much of the infidel in me as to suppose that he has relinquished the government of the world, and given us up to the care of devils; and as I do not, I cannot see on what grounds the king of Britain can look up to heaven for help against us: a common murderer, a highwayman, or a housebreaker, has as good a pretense as he.

It is surprising to see how rapidly a panic will sometimes run through a country. All nations and ages have been subject to them: Britain has trembled like an ague at the report of a French fleet of flat-bottomed boats; and in the fourteenth century the whole English army, after ravaging the kingdom of France, was driven back like men petrified with fear; and this brave exploit was performed by a few broken forces collected and headed by a woman, Joan of Arc. Would that heaven might inspire some Jersey maid to spirit up her countrymen, and save her fair fellow sufferers from ravage and ravishment! Yet panics, in some cases, have their uses; they produce as much good as hurt. Their duration is always short; the mind soon grows through them, and acquires a firmer habit than before. But their peculiar advantage is, that they are the touchstones of sincerity and hypocrisy, and bring things and men to light, which might otherwise have lain forever undiscovered. In fact, they have the same effect on secret traitors which an imaginary apparition would have upon a private murderer. They sift out the hidden thoughts of man, and hold them up in public to the world. Many a disguised tory has lately shown his head, that shall penitentially solemnize with curses the day on which Howe arrived upon the Delaware.

As I was with the troops at Fort Lee, and marched with them to the edge of Pennsylvania, I am well acquainted with many circumstances which those who live at a distance know but little or nothing of. Our situation there was exceedingly cramped, the place being a narrow neck of land between the North River and the Hackensack. Our force was inconsiderable, being not one-fourth so great as Howe could bring against us. We had no army at hand to have relieved the garrison, had we shut ourselves up and stood on our defense. Our ammunition, light artillery, and the best part of our stores, had been removed, on the apprehension that Howe would endeavor to penetrate the Jerseys, in which case Fort Lee could be of no use to us; for it must occur to every thinking man, whether in the army or not, that these kind of field forts are only for temporary purposes, and last in use no longer than the enemy directs his force against the particular object which such forts are raised to defend. Such was our situation and condition at Fort Lee on the morning of the 20th of November, when an officer arrived with information that the enemy with 200 boats had landed about seven miles above. Major General Green, who commanded the garrison, immediately ordered them under arms, and sent express to General Washington at the town of Hackensack, distant by the way of the ferry, six miles. Our first object was to secure the bridge over the Hackensack, which laid up the river between the enemy and us, about six miles from us, three from them. General Washington arrived in about three-quarters of an hour, and marched at the head of the troops towards the bridge, which place I expected we should have a brush for; however, they did not choose to dispute it with us, and the greatest part of our troops went over the bridge, the rest over the ferry, except some which passed at a mill on a small creek between the bridge and the ferry, and made their way through some marshy grounds up to the town of Hackensack, and there passed the river. We brought off as much baggage as the wagons could contain, the rest was lost. The simple object was to bring off the garrison and march them on till they could be strengthened by the Jersey or Pennsylvania militia, so as to be enabled to make a stand. We staid four days at Newark, collected our outposts with some of the Jersey militia, and marched out twice to meet the enemy on being informed that they were advancing, though our numbers were greatly inferior to theirs. Howe, in my little opinion, committed a great error in generalship in not throwing a body of forces off from Staten Island through Amboy, by which means he might have seized all our stores at Brunswick and intercepted our march into Pennsylvania; but if we believe the power of hell to be limited, we must likewise believe that their agents are under some providential control.

I shall not now attempt to give all the particulars of our retreat to the Delaware; suffice it for the present to say that both officers and men, though greatly harassed and fatigued, frequently without rest, covering, or provision—the inevitable consequences of a long retreat—bore it with a manly and martial spirit. All their wishes centered in one; which was, that the country would turn out and help them to drive the enemy back. Voltaire has remarked that King William never appeared to full advantage but in difficulties and in action; the same remark may be made on General Washington, for the character fits him. There is a natural firmness in some minds which cannot be unlocked by trifles, but which, when unlocked, discovers a cabinet of fortitude; and I reckon it among those kinds of public blessings, which we do not immediately see, that God hath blessed him with uninterrupted health, and given him a mind that can even flourish upon care.

I shall conclude this paper with some miscellaneous remarks on the state of our affairs; and shall begin with asking the following question, Why is it that the enemy have left the New England provinces, and made these middle ones the seat of war? The answer is easy: New England is not infested with tories, and we are. I have been tender in raising the cry against these men, and used numberless arguments to show them their danger, but it will not do to sacrifice a world either to their folly or their baseness. The period is now arrived in which either they or we must change our sentiments, or one or both must fall. And what is a tory? Good God! what is he? I should not be afraid to go with a hundred Whigs against a thousand tories, were they to attempt to get into arms. Every tory is a coward; for servile, slavish, self-interested fear is the foundation of toryism; and a man under such influence, though he may be cruel, never can be brave.

But, before the line of irrecoverable separation be drawn between us, let us reason the matter together: Your conduct is an invitation to the enemy, yet not one in a thousand of you has heart enough to join him. Howe is as much deceived by you as the American cause is injured by you. He expects you will all take up arms and flock to his standard with muskets on your shoulders. Your opinions are of no use to him unless you support him personally, for it is soldiers, and not tories, that he wants.

I once felt all that kind of anger, which a man ought to feel, against the mean principles that are held by the tories: A noted one, who kept a tavern at Amboy, was standing at his door, with as pretty a child in his hand, about eight or nine years old, as I ever saw, and after speaking his mind as freely as he thought was prudent, finished with this unfatherly expression, *"Well! give me peace in my day."* Not a man lives on the continent but fully believes that a separation must some time or other finally take place, and a generous parent should have said, *"If there must be trouble, let it be in my day, that my child may have peace"*; and this single reflection, well applied, is sufficient to awaken every man to duty. Not a place upon earth might be so happy as America. Her situation is remote from all the wrangling world, and she has nothing to do but to trade with them. A man can distinguish himself between temper and principle; and I am as confident as I am that God governs the world, that America will never be happy till she gets clear of foreign dominion. Wars, without ceasing, will break out till that period arrives, and the continent must in the end be conqueror; for though the flame of liberty may sometimes cease to shine, the coal can never expire.

America did not, nor does not want force; but she wanted a proper application of that force. Wisdom is not the purchase of a day, and it is no wonder that we should err at the first setting off. From an excess of tenderness, we were unwilling to raise an army, and trusted our cause to the temporary defense of a well-meaning militia. A summer's experience has now taught us better; yet with those troops, while they were collected, we were able to set bounds to the progress of the enemy, and thank God! they are again assembling. I always considered militia as the best troops in the world for a sudden exertion, but they will not do for a long campaign. Howe, it is probable, will make an attempt on this city; should he fail on this side the Delaware, he is ruined. If he succeeds, our cause is not ruined. He stakes all on his side against a part on ours; admitting he succeeds, the consequences will be that armies from both ends of the continent will march to assist their suffering friends in the middle states; for he cannot go everywhere—it is impossible. I consider Howe as the greatest enemy the tories have; he is bringing a war into their country, which, had it not been for him and partly for themselves, they had been clear of. Should he now be expelled, I wish with all the devotion of a Christian, that the names of Whig and Tory may never more be mentioned; but should the tories give him encouragement to come, or assistance if he come, I as sincerely wish that our next year's arms may expel them from the continent, and the Congress appropriate their possessions to the relief of those who have suffered in well-doing. A single successful battle next year will settle the whole. America could carry on a two years' war by the confiscation of the property of disaffected persons, and be made happy by their expulsion. Say not that this is revenge; call it rather the soft resentment of a suffering people, who, having no object in view but the *good* of *all,* have staked their *own all* upon a seemingly doubtful event. Yet it is folly to argue against determined hardness; eloquence may strike the ear, and the language of sorrow draw forth the tear of compassion, but nothing can reach the heart that is steeled with prejudice.

Quitting this class of men, I turn with the warm ardor of a friend to those who have nobly stood, and are yet determined to stand the matter out: I call not upon a few, but upon all: not on *this* State or *that* State, but on *every* State: up and help us; lay your shoulders to the wheel; better have too much force than too little, when so great an object is at stake. Let it be told to the future world, that in the depth of winter, when nothing but hope and virtue could survive, that the city and the country alarmed at one common danger, came forth to meet and to repulse it. Say not that thousands are gone—turn out your tens of thousands; throw not the burden of the day upon Providence, but *"show your faith by your works,"* that God may bless you. It matters not where you live, or what rank of life you hold, the evil or the blessing will reach you all. The far and the near, the home counties and the back, the rich and the poor, will suffer or rejoice alike. The heart that feels not now is dead; the blood of his children will curse his cowardice who shrinks back at a time when a little might have saved the whole and made *them* happy. I love the man that can smile in trouble, that can gather strength from distress and grow brave by reflection. It is the business of little minds to shrink; but he whose heart is firm, and whose conscience approves his conduct, will pursue his principles unto death. My own line of reasoning is to myself as straight and clear as a ray of light. Not all the treasures of the world, so far as I believe, could have induced me to support an offensive war, for I think it murder; but if a thief breaks into my house, burns and destroys my property, and kills or threatens to kill me or those that are in it, and to *"bind me in all cases whatsoever"* to his absolute will, am I to suffer it? What signifies it to me whether he who does it is a king or a common man; my countryman or not my countryman; whether it be done by an individual villain, or an army of them? If we reason to the root of things we shall find no difference; neither can any just cause be assigned why we should punish in the one case and pardon in the other. Let them call me rebel and welcome—I feel no concern from it; but I should suffer the misery of devils, were I to make a whore of my soul by swearing allegiance to one whose character is that of a sottish, stupid, stubborn, worthless, brutish man. I conceive likewise a horrid idea in receiving mercy from a being, who at the last day shall be shrieking to the rocks and mountains to cover him, and fleeing with terror from the orphan, the widow, and the slain of America.

There are cases which cannot be overdone by language, and this is one. There are persons, too, who see not the full extent of the evil which threatens them; they solace themselves with hopes that the enemy, if he succeed, will be merciful. It is the madness of folly, to expect mercy from those who have refused to do justice; and even mercy, where conquest is the object, is only a trick of war. The cunning of the fox is as murderous as the violence of the wolf, and we ought to guard equally against both. Howe's first object is, partly by threats and partly by promises, to terrify or seduce the people to deliver up their arms and receive mercy. The ministry recommended the same plan to Gage, and this is what the tories call making their peace, *"a peace which passeth all understanding," indeed!* A peace which would be the immediate forerunner of a worse ruin than any we have yet thought of. Ye men of Pennsylvania, do reason upon these things! Were the back counties to give up their arms, they would fall an easy prey to the Indians, who are all armed: this perhaps is what some tories would not be sorry for. Were the home counties to deliver up their arms, they would be exposed to the resentment of the back counties, who would then have it in their power to chastise their defection at pleasure. And were any one State to give up its arms, *that* State must be garrisoned by all Howe's army of Britons and Hessians to preserve it from the anger of the rest. Mutual fear is the principal link in the chain of mutual love; and woe be to that State that breaks the compact. Howe is mercifully inviting you to barbarous destruction, and men must be either rogues or fools that will not see it. I dwell not upon the vapors of imagination; I bring reason to your ears, and, in language as plain as A B C, hold up truth to your eyes.

I thank God that I fear not. I see no real cause for fear. I know our situation well, and can see the way out of it. While our army was collected, Howe dared not risk a battle; and it is no credit to him that he decamped from the White Plains, and waited a mean opportunity to ravage the defenseless Jerseys; but it is great credit to us, that with a handful of men, we sustained an orderly retreat for near a hundred miles, brought off our ammunition, all our fieldpieces, the greatest part of our stores, and had four rivers to pass. None can say that our retreat was precipitate; for we were near three weeks in performing it, that the country might have time to come in. Twice we marched back to meet the enemy, and remained out till dark. The sign of fear was not seen in our camp, and had not some of the cowardly and disaffected inhabitants spread false alarms through the country, the Jerseys had never been ravaged. Once more we are again collected and collecting, our new army at both ends of the continent is recruiting fast, and we shall be able to open the next campaign with sixty thousand men, well-armed and clothed. This is our situation, and who will may know it. By perseverance and fortitude we have the prospect of a glorious issue; by cowardice and submission, the sad choice of a variety of evils: a ravaged country—a depopulated city—habitations without safety, and slavery without hope—our homes turned into barracks and bawdy-houses for Hessians—and a future race to provide for, whose fathers we shall doubt of. Look on this picture and weep over it! and if there yet remains one thoughtless wretch who believes it not, let him suffer it unlamented.

COMMON SENSE

December 23, 1776

from THE RIGHTS OF MAN

PART II

COMBINING PRINCIPLES AND PRACTICE

INTRODUCTION

What Archimedes said of the mechanical powers, may be applied to reason and liberty: *"Had we,"* said he, *"a place to stand upon, we might raise the world."*

The revolution in America presented in politics what was only theory in mechanics. So deeply rooted were all the governments of the old world, and so effectually had the tyranny and the antiquity of habit established itself over the mind, that no beginning could be made in Asia, Africa, or Europe, to reform the political condition of man. Freedom had been hunted round the globe; reason was considered as rebellion; and the slavery of fear had made men afraid to think.

But such is the irresistible nature of truth that all it asks, and all it wants, is the liberty of appearing. The sun needs no inscription to distinguish him from darkness, and no sooner did the American governments display themselves to the world than despotism felt a shock and man began to contemplate redress.

The independence of America, considered merely as a separation from England, would have been a matter but of little importance had it not been accompanied by a revolution in the principles and practice of government. She made a stand, not for herself only, but for the world, and looked beyond the advantages which *she* could receive. Even the Hessian, though hired to fight against her, may live to bless his defeat; and England, condemning the viciousness of its government, rejoice in its miscarriage.

As America was the only spot in the political world where the principles of universal reformation could begin, so also was it the best in the natural world. An assemblage of circumstances conspired not only to give birth but to add gigantic maturity to its principles. The scene which that country presents to the eye of the spectator has something in it which generates and enlarges great ideas. Nature appears to him in magnitude. The mighty objects he beholds act upon his mind by enlarging it, and he partakes of the greatness he contemplates. Its first settlers were emigrants from different European nations, and of diversified professions of religion, retiring from the governmental persecutions of the old world, and meeting in the new not as enemies but as brothers. The wants which necessarily accompany the cultivation of a wilderness produced among them a state of society which countries long harassed by the quarrels and intrigues of governments had neglected to cherish. In such a situation man becomes what he ought to be. He sees his species not with the inhuman idea of a natural enemy but as kindred; and the example shows to the artificial world that man must go back to nature for information.

From the rapid progress which America makes in every species of improvement, it is rational to conclude that if the governments of Asia, Africa and Europe had begun on a principle similar to that of America, or had they not been very early corrupted therefrom, those countries must by this time have been in a far superior condition to what they are. Age after age has passed away for no other purpose than to behold their wretchedness. Could we suppose a spectator who knew nothing of the world and who was put into it merely to make his observations, he would take a great part of the old world to be new, just struggling with the difficulties and hardships of an infant settlement. He could not suppose that the hordes of miserable poor, with which old countries abound, could be any other than those who had not yet been able to provide for themselves. Little would he think they were the consequence of what in such countries is called government.

If, from the more wretched parts of the old world, we look at those which are in an advanced state of improvement, we still find the greedy hand of government thrusting itself into every corner and crevice of industry, and grasping the spoil of the multitude. Invention is continually exercised to furnish new pretenses for revenue and taxation. It watches prosperity as its prey, and permits none to escape without a tribute.

As revolutions have begun (and as the probability is always greater against a thing beginning, than of proceeding after it has begun), it is natural to expect that other revolutions will follow. The amazing and still increasing expenses with which old governments are conducted, the numerous wars they engage in or provoke, the embarrassments they throw in the way of universal civilization and commerce, and the oppression and usurpation acted at home, have wearied out the patience and exhausted the property of the world. In such a situation, and with such examples already existing, revolutions are to be looked for. They are become subjects of universal conversation, and may be considered as the *order of the day*.

If systems of government can be introduced less expensive and more productive of general happiness than those which have existed, all attempts to oppose their progress will in the end prove fruitless. Reason, like time, will make its own way, and prejudice will fall in the combat with interest. If universal peace, harmony, civilization, and commerce are ever to be the happy lot of man, it cannot be accomplished but by a revolution in the present system of governments. All the monarchical governments are military. War is their trade, plunder and revenue their objects. While such governments continue, peace has not the absolute security of a day. What is the history of all monarchical governments but a disgustful picture of human wretchedness, and the accidental respite of a few years repose? Wearied with war, and tired with human butchery, they sat down to rest and called it peace. This certainly is not the condition that heaven intended for man; and if *this be monarchy,* well might monarchy be reckoned among the sins of the Jews.

The revolutions which formerly took place in the world had nothing in them that interested the bulk of mankind. They extended only to a change of persons and measures but not of principles, and rose or fell among the common transactions of the moment. What we now behold may not improperly be called a *"counter revolution."* Conquest and tyranny, at some early period, dispossessed man of his rights, and he is now recovering them. And as the tide of human affairs has its ebb and flow in directions contrary to each other, so also is it in this. Government founded on a *moral theory, on a system of universal peace, on the indefeasible, hereditary rights of man,* is now revolving from west to east by a stronger impulse than the government of the sword revolved from east to west. It interests not particular individuals but nations in its progress, and promises a new era to the human race.

The danger to which the success of revolutions is most exposed is that of attempting them before the principles on which they proceed, and the advantages to result from them, are sufficiently understood. Almost everything appertaining to the circumstances of a nation has been absorbed and confounded under the general and mysterious word *government.* Though it avoids taking to its account the errors it commits and the mischiefs it occasions, it fails not to arrogate to itself whatever has the appearance of prosperity. It robs industry of its honors by pedantically making itself the cause of its effects; and purloins from the general character of man the merits that appertain to him as a social being.

It may therefore be of use, in this day of revolutions, to discriminate between those things which are the effect of government, and those which are not. This will best be done by taking a review of society and civilization, and the consequences resulting therefrom, as things distinct from what are called governments. By beginning with this investigation, we shall be able to assign effects to their proper causes, and analyze the mass of common errors.

CHAPTER I

OF SOCIETY AND CIVILIZATION

A great part of that order which reigns among mankind is not the effect of government. It had its origin in the principles of society and the natural constitution of man. It existed prior to government, and would exist if the formality of government was abolished. The mutual dependence and reciprocal interest which man has in man, and all the parts of a civilized community upon each other, create that great chain of connection which holds it together. The landholder, the farmer, the manufacturer, the merchant, the tradesman, and every occupation prospers by the aid which each receives from the other, and from the whole. Common interest regulates their concerns and forms their laws; and the laws which common usage ordains have a greater influence than the laws of government. In fine, society performs for itself almost everything which is ascribed to government.

To understand the nature and quantity of government proper for man, it is necessary to attend to his character. As nature created him for social life, she fitted him for the station she intended. In all cases she made his natural wants greater than his individual powers. No one man is capable, without the aid of society, of supplying his own wants; and those wants, acting upon every individual, impel the whole of them into society as naturally as gravitation acts to a center.

But she has gone further. She has not only forced man into society by a diversity of wants, which the reciprocal aid of each other can supply, but she has implanted in him a system of social affections, which, though not necessary to his existence, are essential to his happiness. There is no period in life when this love for society ceases to act. It begins and ends with our being.

If we examine with attention into the composition and consituation of man, the diversity of his wants, and the diversity of talents in different men for reciprocally accommodating the wants of each other, his propensity to society, and consequently to preserve the advantages resulting from it, we shall easily discover that a great part of what is called government is mere imposition.

Government is no further necessary than to supply the few cases to which society and civilization are not conveniently competent; and instances are not wanting to show that everything which government can usefully add thereto, has been performed by the common consent of society, without government.

For upwards of two years from the commencement of the American war, and a longer period in several of the American states, there were no established forms of government. The old governments had been abolished, and the country was too much occupied in defense to employ its attention in establishing new governments; yet during this interval order and harmony were preserved as inviolate as in any country in Europe. There is a natural aptness in man, and more so in society, because it embraces a greater variety of abilities and resources to accommodate itself to whatever situation it is in. The instant formal government is abolished, society begins to act. A general association takes place, and common interest produces common security.

So far is it from being true, as has been pretended, that the abolition of any formal government is the dissolution of society, it acts by a contrary impulse, and brings the latter the closer together. All that part of its organization which it had committed to its government devolves again upon itself, and acts through its medium. When men, as well from natural instinct as from reciprocal benefits, have habituated themselves to social and civilized life, there is always enough of its principles in practice to carry them through any changes they may find necessary or convenient to make in their government. In short, man is so naturally a creature of society, that it is almost impossible to put him out of it.

Formal government makes but a small part of civilized life; and when even the best that human wisdom can devise is established, it is a thing more in name and idea than in fact. It is to the great and fundamental principles of society and civilization—to the common usage universally consented to, and mutually and reciprocally maintained—to the unceasing circulation of interest, which, passing through its innumerable channels, invigorates the whole mass of civilized man—it is to these things, infinitely more than to anything which even the best instituted government can perform, that the safety and prosperity of the individual and of the whole depends.

The more perfect civilization is, the less occasion has it for government, because the more does it regulate its own affairs and govern itself; but so contrary is the practice of old governments to the reason of the case, that the expenses of them increase in the proportion they ought to diminish. It is but few general laws that civilized life requires, and those of such common usefulness, that whether they are enforced by the forms of government or not, the effect will be nearly the same. If we consider what the principles are that first condense men into society, and what the motives that regulate their mutual intercourse afterwards, we shall find, by the time we arrive at what is called government, that nearly the whole of the business is performed by the natural operation of the parts upon each other.

Man, with respect to all those matters, is more a creature of consistency than he is aware of, or than governments would wish him to believe. All the great laws of society are laws of nature. Those of trade and commerce, whether with respect to the intercourse of individuals or of nations, are laws of mutual and reciprocal interest. They are followed and obeyed, because it is the interest of the parties so to do, and not on account of any formal laws their governments may impose or interpose.

But how often is the natural propensity to society disturbed or destroyed by the operations of government! When the latter, instead of being ingrafted on the principles of the former, assumes to exist for itself, and acts by partialities of favor and oppression, it becomes the cause of the mischiefs it ought to prevent.

If we look back to the riots and tumults which at various times have happened in England, we shall find, that they did not proceed from the want of a government, but that government was itself the generating cause; instead of consolidating society, it divided it; it deprived it of its natural cohesion, and engendered discontents and disorders, which otherwise would not have existed. In those associations which men promiscuously form for the purpose of trade, or of any concern in which government is totally out of the question and in which they act merely on the principles of society, we see how naturally the various parties unite; and this shows, by comparison, that governments, so far from being always the cause or means of order, are often the destruction of it. The riots of 1780 had no other source than the remains of those prejudices which the government itself had encouraged. But with respect to England there are also other causes.

Excess and inequality of taxation, however disguised in the means, never fail to appear in their effect. As a great mass of the community are thrown thereby into poverty and discontent, they are constantly on the brink of commotion; and, deprived as they unfortunately are of the means of information, are easily heated to outrage. Whatever the apparent cause of any riots may be, the real one is always want of happiness. It shows that something is wrong in the system of government, that injures the felicity by which society is to be preserved.

But as fact is superior to reasoning, the instance of America presents itself to confirm these observations. If there is a country in the world, where concord, according to common calculation, would be least expected, it is America. Made up, as it is, of people from different nations,[1] accustomed to different forms and habits of government, speaking different languages, and more different in their modes of worship, it would appear that the union of such a people was impracticable; but by the simple operation of constructing government on the principles of society and the rights of man, every difficulty retires, and all the parts are brought into cordial unison. There, the poor are not oppressed, the rich are not privileged. Industry is not mortified by the splendid extravagance of a court rioting at its expense. Their taxes are few, because their government is just; and as there is nothing to render them wretched, there is nothing to engender riots and tumults.

A metaphysical man, like Mr. Burke, would have tortured his invention to discover how such a people could be governed. He would have supposed that some must be managed by fraud, others by force, and all by some contrivance; that genius must be hired to impose upon ignorance, and show and parade to fascinate the vulgar. Lost in the abundance of his researches, he would have resolved and re-resolved, and finally overlooked the plain and easy road that lay directly before him.

One of the great advantages of the American revolution has been that it led to a discovery of the principles and laid open the imposition of governments. All the revolutions till then had been worked within the atmosphere of a court, and never on the

---

[1] That part of America which is generally called New England, including New Hampshire, Massachusetts, Rhode Island, and Connecticut, is peopled chiefly by English descendants. In the state of New York, about half are Dutch, the rest English, Scotch, and Irish. In New Jersey, a mixture of English and Dutch, with some Scotch and Irish. In Pennsylvania, about one third are English, another Germans, and the remainder Scotch and Irish, with some Swedes. The states to the southward have a greater proportion of English than the middle states, but in all of them there is a mixture; and besides those enumerated, there are a considerable number of French, and some few of all the European nations, lying on the coast. The most numerous religious denomination are the Presbyterians; but no one sect is established above another, and all men are equally citizens.—*Paine*.

great floor of a nation. The parties were always of the class of courtiers; and whatever was their rage for reformation, they carefully preserved the fraud of the profession.

In all cases they took care to represent government as a thing made up of mysteries which only themselves understood: and they hid from the understanding of the nation the only thing that was beneficial to know, namely, *that government is nothing more than a national association acting on the principles of society*.

Having thus endeavored to show that the social and civilized state of man is capable of performing within itself almost everything necessary to its protection and government, it will be proper, on the other hand, to take a review of the present old governments, and examine whether their principles and practice are correspondent thereto.

CHAPTER II

OF THE ORIGIN OF THE PRESENT OLD GOVERNMENTS

It is impossible that such governments as have hitherto existed in the world could have commenced by any other means than a total violation of every principle, sacred and moral. The obscurity in which the origin of all the present old governments is buried, implies the iniquity and disgrace with which they began. The origin of the present governments of America and France will ever be remembered, because it is honorable to record it; but with respect to the rest, even flattery has consigned them to the tomb of time, without an inscription.

It could have been no difficult thing in the early and solitary ages of the world, while the chief employment of men was that of attending flocks and herds, for a banditti of ruffians to overrun a country, and lay it under contribution. Their power being thus established, the chief of the band contrived to lose the name of robber in that of monarch; and hence the origin of monarchy and kings.

The origin of the government of England, so far as relates

to what is called its line of monarchy, being one of the latest, is perhaps the best recorded. The hatred which the Norman invasion and tyranny begat must have been deeply rooted in the nation to have outlived the contrivance to obliterate it. Though not a courtier will talk of the curfew-bell, not a village in England has forgotten it.

Those bands of robbers having parcelled out the world and divided it into dominions, began, as is naturally the case, to quarrel with each other. What at first was obtained by violence was considered by others as lawful to be taken, and a second plunderer succeeded the first. They alternately invaded the dominions which each had assigned to himself, and the brutality with which they treated each other explains the original character of monarchy. It was ruffian torturing ruffian. The conqueror considered the conquered not as his prisoner, but his property. He led him in triumph rattling in chains, and doomed him, at pleasure, to slavery or death. As time obliterated the history of their beginning, their successors assumed new appearances to cut off the entail of their disgrace, but their principles and objects remained the same. What at first was plunder assumed the softer name of revenue; and the power originally usurped, they affected to inherit.

From such beginning of governments, what could be expected but a continual system of war and extortion? It has established itself into a trade. The vice is not peculiar to one more than to another, but is the common principle of all. There does not exist within such governments a stamina whereon to ingraft reformation; and the shortest and most effectual remedy is to begin anew.

What scenes of horror, what perfection of inquity, present themselves in contemplating the character and reviewing the history of such governments! If we would delineate human nature with a baseness of heart and hypocrisy of countenance that reflection would shudder at and humanity disown, it is kings, courts, and cabinets, that must sit for the portrait. Man, as he is naturally, with all his faults about him, is not up to the character.

Can we possibly suppose that if government had originated in a right principle, and had not an interest in pursuing a wrong one, that the world could have been in the wretched and quarrelsome condition we have seen it? What inducement has the farmer, while following the plough, to lay aside his peaceful pursuits and go to war with the farmer of another country? Or what inducement has the manufacturer? What is dominion to them, or to any class of men in a nation? Does it add an acre to any man's estate, or raise its value? Are not conquest and defeat each of the same price, and taxes the never-failing consequence? Though this reasoning may be good to a nation, it is not so to a government. War is the faro-table of governments, and nations the dupes of the game.

If there is anything to wonder at in this miserable scene of governments, more than might be expected, it is the progress which the peaceful arts of agriculture, manufacture, and commerce have made, beneath such a long accumulating load of discouragement and oppression. It serves to show that instinct in animals does not act with stronger impulse than the principles of society and civilization operate in man. Under all discouragements, he pursues his object and yields to nothing but impossibilities.

CHAPTER III

OF THE OLD AND NEW SYSTEMS OF GOVERNMENT

Nothing can appear more contradictory than the principles on which the old governments began, and the condition to which society, civilization, and commerce, are capable of carrying mankind. Government on the old system is an assumption of power for the aggrandizement of itself; on the new, a delegation of power for the common benefit of society. The former supports itself by keeping up a system of war; the latter promotes a system of peace as the true means of enriching a nation. The one encourages national prejudices; the other promotes universal society as the means of universal commerce. The one measures its prosperity by the quantity of revenue it extorts; the other proves its excellence by the small quantity of taxes it requires.

Mr. Burke has talked of old and new whigs. If he can amuse himself with childish names and distinctions, I shall not interrupt his pleasure. It is not to him, but to the Abbé Sièyes, that I address this chapter. I am already engaged to the latter gentleman to discuss the subject of monarchical government; and as it naturally occurs in comparing the old and new systems, I make this the opportunity of presenting to him my observations. I shall occasionally take Mr. Burke in my way.

Though it might be proved that the system of government now called the *new* is the most ancient in principle of all that have existed, being founded on the original inherent rights of man: yet, as tyranny and the sword have suspended the exercise of those rights for many centuries past, it serves better the purpose of distinction to call it the *new* than to claim the right of calling it the old.

The first general distinction between those two systems is that the one now called the old is *hereditary,* either in whole or in part; and the new is entirely *representative*. It rejects all hereditary government:

1st, As being an imposition on mankind.

2d, As inadequate to the purposes for which government is necessary.

With respect to the first of these heads, it cannot be proved by what right hereditary government could begin; neither does there exist, within the compass of mortal power, a right to establish it. Man has no authority over posterity in matters of personal right; and therefore no man or body of men had, or can have, a right to set up hereditary government. Were even ourselves to come again into existence, instead of being succeeded by posterity, we have not now the right of taking from ourselves the rights which would then be ours. On what ground, then, do we pretend to take them from others?

All hereditary government is in its nature tyranny. A heritable crown, or a heritable throne, or by what other fanciful name such things may be called, have no other significant explanation than that mankind are heritable property. To inherit a government is to inherit the people, as if they were flocks and herds.

With respect to the second head, that of being inadequate to the purposes for which government is necessary, we have only to consider what government essentially is and compare it with the circumstances to which hereditary succession is subject.

Government ought to be a thing always in full maturity. It ought to be so constructed as to be superior to all the accidents to which individual man is subject; and therefore, hereditary succession, by being *subject to them all,* is the most irregular and imperfect of all the systems of government.

We have heard the *rights of man* called a *leveling* system; but the only system to which the word *leveling* is truly applicable is the hereditary monarchical system. It is a system of *mental leveling.* It indiscriminately admits every species of character to the same authority. Vice and virtue, ignorance and wisdom, in short, every quality, good or bad, is put on the same level. Kings succeed each other, not as rationals, but as animals. Can we then be surprised at the abject state of the human mind in monarchical countries, when the government itself is formed on such an abject leveling system? It has no fixed character. Today it is one thing; and tomorrow it is something else. It changes with the temper of every succeeding individual, and is subject to all the varieties of each. It is government through the medium of passions and accidents. It appears under all the various characters of childhood, decrepitude, dotage, a thing at nurse, in leading strings, or on crutches. It reverses the wholesome order of nature. It occasionally puts children over men, and the conceits of non-age over wisdom and experience. In short, we cannot conceive a more ridiculous figure of government than hereditary succession, in all its cases, presents.

Could it be made a decree in nature, or an edict registered in heaven, and man could know it, that virtue and wisdom should invariably appertain to hereditary succession, the objections to it would be removed; but when we see that nature acts as if she disowned and sported with the hereditary system; that the mental characters of successors, in all countries, are below the average of human understanding; that one is a tyrant, another an idiot, a third insane, and some all three together, it is impossible to attach confidence to it, when reason in man has power to act.

It is not to the Abbé Sièyes that I need apply this reasoning; he has already saved me that trouble by giving his own opinion upon the case. "If it be asked," says he, "what is my opinion with respect to hereditary right, I answer, without hesitation that, in good theory, an hereditary transmission of any power or office can never accord with the laws of true representation. Hereditaryship is, in this sense, as much an attaint upon principle as an outrage upon society. But let us," continues he, "refer to the history of all elective monarchies and principalities; is there one in which the elective mode is not worse than the hereditary succession?"

As to debating on which is the worst of the two, is admitting both to be bad; and herein we are agreed. The preference which the abbé has given, is a condemnation of the thing he prefers. Such a mode of reasoning on such a subject is inadmissible, because it finally amounts to an accusation of providence, as if she had left to man no other choice with respect to government than between two evils, the best of which he admits to be *"an attaint upon principle, and an outrage upon society."*

Passing over, for the present, all the evils and mischiefs which monarchy has occasioned in the world, nothing can more effectually prove its uselessness in a state of *civil government* than making it hereditary. Would we make any office hereditary that required wisdom and abilities to fill it? And where wisdom and abilities are not necessary, such an office, whatever it may be, is superfluous or insignificant.

Hereditary succession is a burlesque upon monarchy. It puts it in the most ridiculous light by presenting it as an office which any child or idiot may fill. It requires some talents to be a common mechanic; but to be a king requires only the animal figure of man—a sort of breathing automaton. This sort of superstition may last a few years more, but it cannot long resist the awakened reason and interest of man.

As to Mr. Burke, he is a stickler for monarchy, not altogether as a pensioner, if he is one, which I believe, but as a political man. He has taken up a contemptible opinion of mankind, who, in their turn, are taking up the same of him. He considers them as a herd of beings that must be governed by fraud, effigy, and show; and an idol would be as good a figure of monarchy with him, as a man. I will, however, do him the justice to say that, with respect to America, he has been very complimentary. He always contended, at least in my hearing, that the people of America were more enlightened than those of England, or of any country in Europe; and that therefore the imposition of show was not necessary in their governments.

Though the comparison between hereditary and elective monarchy, which the abbé had made, is unnecessary to the case, because the representative system rejects both; yet were I to make the comparison, I should decide contrary to what he has done.

The civil wars which have originated from contested hereditary claims are more numerous, and have been more dreadful, and of longer continuance than those which have been occasioned by election. All the civil wars in France arose from the hereditary system; they were either produced by hereditary claims, or by the imperfection of the hereditary form, which admits of regencies, or monarchy at nurse. With respect to England, its history is full of the same misfortunes. The contests for succession between the houses of York and Lancaster lasted a whole century; and others of a similar nature have renewed themselves since that period. Those of 1715 and 1745 were of the same kind. The succession-war for the crown of Spain embroiled almost half of Europe. The disturbances in Holland are generated from the hereditaryship of the stadtholder. A government calling itself free, with an hereditary office, is like a thorn in the flesh that produces a fermentation which endeavors to discharge it.

But I might go further, and place also foreign wars, of whatever kind, to the same cause. It is by adding the evil of hereditary succession to that of monarchy that a permanent family interest is created, whose constant objects are dominion and revenue. Poland, though an elective monarchy, has had fewer wars than those which are hereditary; and it is the only government that has made a voluntary essay, though but a small one, to reform the condition of the country.

Having thus glanced at a few of the defects of the old, or hereditary systems of government, let us compare it with the new, or representative system.

The representative system takes society and civilization for its basis; nature, reason, and experience for its guide.

Experience, in all ages and in all countries, has demonstrated that it is impossible to control nature in her distribution of mental powers. She gives them as she pleases. Whatever is the rule by which she, apparently to us, scatters them among mankind, that rule remains a secret to man. It would be as ridiculous to attempt to fix the hereditaryship of human beauty, as of wisdom.

Whatever wisdom constituently is, it is like a seedless plant; it may be reared when it appears; but it cannot be voluntarily produced. There is always a sufficiency somewhere in the general mass of society for all purposes; but with respect to the parts of society, it is continually changing its place. It rises in one today, in another tomorrow and has most probably visited in rotation every family of the earth, and again withdrawn.

As this is the order of nature, the order of government must necessarily follow it, or government will, as we see it does, degenerate into ignorance. The hereditary system, therefore, is as repugnant to human wisdom as to human rights; and is as absurd as it is unjust.

As the republic of letters brings forward the best literary productions by giving to genius a fair and universal chance; so the representative system of government is calculated to produce the wisest laws by collecting wisdom where it can be found. I smile to myself when I contemplate the ridiculous insignificance into which literature and all the sciences would sink, were they made hereditary; and I carry the same idea into governments. An hereditary governor is as inconsistent as an hereditary author. I know not whether Homer or Euclid had sons; but I will venture an opinion that if they had, and had left their works unfinished, those sons could not have completed them.

Do we need a stronger evidence of the absurdity of hereditary government than is seen in descendants of those men, in any line of life, who once were famous? Is there scarcely an instance in which there is not a total reverse of the character? It appears as if the tide of mental faculties flowed as far as it could in certain channels, and then forsook its course and arose in others. How irrational then is the hereditary system which establishes channels of power in company with which wisdom refuses to flow! By continuing this absurdity, man is perpetually in contradiction with himself; he accepts, for a king, or a chief magistrate, or a legislator, a person whom he would not elect for a constable.

It appears to general observation that revolutions create genius and talents; but those events do no more than bring them forward. There exists in man a mass of sense lying in a dormant state, and which, unless something excites it to action, will descend with him, in that condition, to the grave. As it is to the advantage of society that the whole of its faculties should be employed, the construction of government ought to be such as to bring forward, by a quiet and regular operation, all that extent of capacity which never fails to appear in revolutions.

This cannot take place in the insipid state of hereditary government, not only because it prevents, but because it operates to benumb. When the mind of a nation is bowed down by any political superstition in its government, such as hereditary succession is, it loses a considerable portion of its powers on all other subjects and objects. Hereditary succession requires the same obedience to ignorance as to wisdom; and when once the mind can bring itself to pay this indiscriminate reverence, it descends below the stature of mental manhood. It is fit to be great only in little things. It acts a treachery upon itself, and suffocates the sensations that urge to detection.

Though the ancient governments present to us a miserable picture of the condition of man, there is one which above all others exempts itself from the general description. I mean the democracy of the Athenians. We see more to admire and less to condemn, in that great, extraordinary people, than in anything which history affords.

Mr. Burke is so little acquainted with constituent principles of government that he confounds democracy and representation together. Representation was a thing unknown in the ancient democracies. In those the mass of the people met and enacted laws (grammatically speaking) in the first person. Simple democracy was no other than the common hall of the ancients. It signifies the *form* as well as the public principle of the government. As these democracies increased in population, and the territory extended, the simple democratical form became unwieldy and impracticable; and as the system of representation was not known, the consequence was they either degenerated convulsively into monarchies or became absorbed into such as then existed. Had the system of representation been then understood, as it now is, there is no reason to believe that those forms of government now called monarchical or aristocratical would ever have taken place. It was the want of some method to consolidate the parts of society after it became too populous and too extensive for the simple democratical form, and also the lax and solitary condition of shepherds and herdsmen in other parts of the world, that afforded opportunities to those unnatural modes of government to begin.

As it is necessary to clear away the rubbish of errors into which the subject of government has been thrown, I shall proceed to remark on some others.

It has always been the political craft of courtiers and court governments to abuse something which they called republicanism; but what republicanism was, or is, they never attempt to explain. Let us examine a little into this case.

The only forms of government are the democratical, the aristocratical, the monarchical, and what is now called the representative.

What is called a *republic* is not any *particular form* of government. It is wholly characteristical of the purport, matter, or object for which government ought to be instituted, and on which it is to be employed, *res-publica,* the public affairs, or the public good; or, literally translated, the *public thing.* It is a word of a good original, referring to what ought to be the character and business of government; and in this sense it is naturally opposed to the word *monarchy,* which has a base original signification. It means arbitrary power in an individual person; in the exercise of which, *himself,* and not the *res-publica,* is the object.

Every government that does not act on the principle of a republic, or, in other words, that does not make the *res-publica* its whole and sole object, is not a good government. Republican government is no other than government established and conducted for the interest of the public, as well individually as collectively. It is not necessarily connected with any particular form, but it most naturally associates with the representative form, as being best calculated to secure the end for which a nation is at the expense of supporting it.

Various forms of government have affected to style themselves republics. Poland calls itself a republic, but is in fact an hereditary aristocracy, with what is called an elective monarchy. Holland calls itself a republic, which is chiefly aristocratical, with an hereditary stadtholdership. But the government of America, which is wholly on the system of representation, is the only real republic in character and practice that now exists. Its government has no other object than the public business of the nation, and therefore it is properly a republic; and the Americans have taken care that *this,* and no other, shall be the object of their government, by their rejecting everything hereditary and establishing government on the system of representation only.

Those who have said that a republic is not a *form* of government calculated for countries of great extent mistook, in the first place, the *business* of a government for a *form* of government; for the *res-publica* equally appertains to every extent of territory and population. And in the second place, if they meant anything with respect to *form,* it was the simple democratical form, such as was the mode of government in the ancient democracies, in which there was no representation. The case, therefore, is not that a republic cannot be extensive, but that it cannot be extensive on the simple democratic form; and the question naturally presents itself, *What is the best form of government for conducting the* RES-PUBLICA *or* PUBLIC BUSINESS *of a nation after it becomes too extensive and populous for the simple democratical form?*

It cannot be monarchy, because monarchy is subject to an objection of the same amount to which the democratical form was subject.

It is possible that an individual may lay down a system of principles on which government shall be constitutionally established to any extent of territory. This is no more than an operation of the mind, acting by its own powers. But the practice upon those principles, as applying to the various and numerous circumstances of a nation, its agriculture, manufactures, trade, commerce, &c. require a knowledge, of a different kind, and which can be had only from the various parts of society. It is an assemblage of practical knowledge which no one individual can possess; and therefore the monarchical form is as much limited, in useful practice, from the incompetency of knowledge, as was the democratical form from the multiplicity of population. The one degenerates, by extension, into confusion; the other, into ignorance and incapacity, of which all the great monarchies are an evidence. The monarchical form, therefore, could not be a substitute for the democratical, because it has equal inconveniences.

Much less could it when made hereditary. This is the most effectual of all forms to preclude knowledge. Neither could the high democratical mind have voluntarily yielded itself to be governed by children and idiots, and all the motley insignificance of character, which attends such a mere animal system, the disgrace and the reproach of reason and of man.

As to the aristocratical form, it has the same vices and defects with the monarchical, except that the chance of abilities is better from the proportion of numbers, but there is still no security for the right use and application of them.

Referring, then, to the original simple democracy, it affords the true data from which government on a large scale can begin. It is incapable of extension, not from its principle, but from the inconvenience of its form; and monarchy and aristocracy from their incapacity. Retaining, then, democracy as the ground, and rejecting the corrupt systems of monarchy and aristocracy, the representative system naturally presents itself; remedying at once the defects of the simple democracy as to form, and the incapacity of the other two with regard to knowledge.

Simple democracy was society governing itself without the use of secondary means. By ingrafting representation upon democracy, we arrive at a system of government capable of embracing and confederating all the various interests and every extent of territory and population; and that also with advantages as much superior to hereditary government as the republic of letters is to hereditary literature.

It is on this system that the American government is founded. It is representation ingrafted upon democracy. It has settled the form by a scale parallel in all cases to the extent of the principle. What Athens was in miniature, America will be in magnitude. The one was the wonder of the ancient world—the other is becoming the admiration and model of the present. It is the easiest of all the forms of government to be understood and the most eligible in practice; and excludes at once the ignorance and insecurity of the hereditary mode and the inconvenience of the simple democracy.

It is impossible to conceive a system of government capable of acting over such an extent of territory, and such a circle of interests, as is produced by the operation of representation. France, great and populous as it is, is but a spot in the capaciousness of the system. It adapts itself to all possible cases. It is preferable to simple democracy even in small territories. Athens, by representation, would have surpassed her own democracy.

That which is called government, or rather that which we ought to conceive government to be, is no more than some common center in which all the parts of society unite. This cannot be established by any method so conducive to the various interests of the community as by the representative system. It concentrates the knowledge necessary to the interests of the parts and of the whole. It places government in a state of constant maturity. It is, as has been already observed, never young, never old. It is subject neither to nonage nor dotage. It is never in the cradle nor on crutches. It admits not of a separation between knowledge and power, and is superior, as government ought always to be, to all the accidents of individual man, and is therefore superior to what is called monarchy.

A nation is not a body, the figure of which is to be represented by the human body; but is like a body contained within a circle, having a common center in which every radius meets; and that center is formed by representation. To connect representation with what is called monarchy is eccentric government. Representation is of itself the delegated monarchy of a nation, and cannot debase itself by dividing it with another.

Mr. Burke has two or three times in his parliamentary speeches, and in his publications, made use of a jingle of words that convey no ideas. Speaking of government, he says, "It is better to have monarchy for its basis, and republicanism for its corrective, than republicanism for its basis, and monarchy for its corrective." If he means that it is better to correct folly with wisdom than wisdom with folly, I will no otherwise contend with him than to say it would be much better to reject the folly altogether.

But what is this thing which Mr. Burke calls monarchy? Will he explain it: all mankind can understand what representation is; and that it must necessarily include a variety of knowledge and talents. But what security is there for the same qualities on the part of monarchy? Or, when this monarchy is a child, where then is the wisdom? What does it know about government? Who then is the monarch? Or where is the monarchy? If it is to be performed by regency, it proves it to be a farce. A regency is a mock species of republic, and the whole of monarchy deserves no better appellation. It is a thing as various as imagination can paint. It has none of the stable character that government ought to possess. Every succession is a revolution, and every regency a counter-revolution. The whole of it is a scene of perpetual court cabal and intrigue, of which Mr. Burke is himself an instance.

Whether I have too little sense to see, or too much to be imposed upon; whether I have too much or too little pride, or of anything else, I leave out of the question; but certain it is that what is called monarchy always appears to me a silly, contemptible thing. I compare it to something kept behind a curtain, about which there is a great deal of bustle and fuss, and a wonderful air of seeming solemnity; but when, by any accident, the curtain happens to be open and the company see what it is, they burst into laughter.

In the representative system of government, nothing like this can happen. Like the nation itself, it possesses a perpetual stamina as well of body as of mind, and presents itself on the open theater of the world in a fair and manly manner. Whatever are its excellencies or its defects, they are visible to all. It exists not by fraud and mystery; it deals not in cant and sophistry; but inspires a language that, passing from heart to heart, is felt and understood.

We must shut our eyes against reason, we must basely degrade our understanding, not to see the folly of what is called monarchy. Nature is orderly in all her works; but this is a mode of government that counteracts nature. It turns the progress of the human faculties upside down. It subjects age to be governed by children, and wisdom by folly.

On the contrary, the representative system is always parallel with the order and immutable laws of nature, and meets the reason of man in every part. For example:

In the American federal government, more power is delegated to the President of the United States, than to any other individual member of congress. He cannot, therefore, be elected to this office under the age of thirty-five years. By this time the judgment of man becomes matured, and he has lived long enough to be acquainted with men and things, and the country with him. But on the monarchical plan (exclusive of the numerous chances there are against every man born into the world, of drawing a prize in the lottery of human faculties), the next in succession, whatever he may be, is put at the head of a nation, and of a government at the age of eighteen years. Does this appear like an act of wisdom? Is it consistent with the proper dignity and the manly character of a nation? Where is the propriety of calling such a lad the father of the people? In all other cases, a person is a minor until the age of twenty-one years. Before this period he is not trusted with the management of an acre of land, or with the heritable property of a flock of sheep, or a herd of swine; but wonderful to tell! he may at the age of eighteen years be trusted with a nation.

That monarchy is all a bubble, a mere court artifice to procure money, is evident (at least to me) in every character in which it can be viewed. It would be almost impossible, on the rational system of representative government, to make out a bill of expenses to such an enormous amount as this deception admits. Government is not of itself a very chargeable institution. The whole expense of the federal government of America, founded, as I have already said, on the system of representation, and extending over a country nearly ten times as large as England, is but six hundred thousand dollars, or one hundred and thirty thousand pounds sterling.

I presume that no man in his sober senses will compare the character of any of the kings of Europe, with that of General Washington. Yet, in France, and also in England, the expense of the civil list only, for the support of one man, is eight times greater than the whole expense of the federal government of America. To assign a reason for this appears almost impossible. The generality of people in America, especially the poor, are more able to pay taxes than the generality of people either in France or England.

But the case is that the representative system diffuses such a body of knowledge throughout the nation, on the subject of government, as to explode ignorance and preclude imposition. The craft of courts cannot be acted on that ground. There is no place for mystery; nowhere for it to begin. Those who are not in the representation know as much of the nature of business as those who are. An affectation of mysterious importance would there be scouted. Nations can have no secrets; and the secrets of courts, like those of individuals, are always their defects.

In the representative system, the reason for everything must publicly appear. Every man is a proprietor in government, and considers it a necessary part of his business to understand. It concerns his interest because it affects his property. He examines the cost, and compares it with the advantages; and above all, he does not adopt the slavish custom of following what in other governments are called *leaders*.

It can only be by blinding the understanding of man, and making him believe that government is some wonderful mysterious thing, that excessive revenues are obtained. Monarchy is well calculated to ensure this end. It is the popery of government; a thing kept up to amuse the ignorant, and quiet them into paying taxes.

The government of a free country, properly speaking, is not

in the persons, but in the laws. The enacting of those requires no great expense; and when they are administered, the whole of civil government is performed—the rest is all court contrivance.

. . . . .

When it shall be said in any country in the world, my poor are happy: neither ignorance nor distress is to be found among them; my jails are empty of prisoners, my streets of beggars; the aged are not in want, the taxes are not oppressive; the rational world is my friend, because I am the friend of its happiness: when these things can be said, then may that country boast of its constitution and its government.

Within the space of a few years we have seen two revolutions, those of America and France. In the former the contest was long and the conflict severe; in the latter the nation acted with such a consolidated impulse that, having no foreign enemy to contend with, the revolution was complete in power the moment it appeared. From both those instances it is evident that the greatest forces that can be brought into the field of revolutions are reason and common interest. Where these can have the opportunity of acting, opposition dies with fear or crumbles away by conviction. It is a great standing which they have now universally obtained; and we may hereafter hope to see revolutions, or changes in governments, produced with the same quiet operation by which any measure, determinable by reason and discussion is accomplished.

Formerly when divisions arose respecting governments, recourse was had to the sword and a civil war ensued. That savage custom is exploded by the new system, and reference is had to national conventions. Discussion and the general will arbitrates the question, and to this private opinion yields with a good grace, and order is preserved uninterrupted.

Some gentlemen have affected to call the principles, upon which this work and the former part of *The Rights of Man* are founded, "a new-fangled doctrine." The question is not whether these principles are new or old, but whether they are right or wrong. Suppose the former, I will show their effect by a figure easily understood.

It is now towards the middle of February. Were I to take a turn into the country, the trees would present a leafless, wintery appearance. As people are apt to pluck twigs as they go along, I perhaps might do the same, and by chance might observe that a *single bud* on that twig had begun to swell. I should reason very unnaturally, or rather not reason at all, to suppose *this* was the *only* bud in England which had this appearance. Instead of deciding thus, I should instantly conclude that the same appearance was beginning or about to begin everywhere; and though the vegetable sleep will continue longer on some trees and plants than on others, and though some of them may not *blossom* for two or three years, all will be in leaf in the summer, except those which are *rotten*. What pace the political summer may keep with the natural, no human foresight can determine. It is, however, not difficult to perceive that the spring is begun.

THOMAS PAINE

London, Feb. 9, 1792

from THE AGE OF REASON

BEING AN INVESTIGATION OF TRUE
AND OF FABULOUS THEOLOGY

CREDO

. . . .

I believe in one God, and no more; and I hope for happiness beyond this life.

I believe in the equality of man, and I believe that religious duties consist in doing justice, loving mercy, and endeavoring to make our fellow-creatures happy.

But lest it should be supposed that I believe many other things in addition to these, I shall, in the progress of this work, declare the things I do not believe and my reasons for not believing them.

I do not believe in the creed professed by the Jewish church, by the Roman church, by the Greek church, by the Turkish church, by the Protestant church, nor by any church that I know of. My own mind is my own church.

All national institutions of churches—whether Jewish, Christian, or Turkish—appear to me no other than human inventions set up to terrify and enslave mankind and monopolize power and profit.

I do not mean by this declaration to condemn those who believe otherwise. They have the same right to their belief as I have to mine. But it is necessary to the happiness of man that he be mentally faithful to himself. Infidelity does not consist in believing or in disbelieving; it consists in professing to believe what he does not believe.

It is impossible to calculate the moral mischief, if I may so express it, that mental lying has produced in society. When a man has so far corrupted and prostituted the chastity of his mind as to subscribe his professional belief to things he does not believe, he has prepared himself for the commission of every other crime. He takes up the trade of a priest for the sake of gain, and, in order to *qualify* himself for that trade, he begins with a perjury. Can we conceive anything more destructive to morality than this?

Soon after I had published the pamphlet, COMMON SENSE, in America, I saw the exceeding probability that a revolution in the system of government would be followed by a revolution in the system of religion. The adulterous connection of church and state, wherever it had taken place, whether Jewish, Christian, or Turkish, had so effectually prohibited, by pains and penalties, every discussion upon established creeds and upon first principles of religion, that until the system of government should be changed those subjects could not be brought fairly and openly before the world; but that whenever this should be done, a revolution in the system of religion would follow. Human inventions and priestcraft would be detected, and man would return to the pure, unmixed, and unadulterated belief of one God, and no more.

MERCY WARREN
(1728-1814)

As the sister of James Otis, wife of James Warren, and life-long friend of the Adamses, Mercy Otis Warren was close to great men and events during the making of the republic. In her poetry and plays the dominant notes are piety and nationalism. In spite of her friendship for the Adamses, she was a firm follower of her husband when, after the war, he took the Jeffersonian side which was so unpopular in good Massachusetts society that, as Elbridge Gerry said, allegiance to it excluded one from the ranks of gentlemen. In Mercy Warren's *History* these appear, and, along with them, a firm optimism and certainty of the goodness of the American cause and of the future of the American experiment which is strikingly missing from such a high-Federalist as Fisher Ames. The scrupulous care with which, over a thirty-year period, she wrote, and her intimate knowledge of both human and documentary sources, give her *History* particular interest and authority.

Bibliography: Alice Brown, *Mercy Warren*, New York, 1896; Charles and Mary Beard, *The American Spirit*, New York, 1942.

Text: Mercy Warren, *History of the Rise, Progress and Termination of the American Revolution*, Boston, 1805.

from THE HISTORY OF THE RISE, PROGRESS, AND TERMINATION OF THE AMERICAN REVOLUTION

CHAPTER XXX

We have seen the banners of Albion displayed, and the pendants of her proud navy waving over the waters of the western world, and threatening terror, servitude, or desolation, to resisting millions. We have seen through the tragic tale of war, all political connexion with Great Britain broken off, the authority of the parent state renounced, and the independence of the American states sealed by the definitive treaty. The mind now willingly draws a veil over the unpleasing part of the drama, and indulges the imagination in future prospects of peace and felicity; when the soldier shall retreat from the field, lay by the sword, and resume the implements of husbandry—the mechanic return to his former occupation, and the merchant rejoice in the prosperous view of commerce; when trade shall not be restricted by the unjust or partial regulations of foreigners; and when the ports of America shall be thrown open to all the world, and an intercourse kept free, to reap the advantages of commerce extended to all nations.

The young government of this newly established nation had, by the recent articles of peace, a claim to a jurisdiction over a vast territory, reaching from the St. Mary's on the south, to the river St. Croix, the extreme boundary of the east, containing a line of post-roads of eighteen hundred miles, exclusive of the northern and western wilds, but partially settled, and whose limits have not yet been explored. Not the Lycian league, nor any of the combinations of the Grecian states, encircled such an extent of territory; nor does modern history furnish any example of a confederacy of equal magnitude and respectability with that of the United States of America.

We look back with astonishment when we reflect, that it was only in the beginning of the seventeenth century, that the first Europeans landed in Virginia, and that nearly at the same time, a few wandering strangers coasted about the unknown bay of Massachusetts, until they found a footing in Plymouth. Only a century and an half had elapsed, before their numbers and their strength accumulated, until they bade defiance to foreign oppression, and stood ready to meet the power of Britain, with courage and magnanimity scarcely paralleled by the progeny of nations, who had been used to every degree of subodination and obedience.

The most vivid imagination cannot realize the contrast, when it surveys the vast surface of America now enrobed with fruitful fields, and the rich herbage of the pastures, which had been so recently covered with a thick mattress of woods; when it beholds the cultivated vista, the orchards and the beautiful gardens which have arisen within the limits of the Atlantic states, where the deep embrowned, melancholy forest, had from time immemorial sheltered only the wandering savage; where the sweet notes of the feathered race, that follow the track of cultivation, had never chanted their melodious songs: the wild waste had been a haunt only for the hoarse birds of prey, and the prowling quadrupeds that filled the forest.

In a country like America, including a vast variety of soil and climate, producing every thing necessary for convenience and pleasure, every man might be lord of his own acquisition. It was a country where the standard of freedom had recently been erected, to allure the liberal minded to her shores, and to receive and to protect the persecuted subjects of arbitrary power, who might there seek an asylum from the chains of servitude to which they had been subjected in any part of the globe. Here it might rationally be expected, that beside the natural increase, the emigrations to a land of such fair promise of the blessings of plenty, liberty, and peace, to which multitudes would probably resort, there would be exhibited in a few years, a population almost beyond the calculation of figures.

The extensive tract of territory above described, on the borders of the Atlantic, had, as we have seen, been divided into several distinct governments, under the control of the crown of Great Britain; these governments were now united in a strong confederacy, absolutely independent of all foreign domination: the several states retained their own legislative powers; they were proud of their individual independence, tenacious of their republican principles, and newly emancipated from the degrading ideas of foreign control, and the sceptred hand of monarchy. With all these distinguished privileges, deeply impressed with the ideas of internal happiness, we shall see they grew jealous of each other, and soon after the peace, even of the powers of the several governments erected by themselves: they were eager for the acquisition of wealth, and the possession of the new advantages dawning on their country, from their friendly connexions abroad, and their abundant resources at home.

At the same time that these wayward appearances began early

to threaten their internal felicity, the inhabitants of America were in general sensible, that the freedom of the people, the virtue of society, and the stability of their commonwealth, could only be preserved by the strictest union; and that the independence of the United States must be secured by an undeviating adherence to the principles that produced the revolution.

These principles were grounded on the natural equality of man, their right of adopting their own modes of government, the dignity of the people, and that sovereignty which cannot be ceded either to representatives or to kings. But, as a certain writer has expressed it,—"Powers may be delegated for particular purposes; but the omnipotence of society, if any where, is in itself. Princes, senates, or parliaments, are not proprietors or masters; they are subject to the people, who form and support that society, by an eternal law of nature, which has ever subjected a part to the whole."[1]

These were opinions congenial to the feelings, and were disseminated by the pens, of political writers; of Otis, Dickinson, Quincy,[2] and many others, who with pathos and energy had defended the liberties of America, previous to the commencement of hostilities.

On these principles, a due respect must ever be paid to the general will; to the right in the people to dispose of their own monies by a representative voice; and to liberty of conscience without religious tests: on these principles, frequent elections, and rotations of office, were generally thought necessary, without

---

[1] See Lessons to a Prince, by an anonymous writer.—*Warren*.

[2] The characters of Dickinson and Otis are well known, but the early death of Mr. *Quincy* prevented his name from being conspicuous in the history of American worthies. He was a gentleman of abilities and principles which qualified him to be eminently useful, in the great contest to obtain and support the freedom of his country. He had exerted his eloquence and splendid talents for this purpose, until the premature hand of death deprived society of a man, whose genius so well qualified him for the investigation of the claims, and the defence of the rights of mankind. He died on his return from a voyage to Europe, a short time before war was actually commenced between Great Britain and the colonies.

The writings of the above named gentlemen, previous to the commencement of the war, are still in the hands of many.—*Warren*.

precluding the indispensable subordination and obedience due to rulers of their own choice. From the principles, manners, habits, and education of the Americans, they expected from their rulers, economy in expenditure, (both public and private,) simplicity of manners, pure morals, and undeviating probity. These they considered as the emanations of virtue, grounded on a sense of duty, and a veneration for the Supreme Governor of the universe, to whom the dictates of nature teach all mankind to pay homage, and whom they had been taught to worship according to revelation, and the divine precepts of the gospel. Their ancestors had rejected and fled from the impositions and restrictions of men, vested either with princely or priestly authority: they equally claimed the exercise of private judgment, and the rights conscience, unfettered by religious establishments in favor of particular denominations.

They expected a simplification of law; clearly defined distinctions between executive, legislative, and judiciary powers: the right of trial by jury, and a sacred regard to personal liberty and the protection of private property, were opinions embraced by all who had any just ideas of government, law, equity, or morals.

These were the rights of men, the privileges of Englishmen, and the claim of Americans: these were the principles of the Saxon ancestry of the British empire, and of all the free nations of Europe, previous to the corrupt systems introduced by intriguing and ambitious individuals.

These were the opinions of Ludlow and Sydney, of Milton and Harrington: these were principles defended by the pen of the learned, enlightened, and renowned Locke; and even judge Blackstone, in his excellent commentaries on the laws of England, has observed, "that trial by jury and the liberties of the people went out together." Indeed, most of the learned and virtuous writers that have adorned the pages of literature from generation to generation, in an island celebrated for the erudite and comprehensive genius of its inhabitants, have enforced these rational and liberal opinions.

These were the principles which the ancestors of the inhabitants of the United States brought with them from the polished shores of Europe, to the dark wilds of America: these opinions were deeply infixed in the bosoms of their posterity, and nurtured with zeal, until necessity obliged them to announce the declaration of the independence of the United States. We have seen that the instrument which announced the final separation of the American colonies from Great Britain, was drawn by the elegant and energetic pen of Jefferson, with that correct judgment, precision, and dignity, which have ever marked his character.

The declaration of independence, which has done so much honor to the then existing congress, to the inhabitants of the United States, and to the genius and heart of the gentlemen who drew it, in the belief, and under the awe, of the Divine Providence, ought to be frequently read by the rising youth of the American states, as a palladium of which they should never lose sight, so long as they wish to continue a free and independent people.

This celebrated paper, which will be admired in the annals of every historian, begins with an assertion, that all men are created equal, and endowed by their Creator with certain unalienable rights, which nature and nature's God entitle them to claim; and, after appealing to the Supreme Judge of the world for the rectitude of their intentions, it concludes in the name of the *good people* of the *colonies,* by their representatives assembled in congress, they publish and declare, that they are, and of right ought to be, Free and Independent States: in the *name* of the *people,* the fountain of all just authority, relying on the protection of Divine Providence, they mutually pledged themselves to maintain these rights, with their lives, fortunes, and honor.

These principles the *Sons of Columbia* had supported by argument, defended by the sword, and have now secured by negociation, as far as the pledges of national faith and honor will blind society to a strict adherence to equity. This however is seldom longer than it appears to be the interest of nations, or designing individuals of influence and power. Virtue in the sublimest sense, operates only on the minds of a chosen few: in their breasts it will ever find its own reward.

In all ages, mankind are governed less by reason and justice, than by interest and passion: the caprice of a day, or the impulse of a moment, will blow them about as with a whirlwind, and bear them down the current of folly, until awakened by their misery: by these they are often led to breaches of the most solemn engagements, the consequences of which may involve whole nations in wretchedness. It is devoutly to be hoped, that the conduct of America will never stand upon record as a striking example of the truth of this observation. She has fought for her liberties; she has purchased by them the most costly sacrifices: we have seen her embark in the enterprise, with a spirit that gained her the applause of mankind. The United States have procured their own emancipation from foreign thraldom, by the sacrifice of their heroes and their friends: they are now ushered on to the temple of peace, who holds out her wand, and beckons them to make the wisest improvements of the advantages they had acquired, by their patience, perseverance, and valor.

They had now only to close the scenes of war by a quiet dispersion of their own armies, and to witness the last act of hostile parade, the decampment of the battalions of Britain, and the retirement of the potent fleets that had long infested their coasts.

GEORGE WASHINGTON
(1732-1799)

For an out-doors man of action, soldier, and large scale farmer, Washington was forced to do an unconscionable amount of writing, much of it more or less ceremonial in nature. By long practice, on the basis of his laborious youthful training in the mode of the Virginia gentry's style, he eventually learned to express his masculine and thoughtful personality as well as his ideas. The "Circular to the States" has been chosen here in place of such pieces as the familiar "Farewell Address" for several reasons. It is more clearly Washington's own. It represents him at the height rather than the decline of his powers. It expresses the man himself, not the retiring Father of His Country oppressed by the demands of an oracular moment. And, finally, it represents Washington's serious concerns and proposals for his country's future.

Bibliography: Douglas Southall Freeman, *George Washington, a Biography,* New York, 1948; N. W. Stephenson and W. H. Dunn, *George Washington,* New York, 1940.

Text: *The Writings of George Washington from the Original Manuscript Sources,* ed. John C. Fitzpatrick, Washington, 1931.

CIRCULAR TO THE STATES

Head Quarters, Newburgh, June 8, 1783

Sir: The great object for which I had the honor to hold an appointment in the Service of my Country, being accomplished, I am now preparing to resign it into the hands of Congress, and to return to that domestic retirement, which, it is well known, I left with the greatest reluctance, a Retirement, for which I have never ceased to sigh through a long and painful absence, and in which (remote from the noise and trouble of the World) I meditate to pass the remainder of life in a state of undisturbed repose; But before I carry this resolution into effect, I think it a duty incumbent on me, to make this my last official communication, to congratulate you on the glorious events which Heaven has been pleased to produce in our favor, to offer my sentiments respecting some important subjects, which appear to me, to be intimately connected with the tranquility of the United States, to take my leave of your Excellency as a public Character, and to give my final blessing to that Country, in whose service I have spent the prime of my life, for whose sake I have consumed so many anxious days and watchfull nights, and whose happiness being extremely dear to me, will always constitute no inconsiderable part of my own.

Impressed with the liveliest sensibility on this pleasing occasion, I will claim the indulgence of dilating the more copiously on the subjects of our mutual felicitation. When we consider the magnitude of the prize we contended for, the doubtful nature of the contest, and the favorable manner in which it has terminated, we shall find the greatest possible reason for gratitude and rejoicing; this is a theme that will afford infinite delight to every benevolent and liberal mind, whether the event in contemplation, be considered as the source of present enjoyment or the parent of future happiness; and we shall have equal occasion to felicitate ourselves on the lot which Providence has assigned us, whether we view it in a natural, a political or moral point of light.

The Citizens of America, placed in the most enviable condition, as the sole Lords and Proprietors of a vast Tract of Continent, comprehending all the various soils and climates of the World, and abounding with all the necessaries and conveniencies of life, are now by the late satisfactory pacification, acknowledged to be possessed of absolute freedom and Independency; They are, from this period, to be considered as the Actors on a most conspicuous Theatre, which seems to be peculiarly designated by Providence for the display of human greatness and felicity; Here, they are not only surrounded with every thing which can contribute to the completion of private and domestic enjoyment, but Heaven has crowned all its other blessings, by giving a fairer oppertunity for political happiness, than any other Nation has ever been favored with. Nothing can illustrate these observations more forcibly, than a recollection of the happy conjuncture of times and circumstances, under which our Republic assumed its rank among the Nations; The foundation of our Empire was not laid in the gloomy age of Ignorance and Superstition, but at an Epocha when the rights of mankind were better understood and more clearly defined, than at any former period, the researches of the human mind, after social happiness, have been carried to a great extent, the Treasures of knowledge, acquired by the labours of Philosophers, Sages and Legislatures, through a long succession of years, are laid open for our use, and their collected wisdom may be happily applied in the Establishment of our forms of Government; the free cultivation of Letters, the unbounded extension of Commerce, the progressive refinement of Manners, the growing liberality of sentiment, and above all, the pure and benign light of Revelation, have had a meliorating influence on mankind and increased the blessings of Society. At this auspicious period, the United States came into existence as a Nation, and if their Citizens should not be completely free and happy, the fault will be intirely their own.

Such is our situation, and such are our prospects: but notwithstanding the cup of blessing is thus reached out to us, notwithstanding happiness is ours, if we have a disposition to seize the occasion and make it our own; yet, it appears to me there is an option still left to the United States of America, that it is in their choice, and depends upon their conduct, whether they will be respectable and prosperous, or contemptible and miserable as a Nation; This is the time of their political probation, this is the moment when the eyes of the whole World are turned upon them, this is the moment to establish or ruin their national Character forever, this is the favorable moment to give such a tone to our Federal Government, as will enable it to answer the ends of its institution, or this may be the ill-fated moment for relaxing the powers of the Union, annihilating the cement of the Confederation, and exposing us to become the sport of European politics, which may play one State against another to prevent their growing importance, and to serve their own interested purposes. For, according to the system of Policy the States shall adopt at this moment, they will stand or fall, and by their confirmation or lapse, it is yet to be decided, whether the Revolution must ultimately be considered as a blessing or a curse: a blessing or a curse, not to the present age alone, for with our fate will the destiny of unborn Millions be involved.

With this conviction of the importance of the present Crisis, silence in me would be a crime; I will therefore speak to your Excellency, the language of freedom and of sincerity, without disguise; I am aware, however, that those who differ from me in political sentiment, may perhaps remark, I am stepping out of the proper line of my duty, and they may possibly ascribe to arrogance or ostentation, what I know is alone the result of the purest intention, but the rectitude of my own heart, which disdains such unworthy motives, the part I have hitherto acted in life, the determination I have formed, of not taking any share in public business hereafter, the ardent desire I feel, and shall continue to manifest, of quietly enjoying in private life, after all the toils of War, the benefits of a wise and liberal Government, will, I flatter myself, sooner or later convince my Countrymen, that I could have no sinister views in delivering with so little reserve, the opinions contained in this Address.

There are four things, which I humbly conceive, are essential to the well being, I may even venture to say, to the existence of the United States as an Independent Power:

1st. An indissoluble Union of the States under one Federal Head.

2dly. A sacred regard to Public Justice.

3dly. The adoption of a proper Peace Establishment, and

4thly. The prevalence of that pacific and friendly Disposition, among the People of the United States, which will induce them to forget their local prejudices and policies, to make those mutual concessions which are requisite to the general prosperity, and in some instances, to sacrifice their individual advantages to the interest of the Community.

These are the Pillars on which the glorious Fabrick of our Independency and National Character must be supported; Liberty is the Basis, and whoever would dare to sap the foundation, or overturn the Structure, under whatever specious pretexts he may attempt it, will merit the bitterest execration, and the severest punishment which can be inflicted by his injured Country.

On the three first Articles I will make a few observations, leaving the last to the good sense and serious consideration of those immediately concerned.

Under the first head, altho' it may not be necessary or proper for me in this place to enter into a particular disquisition of the principles of the Union, and to take up the great question which has been frequently agitated, whether it be expedient and requisite for the States to delegate a larger proportion of Power to Congress, or not, Yet it will be a part of my duty, and that of every true Patriot, to assert without reserve, and to insist upon the following positions, That unless the States will suffer Congress to exercise those prerogatives, they are undoubtedly invested with by the Constitution, every thing must very rapidly tend to Anarchy and confusion, That it is indispensable to the happiness of the individual States, that there should be lodged somewhere, a Supreme Power to regulate and govern the general concerns of the Confederated Republic, without which the Union cannot be of long duration. That there must be a faithful and pointed compliance on the part of every State, with the late proposals and demands of Congress, or the most fatal consequences will ensue, That whatever measures have a tendency to dissolve the Union, or contribute to violate or lessen the Sovereign Authority, ought to be considered as hostile to the Liberty and Independency of America, and the Authors of them treated accordingly, and lastly, that unless we can be enabled by the concurrence of the States, to participate of the fruits of the Revolution, and enjoy the essential benefits of Civil Society, under a form of Government so free and uncorrupted, so happily guarded against the danger of oppression, as has been devised and adopted by the Articles of Confederation, it will be a subject of regret, that so much blood and treasure have been lavished for no purpose, that so many sufferings have been encountered without a compensation, and that so many sacrifices have been made in vain. Many other considerations might here be adduced to prove, that without an entire conformity to the Spirit of the Union, we cannot exist as an Independent Power; it will be sufficient for my purpose to mention but one or two which seem to me of the greatest importance. It is only in our united Character as an Empire, that our Independence is acknowledged, that our power can be regarded, or our Credit supported among Foreign Nations. The Treaties of the European Powers with the United States of America, will have no validity on a dissolution of the Union. We shall be left nearly in a state of Nature, or we may find by our own unhappy experience, that there is a natural and necessary progression, from the extreme of anarchy to the extreme of Tyranny; and that arbitrary power is most easily established on the ruins of Liberty abused to licentiousness.

As to the second Article, which respects the performance of Public Justice, Congress have, in their late Address to the United States, almost exhausted the subject, they have explained their Ideas so fully, and have enforced the obligations the States are under, to render compleat justice to all the Public Creditors, with so much dignity and energy, that in my opinion, no real friend to the honor and Independency of America, can hesitate a single moment respecting the propriety of complying with the just and honorable measures proposed; if their Arguments do not produce conviction, I know of nothing that will have greater influence; especially when we recollect that the System referred to, being the result of the collected Wisdom of the Continent, must be esteemed, if not perfect, certainly the least objectionable of any that could be devised; and that if it shall not be carried into immediate execution, a National Bankruptcy, with all its deplorable consequences will take place, before any different Plan can possibly be proposed and adopted; So pressing are the present circumstances! and such is the alternative now offered to the States!

The ability of the Country to discharge the debts which have been incurred in its defence, is not to be doubted, an inclination, I flatter myself, will not be wanting, the path of our duty is plain before us, honesty will be found on every experiment, to be the best and only true policy, let us then as a Nation be just, let us fulfil the public Contracts, which Congress had undoubtedly a right to make for the purpose of carrying on the War, with the same good faith we suppose ourselves bound to perform our private engagements; in the mean time, let an attention to the chearfull performance of their proper business, as Individuals, and as members of Society, be earnestly inculcated on the Citizens of America, that will they strengthen the hands of Government, and be happy under its protection: every one will reap the fruit of his labours, every one will enjoy his own acquisitions without molestation and without danger.

In this state of absolute freedom and perfect security, who will grudge to yield a very little of his property to support the common interest of Society, and insure the protection of Government? Who does not remember, the frequent declarations, at the commencement of the War, that we should be compleatly satisfied, if at the expence of one half, we could defend the remainder of our possessions? Where is the Man to be found, who wishes to remain indebted, for the defence of his own person and property, to the exertions, the bravery, and the blood of others, without making one generous effort to repay the debt of honor and of gratitude? In what part of the Continent shall we find any Man, or body of Men, who would not blush to stand up and propose measures, purposely calculated to rob the Soldier of his Stipend, and the Public Creditor of his due? and were it possible that such a flagrant instance of Injustice could ever happen, would it not excite the general indignation, and tend to bring down, upon the Authors of such measures, the aggravated vengeance of Heaven? If after all, a spirit of disunion or a temper of obstinacy and perverseness, should manifest itself in any of the States, if such an ungracious disposition should attempt to frustrate all the happy effects that might be expected to flow from the Union, if there should be a refusal to comply with the requisitions for Funds to discharge the annual interest of the public debts, and if that refusal should revive again all those jealousies and produce all those evils, which are now happily removed, Congress, who have in all their Transaction shewn a great degree of magnanimity and justice, will stand justified in the sight of God and Man, and the State alone which puts itself in opposition to the aggregate Wisdom of the Continent, and follows such mistaken and pernicious Councils, will be responsible for all the consequences.

For my own part, conscious of having acted while a Servant of the Public, in the manner I conceived best suited to promote the real interests of my Country; having in consequence of my fixed belief in some measure pledged myself to the Army, that their Country would finally do them compleat and ample Justice; and not wishing to conceal any instance of my official conduct from the eyes of the World, I have thought proper to transmit to your Excellency the inclosed collection of Papers, relative to the half pay and commutation granted by Congress to the Officers of the Army; From these communications, my decided sentiment will be clearly comprehended, together with the conclusive reasons which induced me, at an early period, to recommend the adoption of the measure, in the most earnest and serious manner. As the proceedings of Congress, the Army, and myself are open to all, and contain in my opinion, sufficient information to remove the prejudices and errors which may have been entertained by any; I think it unnecessary to say any thing more, than just to observe, that the Resolutions of Congress, now alluded to, are undoubtedly as absolutely binding upon the United States, as the most solemn Acts of Confederation or Legislation. As to the Idea, which I am informed has in some instances prevailed, that the half pay and commutation are to be regarded merely in the odious light of a Pension, it ought to be exploded forever; that Provision, should be viewed as it really was, a reasonable compensation offered by Congress, at a time when they had nothing else to give, to the Officers of the Army, for services then to be performed. It was the only means to prevent a total dereliction of the Service, It was a part of their hire, I may be allowed to say, it was the price of their blood and of your Independency, it is therefore more than a common debt, it is a debt of honour, it can never be considered as a Pension or gratuity, nor be cancelled until it is fairly discharged.

With regard to a distinction between Officers and Soldiers, it is sufficient that the uniform experience of every Nation of the World, combined with our own, proves the utility and propriety of the discrimination. Rewards in proportion to the aids the public derives from them, are unquestionably due to all its Servants; In some Lines, the Soldiers have perhaps generally had as ample a compensation for their Services, by the large Bounties which have been paid to them, as their Officers will receive in the proposed Commutation, in others, if besides the donation of Lands, the payment of Arrearages of Cloathing and Wages (in which Articles all the component parts of the Army must be put upon the same footing) we take into the estimate, the Bounties many of the Soldiers have received and the gratuity of one Year's full pay, which is promised to all, possibly their situation (every circumstance being duly considered) will not be deemed less eligible than that of the Officers. Should a farther reward, however, be judged equitable, I will venture to assert, no one will enjoy greater satisfaction than myself, on seeing an exemption from Taxes for a limited time, (which has been petitioned for in some instances) or any other adequate immunity or compensation, granted to the brave defenders of their Country's Cause; but neither the adoption or rejection of this proposition will in any manner affect, much less militate against, the Act of Congress, by which they have offered five years full pay, in lieu of the half pay for life, which had been before promised to the Officers of the Army.

Before I conclude the subject of public justice, I cannot omit to mention the obligations this Country is under, to that meritorious Class of veteran Non-commissioned Officers and Privates, who have been discharged for inability, in consequence of the Resolution of Congress of the 23d of April 1782, on an annual pension for life, their peculiar sufferings, their singular merits and claims to that provision need only be known, to interest all the feelings of humanity in their behalf: nothing but a punctual payment of their annual allowance can rescue them from the most complicated misery, and nothing could be a more melancholy and distressing sight, than to behold those who have shed their blood or lost their limbs in the service of their Country, without a shelter, without a friend, and without the means of obtaining any of the necessaries or comforts of Life; compelled to beg their daily bread from door to door! suffer me to recommend those of this discription, belonging to your State, to the warmest patronage of your Excellency and your Legislature.

It is necessary to say but a few words on the third topic which was proposed, and which regards particularly the defence of the Republic, As there can be little doubt but Congress will recommend a proper Peace Establishment for the United States, in which a due attention will be paid to the importance of placing the Militia of the Union upon a regular and respectable footing; If this should be the case, I would beg leave to urge the great advantage of it in the strongest terms. The Militia of this Country must be considered as the Palladium of our security, and the first effectual resort in case of hostility; It is essential therefore, that the same system should pervade the whole; that the formation and discipline of the Militia of the Continent should be absolutely uniform, and that the same species of Arms, Accoutrements and Military Apparatus, should be introduced in every part of the United States; No one, (who has not learned it from experience,) can conceive the difficulty, expence, and confusion which result from a contrary system, or the vague Arrangements which have hitherto prevailed.

If in treating of political points, a greater latitude than usual has been taken in the course of this Address, the importance of the Crisis, and the magnitude of the objects in discussion, must be my apology: It is, however, neither my wish or expectation, that the preceeding observations should claim any regard, except so far as they shall appear to be dictated by a good intention, consonant to the immutable rules of Justice; calculated to produce a liberal system of policy, and founded on whatever experience may have been acquired by a long and close attention to public business. Here I might speak with the more confidence from my actual observations, and, if it would not swell this Letter (already too prolix) beyond the bounds I had prescribed myself: I could demonstrate to every mind open to conviction, that in less time and with much less expence than has been incurred, the War might have been brought to the same happy conclusion, if the resourses of the Continent could have been properly drawn forth, that the distresses and disappointments which have very often occurred, have in too many instances, resulted more from a want of energy, in the Continental Government, than a deficiency of means in the particular States. That the inefficiency of measures, arising from the want of an adequate authority in the Supreme Power, from a partial compliance with the Requisitions of Congress in some of the States, and from a failure of punctuality in others, while it tended to damp the zeal of those which were more willing to exert themselves; served also to accumulate the expences of the War, and to frustrate the best concerted Plans, and that the discouragement occasioned by the complicated difficulties and embarrassments, in which our affairs were, by this means involved, would have long ago produced the dissolution of any Army, less patient, less virtuous and less persevering, than that which I have had the honor to command. But while I mention these things, which are notorious facts, as the defects of our Federal Constitution, particularly in the prosecution of a War, I beg it may be understood, that as I have ever taken a pleasure in gratefully acknowledging the assistance and support I have derived from every Class of Citizens, so shall I always be happy to do justice to the unparalleled exertion of the individual States, on many interesting occasions.

ALEXANDER HAMILTON
(*1757-1804*)

AND

JAMES MADISON
(*1751-1836*)

The Federalist transcended an origin in mere propaganda to achieve the permanence of political philosophy. Conceived by Alexander Hamilton as a series of *ad hoc* publications to win New York State's ratification of the Constitution, it grew under the hands of Hamilton and James Madison and John Jay into an enduringly important analysis of the nature of federal government, a stature far greater than the simply historic importance which its 85 installments in various New York newspapers of 1787 and 1788 could possibly give it.

One of the interesting developments of the mid-twentieth century has been the increased attention given to Madison and his part, not only in the *Federalist* but in the entire period. The intensely controversial and mercurial figure of Hamilton, political conservative, industrial radical, potential Man on Horseback, tended in the past to obscure that of the subtle little Virginia squire. But now the true importance of Madison's philosophic and astute mind is being recognized. The selections that follow reveal the two men in an interesting juxtaposition.

Bibliography: Paul L. Ford, *The Federalist,* New York, 1898; F. C. Prescott, *Alexander Hamilton and Thomas Jefferson,* New York, 1934; Irving Brant, *James Madison, Father of the Constitution,* New York, 1950.

Text: H. C. Lodge, ed., *The Federalist,* 1888.

from THE FEDERALIST

FOR THE INDEPENDENT JOURNAL

THE FEDERALIST. NO. I

(HAMILTON)

To the People of the State of New York:

After an unequivocal experience of the inefficiency of the subsisting federal government, you are called upon to deliberate on a new Constitution for the United States of America. The subject speaks its own importance; comprehending in its consequences nothing less than the existence of the UNION, the safety and welfare of the parts of which it is composed, the fate of an empire in many respects the most interesting in the world. It has been frequently remarked that it seems to have been reserved to the people of this country, by their conduct and example, to decide the important question, whether societies of men are really capable or not of establishing good government from reflection and choice, or whether they are forever destined to depend for their political constitutions on accident and force. If there be any truth in the remark, the crisis at which we are arrived may with propriety be regarded as the era in which that decision is to be made; and a wrong election of the part we shall act may, in this view, deserve to be considered as the general misfortune of mankind.

This idea will add the inducements of philanthropy to those of patriotism, to heighten the solicitude which all considerate and good men must feel for the event. Happy will it be if our choice should be directed by a judicious estimate of our true interests, unperplexed and unbiased by considerations not connected with the public good. But this is a thing more ardently to be wished than seriously to be expected. The plan offered to our deliberations affects too many particular interests, innovates upon too many local institutions, not to involve in its discussion a variety of objects foreign to its merits, and of views, passions and prejudices little favourable to the discovery of truth.

Among the most formidable of the obstacles which the new Constitution will have to encounter may readily be distinguished the obvious interest of a certain class of men in every State to resist all changes which may hazard a diminution of the power, emolument, and consequence of the offices they hold under the State establishments; and the perverted ambition of another class of men, who will either hope to aggrandise themselves by the confusions of their country, or will flatter themselves with fairer prospects of elevation from the subdivision of the empire into several partial confederacies than from its union under one government.

It is not, however, my design to dwell upon observations of this nature. I am well aware that it would be disingenuous to resolve indiscriminately the opposition of any set of men (merely because their situations might subject them to suspicion) into interested or ambitious views. Candour will oblige us to admit that even such men may be actuated by upright intentions; and it cannot be doubted that much of the opposition which has made its appearance, or may hereafter make its appearance, will spring from sources, blameless at least, if not respectable—the honest errors of minds led astray by preconceived jealousies and fears. So numerous indeed and so powerful are the causes which serve to give a false bias to the judgment, that we, upon many occasions, see wise and good men on the wrong as well as on the right side of questions of the first magnitude to society. This circumstance, if duly attended to, would furnish a lesson of moderation to those who are ever so much persuaded of their being in the right in any controversy. And a further reason for caution, in this respect, might be drawn from the reflection that we are not always sure that those who advocate the truth are influenced by purer principles than their antagonists. Ambition, avarice, personal animosity, party opposition, and many other motives not more laudable than these, are apt to operate as well upon those who support as those who oppose the right side of a question. Were there not even these inducements to moderation, nothing could be more ill-judged than that intolerant spirit which has, at all times, characterised political parties. For in politics, as in religion, it is equally absurd to aim at making proselytes by fire and sword. Heresies in either can rarely be cured by persecution.

And yet, however just these sentiments will be allowed to be, we have already sufficient indications that it will happen in this as in all former cases of great national discusssion. A torrent of angry and malignant passions will be let loose. To judge from the conduct of the opposite parties, we shall be led to conclude that they will mutually hope to evince the justness of their opinions, and to increase the number of their converts by the loudness of their declamations and the bitterness of their invectives. An enlightened zeal for the energy and efficiency of government will be stigmatised as the offspring of a temper fond of despotic power and hostile to the principles of liberty. An over-scrupulous jealousy of danger to the rights of the people, which is more commonly the fault of the head than of the heart, will be represented as mere pretence and artifice, the stale bait for popularity at the expense of the public good. It will be forgotten, on the one hand, that jealousy is the usual concomitant of love, and that the noble enthusiasm of liberty is apt to be infected with a spirit of narrow and illiberal distrust. On the other hand, it will be equally forgotten that the vigour of government is essential to the security of liberty; that, in the contemplation of a sound and well-informed judgment, their interest can never be separated; and that a dangerous ambition more often lurks behind the specious mask of zeal for the rights of the people than under the forbidding appearance of zeal for the firmness and efficiency of government. History will teach us that the former has been found a much more certain road to the introduction of despotism than the latter, and that of those men who have overturned the liberties of republics, the greatest number have begun their career by paying an obsequious court to the people; commencing demagogues, and ending tyrants.

In the course of the preceding observations, I have had an eye, my fellow-citizens, to putting you upon your guard against all attempts, from whatever quarter, to influence your decision, in a matter of the utmost moment to your welfare, by any impressions other than those which may result from the evidence of truth. You will, no doubt, at the same time, have collected from the general scope of them, that they proceed from a source not unfriendly to the new Constitution. Yes, my countrymen, I own to you that, after having given it an attentive consideration, I am clearly of opinion it is your interest to adopt it. I am convinced that this is the safest course for your liberty, your dignity, and your happiness. I affect not reserves which I do not feel. I will not amuse you with an appearance of deliberation when I have decided. I frankly acknowledge to you my convictions, and I will freely lay before you the reasons on which they are founded. The consciousness of good intentions disdains ambiguity. I shall not, however, multiply professions on this head. My motives must remain in the depository of my own breast. My arguments will be open to all, and may be judged of by all. They shall at least be offered in a spirit which will not disgrace the cause of truth.

I propose, in a series of papers, to discuss the following interesting particulars:—*The utility of the UNION to your political prosperity—The insufficiency of the present Confederation to preserve that Union—The necessity of a government at least equally energetic with the one proposed, to the attainment of this object—The conformity of the proposed Constitution to the true principles of republican government—Its analogy to your own State constitution—and lastly, The additional security which its adoption will afford to the preservation of that species of government, to liberty, and to property.*

In the progress of this discussion I shall endeavour to give a satisfactory answer to all the objections which shall have made their appearance, that may seem to have any claim to your attention.

It may perhaps be thought superfluous to offer arguments to prove the utility of the UNION, a point, no doubt, deeply engraved on the hearts of the great body of the people in every State, and one which, it may be imagined, has no adversaries. But the fact is, that we already hear it whispered in the private circles of those who oppose the new Constitution, that the thirteen States are of too great extent for any general system, and that we must of necessity resort to separate confederacies of distinct portions of the whole.[1] This doctrine will, in all probability, be gradually propagated, till it has votaries enough to countenance an

---

[1] The same idea, tracing the arguments to their consequences, is held out in several of the late publications against the new Constitution.—PUBLIUS.—*Hamilton.*

open avowal of it. For nothing can be more evident, to those who are able to take an enlarged view of the subject, than the alternative of an adoption of the new Constitution or a dismemberment of the Union. It will therefore be of use to begin by examining the advantages of that Union, the certain evils, and the probable dangers, to which every State will be exposed from its dissolution. This shall accordingly constitute the subject of my next address. PUBLIUS.

FROM THE NEW YORK PACKET, FRIDAY, NOVEMBER 23, 1787

THE FEDERALIST. NO. X

(MADISON)

To the People of the State of New York:

Among the numerous advantages promised by a well-constructed Union, none deserves to be more accurately developed than its tendency to break and control the violence of faction. The friend of popular governments never finds himself so much alarmed for their character and fate as when he contemplates their propensity to this dangerous vice. He will not fail, therefore, to set a due value on any plan which, without violating the principles to which he is attached, provides a proper cure for it. The instability, injustice, and confusion introduced into the public councils, have, in truth, been the mortal diseases under which popular governments have everywhere perished; as they continue to be the favourite and fruitful topics from which the adversaries to liberty derive their most specious declamations. The valuable improvements made by the American constitutions on the popular models, both ancient and modern, cannot certainly be too much admired; but it would be an unwarrantable partiality, to contend that they have as effectually obviated the danger on this side, as was wished and expected. Complaints are everywhere heard from our most considerate and virtuous citizens, equally the friends of public and private faith, and of public and personal liberty, that our governments are too unstable, that the public good is disregarded in the conflicts of rival parties, and that measures are too often decided, not according to the rules of justice and the rights of the minor party, but by the superior force of an interested and overbearing majority. However anxiously we may wish that these complaints had no foundation, the evidence of known facts will not permit us to deny that they are in some degree true. It will be found, indeed, on a candid review of our situation, that some of the distresses under which we labour have been erroneously charged on the operation of our governments; but it will be found, at the same time, that other causes will not alone account for many of our heaviest misfortunes; and, particularly, for that prevailing and increasing distrust of public engagements, and alarm for private rights, which are echoed from one end of the continent to the other. These must be chiefly, if not wholly, effects of the unsteadiness and injustice with which a factious spirit has tainted our public administrations.

By a faction, I understand a number of citizens, whether amounting to a majority or minority of the whole, who are united and actuated by some common impulse of passion, or of interest, adverse to the rights of other citizens, or to the permanent and aggregate interests of the community.

There are two methods of curing the mischiefs of faction: the one, by removing its causes; the other, by controlling its effects.

There are again two methods of removing the causes of faction: the one, by destroying the liberty which is essential to its existence; the other, by giving to every citizen the same opinions, the same passions, and the same interests.

It could never be more truly said than of the first remedy, that it was worse than the disease. Liberty is to faction what air is to fire, an ailment without which it instantly expires. But it could not be less folly to abolish liberty, which is essential to political life, because it nourishes faction, than it would be to wish the annihilation of air, which is essential to animal life, because it imparts to fire its destructive agency.

The second expedient is as impracticable as the first would be unwise. As long as the reason of man continues fallible, and he is at liberty to exercise it, different opinions will be formed. As long as the connection subsists between his reason and his self-love, his opinions and his passions will have a reciprocal influence on each other; and the former will be objects to which the latter will attach themselves. The diversity in the faculties of men, from which the rights of property originate, is not less an insuperable obstacle to a uniformity of interests. The protection of these faculties is the first object of government. From the protection of different and unequal faculties of acquiring property, the possession of different degrees and kinds of property immediately results; and from the influence of these on the sentiments and views of the respective proprietors, ensues a division of the society into different interests and parties.

The latent causes of faction are thus sown in the nature of man; and we see them everywhere brought into different degrees of activity, according to the different circumstances of civil society. A zeal for different opinions concerning religion, concerning government, and many other points, as well of speculation as of practice; an attachment of different leaders ambitiously contending for pre-eminence and power; or to persons of other descriptions whose fortunes have been interesting to the human passions, have, in turn, divided mankind into parties, inflamed them with mutual animosity, and rendered them much more disposed to vex and oppress each other than to co-operate for their common good. So strong is this propensity of mankind to fall into mutual animosities, that where no substantial occasion presents itself, the most frivolous and fanciful distinctions have been sufficient to kindle their unfriendly passions and excite their most violent conflicts. But the most common and durable source of factions has been the various and unequal distribution of property. Those who hold and those who are without property have ever formed distinct interests in society. Those who are creditors, and those who are debtors, fall under a like discrimination. A landed interest, a manufacturing interest, a mercantile interest, a moneyed interest, with many lesser interests, grow up of necessity in civilised nations, and divide them into different classes, activated by different sentiments and views. The regulation of these various and interfering interests forms the principal task of modern legislation, and involves the spirit of party and faction in the necessary and ordinary operations of the government.

No man is allowed to be a judge in his own cause, because his interest would certainly bias his judgment, and, not improbably, corrupt his integrity. With equal, nay, with greater reason, a body of men are unfit to be both judges and parties at the same time; yet what are many of the most important acts of legislation but so many judicial determinations, not indeed concerning the rights of single persons, but concerning the rights of large bodies of citizens? And what are the different classes of legislators but advocates and parties to the causes which they determine? Is a law proposed concerning private debts? It is a question to which the creditors are parties on one side and the debtors on the other. Justice ought to hold the balance between them. Yet the parties are, and must be, themselves the judges; and the most numerous party, or, in other words, the most powerful faction must be expected to prevail. Shall domestic manufactures be encouraged, and in what degree, by restrictions on foreign manufactures? are questions which would be differently decided by the landed and the manufacturing classes, and probably by neither with a sole regard to justice and the public good. The apportionment of taxes on the various descriptions of property is an act which seems to require the most exact impartiality; yet there is, perhaps, no legislative act in which greater opportunity and temptation are given to a predominant party to trample on the rules of justice. Every shilling with which they overburden the inferior number is a shilling saved to their own pockets.

It is in vain to say that enlightened statesmen will be able to adjust these clashing interests, and render them all subservient to the public good. Enlightened statesmen will not always be at the helm. Nor, in many cases, can such an adjustment be made at all without taking into view indirect and remote considerations, which will rarely prevail over the immediate interest which one party may find in disregarding the rights of another or the good of the whole.

The inference to which we are brought is, that the *causes* of faction cannot be removed, and that relief is only to be sought in the means of controlling its *effects*.

If a faction consists of less than a majority, relief is supplied by the republican principle, which enables the majority to defeat its sinister views by regular vote. It may clog the administration, it may convulse the society; but it will be unable to execute and mask its violence under the forms of the Constitution. When a majority is included in a faction, the form of popular government, on the other hand, enables it to sacrifice to its ruling passion or interest both the public good and the rights of other citizens. To secure the public good and private rights against the danger of such a faction, and at the same time to preserve the spirit and the form of popular government, is then the great object to which our inquiries are directed. Let me add that it is the great desideratum by which this form of government can be rescued from the opprobrium under which it has so long laboured, and be recommended to the esteem and adoption of mankind.

By what means is this object obtainable? Evidently by one of two only. Either the existence of the same passion or interest in a majority at the same time must be prevented, or the majority, having such co-existent passion or interest, must be rendered, by their number and local situation, unable to concert and carry into effect schemes of oppression. If the impulse and the opportunity be suffered to coincide, we well know that neither moral nor religious motives can be relied on as an adequate control. They are not found to be such on the injustice and violence of individuals, and lose their efficacy in proportion to the number combined together, that is, in proportion as their efficacy becomes needful.

From this view of the subject it may be concluded that a pure democracy, by which I mean a society consisting of a small number of citizens, who assemble and administer the government in person, can admit of no cure for the mischiefs of faction. A common passion or interest will, in almost every case, be felt by a majority of the whole; a communication and concert result from the form of government itself; and there is nothing to check the inducements to sacrifice the weaker party or an obnoxious individual. Hence it is that such democracies have ever been spectacles of turbulence and contention; have ever been found incompatible with personal security or the rights of property; and have in general been as short in their lives as they have been violent in their deaths. Theoretic politicians, who have patronised this species of government, have erroneously supposed that by reducing mankind to a perfect equality in their political rights, they would, at the same time, be perfectly equalised and assimilated in their possessions, their opinions, and their passions.

A republic, by which I mean a government in which the scheme of representation takes place, opens a different prospect, and promises the cure for which we are seeking. Let us examine the points in which it varies from pure democracy, and we shall comprehend both the nature of the cure and the efficacy which it must derive from the Union.

The two great points of difference between a democracy and a republic are: first, the delegation of the government, in the latter, to a small number of citizens elected by the rest; secondly, the greater number of citizens, and greater sphere of country, over which the latter may be extended.

The effect of the first difference is, on the one hand, to refine and enlarge the public views, by passing them through the medium of a chosen body of citizens, whose wisdom may best discern the true interest of their country, and whose patriotism and love of justice will be least likely to sacrifice it to temporary or partial considerations. Under such a regulation, it may well happen that the public voice, pronounced by the representatives of the people, will be more consonant to the public good than if pronounced by the people themselves, convened for the purpose. On the other hand, the effect may be inverted. Men of factious tempers, of local prejudices, or of sinister designs, may, by intrigue, by corruption, or by other means, first obtain the suffrages, and then betray the interests, of the people. The question resulting is, whether small or extensive republics are more favourable to the election of proper guardians of the public weal; and it is clearly decided in favour of the latter by two obvious considerations:

In the first place, it is to be remarked that, however small the republic may be, the representatives must be raised to a certain number, in order to guard against the cabals of a few; and that, however large it may be, they must be limited to a certain number, in order to guard against the confusion of a multitude. Hence the number of representatives in the two cases not being in proportion to that of the two constituents, and being proportionally greater in the small republic, it follows that, if the proportion of fit characters be not less in the large than in the small republic, the former will present a greater option, and consequently a greater probability of a fit choice.

In the next place, as each representative will be chosen by a greater number of citizens in the large than in the small republic, it will be more difficult for unworthy candidates to practise with success the vicious arts by which elections are too often carried; and the suffrages of the people being more free, will be more likely to centre in men who possess the most attractive merit and the most diffusive and established character.

It must be confessed that in this, as in most other cases, there is a mean, on both sides of which inconveniences will be found to lie. By enlarging too much the number of electors, you render the representative too little acquainted with all their local circumstances and lesser interests; as by reducing it too much, you render him unduly attached to these, and too little fit to comprehend and pursue great and national objects. The federal Constitution forms a happy combination in this respect; the great and aggregate interests being referred to the national, the local and particular to the State legislatures.

The other point of difference is, the greater number of citizens and extent of territory which may be brought within the compass of republican than of democratic government; and it is this circumstance principally which renders factious combinations less to be dreaded in the former than in the latter. The smaller the society, the fewer probably will be the distinct parties and interests composing it; the fewer the distinct parties and interests, the more frequently will a majority be found of the same party; and the smaller the number of individuals composing a majority, and the smaller the compass within which they are placed, the more easily will they concert and execute their plans of oppression. Extend the sphere, and you take in a greater variety of parties and interests; you make it less probable that a majority of the whole will have a common motive to invade the rights of other citizens; or if such a common motive exists, it will be more difficult for all who feel it to discover their own strength, and to act in unison with each other. Besides other impediments, it may be remarked that, where there is a consciousness of unjust or dishonourable purposes, communication is always checked by distrust in proportion to the number whose concurrence is necessary.

Hence, it clearly appears, that the same advantage which a republic has over a democracy, in controlling the effects of faction, is enjoyed by a large over a small republic—is enjoyed by the Union over the States composing it. Does the advantage consist in the substitution of representatives whose enlightened views and virtuous sentiments render them superior to local prejudices and to schemes of injustice? It will not be denied that the representation of the Union will be most likely to possess these requisite endowments. Does it consist in the greater security afforded by a greater variety of parties, against the event of any one party being able to outnumber and oppress the rest? In an equal degree does the increased variety of parties comprised within the Union increase this security? Does it, in fine, consist in the greater obstacles opposed to the concert and accomplishment of the secret wishes of an unjust and interested majority? Here, again, the extent of the Union gives it the most palpable advantage.

The influence of factious leaders may kindle a flame within their particular States, but will be unable to spread a general conflagration through the other States. A religious sect may degenerate into a political faction in a part of the Confederacy; but the variety of sects dispersed over the entire face of it must secure the national councils against any danger from that source. A rage for paper money, for an abolition of debts, for an equal division of property, or for any other improper or wicked project, will be less apt to pervade the whole body of the Union than a particular member of it; in the same proportion as such a malady is more likely to taint a particular county or district, than an entire State.

In the extent and proper structure of the Union, therefore, we behold a republican remedy for the diseases most incident to republican government. And according to the degree of pleasure and pride we feel in being republicans, ought to be our zeal in cherishing the spirit and supporting the character of Federalists. PUBLIUS.

FROM THE NEW YORK PACKET, TUESDAY, DECEMBER 18, 1787

THE FEDERALIST. NO. XXIII

(HAMILTON)

To the People of the State of New York:

The necessity of a Constitution, at least equally energetic with the one proposed, to the preservation of the Union, is the point at the examination of which we are now arrived.

This inquiry will naturally divide itself into three branches —the objects to be provided for by the federal government, the quantity of power necessary to the accomplishment of those objects, the persons upon whom that power ought to operate.

ALEXANDER HAMILTON

Its distribution and organisation will more properly claim our attention under the succeeding head.

The principal purposes to be answered by union are these—the common defence of the members; the preservation of the public peace, as well against internal convulsions as external attacks; the regulation of commerce with other nations and between the States; the superintendence of our intercourse, political and commercial, with foreign countries.

The authorities essential to the common defence are these: to raise armies; to build and equip fleets; to prescribe rules for the government of both; to direct their operations; to provide for their support. These powers ought to exist without limitation, *because it is impossible to foresee or define the extent and variety of national exigencies, or the correspondent extent and variety of the means which may be necessary to satisfy them.* The circumstances that endanger the safety of nations are infinite, and for this reason no constitutional shackles can wisely be imposed on the power to which the care of it is committed. This power ought to be co-extensive with all the possible combinations of such circumstances; and ought to be under the direction of the same councils which are appointed to preside over the common defence.

This is one of those truths which, to a correct and unprejudiced mind, carries its own evidence along with it; and may be obscured, but cannot be made plainer by argument or reasoning. It rests upon axioms as simple as they are universal; the *means* ought to be proportioned to the *end;* the persons, from whose agency the attainment of any *end* is expected, ought to possess the *means* by which it is to be attained.

Whether there ought to be a federal government intrusted with the care of the common defence, is a question in the first instance open for discussion; but the moment it is decided in the affirmative, it will follow, that that government ought to be clothed with all the powers requisite to complete execution of its trust. And unless it can be shown that the circumstances which may affect the public safety are reducible within certain determinate limits; unless the contrary of this position can be fairly and rationally disputed, it must be admitted, as a necessary consequence, that there can be no limitation of that authority which is to provide for the defence and protection of the community, in any matter essential to its efficacy—that is, in any matter essential to the *formation, direction,* or *support* of the NATIONAL FORCES.

Defective as the present Confederation has been proved to be, this principle appears to have been fully recognised by the framers of it; though they have not made proper or adequate provision for its exercise. Congress have an unlimited discretion to make requisitions of men and money; to govern the army and navy; to direct their operations. As their requisitions are made constitutionally binding upon the States, who are in fact under the most solemn obligation to furnish the supplies required of them, the intention evidently was, that the United States should command whatever resources were by them judged requisite to the "common defence and general welfare." It was presumed that a sense of their true interests, and a regard to the dictates of good faith, would be found sufficient pledges for the punctual performance of the duty of the members to the federal head.

The experiment has, however, demonstrated that this expectation was ill-founded and illusory; and the observations, made under the last head, will, I imagine, have sufficed to convince the impartial and discerning, that there is an absolute necessity for an entire change in the first principles of the system; that if we are in earnest about giving the Union energy and duration, we must abandon the vain project of legislating upon the States in their collective capacities; we must extend the laws of the federal government to the individual citizens of America; we must discard the fallacious scheme of quotas and requisitions, as equally impracticable and unjust. The result from all this is that the Union ought to be invested with full power to levy troops; to build and equip fleets; and to raise the revenues which will be required for the formation and support of an army and navy, in the customary and ordinary modes practised in other governments.

If the circumstances of our country are such as to demand a compound instead of a simple, a confederate instead of a sole, government, the essential point which will remain to be adjusted will be to discriminate the OBJECTS, as far as it can be done, which shall appertain to the different provinces or departments of power; allowing to each the most ample authority for fulfilling the objects committed to its charge. Shall the Union be constituted the guardian of the common safety? Are fleets and armies and revenues necessary to this purpose? The government of the Union must be empowered to pass all laws, and to make all regulations which have relation to them. The same must be the case in respect to commerce, and to every other matter to which its jurisdiction is permitted to extend. Is the administration of justice between the citizens of the same State the proper department of the local governments? These must possess all the authorities which are connected with this object, and with every other that may be allotted to their particular cognisance and direction. Not to confer in each case a degree of power commensurate to the end, would be to violate the most obvious rules of prudence and propriety, and improvidently to trust the great interests of the nation to hands which are disabled from managing them with vigour and success.

Who so likely to make suitable provisions for the public defence as that body to which the guardianship of the public safety is confided; which, as the centre of information, will best understand the extent and urgency of the dangers that threaten; as the representative of the WHOLE, will feel itself most deeply interested in the preservation of every part; which, from the responsibility implied in the duty assigned to it, will be most sensibly impressed with the necessity of proper exertions; and which, by the extension of its authority throughout the States, can alone establish uniformity and concert in the plans and measures by which the common safety is to be secured? Is there not a manifest inconsistency in devolving upon the federal government the care of the general defence, and leaving in the State governments the *effective* powers by which it is to be provided for? Is not a want of co-operation the infallible consequence of such a system? And will not weakness, disorder, an undue distribution of the burdens and calamities of war, an unnecessary and intolerable increase of expense, be its natural and inevitable concomitants? Have we not had unequivocal experience of its effects in the course of the revolution which we have just accomplished?

Every view we may take of the subject, as candid inquirers after truth, will serve to convince us, that it is both unwise and dangerous to deny the federal government an unconfined authority, as to all those objects which are intrusted to its management. It will indeed deserve the most vigilant and careful attention of the people, to see that it be modelled in such a manner as to admit of its being safely vested with the requisite powers. If any plan which has been, or may be, offered to our consideration, should not, upon a dispassionate inspection, be found to answer this description, it ought to be rejected. A government, the constitution of which renders it unfit to be trusted with all the powers which a free people *ought to delegate to any government,* would be an unsafe and improper depositary of the NATIONAL INTERESTS. Wherever THESE can with propriety be confided, the coincident powers may safely accompany them. This is the true result of all just reasoning upon the subject. And the adversaries of the plan promulgated by the convention ought to have confined themselves to showing that the internal structure of the proposed government was such as to render it unworthy of the confidence of the people. They ought not to have wandered into inflammatory declamations and unmeaning cavils about the extent of the powers. The POWERS are not too extensive for the OBJECTS of federal administration, or, in other words, for the management of our NATIONAL INTERESTS; nor can any satisfactory argument be framed to show that they are chargeable with such an excess. If it be true, as has been insinuated by some of the writers on the other side, that the difficulty arises from the nature of the thing, and that the extent of the country will not permit us to form a government in which such ample powers can safely be reposed, it would prove that we ought to contract our views, and resort to the expedient of separate confederacies, which will move within more practicable spheres. For the absurdity must continually stare us in the face of confiding to a government the direction of the most essential national interests, without daring to trust it to the authorities which are indispensable to their proper and efficient management. Let us not attempt to reconcile contradictions, but firmly embrace a rational alternative.

I trust, however, that the impracticability of one general system cannot be shown. I am greatly mistaken, if anything of weight has yet been advanced of this tendency; and I flatter myself that the observations which have been made in the course of these papers have served to place the reverse of that position in as clear a light as any matter still in the womb of time and experience can be susceptible of. This, at all events, must be evident, that the very difficulty itself, drawn from the extent of the country, is the strongest argument in favour of an energetic government; for any other can certainly never preserve the Union of so large an empire. If we embrace the tenets of those who oppose the adoption of the proposed Constitution, as the standard of our political creed, we cannot fail to verify the gloomy doctrines which predict the impracticability of a national system pervading entire limits of the present Confederacy.   PUBLIUS.

PHILIP FRENEAU

(1752-1832)

Philip Freneau's career was notably stormy in a far from tranquil age. One can only guess what the final effect of his political and journalistic struggles was upon his promising but stifled poetic life. Certainly a characteristic personal cycle through which he passed at least five times did his poetry no good. As a typical cycle, Freneau took over a printing-office and began a newspaper, plunged furiously into a political battle, meanwhile producing most of the prose and poetic content of his paper. Since he regularly chose the radical-democratic side in the years of patrician dominance between 1783 and Jefferson's victory in 1800, he regularly lost the battles and the papers and went either to sea or back to the ancestral farm to recoup his financial and psychic capital.

In spite of his personal defeats, he contributed fundamentally to the eventual Jeffersonian triumph. Jefferson, who had encouraged him to found the *National Gazette* in Philadelphia in 1791 as the primary voice of Anti-Federalism, testified that he had saved the country "when it was galloping fast into monarchy." And when Jefferson came to power Freneau had the satisfaction of distinguishing himself from the petty editors of a venal era by turning down his share of the political spoils, in spite of his growing poverty.

Nothing among all his excellent prose writings was more shrewdly calculated than the letters of Robert Slender, O. S. M. In the period of the Alien and Sedition Acts, when editorial criticism of the government was legally dangerous, Freneau struck, in creating poor little Robert, upon an ironic device which penetrated the Federalist screen of bluster, fear and violence. To assault Robert Slender, so timid, so innocent, so stupid, for his embarrassing questions and naive comment, would be to make oneself a laughing-stock—and to confess the force of what he intimated.

Bibliography: H. H. Clark, *Poems of Freneau,* New York, 1929; H. H. Clark, "Introduction" to *Letters on Various Interesting and Important Subjects, by Philip Freneau,* New York, 1943; Lewis Leary, *That Rascal Freneau,* New Brunswick, 1941.

Text: H. H. Clark, ed., *Letters on Various Interesting and Important Subjects, by Philip Freneau,* Scholars' Facsimiles and Reprints, New York, 1943.

from LETTERS ON VARIOUS INTERESTING AND IMPORTANT SUBJECTS

FELLOW CITIZENS

After having debated the matter with myself at least twenty times, at last I determined to publish all my letters, agreeable to the request of my friends, with several others which I have prepared, and some trifles, that may at least amuse the ignorant, whose brains, like my own, are not able to bear deep reasoning, because they have never learned Latin.

Having come to this conclusion, in I stepped to my neighbour the Latinist, and told him the scheme, with as few round-about disgressions as I could: he heard me to the end of my tale with great patience, and then, emphatically shaking his head, exclaimed, Ah! Robert, I much fear you'll find the truth of the old Latin proverb, *Sutor ne ultra crepidam,*—let the cobler stick to his last. 'Tis a mad thing of you to commence author; for, first, you know you are not *rich*: you don't boast of great connexions, but stand, as you yourself have said a timorous little fellow, undistinguished among the swinish herd. Secondly, you cannot come before the public with a flourish, thus—By Robert Slender, A.M. or D.M. or LL.D. or F.R.S. And in the last place, you have no great man to whom you can dedicate your performance: and let me tell you, that a number of the poets and historians, of both modern and ancient times, would never have obtained the celebrity they enjoy, if they had not been patronized by some great men—Odds my heart, cried I, for I could hold no longer, I thought you would have applauded my resolution, and offered me your assistance; but instead of that, you come forward with your doubts and difficulties. To be sure I am not rich, but what says that to my letters; the public say they like them, and why should I deny them that gratification? —Indeed, I grant that I cannot write myself, with truth, A.M. or D.M. or LL.D. or F.R.S.; but I can write myself, O.S.M. and that will do quite as well. In the name of common sense, said my friend, what do you mean by O.S.M. I'm sure I never heard of it before? Why, answered I, I believe it has very seldom been chosen by any of your great men and great scholars; but it suits me exactly—its meaning is, one of the swinish multitude: and for dedicating, continued I, I'll dedicate to the President of the United States. Nay, replied my friend, that could not otherwise be construed than daring presumption—Well then, to Timothy Pickering—That would be deemed an insult—I'll dedicate, answered I, much agitated, to our own governor Thomas M'Kean, for whom I have more real respect than I have for them both— Why Robert, that would argue too great familiarity—It don't signify, said I, leaping to my feet, I'll dedicate to all their masters —To the Freemen of the United States; and I'll bet you a pair of boots, that my plain stories, shall be by them as well received, with my plain name, and O.S.M. as some of the productions of these flashy fellows with a string of titles, which are of no other use to American freemen, than to lull them to sleep. Robert, replied my friend, I'll not bet with you; I have gotten more boots, shoes and hats, by the election, than I'll wear these three years; but I doubt you will make a poor job of it—dedications are of all others, the most difficult—Have you studied the art of flattery? Can you new vamp a character as easily as you would a pair of old boots; and make it appear fair and unsullied though many years have passed since a single virtuous trait was found in it? Can you collect as many mouthfulls of moonshine as the pallet of vanity can easily admit? Or with a good grace and pious countenance, offer incense to a mortal, who is only clothed with a little brief authority?—If you can do these things, go, dedicate to any great man you please, he'll be your patron; and though your pages be as dull and as stupid as ever disgraced the republic of letters, yet the great man's nod of approbation will place *sterling* value on the performance; but if you dedicate to the freemen of the United States, you—I'll have none of your buts, said I, out of all patience—I'll never flatter vice as long as I live: nay, first, as your book says, I'll "sow nether socks, foot them and mend them too;" and placing my hands in my sides and looking as big as if I was worth a 1000 a-year, Do you think sir, said I, I'd gather moonshine for any man? No sir, if the sides of vanity never stand prominent till they are puffed out by the breath of Robert Slender's flattery, they will be as lean as a lath to the day of judgment—I say, I will dedicate my works to the Freemen, the Lovers of Liberty, the Asserters, Maintainers and Supporters of Independence throughout the United States—And not my works only, added I, but my life also, and all I have, and God knows that's not much, shall be ever at their service, to defend and preserve that invaluable CONSTITUTION and glorious Independence, which is their indescribable honour, and the richest patrimony that true republicans can hand down untarnished to posterity—And if my plain told stories, continued I, can have the effect of calling up the republican spirits to a more ardent love of their country's rights—to more watchfulness, and stricter enquiry, I shall abundantly receive that which I expect—For the good of his country, must undoubtedly be the good of Robert Slender—

And, said my friend, feeling I had talked myself out of breath, What will you do now?—Why, answered I, go home and write my dedication.—Why, answered he, you have done it already. Out of a frolic, when I saw you so earnest, I took down your last reply—here it is—I pronounce it a complete dedication, and any thing you could say after this, would be as fulsome as the flatteries of Dryden—Odds my heart, said I, I did not intend to have been cheated into a dedication neither, I would have— Hold, hold, says he, placing his hand before my mouth, not another word, or all's ruined. Well, well, said I, so be it, if it must be so—only with your consent, I would add, that with the sincerest wishes for your real happiness,

I am,
Fellow Citizens,
Your very humble servant,
ROBERT SLENDER.

LETTER XIX

Mr. Editor,

In reading the history of man, and attending to the important and noble struggles of eminent individuals, either for the preserving their liberty when assailed by rapacious tyrants, or freeing themselves from the galling yoke of slavery and oppression, I have, said my friend the Latinist, as we sat chatting the other day under a tree, felt for them in all their troubles; my heart has bled for their wounds, and gladly, were it in my power, would I have acted the good Samaritan, and poured in the wine and oil. But, continued he, I do not remember that ever my feelings were excited to a higher pitch, than by the fate of Jonathan Robbins. Why, what of him? said I; I think I never heard his name before. I do not remember any of our ministers, or consuls, our generals, or commodores, added I, of that name: if he was one of them, to be sure he might be an object of pity—for, says I, he might have been *recalled,* and disgraced, without knowing for what—or *dishonoured,* by having a young officer placed over his head—or, when almost worn out, and grown grey in the service of his country, a number of men might come forward in the face of the world, and pledge themselves to support and protect all such, as from envy or malevolence might be inclined to raise and circulate stories calculated to injure his reputation, and sully his fair fame.—In the half of the time, said my friend, that you have been conjecturing, I would have told you his story—Odds my life, replied I, let me hear it—has poor Robbins been carbonadoed for going to France (as Dr. Logan did) to make peace, and keep us from murdering one another?—or has he been flogged, like SCHNEIDER and DUANE, for writing the truth, as many people say?—or—If you go on at this rate Robert, said my friend, the moon may change before I'll get time to tell you the story—Why, said I, you well know I would fifty times rather find out a thing myself, than be informed of it by any man alive—but I hope you will go on, and tell the story your own way—Some time ago, said my friend, a British ship called the Hermoine, was taken by the crew—the captain, and some others, fell in the contest—she was carried into a Spanish port, and then sold by those who carried her in, who made off with the booty. After some time, however, the affair was found out, and it was made appear that a Jonathan Robbins was somehow concerned in this business—This Robbins, a citizen of the United States, had before that fatal affair been pressed aboard the Hermoine, and there forced to work and fight in a cause *contrary* to his conscience—yet this man was taken in the United States, imprisoned—tried—not by a jury, mind that—and delivered over in chains to the commander of a British frigate, who immediately sailed for Jamaica, where he will undoubtedly be hanged like a dog. 'Tis all a joke, said I, there is no more truth in it than there is in the Alcoran—A Citizen of the United States delivered up to the British to be hanged because he used every means in his power to obtain his freedom, when actually a slave!!—No, no, says I, 'tis by circulating such stories as this, that your Democrats will lose any little credit they may have acquired—Don't labour under a mistake Robert, replied my friend, 'tis as true as the gospel—Well, answered I, if it is indeed true, I am as sure as I live, that if any state government has given him up, our President will immediately claim him—Softly good friend, returned he, the President advised and requested them to give him up. Did he indeed? says I, then if he did—but I cannot believe it—'tis all over, we must be once more a British colony—for if that were not the case, could any man be blamed, at the risque of his life to obtain his freedom? I think, says I, I have as much of the milk of human kindness flowing in my veins as any a president or king in the world, and yet I believe in my heart, added I, if I were taken prisoner by an Algerine cruiser, if I had it in my power to gain my liberty by sending the whole ship's crew to Davy Jones, bag and baggage, I would not hesitate a moment—Nor would any one blame you for so doing, said my friend—but you must remember, this was a frigate belonging to his Britannic Majesty; the chief supporter of order, good government, humanity and religion in the world—it matters not, says I, somewhat ruffled, what she was, a sloop or frigate, shallop or what you please—or whether she belonged to Dick, Billy, Tom or Harry—answer me only this plain question, Was Robbins kept there against his will, or not? if against his mind, then he was as completely a slave on board the Hermoine as if he had been in Algiers; and is it possible that any freeborn republican, who loves, or ought to love his freedom more than his life, can condemn his equal in rights and in liberty, for breaking the chains with which he is unjustly bound, and which every moment rankle in his flesh?—My God! continued I, is it possible, that if a British rascal makes me a slave, beat, abuse, and compel me to fight contrary to my conscience, and if an opportunity offers by which I may regain my liberty, once more revisit my country, my beloved relations, and dear friends, by the destruction of my violent oppressor and tyrannical enslaver—must I for this be delivered up by my country?—must I for this be delivered up to die?—for asserting my native right, for repelling the unjust attack of a cruel tyrant, for supporting my independence at the risque of my life, must I be sacrificed on the altar of despotic power?—If this be true, added I, what language does the unaccountable action speak to the poor American sailors?—Does it not speak thus—sailors of America, remember, that should you be pressed by any of the ships of war belonging to his Britannic Majesty, ye must there do duty faithfully and truly—if you be set at liberty, 'tis well; if not, though it were in your power to regain your liberty, you *must not;* for in the attempt, should you kill any of his Majesty's subjects, your country will undoubtedly give you up to his Majesty, the king of Great Britain—and God have mercy on your souls?—Why Robert, said my friend, you talk on this subject as if you felt it— Feel it, replied I, is it possible for an American citizen not to feel it? If he be not actually blinded by prejudice, or money, which is ten times worse, his lost dignity, his injured independence, his degraded situation, from a citizen of the American republic, FREE and INDEPENDENT, to be a SLAVE in a British galley, must render him completely miserable—Good heavens! says I, if his blood does not run cold—if he is not agonizing through every pore—'tis because he is BOUGHT WITH A PRICE—This is just your way, said my friend, you always get so warm on the subject you discourse of, that I am glad always to withdraw, lest it should injure your health—Health, rejoined I, what is health? what is life? what is house, or home, without liberty? but painted baubles fit only for children—that I do not carry my reasoning too far, said I, I'll put a case, which I would wish the Judge Bee's of the day would rightly consider—Suppose an English frigate, to make up her complement of men, sends a part of her crew and presses fifty Americans—after some time, these men find that it is in their power to take the frigate—they do so; but fifty Britons are slain in the struggle—they run the vessel into the nearest port—suppose a Spanish—dispose of her, and so return home, and openly avow what they have done—Sir Robert Liston prosecutes them—pleads the article of the treaty—and, astonishing! "our President gives his advice that *they ought to be given up.*" Judge Bee presides—and these fifty men are delivered over to be sacrificed to *Molech*—Spirits of seventy-six! said I, whither are you flown? What shall arouse you from your lethargy? Free-born American! —AWAKE! AWAKE! ere thou sleepest a sleep unto death—But stay Robert, said my friend, have you not stated this case wrong?—You know that these fifty men perpetrated an high crime on, or in British territory, that is, on board a British vessel, and by the treaty they must be given up. 'Tis false, said I, I know no such thing; they acted virtuously, they acted nobly—they so acted, said I, that Great Britain, were they her subjects, would load them with honour—But let us, added I, examine this case—suppose says I, this frigate's crew had landed, and instead of taking men, had gutted two or three merchants' stores, and carried away whatever they could find valuable, what would you call them? Pirates undoubtedly, answered my friend. And would they not forfeit, said I, both the ship and their lives? I am of opinion, said he, they would. Suppose I, or Jonathan, or Nathan, or Dick, or Tom, says I, should kill a dozen of them, or the whole of them—have I or he committed a crime?—By no means said he—but they did not do this. I'll prove they did worse, added I—do not you know, says I, that in the law of God, *which we say we reverence,* it is fairly stated, that he who steals from me any of my property, must restore it four-fold; but he who steals a man, shall, says the scripture, *die* the Death? But still, says my friend, admitting the full force of this reasoning, for indeed it cannot be denied—they did not come ashore and take away Jonathan Robbins—but pressed him out of one of our ships—That, says I, does not alter the case—You know the British council argued, that on board a British ship is British territory, and hence I would suppose that an American ship is American territory, at least my weak brain cannot see the difference—And, says I, by this mode of reasoning, I prove that a British officer pressing, enslaving, and confining an American citizen, is a man-stealer, a pirate, a robber of the worst possible description—and that any American, confined and enslaved aboard any vessel of any power whatever, as, by his confinement and slavery all ties of amity are broken which did formerly subsist between him and them, is justifiable, in the sight of God and man, to regain his liberty, even with the destruction of the ship's crew—and deserves the highest approbation of his country, for asserting his right in so noble a manner—And, added I, 'tis all a joke to talk about the treaty, because they, by pressing a single American, broke the treaty effectually—unless, added I, there be a secret treaty, by which they are permitted to press American citizens to aid the cause of kings against the cause of republicans—which I have oftentimes thought before now, to be the case—One thing, said I, is pretty certain, there are secrets, there are clues, there are conspiracies;—but, whether the sagacious Harper will be able to ferret them out—or whether Peter will blab them, Robert acknowledge them—or the Rossian committee open the way for them, is as great a secret as the secrets themselves. But, honest Americans, 'tis full time ye were undeceived; 'tis time ye should think for yourselves, 'tis full time ye should see what the fate of Jonathan Robbins leads to—and what security it holds out, for the safety of our hardy sailor, and infant navy—And ye shall be made acquainted with it, said I, snatching up my hat, and adjusting my wig, which I had much ruffled in my passion—for I'll go this instant, and send it to my friend Duane, and my friend Callendar; and, says I, to that noble fellow, that I would be very glad to be acquainted with, the editor of the Albany Register—and, says I, we'll hold up the A's, and B's, and C's, and D's, and E's, who yielded up poor Robbins to that infamous government, that they may be branded with eternal execration.—

LETTER XX

MR. EDITOR,

As I sat musing the other evening, after a very hard week's work, who should come in but my old friend the Latinist. His cheerful countenance and friendly address always give me new spirits, and although he is a man of great learning, yet you see he talks as familiarly with me as if I were as great a scholar as himself. After having taken a stool—(for you must know, Mr. Editor, that in a country where taxes are pretty *high,* provisions not very *cheap,* and house rent enormous, it is not easy for a poor mechanic, who has five or six children, to purchase chairs)— after taking a stool, in his friendly manner laying his hand upon my knee, he thus began: Friend Robert, what's the matter? you seem in but poor spirits. Very true, says I; I have just seen the end of Robbins—poor, brave, injured, betrayed, unfortunate Robbins!—Are you crazy—or,—No, answered I, I am much as usual; I have seen him with my "mind's eye," as Hamlet says—and a horrid spectacle it was. I have just been composing his epitaph, which, says I, it is probable will never be engraven upon his tomb-stone—though it is certain it will go down to posterity on the faithful and impartial page of history—and perhaps in the very words—Here it is.

Reader,
If thou be a Christian and a Freeman,
consider
By what unexampled causes

It has become necessary to construct
This Monument
Of national degradation
and
Individual Injustice
which is erected
To the Memory of a Citizen of the United States
JONATHAN ROBBINS, Mariner;
A native of Danbury, in the pious and industrious state of Connecticut:
who,
Under the Presidency of John Adams,
And by his advice,
Timothy Pickering being Secretary of State,
Was delivered up to the British government,
By whom he was ignominiously put to death;
because,
Though an American Citizen,
He was barbarously forced into the service of his country's worst enemy,
And compelled to fight
Against his conscience and his country's good,
On board the British frigate Hermoine,
Commanded by a monster of the name of Pigot,
He
Bravely asserted his right to freedom as a man, and boldly extricated himself from the bondage of his tyrannical oppressors,
After devoting them to merited destruction.
If you are a Seaman,
Pause:—
Cast your eyes into your soul and ask,
If you had been as Robbins was
What would you have done?
What ought you not to do?
And look at Robbins

Hanging at a British yard-arm!
He was your comrade—
And as true a tar as ever strapped a block:
He was your fellow-citizen
And as brave a heart as bled at Lexington or Trenton.
Like you,
He was a member of a Republic
Proud of past glories,
and
Boastful of national honour, virtue, and independence.
Like him,
You one day may be trussed up, to satiate British vengeance;
Your heinous crime,
Daring to prefer danger or death
To a base bondage—
Alas poor Robbins!
Alas poor Liberty!
Alas my country!

Indeed, said my friend, I see you have wrought yourself up to a very serious state of mind; but I much fear, as the scripture saith, that this case of poor Robbins is only "the beginning of sorrows." When the liberty of nations, and the freedom of states, are depending on almost the turn of a beam—when corruption lifts its head in open day unashamed—when bribery is reduced to a regular and avowed system—when religion has degenerated into hypocrisy, and men with brazen front assert that they love God, and yet plot to destroy their brother, covering the earth with blood, rapine, and horrid cruelty—when such is the state of things, said my friend, the destruction of an obscure individual, however dishonourable and perfidious the sacrifice, will be easily looked over, and perhaps forgotten—for who would attend to the burning of a taper, when Etna or Vesuvius blazes?

To enslave men, continued my friend, is now as earnest an object, as to free them was twenty years ago—Look at the combination, and mark the intrigues of kings and emperors, popes and muftis, princes and bishops, nobles and priests, with the whole train of their dependants and adherents, united as one man—and above all, see republics betrayed into the conspiracy against themselves—It is vain, friend Robert, to repine over the fate of poor Robbins; we may 'tis true deplore the man—but we must consider what is to become of the republic under such a precedent of dishonour and indignity!—Liberty or its enemies must triumph—one or the other must fall; and, however gloomy you may be, considering the state of this martyr to British tyranny and influence, his death may be the salvation of our liberties. My friend never displayed so much sensibility, the tears trickled from his eyes—and I was so much overcome, that I could only squeeze his hand as he laid it once more on my knee, and proceeded again.

My friend Robert, this sacrifice of Robbins is a very serious transaction—and whether sailor, or farmer, every man must think upon so strange and cruel a subject—the scheme for restoring universal slavery is unfolding fast, by the principal actors in our country; but it will destroy itself. In other countries liberty has been destroyed by one bold stroke—here it is attacked by piecemeal—The British arms could not prevail twenty years ago—they now use other weapons, they gain upon us inch by inch—The British treaty was a bold stroke—We now are forced to acknowledge that Grenville outgeneralled Jay—and the commissioners for settling British claims have discovered, that we are completely entrapped, saddled with an enormous debt, which for ages we could not discharge—and for which wise behaviour, the finger of discernment, throughout the world, is pointed with rebuke at our degraded forehead—Why need I mention, added my friend, the alien and sedition bills, stamp act—standing army—excise law—and many others; they are but so many features of the grand system that is so well understood, and so warmly advocated by the friends of order and good government—God bless me, says I, why you almost make my hair stand on end—I think, I see slavery rattling her chains and sharpening all her instruments of torture—What shall we do?—how shall we escape?

Must we sit still until the label "SLAVE" is stigmatized upon our cheek, or branded on our forehead?—Is there no help?—Yes, answered my friend, there is, thanks to the wise, the virtuous framers of our glorious constitution—the invaluable right of election is still ours—Let us but use this right well—let us be diligent to canvass the character of these men that are candidates for any office of power or trust—let our pointed disapprobation ever attend those who are known to have advocated the British treaty, alien and sedition bills, stamp act, standing army, &c; and in a special manner, let us be careful of trusting any man who maintains, that a republican form of government may mean any thing or nothing. Indeed, said I, I think we ought to be careful—If we can do any good, and do not do it, then we are criminal, as my good old father used to say—but it has long been a question with me, as well as with many of my well-meaning neighbours, whether we can do any good by going and voting at elections. I have often heard this argument made use of—What need I go to the election?—let them put in whom they will, to me it makes no difference. I must obey, let them choose who they may. And so reasoning, they stay at home. And if a bad man is chosen, then they comfort themselves thus—Well, God be thanked, we had no hand in it. Indeed, said my friend, they are much mistaken, but they had a hand in it, and a strong one too; for by one man's staying away, the man who would honestly and faithfully serve his country, might lose his election—and every free elector ought to consider his vote of that consequence, as that thereby an able man is chosen to act for the common good; and therefore it is a duty which every man owes to God, his country, and himself, to inform himself of the character of every candidate for any public office, as I said before, with the greatest strictness and impartiality—If he be a man of true honour and of Christian-like deportment; if he be the poor man's friend, and ever ready to curb the rich in their domineering strides; at every time, and in God's name, let us ever support him; for such a man is undoubtedly a treasure—Having thus said, my friend perceiving it grew late, bade me good night.

FISHER AMES
(*1758-1808*)

Regarded as the most brilliant oratorical gladiator of his party in Congress before his retirement because of ill health in 1798, Fisher Ames represented mercantile Federalism in its extreme form. As a Congressman he pleaded for the Hamiltonian principles of strong central government and national support of business. When Federalism went out of power he became an advocate of States' Rights and a vituperative opponent of Jefferson. Some of this was based on adherence to the merchant class of Massachusetts, the remainder was the result of a post-Calvinistic, perhaps Hobbesian, conviction of the innate depravity of human nature. A major reason for the demise of the Federalist party can be seen in the vivid but completely negative horror of popular government expressed by Ames. The extremity of these sentiments made John Quincy Adams think Ames had gone out of his head in his last years.

Bibliography: Charles Warren, *Jacobin and Junto,* Cambridge, 1931; Claude G. Bowers, *Jefferson and Hamilton,* Boston, 1925.

Text: *Works of Fisher Ames,* Boston, 1809.

from THE DANGERS OF AMERICAN LIBERTY

. . . . .

They are certainly blind who do not see, that we are descending from a supposed orderly and stable republican government into a licentious democracy, with a progress that baffles all means to resist, and scarcely leaves leisure to deplore its celerity. The institutions and the hopes that Washington raised are nearly prostrate; and his name and memory would perish, if the rage of his enemies had any power over history. But they have not—history will give scope to her vengeance, and posterity will not be defrauded.

But, if our experience had not clearly given warning of our approaching catastrophe, the very nature of democracy would inevitably produce it.

A government by the passions of the multitude, or, no less correctly, according to the vices and ambition of their leaders, is a democracy. We have heard so long of the indefeasible sovereignty of the people, and have admitted so many specious theories of the rights of man, which are contradicted by his nature and experience, that few will dread at all, and fewer still will dread as they ought, the evils of an American democracy. They will not believe them near, or they will think them tolerable or temporary. Fatal delusion!

When it is said, there may be a tyranny of the *many* as well as of the *few,* every democrat will yield at least a cold and speculative assent; but he will at all times act, as if it were a thing incomprehensible, that there should be any evil to be apprehended in the uncontrolled power of the people. He will say, arbitrary power may make a tyrant, but how can it make its possessor a slave?

In the first place, let it be remarked, the power of individuals is a very different thing from their liberty. When I vote for the man I prefer, he may happen not to be chosen; or he may disappoint my expectations, if he is; or he may be out-voted by others in the publick body to which he is elected. I may, then, hold and exercise all the power that a citizen can have or enjoy, and yet such laws may be made and such abuses allowed as shall deprive me of all liberty. I may be tried by a jury, and that jury may be culled and picked out from my political enemies by a federal marshal. Of course, my life and liberty may depend on the good pleasure of the man who appoints that marshal. I may be assessed arbitrarily for my faculty, or upon conjectural estimation of my property, so that all I have shall be at the control of the government, whenever its displeasure shall exact the sacrifice. I may be told, that I am a federalist, and, as such, bound to submit, in all cases whatsoever, to the will of the majority, as the ruling faction ever pretend to be. My submission may be tested by my resisting or obeying commands that will involve me in disgrace, or drive me to despair. I may become a fugitive, because the ruling party have made me afraid to stay at home; or, perhaps, while I remain at home, they may, nevertheless, think fit to inscribe my name on the list of emigrants and proscribed persons.

All this was done in France, and many of the admirers of French examples are impatient to imitate them. All this time the people may be told, they are the freest in the world; but what ought my opinion to be? What would the threatened clergy, the *aristocracy* of wealthy merchants, as they have been called already, and thirty thousand more in Massachusetts, who vote for governour Strong, and whose case might be no better than mine, what would they think of their condition? Would they call it liberty? Surely, here is oppression sufficient in extent and degree to make the government that inflicts it both odious and terrible; yet this and a thousand times more than this was practised in France, and will be repeated, as often as it shall please God in his wrath to deliver a people to the dominion of their licentious passions.

The people, as a body, cannot deliberate. Nevertheless, they will feel an irresistible impulse to act, and their resolutions will be dictated to them by their demagogues. The consciousness, or the opinion, that they possess the supreme power, will inspire inordinate passions; and the violent men, who are the most forward to gratify those passions, will be their favourites. What is called the government of the people is in fact too often the arbitrary power of such men. Here, then, we have the faithful portrait of democracy. What avails the boasted *power* of individual citizens? or of what value is the will of the majority, if that will is dictated by a committee of demagogues, and law and right are in fact at the mercy of a victorious faction? To make a nation free, the crafty must be kept in awe, and the violent in restraint. The weak and the simple find their liberty arise not from their own individual sovereignty, but from the power of law and justice over all. It is only by the due restraint of others, that I am free.

Popular sovereignty is scarcely less beneficent than awful, when it resides in their courts of justice; there its office, like a sort of human providence, is to warn, enlighten, and protect; when the people are inflamed to seize and exercise it in their assemblies, it is competent only to kill and destroy. Temperate liberty is like the dew, as it falls unseen from its own heaven; constant without excess, it finds vegetation thirsting for its refreshment, and imparts to it the vigour to take more. All nature, moistened with blessings, sparkles in the morning ray. But democracy is a water spout, that bursts from the clouds, and lays the ravaged earth bare to its rocky foundations. The labours of man lie whelmed with his hopes beneath masses of ruin, that bury not only the dead, but their monuments.

It is the almost universal mistake of our countrymen, that democracy would be mild and safe in America. They charge the horrid excesses of France not so much to human nature, which will never act better, when the restraints of government, morals, and religion are thrown off, but to the characteristick cruelty and wickedness of Frenchmen.

The truth is, and let it humble our pride, the most ferocious of all animals, when his passions are roused to fury and are uncontrolled, is man; and of all governments, the worst is that which never fails to excite, but was never found to restrain those passions, that is, democracy. It is an illuminated hell, that in the midst of remorse, horrour, and torture, rings with festivity; for experience shews, that one joy remains to this most malignant description of the damned, the power to make others wretched. When a man looks round and sees his neighbours mild and merciful, he cannot feel afraid of the abuse of their power over him: and surely if they oppress me, he will say, they will spare their own liberty, for that is dear to all mankind. It is so. The human heart is so constituted, that a man loves liberty as naturally as himself. Yet liberty is a rare thing in the world, though the love of it is so universal.

Before the French revolution, it was the prevailing opinion of our countrymen, that other nations were not free, because their despotick governments were too strong for the people. Of course, we were admonished to detest all existing governments, as so many lions in liberty's path; and to expect by their downfal the happy opportunity that every emancipated people would embrace to secure their own equal rights for ever. France is supposed to have had this opportunity, and to have lost it. Ought we not, then, to be convinced, that something more is necessary to preserve liberty than to love it? Ought we not to see, that, when the people have destroyed all power but their own, they are the nearest possible to a despotism, the more uncontrolled for being new, and tenfold the more cruel for its hypocrisy?

The steps by which a people must proceed to change a government, are not those to enlighten their judgment or to sooth their passions. They cannot stir without following the men before them, who breathe fury into their hearts and banish nature from them. On whatever grounds and under whatever leaders the contest may be commenced, the revolutionary work is the same, and the characters of the agents will be assimilated to it. A revolution is a mine that must explode with destructive violence. The men who were once peaceable like to carry firebrands and daggers too long. Thus armed, will they submit to salutary restraint? How will you bring them to it? Will you undertake to reason down fury? Will you satisfy revenge without blood? Will you preach banditti into habits of self-denial? If you can, and in times of violence and anarchy, why do you ask any other guard than sober reason for your life and property in times of peace and order, when men are most disposed to listen to it? Yet even at such times, you impose restraints; you call out for your defence the whole array of law with its instruments of punishment and terrour; you maintain ministers to strengthen force with opinion, and to make religion the auxiliary of morals. With all this, however, crimes are still perpetrated; society is not any too safe or quiet. Break down all these fences; make what is called law an assassin; take what it ought to protect, and divide it; extinguish by acts of rapine and vengeance the spark of mercy in the heart; or, if it should be found to glow there, quench it in that heart's blood; make your people scoff at their morals, and unlearn an education to virtue; displace the christian sabbath by a profane one, for a respite once in ten days from the toils of murder, because men, who first shed blood for revenge, and proceed to spill it for plunder, and in the progress of their ferocity, for sport, want a festival—what sort of society would you have? Would not rage grow with its indulgence? The coward fury of a mob rises in proportion as there is less resistance; and their inextinguishable thirst for slaughter grows more ardent as more blood is shed to slake it. In such a state is liberty to be gained or guarded from violation? It could not be kept an hour from the daggers of those who, having seized despotick power, would claim it as their lawful prize.—I have written the history of France. Can we look back upon it without terrour, or forward without despair?

The nature of arbitrary power is always odious; but it cannot be long the arbitrary power of the multitude. There is, probably, no form of rule among mankind, in which the progress of the government depends so little on the particular character of those who administer it. Democracy is the creature of impulse and violence; and the intermediate stages towards the tyranny of one are so quickly passed, that the vileness and cruelty of men are displayed with surprising uniformity. There is not time for great talents to act. There is no sufficient reason to believe, that we should conduct a revolution with much more mildness than the French. If a revolution find the citizens lambs, it will soon make them carnivorous, if not cannibals. We have many thousands of the Paris and St. Domingo assassins in the United States, not as fugitives, but as patriots, who merit reward, and disdain to take any but power. In the progress of our confusion, these men will effectually assert their claims and display their skill. There is no governing power in the state but party. The moderate and thinking part of the citizens are without power or influence; and it must be so, because all power and influence are engrossed by a factious combination of men, who can overwhelm uncombined individuals, with numbers, and the wise and virtuous with clamour and fury.

It is indeed a law of politicks as well as of physicks, that a body in action must overcome an equal body at rest. The attacks that have been made on the constitutional barriers proclaim in a tone that would not be louder from a trumpet, that party will not tolerate any resistance to its will. All the supposed independent orders of the commonwealth must be its servile instruments, or its victims. We should experience the same despotism in Massachusetts, New-Hampshire, and Connecticut, but the battle is not yet won. It will be won; and they who already display the temper of their Southern and French allies, will not linger or reluct in imitating the worst extremes of their example.

What, then, is to be our condition?

Faction will inevitably triumph. Where the government is both stable and free, there may be parties. There will be differences of opinion, and the pride of opinion will be sufficient to generate contests, and to inflame them with bitterness and rancour. There will be rivalships among those whom genius, fame, or station have made great, and these will deeply agitate the state without often hazarding its safety. Such parties will excite alarm, but they may be safely left, like the elements, to exhaust their fury upon each other.

The object of their strife is to get power *under* the government; for, where that is constituted as it should be, the power *over* the government will not seem attainable, and, of course, will not be attempted.

But in democratick states there will be *factions*. The sovereign power being nominally in the hands of all, will be effectively within the grasp of a FEW; and, therefore, by the very laws of our nature, a few will combine, intrigue, lie, and fight to engross it to themselves. All history bears testimony, that this attempt has never yet been disappointed.

Who will be the associates? Certainly not the virtuous, who do not wish to control the society, but quietly to enjoy its protection. The enterprising merchant, the thriving tradesman, the careful farmer will be engrossed by the toils of their business, and will have little time or inclination for the unprofitable and disquieting pursuits of politicks. It is not the industrious, sober husbandman, who will plough that barren field; it is the lazy and dissolute bankrupt, who has no other to plough. The idle, the ambitious, and the needy will band together to break the hold that law has upon them, and then to get hold of law. Faction is a Hercules, whose first labour is to strangle this lion, and then to make armour of his skin. In every democratick state the ruling faction will have law to keep down its enemies; but it will arrogate to itself an undisputed power over law. If our ruling faction has found any impediments, we ask, which of them is now remaining? And is it not absurd to suppose, that the conquerors will be contented with half the fruits of victory?

We are to be subject, then, to a *despotick* faction, irritated by the resistance that has delayed, and the scorn that pursues their triumph, elate with the insolence of an arbitrary and uncontrollable domination, and who will exercise their sway, not according to the rules of integrity or national policy, but in conformity with their own exclusive interests and passions.

This is a state of things, which admits of progress, but not of reformation: it is the beginning of a revolution, which must *advance*. Our affairs, as first observed, no longer depend on counsel. The opinion of a majority is no longer invited or permitted to control our destinies, or even to retard their consummation. The men in power may, and, no doubt, will give place to some other faction, who will succeed, because they are abler men, or, possibly, in candour we say it, because they are worse. Intrigue will for some time answer instead of force, or the mob will supply it. But by degrees force only will be relied on by those who are *in,* and employed by those who are *out*. The vis major will prevail, and some bold chieftain will *conquer* liberty, and triumph and reign in her name.

Yet, it is confessed we have hopes, that this event is not very near. We have no cities as large as London or Paris; and, of course, the ambitious demagogues may find the ranks of their STANDING ARMY too thin to rule by them alone. It is also worth remark, that our mobs are not, like those of Europe, excitable by the cry of *no bread*. The dread of famine is every where else a power of political electricity, that glides through all the haunts of filth, and vice, and want in a city with incredible speed, and in times of insurrection rives and scorches with a sudden force, like heaven's own thunder. Accordingly, we find the sober men of Europe more afraid of the despotism of the rabble than of the government.

But, as in the United States we see less of this description of low vulgar, and as, in the essential circumstance alluded to, they are so much less manageable by their demagogues, we are to expect, that our affairs will be long guided by courting the mob, before they are violently changed by employing them. While the passions of the multitude can be conciliated to confer power and to overcome all impediments to its action, our rulers have a plain and easy task to perform. It costs them nothing but hypocrisy. As soon, however, as rival favourites of the people may happen to contend by the practice of the same arts, we are to look for the sanguinary strife of ambition. Brissot will fall by the hand of Danton, and *he* will be supplanted by Robespiere. The revolution will proceed in exactly the same way, but not with so rapid a pace, as that of France.

JOHN ADAMS
(*1735-1826*)

AND

THOMAS JEFFERSON
(*1743-1826*)

Adams and Jefferson became warm friends in the Congress of 1776 in spite of sharp contrasts in personality and background which each had to forgive in the other. Adams was charmed by Jefferson's gentleness and cordiality and by the astonishing range of his mind. Jefferson was delighted at Adams's energy and drive and deeply respectful of his friend's extraordinary integrity. But when the war was over their ways divided sharply. Jefferson went as Minister to France, and his own democratic ideas and commitments were intensified. Adams stayed home, where the issues of constructing a workable post-revolutionary government had to be faced. Like many another successful revolutionist, he found himself receding from earlier ideals under the pressures of responsibility and power. Consequently, when Jefferson came home to take his post as Secretary of State under Washington, with Adams as Vice-President, he found himself out of sympathy both with Adams and with the other members of the government. And as the Washington administrations wore on and the first two political parties emerged, Jefferson became the head of the Republicans; and Adams, uneasily supported by Hamilton, head of the Federalists. In the ensuing political campaigns the two old friends were alienated over the venomous personal smear campaigns conducted by irresponsible newspaper editors.

But when both had retired, mutual friends, especially Dr. Benjamin Rush, led them gradually to a reconciliation by mail. The first tentative notes brought warm responses, and the responses blossomed into a steady exchange. This sunset correspondence is a great one for a number of reasons. Both men were accomplished letter writers, and it seems clear that they put themselves out to impress each other. They had minds richly stocked both with scholarship and significant experience. Since each had contributed importantly to the design of the foundations of the Republic, their reminiscences and interpretations cast authoritative light on our national origins. Finally, they were heroic men—as Jefferson himself put it, Argonauts. That they should deliberately have set out to record their self-explanations so cordially is an event almost without parallel. It gives one the same sense of participating in history as was given the entire nation when, close to high noon, on the fiftieth anniversary of Independence Day, July 4, 1826, both died, the last survivors of the event.

Bibliography: Paul Wilstach has edited selected portions of *Correspondence of John Adams and Thomas Jefferson, 1812-1826*, Indianapolis, 1925. Almost any collection of either man prints a few of the letters: e.g., F. C. Prescott, *Alexander Hamilton and Thomas Jefferson*, New York, 1934; Adrienne Koch and William Peden, *The Selected Writings of John and John Quincy Adams*, New York, 1946, and *The Life and Selected Writings of Thomas Jefferson*, New York, 1944.

Text: *The Works of Thomas Jefferson*, ed., H. A. Washington, New York, 1884.

from CORRESPONDENCE OF JOHN ADAMS AND THOMAS JEFFERSON, 1813-1826

TO JOHN ADAMS

Monticello, June 27, 1813.

Ιδαν ες πολυδενδρον ανηρ 'υλητομος ελθων
Παπταινει, παρεοντος αδην, ποθεν αρξεται εργ⁸
Τι πρατον καταλεξω; επει παρα μυρια ειπην.[1]

And I too, my dear Sir, like the wood-cutter of Ida, should doubt where to begin, were I to enter the forest of opinions, discussions, and contentions which have occurred in our day. I should say with Theocritus, Τι πρατον καταλεξω; επει παρα μυρια ειπην.[2] But I shall not do it. The summum bonum[3] with me is now truly epicurian, ease of body and tranquillity of mind; and to these I wish to consign my remaining days. Men have differed in opinion, and been divided into parties by these opinions, from the first origin of societies, and in all governments where they

---

[1] "A wood-cutter, come to thickly-wooded Ida, hesitated as to where to begin work: 'which shall I pick out, since there is a myriad of trees?'"
[2] A repetition of the third line above, the implied question.
[3] "highest good"

have been permitted freely to think and to speak. The same political parties which now agitate the United States, have existed through all time. Whether the power of the people or that of the αριστοι should prevail, were questions which kept the states of Greece and Rome in eternal convulsions, as they now schismatize every people whose minds and mouths are not shut up by the gag of a despot. And in fact, the terms of whig and tory belong to natural as well as to civil history. They denote the temper and constitution of mind of different individuals. To come to our own country, and to the times when you and I became first acquainted, we well remember the violent parties which agitated the old Congress, and their bitter contests. There you and I were together, and the Jays, and the Dickinsons, and other anti-independents, were arrayed against us. They cherished the monarchy of England, and we the rights of our countrymen. When our present government was in the mew, passing from Confederation to Union, how bitter was the schism between the Feds and Antis. Here you and I were together again. For although, for a moment, separated by the Atlantic from the scene of action, I favored the opinion that nine States should confirm the constitution, in order to secure it, and the others hold off until certain amendments, deemed favorable to freedom, should be made. I rallied in the first instant to the wiser proposition of Massachusetts, that all should confirm, and then all instruct their delegates to urge those amendments. The amendments were made, and all were reconciled to the government. But as soon as it was put into motion, the line of division was again drawn. We broke into two parties, each wishing to give the government a different direction; the one to strengthen the most popular branch, the other the more permanent branches, and to extend their permanence. Here you and I separated for the first time, and as we had been longer than most others on the public theatre, and our names therefore were more familiar to our countrymen, the party which considered you as thinking with them, placed your name at their head; the other, for the same reason, selected mine. But neither decency nor inclination permitted us to become the advocates of ourselves, or to take part personally in the violent contests which followed. We suffered ourselves, as you so well expressed it, to be passive subjects of public discussion. And these discussions, whether relating to men, measures or opinions, were conducted by the parties with an animosity, a bitterness and an indecency which had never been exceeded. All the resources of reason and of wrath were exhausted by each party in support of its own, and to prostrate the adversary opinions; one was upbraided with receiving the anti-federalists, the other the old tories and refugees, into their bosom. Of this acrimony, the public papers of the day exhibit ample testimony, in the debates of Congress, of State Legislatures, of stump-orators, in addresses, answers, and newspaper essays; and to these, without question, may be added the private correspondences of individuals; and the less guarded in these, because not meant for the public eye, not restrained by the respect due to that, but poured forth from the overflowings of the heart into the bosom of a friend, as a momentary easement of our feelings. In this way, and in answers to addresses, you and I could indulge ourselves. We have probably done it, sometimes with warmth, often with prejudice, but always, as we believed, adhering to truth. I have not examined my letters of that day. I have no stomach to revive the memory of its feelings. But one of these letters, it seems, has got before the public, by accident and infidelity, by the death of one friend to whom it was written, and of his friend to whom it had been communicated, and by the malice and treachery of a third person, of whom I had never before heard, merely to make mischief, and in the same satanic spirit in which the same enemy had intercepted and published, in 1776, your letter animadverting on Dickinson's character. How it happened that I quoted you in my letter to Doctor Priestley, and for whom, and not for yourself, the strictures were meant, has been explained to you in my letter of the 15th, which had been committed to the post eight days before I received yours of the 10th, 11th and 14th. That gave you the reference which these asked to the particular answer alluded to in the one to Priestley.

The renewal of these old discussions, my friend, would be equally useless and irksome. To the volumes then written on these subjects, human ingenuity can add nothing new, and the rather, as lapse of time has obliterated many of the facts. And shall you and I, my dear Sir, at our age, like Priam of old, gird on the *"arma, diu desueta, trementibus ævo humeris?"* [4] Shall we, at our age, become the Athletæ of party, and exhibit ourselves as gladiators in the arena of the newspapers? Nothing in the universe could induce me to it. My mind has been long fixed to bow to the judgment of the world, who will judge by my acts, and will never take counsel from me as to what that judgment shall be. If your objects and opinions have been misunderstood, if the measures and principles of others have been wrongfully imputed to you, as I believe they have been, that you should leave an explanation of them, would be an act of justice to yourself. I will add, that it has been hoped that you would leave such explanations as would place every saddle on its right horse, and replace on the shoulders of others the burthens they shifted on yours.

But all this, my friend, is offered, merely for your consideration and judgment, without presuming to anticipate what you alone are qualified to decide for yourself. I mean to express my own purpose only, and the reflections which have led to it. To me, then, it appears, that there have been differences of opinion and party differences, from the first establishment of governments to the present day, and on the same question which now divides our own country; that these will continue through all future time; that every one takes his side in favor of the many, or of the few, according to his constitution, and the circumstances in which he is placed; that opinions, which are equally honest on both sides, should not affect personal esteem or social intercourse; that as we judge between the Claudii and the Gracchi, the Wentworths and the Hampdens of past ages, so of those among us whose names may happen to be remembered for awhile, the next generations will judge, favorably or unfavorably,

---

[4] "arms, long disused, on shoulders shaking with age"

according to the complexion of individual minds, and the side they shall themselves have taken; that nothing new can be added by you or me to what has been said by others, and will be said in every age in support of the conflicting opinions on government; and that wisdom and duty dictate an humble resignation to the verdict of our future peers. In doing this myself, I shall certainly not suffer moot questions to affect the sentiments of sincere friendship and respect, consecrated to you by so long a course of time, and of which I now repeat sincere assurances.

TO THOMAS JEFFERSON

QUINCY, June 28, 1813.

DEAR SIR,—It is very true that the denunciations of the priesthood are fulminated against every advocate for a complete freedom of religion. Comminations, I believe, would be plenteously pronounced by even the most liberal of them, against Atheism, Deism, against every man who disbelieved or doubted the resurrection of Jesus, or the miracles of the New Testament. Priestley himself would denounce the man who should deny the Apocalypse, or the Prophecies of Daniel. Priestley and Lindsay both have denounced as idolaters and blasphemers all the Trinitarians, and even the Arians.

Poor weak man, when will thy perfection arrive? Thy perfectability I shall not deny; for a greater character than Priestley or Godwin has said, "Be ye perfect," &c. For my part I can not deal damnation round the land on all I judge the foes of God and man. But I did not intend to say a word on this subject in this letter. As much of it as you please hereafter, but let me return to politics.

With some difficulty I have hunted up, or down, the "address of the young men of the city of Philadelphia, the district of Southwark, and the Northern Liberties," and the answer.

The addresses say, "Actuated by the SAME PRINCIPLES on which our forefathers achieved their independence, the recent attempts of a foreign power to derogate from the dignity and rights of our country, awaken our liveliest sensibility, and our strongest indignation." Huzza my brave boys! Could Thomas Jefferson or John Adams hear those words with insensibility, and without emotion? These boys afterwards add, "We regard our liberty and independence as the richest portion given us by our ancestors." And who were those ancestors? Among them were Thomas Jefferson and John Adams. And I very coolly believe that no two men among those ancestors did more towards it than those two. Could either hear this like statues? If, one hundred years hence, your letters and mine should see the light, I hope the reader will hunt up this address, and read it all; and remember that we were then engaged, or on the point of engaging, in a war with France. I shall not repeat the answer till we come to the paragraph upon which you criticised to Dr. Priestley, though every word of it is true, and I now rejoice to see it recorded, and though I had wholly forgotten it.

The paragraph is, "Science and morals are the great pillars on which this country has been raised to its present population, opulence and prosperity, and these alone can advance, support, and preserve it. Without wishing to damp the ardor of curiosity, or influence the freedom of inquiry, I will hazard a prediction that, after the most industrious and impartial researches, the longest liver of you all will find no principles, institutions, or systems of education more fit, IN GENERAL, to be transmitted to your posterity than those you have received from your ancestors."

Now, compare the paragraph in the answer with the paragraph in the address, as both are quoted above, and see if we can find the extent and the limits of the meaning of both.

Who composed that army of fine young fellows that was then before my eyes? There were among them Roman Catholics, English Episcopalians, Scotch and American Presbyterians, Methodists, Moravians, Anabaptists, German Lutherans, German Calvinists, Universalists, Arians, Priestleyans, Socinians, Independents, Congregationalists, Horse Protestants and House Protestants, Deists and Atheists; and "Protestans qui ne croyent rien."[5] Very few however of several of these species. Neverthe-

---
[5] "Protestants who believe nothing at all"

less, all educated in the GENERAL PRINCIPLES of Christianity; and the general principles of English and American liberty.

Could my answer be understood by any candid reader or hearer, to recommend to all the others the general principles, institutions, or systems of education of the Roman Catholics? Or those of the Quakers? Or those of the Presbyterians? Or those of the Menonists? Or those of the Methodists? Or those of the Moravians? Or those of the Universalists? Or those of the Philosophers? No.

The GENERAL PRINCIPLES on which the fathers achieved independence, were the only principles in which that beautiful assembly of young gentlemen could unite, and these principles only could be intended by them in their address, or by me in my answer.

And what were these GENERAL PRINCIPLES? I answer, the general principles of Christianity, in which all those sects were united; and the GENERAL PRINCIPLES of English and American liberty, in which all these young men united, and which had united all parties in America, in majorities sufficient to assert and maintain her independence.

Now I will avow that I then believed, and now believe, that those general principles of Christianity are as eternal and immutable as the existence and attributes of God; and that those principles of liberty are as unalterable as human nature, and our terrestrial mundane system. I could therefore safely say, consistently with all my then and present information, that I believed they would never make discoveries in contradiction to these GENERAL PRINCIPLES. In favor of these GENERAL PRINCIPLES in philosophy, religion and government, I would fill sheets of quotations from Frederick of Prussia, from Hume, Gibbon, Bolingbroke, Rousseau and Voltaire, as well as Newton and Locke; not to mention thousands of divines and philosophers of inferior fame.

I might have flattered myself that my sentiments were sufficiently known to have protected me against suspicions of narrow thoughts, contracted sentiments, bigoted, enthusiastic, or superstitious principles, civil, political, philosophical, or ecclesiastical. The first sentence of the preface to my defence of the constitution, vol. 1st, printed in 1787, is in these words: "The arts and sciences, in general, during the three or four last centuries, have had a regular course of *progressive* improvement. The inventions in mechanic arts, the discoveries in natural philosophy, navigation, and commerce, and the advancement of civilization and humanity, have occasioned changes in the condition of the world and the human character, which would have astonished the most refined nations of antiquity," &c. I will quote no farther; but request you to read again that whole page, and then say whether the writer of it could be suspected of recommending to youth "to look backward instead of forward" for instruction and improvement.

This letter is already too long. In my next I shall consider the Terrorism of the day. Meantime I am, as ever, your friend.

TO THOMAS JEFFERSON

Quincy, July 9, 1813.

Lord! Lord! What can I do with so much Greek? When I was of your age, young man, *i. e.,* seven, or eight, or nine years ago, I felt a kind of pang of affection for one of the flames of my youth, and again paid my addresses to Isocrates, and Dionysius Hallicarnassensis, &c., &c. I collected all my Lexicons and Grammars, and sat down to περὶ συθησεως ονοματων,[6] &c. In this way I amused myself for some time; but I found, that if I looked a word to-day, in less than a week I had to look it again. It was to little better purpose than writing letters on a pail of water.

Whenever I set down to write to you, I am precisely in the situation of the wood-cutter on Mount Ida. I cannot see wood for trees. So many subjects crowd upon me, that I know not with which to begin. But I will begin, at random, with Belsham; who is, as I have no doubt, a man of merit. He had no malice against you, nor any thought of doing mischief; nor has

---
[6] "on the composition of words"

he done any, though he has been imprudent. The truth is, the dissenters of all denominations in England, and especially the Unitarians, are cowed, as we used to say at College. They are ridiculed, insulted, persecuted. They can scarcely hold their heads above water. They catch at straws and shadows to avoid drowning. Priestley sent your letter to Linsay, and Belsham printed it from the same motive, *i. e.* to derive some countenance from the name of Jefferson. Nor has it done harm here. Priestley says to Linsay, "You see he is almost one of us, and he hopes will soon be altogether such as we are." Even in our New England, I have heard a high Federal Divine say, your letters had increased his respect for you.

"The same political parties which now agitate the United States, have existed through all time;" precisely. And this is precisely the complaint in the preface to the first volume of my defence. While all other sciences have advanced, that of government is at a stand; little better understood; little better practiced now, than three or four thousand years ago. What is the reason? I say, parties and factions will not suffer, or permit improvements to be made. As soon as one man hints at an improvement, his rival opposes it. No sooner has one party discovered or invented an amelioration of the condition of man, or the order of society, than the opposite party belies it, misconstrues, misrepresents it, ridicules it, insults it, and persecutes it. Records are destroyed. Histories are annihilated, or interpolated, or prohibited: sometimes by popes, sometimes by emperors, sometimes by aristocratical, and sometimes by democratical assemblies, and sometimes by mobs.

Aristotle wrote the history of eighteen hundred republics which existed before his time. Cicero wrote two volumes of discourses on government, which, perhaps, were worth all the rest of his works. The works of Livy and Tacitus, &c., that are lost, would be more interesting than all that remain. Fifty gospels have been destroyed, and where are St. Luke's world of books that have been written? If you ask my opinion who has committed all the havoc, I will answer you candidly,—Ecclesiastical and Imperial despotism has done it, to conceal their frauds.

Why are the histories of all nations, more ancient than the Christian era, lost? Who destroyed the Alexandrian library? I believe that Christian priests, Jewish rabbis, Grecian sages, and emperors, had as great a hand in it as Turks and Mahometans.

Democrats, Rebels and Jacobins, when they possessed a momentary power, have shown a disposition both to destroy and forge records as vandalical as priests and despots. Such has been and such is the world we live in.

I recollect, near some thirty years ago, to have said carelessly to you that I wished I could find time and means to write something upon aristocracy. You seized upon the idea, and encouraged me to do it with all that friendly warmth that is natural and habitual to you. I soon began, and have been writing upon that subject ever since. I have been so unfortunate as never to be able to make myself understood.

Your "ἄριστοι"[7] are the most difficult animals to manage of anything in the whole theory and practice of government. They will not suffer themselves to be governed. They not only exert all their own subtlety, industry and courage, but they employ the commonalty to knock to pieces every plan and model that the most honest architects in legislation can invent to keep them within bounds. Both patricians and plebeians are as furious as the workmen in England, to demolish labor-saving machinery.

But who are these "ἄριστοι"? Who shall judge? Who shall select these choice spirits from the rest of the congregation? Themselves? We must first find out and determine who themselves are. Shall the congregation choose? Ask Xenophon; perhaps hereafter I may quote you Greek. Too much in a hurry at present, English must suffice. Xenophon says that the ecclesia always chooses the worst men they can find, because none others will do their dirty work. This wicked motive is worse than

---

[7] "the best"

birth or wealth. Here I want to quote Greek again. But the day before I received your letter of June 27th, I gave the book to George Washington Adams, going to the academy at Hingham. The title is Ἠθική ποίησις[8] a collection of moral sentences from all the most ancient Greek poets. In one of the oldest of them, I read in Greek, that I cannot repeat, a couplet, the sense of which was: "Nobility in men is worth as much as it is in horses, asses, or rams; but the meanest blooded puppy in the world, if he gets a little money, is as good a man as the best of them." Yet birth and wealth together have prevailed over virtue and talents in all ages. The many will acknowledge no other "ἄριστοι."

Your experience of this truth will not much differ from that of your best friend.

TO THOMAS JEFFERSON

QUINCY, July 13, 1813.

DEAR SIR,—Let me allude to one circumstance more in one of your letters to me, before I touch upon the subject of religion in your letters to Priestley.

The first time that you and I differed in opinion on any material question, was after your arrival from Europe, and that point was the French revolution.

You were well persuaded in your own mind, that the nation would succeed in establishing a free republican government. I was as well persuaded in mine, that a project of such a government over five and twenty millions of people, when four and twenty millions and five hundred thousand of them could neither read nor write, was as unnatural, irrational and impracticable as it would be over the elephants, lions, tigers, panthers, wolves and bears in the royal menagerie at Versailles. Napoleon has lately invented a word which perfectly expresses my opinion, at that time and ever since. He calls the project Ideology; and John Randolph, though he was, fourteen years ago, as wild an enthusiast for equality and fraternity as any of them, appears

---
[8] "Ethics of poetry"

to be now a regenerated proselyte to Napoleon's opinion and mine, that it was all madness.

The Greeks, in their allegorical style, said that the two ladies, Ἀριστοκρατία and δημοκρατία,[9] always in a quarrel, disturbed every neighborhood with their brawls. It is a fine observation of yours, that "Whig and Tory belong to natural history." Inequalities of mind and body are so established by God Almighty, in his constitution of human nature, that no art or policy can ever plane them down to a level. I have never read reasoning more absurd, sophistry more gross, in proof of the Athanasian creed, or Transubstantiation, than the subtle labors of Helvetius and Rousseau, to demonstrate the natural equality of mankind. *Jus cuique,* the golden rule, do as you would be done by, is all the equality that can be supported or defended by reason, or reconciled to common sense.

It is very true, as you justly observe, I can say nothing new on this or any other subject of government. But when Lafayette harangued you and me and John Quincy Adams, through a whole evening in your hotel in the Cul de Sac, at Paris, and developed the plans then in operation to reform France, though I was as silent as you were, I then thought I could say something new to him.

In plain truth, I was astonished at the grossness of his ignorance of government and history, as I had been for years before, at that of Turgot, Rochefaucault, Condorcet and Franklin. This gross Ideology of them all, first suggested to me the thought and the inclination which I afterwards hinted to you in London, of writing something upon aristocracy. I was restrained for years, by many fearful considerations. Who, and what was I? A man of no name or consideration in Europe. The manual exercise of writing was painful and distressing to me, almost like a blow on the elbow or knee. My style was habitually negligent, unstudied, unpolished; I should make enemies of all the French patriots, the Dutch patriots, the English republicans, dissenters, reformers, call them what you will; and what came nearer home

---
[9] "Aristocracy" and "democracy"

to my bosom than all the rest, I knew I should give offence to many if not all of my best friends in America, and very probably destroy all the little popularity I ever had, in a country where popularity had more omnipotence than the British Parliament assumed. Where should I get the necessary books? What printer or bookseller would undertake to print such hazardous writings?

But when the French assembly of notables met, and I saw that Turgot's "government in one centre, and that centre the nation," a sentence as mysterious or as contradictory as the Athanasian creed, was about to take place, and when I saw that Shaise's rebellion was about breaking out in Massachusetts, and when I saw that even my obscure name was often quoted in France as an advocate for simple democracy, when I saw that the sympathies in America had caught the French flame, I was determined to wash my own hands as clean as I could of all this foulness. I had then strong forebodings that I was sacrificing all the honors and emoluments of this life, and so it has happened, but not in so great a degree as I apprehended.

In truth, my defence of the constitutions and "discourses on Davila," laid the foundation for that immense unpopularity which fell, like the tower of Siloam, upon me. Your steady defence of democratical principles, and your invariable favorable opinion of the French revolution, laid the foundation of your unbounded popularity.

Sic transit gloria mundi! [10] Now I will forfeit my life, if you can find one sentence in my defence of the constitutions, or the discourses on Davila, which, by a fair construction, can favor the introduction of hereditary monarchy or aristocracy into America.

They were all written to support and strengthen the constitutions of the United States.

The wood-cutter on Ida, though he was puzzled to find a tree to chop at first, I presume knew how to leave off when he was weary. But I never know when to cease when I begin to write to you.

---

[10] "So passes the glory of this world!"

TO JOHN ADAMS

Monticello, October 28, 1813

. . . . .

I agree with you that there is a natural aristocracy among men. The grounds of this are virtue and talents. Formerly, bodily powers gave place among the aristoi. But since the invention of gunpowder has armed the weak as well as the strong with missile death, bodily strength, like beauty, good humor, politeness and other accomplishments, has become but an auxiliary ground of distinction. There is also an artificial aristocracy, founded on wealth and birth, without either virtue or talents; for with these it would belong to the first class. The natural aristocracy I consider as the most precious gift of nature, for the instruction, the trusts, and government of society. And indeed, it would have been inconsistent in creation to have formed man for the social state, and not to have provided virtue and wisdom enough to manage the concerns of the society. May we not even say, that that form of government is the best, which provides the most effectually for a pure selection of these natural aristoi into the offices of government? The artificial aristocracy is a mischievous ingredient in government, and provision should be made to prevent its ascendency. On the question, what is the best provision, you and I differ; but we differ as rational friends, using the free exercise of our own reason, and mutually indulging its errors. You think it best to put the pseudo-aristoi into a separate chamber of legislation, where they may be hindered from doing mischief by their co-ordinate branches, and where, also, they may be a protection to wealth against the Agrarian and plundering enterprises of the majority of the people. I think that to give them power in order to prevent them from doing mischief, is arming them for it, and increasing instead of remedying the evil. For if the co-ordinate branches can arrest their action, so may they that of the co-ordinates. Mischief may be done negatively as well as positively. Of this, a cabal in the Senate of the United States has furnished many proofs. Nor do I believe them necessary to protect the wealthy; because enough of these will find their way into every branch of the legislation, to protect themselves. From fifteen to twenty legislatures of our own, in action for thirty years past, have proved that no fears of an equalization of property are to be apprehended from them. I think the best remedy is exactly that provided by all our constitutions, to leave to the citizens the free election and separation of the aristoi from the pseudo-aristoi, of the wheat from the chaff. In general they will elect the really good and wise. In some instances, wealth may corrupt, and birth blind them; but not in sufficient degree to endanger the society.

It is probable that our difference of opinion may, in some measure, be produced by a difference of character in those among whom we live. From what I have seen of Massachusetts and Connecticut myself, and still more from what I have heard, and the character given of the former by yourself, who know them so much better, there seems to be in those two States a traditionary reverence for certain families, which has rendered the offices of the government nearly hereditary in those families. I presume that from an early period of your history, members of those families happening to possess virtue and talents, have honestly exercised them for the good of the people, and by their services have endeared their names to them. In coupling Connecticut with you, I mean it politically only, not morally. For having made the Bible the common law of their land, they seem to have modeled their morality on the story of Jacob and Laban. But although this hereditary succession to office with you, may, in some degree, be founded in real family merit, yet in a much higher degree, it has proceeded from your strict alliance of Church and State. These families are canonised in the eyes of the people on common principles, "you tickle me, and I will tickle you." In Virginia we have nothing of this. Our clergy, before the revolution, having been secured against rivalship by fixed salaries, did not give themselves the trouble of acquiring influence over the people. Of wealth, there were great accumulations in particular families, handed down from generation to generation, under the English law of entails. But the only object of ambition for the wealthy was a seat in the King's Council. All their court then was paid to the crown and its creatures; and they Philipised in all collisions between the King and the people. Hence they were unpopular; and that unpopularity continues attached to their names. A Randolph, a Carter, or a Burwell must have great personal superiority over a common competitor to be elected by the people even at this day. At the first session of our legislature after the Declaration of Independence, we passed a law abolishing entails. And this was followed by one abolishing the privilege of primogeniture, and dividing the lands of intestates equally among all their children, or other representatives. These laws, drawn by myself, laid the axe to the foot of pseudo-aristocracy. And had another which I prepared been adopted by the legislature, our work would have been complete. It was a bill for the more general diffusion of learning. This proposed to divide every county into wards of five or six miles square, like your townships; to establish in each ward a free school for reading, writing and common arithmetic; to provide for the annual selection of the best subjects from these schools, who might receive, at the public expense, a higher degree of education at a district school; and from these district schools to select a certain number of the most promising subjects, to be completed at an University, where all the useful sciences should be taught. Worth and genius would thus have been sought out from every condition of life, and completely prepared by education for defeating the competition of wealth and birth for public trusts. My proposition had, for a further object, to impart to these wards those portions of self-government for which they are best qualified, by confiding to them the care of their poor, their roads, police, elections, the nomination of jurors, administration of justice in small cases, elementary exercises of militia; in short, to have made them little republics, with a warden at the head of each, for all those concerns which, being under their eye, they would better manage than the larger republics of the county or State. A general call of ward meetings by their wardens on the same day through the State, would at any time produce the genuine sense of the people on any required point, and would enable the State to act in mass, as your people have so often done, and with so much effect by their town meetings. The law for religious freedom, which made a part of this system, having put down the aristocracy of the clergy, and restored to the citizen the freedom of the mind, and those of entails and descents nurturing an equality of condition among them, this on education would have raised the mass of the people to the high ground of moral respectability necessary to their own safety, and to orderly government; and would have completed the great object of qualifying them to select the veritable aristoi, for the trusts of government, to the exclusion of the pseudalists; and the same Theognis who has furnished the epigraphs of your two letters, assures us that "Οὐδέμων πω, Κυρν', ἄγαθοι πόλιν ὤλεξαν ἄνδρες."[11] Although this law has not yet been acted on but in a small and inefficient degree, it is still considered as before the legislature, with other bills of the revised code, not yet taken up, and I have great hope that some patriotic spirit will, at a favorable moment, call it up, and make it the key-stone of the arch of our government.

With respect to aristocracy, we should further consider, that before the establishment of the American States, nothing was known to history but the man of the old world, crowded within limits either small or overcharged, and steeped in the vices which that situation generates. A government adapted to such men would be one thing; but a very different one, that for the man of these States. Here every one may have land to labor for himself, if he chooses; or, preferring the exercise of any other industry, may exact for it it such compensation as not only to afford a comfortable subsistence, but wherewith to provide for a cessation from labor in old age. Every one, by his property, or by his satisfactory situation, is interested in the support of law and order. And such men may safely and advantageously reserve to themselves a wholesome control over their public affairs, and a de-

---

[11] "Good men have never destroyed a city, Kurnos."

gree of freedom, which, in the hands of the *canaille* of the cities of Europe, would be instantly perverted to the demolition and destruction of everything public and private. The history of the last twenty-five years of France, and of the last forty years in America, nay of its last two hundred years, proves the truth of both parts of this observation.

But even in Europe a change has sensibly taken place in the mind of man. Science had liberated the ideas of those who read and reflect, and the American example had kindled feelings of right in the people. An insurrection has consequently begun, of science, talents, and courage, against rank and birth, which have fallen into contempt. It has failed in its first effort, because the mobs of the cities, the instrument used for its accomplishment, debased by ignorance, poverty, and vice, could not be restrained to rational action. But the world will recover from the panic of this first catastrophe. Science is progressive, and talents and enterprise on the alert. Resort may be had to the people of the country, a more governable power from their principles and subordination; and rank, and birth, and tinsel-aristocracy will finally shrink into insignificance, even there. This, however, we have no right to meddle with. It suffices for us, if the moral and physical condition of our own citizens qualifies them to select the able and good for the direction of their government, with a recurrance of elections at such short periods as will enable them to displace an unfaithful servant, before the mischief he meditates may be irremediable.

I have thus stated my opinion on a point on which we differ, not with a view to controversy, for we are both too old to change opinions which are the result of a long life of inquiry and reflection; but on the suggestions of a former letter of yours, that we ought not to die before we have explained ourselves to each other. We acted in perfect harmony, through a long and perilous contest for our liberty and independence. A constitution has been acquired, which, though neither of us thinks perfect, yet both consider as competent to render our fellow citizens the happiest and the securest on whom the sun has ever shone. If we do not think exactly alike as to its imperfections, it matters little to our country, which, after devoting to it long lives of disinterested labor, we have delivered over to our successors in life, who will be able to take care of it and of themselves.

Of the pamphlet on aristocracy which has been sent to you, or who may be its author, I have heard nothing but through your letter. If the person you suspect, it may be known from the quaint, mystical, and hyperbolical ideas, involved in affected, new-fangled and pedantic terms which stamp his writings. Whatever it be, I hope your quiet is not to be affected at this day by the rudeness or intemperance of scribblers; but that you may continue in tranquillity to live and to rejoice in the prosperity of our country, until it shall be your own wish to take your seat among the aristoi who have gone before you. Ever and affectionately yours.

TO THOMAS JEFFERSON

Quincy, November 15, 1813.

In 1775, Franklin made a morning visit at Mrs. Yard's, to Sam Adams and John. He was unusually loquacious. "Man, a rational creature!" said Franklin. "Come, let us suppose a rational man. Strip him of all his appetites, especially his hunger and thirst. He is in his chamber, engaged in making experiments, or in pursuing some problem. He is highly entertained. At this moment a servant knocks. 'Sir, dinner is on the table.' 'Dinner! pox! pough! but what have you for dinner?' 'Ham and chickens.' 'Ham, and must I break the chain of my thoughts to go down and gnaw a morsel of damned hog's arse? Put aside your ham; I will dine to-morrow.'" Take away appetite, and the present generation would not live a month, and no future generation would ever exist; and thus the exalted dignity of human nature would be annihilated and lost, and in my opinion the whole loss would be of no more importance than putting out a candle, quenching a torch, or crushing a fire-fly, *if in this world we only have hope*. Your distinction between natural and artificial aristocracy, does not appear to me founded. Birth and wealth are conferred upon some men as imperiously by nature as genius, strength, or beauty. The heir to honors, and riches, and power, has often no more merit in procuring these advantages, than he has in obtaining a handsome face, or an elegant figure. When aristocracies are established by human laws, and honor, wealth, and power are made hereditary by municipal laws and political institutions, then I acknowledge artificial aristocracy to commence; but this never commences till corruption in elections become dominant and uncontrollable. But this artificial aristocracy can never last. The everlasting envies, jealousies, rivalries, and quarrels among them; their cruel rapacity upon the poor ignorant people, their followers, compel them to set up Cæsar, a demagogue, to be a monarch, a master; *pour mettre chacun à sa place*.[12] Here you have the origin of all artificial aristocracy, which is the origin of all monarchies. And both artificial aristocracy and monarchy, and civil, military, political, and hierarchical despotism, have all grown out of the natural aristocracy of virtues and talents. We, to be sure, are far remote from this. Many hundred years must roll away before we shall be corrupted. Our pure, virtuous, public-spirited, federative republic will last forever, govern the globe, and introduce the perfection of man; his perfectibility being already proved by Price, Priestley, Condorcet, Rousseau, Diderot, and Godwin. Mischief has been done by the Senate of the United States. I have known and felt more of this mischief, than Washington, Jefferson, and Madison, all together. But this has been all caused by the constitutional power of the Senate, in executive business, which ought to be immediately, totally, and essentially abolished. Your distinction between the Αριστοι and ψευδο αριστοι, will not help the matter. I would trust one as well as the other with unlimited power. The law wisely refuses an oath as a witness in his own case, to the saint as well as the sinner. No romance would be more amusing than the history of your Virginian and our New England aristocratical families. Yet even in Rhode Island there has been no clergy, no church, and I had

---

[12] "to put everyone in his place"

almost said no State, and some people say no religion. There has been a constant respect for certain old families. Fifty-seven or fifty-eight years ago, in company with Colonel, Counsellor, Judge, John Chandler, whom I have quoted before, a newspaper was brought in. The old sage asked me to look for the news from Rhode Island, and see how the elections had gone there. I read the list of Wanbous, Watrous, Greens, Whipples, Malboues, &c. "I expected as much," said the aged gentleman, "for I have always been of opinion that in the most popular governments, the elections will generally go in favor of the most ancient families." To this day, when any of these tribes—and we may add Ellerys, Channings, Champlins, &c.,—are pleased to fall in with the popular current, they are sure to carry all before them.

You suppose a difference of opinion between you and me on the subject of aristocracy. I can find none. I dislike and detest hereditary honors, offices, emoluments, established by law. So do you. I am for excluding legal, hereditary distinctions from the United States as long as possible. So are you. I only say that mankind have not yet discovered any remedy against irresistible corruption in elections to offices of great power and profit, but making them hereditary.

But will you say our elections are pure? Be it so, upon the whole; but do you recollect in history a more corrupt election than that of Aaron Burr to be President, or that of De Witt Clinton last year? By corruption here, I mean a sacrifice of every national interest and honor to private and party objects. I see the same spirit in Virginia that you and I see in Rhode Island and the rest of New England. In New York it is a struggle of family feuds—a feudal aristocracy. Pennsylvania is a contest between German, Irish and old England families. When Germans and Irish unite they give 30,000 majorities. There is virtually a white rose and a red rose, a Cæsar and a Pompey, in every State in this Union, and contests and dissensions will be as lasting. The rivalry of Bourbons and Noaillises produced the French revolution, and a similar competition for consideration and influence exists and prevails in every village in the world. Where will terminate the *rabies agri?* [13] The continent will be scattered over with manors much larger than Livingston's, Van Renselaers's, or Philips's; even our Deacon Strong will have a principality among you Southern folk. What inequality of talents will be produced by these land jobbers. Where tends the mania of banks? At my table in Philadelphia, I once proposed to you to unite in endeavors to obtain an amendment of the constitution prohibiting to the separate States the power of creating banks; but giving Congress authority to establish one bank with a branch in each State, the whole limited to ten millions of dollars. Whether this project was wise or unwise, I know not, for I had deliberated little on it then, and have never thought it worth thinking of since. But you spurned the proposition from you with disdain. This system of banks, begotten, brooded and hatched by Duer, Robert and Gouverneur Morris, Hamilton and Washington, I have always considered as a system of national injustice. A sacrifice of public and private interest to a few aristocratical friends and favorites. My scheme could have had no such effect. Verres plundered temples, and robbed a few rich men, but he never made such ravages among private property in general, nor swindled so much out of the pockets of the poor, and middle class of people, as these banks have done. No people but this would have borne the imposition so long. The people of Ireland would not bear Wood's half-pence. What inequalities of talent have been introduced into this country by these aristocratical banks! Our Winthrops, Winslows, Bradfords, Saltonstalls, Quinceys, Chandlers, Leonards, Hutchinsons, Olivers, Sewalls, &c., are precisely in the situation of your Randolphs, Carters, and Burwells, and Harrisons. Some of them unpopular for the part they took in the late revolution, but all respected for their names and connections; and whenever they fell in with the popular sentiments are preferred *ceteris paribus*,[14] to all others. When I was young the *summum bonum*[15] in Massachusetts was to be worth

---

[13] "lust for land"
[14] "other things being equal"
[15] "highest good"

£10,000 sterling, ride in a chariot, be Colonel of a regiment of militia, and hold a seat in his Majesty's council. No man's imagination aspired to anything higher beneath the skies. But these plumbs, chariots, colonelships, and counsellorships, are recorded and will never be forgotten. No great accumulations of land were made by our early settlers. Mr. Baudoin, a French refugee, made the first great purchases, and your General Dearborne, born under a fortunate star, is now enjoying a large portion of the aristocratical sweets of them. As I have no amanuenses but females, and there is so much about generation in this letter that I dare not ask any of them to copy it, and I cannot copy it myself, I must beg of you to return it to me. Your old friend.

TO JOHN ADAMS

Monticello, August 10, 1815

DEAR SIR,—The simultaneous movements in our correspondence have been remarkable on several occasions. It would seem as if the state of the air, or state of the times, or some other unknown cause, produced a sympathetic effect on our mutual recollections. I had sat down to answer your letters of June the 19th, 20th and 22d, with pen, ink and paper before me, when I received from our mail that of July the 30th. . . .

On the subject of the history of the American Revolution, you ask who shall write it? Who can write it? And who will ever be able to write it? Nobody; except merely its external facts; all its councils, designs and discussions having been conducted by Congress with closed doors, and no members, as far as I know, having even made notes of them. These, which are the life and soul of history, must forever be unknown. Botta, as you observe, has put his own speculations and reasonings into the mouths of persons whom he names, but who, you and I know, never made such speeches. In this he has followed the example of the ancients, who made their great men deliver long speeches, all of them in the same style, and in that of the author himself. The work is nevertheless a good one, more judicious, more chaste, more classical, and more true than the party diatribe of Marshall.

Its greatest fault is in having taken too much from him. I possessed the work, and often recurred to considerable portions of it, although I never read it through. But a very judicious and well-informed neighbor of mine went through it with great attention, and spoke very highly of it. I have said that no member of the old Congress, as far as I knew, made notes of the discussion. I did not know of the speeches you mention of Dickinson and Witherspoon. But on the questions of Independence, and on the two articles of Confederation respecting taxes and votings, I took minutes of the heads of the arguments. On the first, I threw all into one mass, without ascribing to the speakers their respective arguments; pretty much in the manner of Hume's summary digests of the reasonings in parliament for and against a measure. On the last, I stated the heads of the arguments used by each speaker. But the whole of my notes on the question of Independence does not occupy more than five pages, such as of this letter; and on the other questions, two such sheets. They have never been communicated to any one. Do you know that there exists in manuscript the ablest work of this kind ever yet executed, of the debates of the constitutional convention of Philadelphia in 1788? The whole of everything said and done there was taken down by Mr. Madison, with a labor and exactness beyond comprehension.

I presume that our correspondence has been observed at the post offices, and thus has attracted notice. Would you believe, that a printer has had the effrontery to propose to me the letting him publish it? These people think they have a right to everything, however secret or sacred. . . .

TO JOHN ADAMS

Monticello, January 11, 1816.

DEAR SIR,—Of the last five months I have passed four at my other domicil, for such it is in a considerable degree. No letters are forwarded to me there, because the cross post to that place is circuitous and uncertain; during my absence, therefore, they are accumulating here, and awaiting acknowledgments. This has been the fate of your favor of November 13th.

I agree with you in all its eulogies on the eighteenth century. It certainly witnessed the sciences and arts, manners and morals, advanced to a higher degree than the world had ever before seen. And might we not go back to the æra of the Borgias, by which time the barbarous ages had reduced national morality to its lowest point of depravity, and observe that the arts and sciences, rising from that point, advanced gradually through all the sixteenth, seventeenth and eighteenth centuries, softening and correcting the manners and morals of man? I think, too, we may add to the great honor of science and the arts, that their natural effect is, by illuminating public opinion, to erect it into a censor, before which the most exalted tremble for their future, as well as present fame. With some exceptions only, through the seventeenth and eighteenth centuries, morality occupied an honorable chapter in the political code of nations. You must have observed while in Europe, as I thought I did, that those who administered the governments of the greater powers at least, had a respect to faith, and considered the dignity of their government as involved in its integrity. A wound indeed was inflicted on this character of honor in the eighteenth century by the partition of Poland. But this was the atrocity of a barbarous government chiefly, in conjunction with a smaller one still scrambling to become great, while one only of those already great, and having character to lose, descended to the baseness of an accomplice in the crime. France, England, Spain, shared in it only inasmuch as they stood aloof and permitted its perpetration.

How then has it happened that these nations, France especially and England, so great, so dignified, so distinguished by science and the arts, plunged all at once into all the depths of human enormity, threw off suddenly and openly all the restraints of morality, all sensation to character, and unblushingly avowed and acted on the principle that power was right? Can this sudden apostasy from national rectitude be accounted for? The treaty of Pilnitz seems to have begun it, suggested perhaps by the baneful precedent of Poland. Was it from the terror of monarchs, alarmed at the light returning on them from the west, and kindling a volcano under their thrones? Was it a combination to extinguish that light, and to bring back, as their best auxiliaries, those enumerated by you, the Sorbonne, the Inquisition, the Index Expurgatorius, and the knights of Loyola? Whatever it was, the close of the century saw the moral world thrown back again to the age of the Borgias, to the point from which it had departed three hundred years before. France, after crushing and punishing the conspiracy of Pilnitz, went herself deeper and deeper into the crimes she had been chastising. I say France and not Bonaparte; for, although he was the head and mouth, the nation furnished the hands which executed his enormities. England, although in opposition, kept full pace with France, not indeed by the manly force of her own arms, but by oppressing the weak and bribing the strong. At length the whole choir joined and divided the weaker nations among them. . . .

TO JOHN ADAMS

Monticello, September 12, 1821.

DEAR SIR,—I am just returned from my other home, and shall within a week go back to it for the rest of the autumn. I find here your favor of August 20th, and was before in arrear for that of May 19th. I cannot answer, but join in, your question of May 19th. Are we to surrender the pleasing hopes of seeing improvement in the moral and intellectual condition of man? The events of Naples and Piedmont cast a gloomy cloud over that hope, and Spain and Portugal are not beyond jeopardy. And what are we to think of this northern triumvirate, arming their nations to dictate despotisms to the rest of the world? And the evident connivance of England, as the price of secret stipulations for continental armies, if her own should take side with her malcontent and pulverized people? And what of the poor Greeks, and their small chance of amelioration even if the hypocritical Autocrat should take them under the iron cover of his Ukazes. Would this be lighter or safer than that of the Turk? These, my dear friend, are speculations for the new generation, as, before they will be resolved, you and I must join our deceased brother Floyd.

Yet I will not believe our labors are lost. I shall not die without a hope that light and liberty are on steady advance. We have seen, indeed, once within the records of history, a complete eclipse of the human mind continuing for centuries. And this, too, by swarms of the same northern barbarians, conquering and taking possession of the countries and governments of the civilized world. Should this be again attempted, should the same northern hordes, allured again by the corn, wine, and oil of the south, be able again to settle their swarms in the countries of their growth, the art of printing alone, and the vast dissemination of books, will maintain the mind where it is, and raise the conquering ruffians to the level of the conquered, instead of degrading these to that of their conquerors. And even should the cloud of barbarism and despotism again obscure the science and liberties of Europe, this country remains to preserve and restore light and liberty to them. In short, the flames kindled on the 4th of July, 1776, have spread over too much of the globe to be extinguished by the feeble engines of despotism; on the contrary, they will consume these engines and all who work them.

I think with you that there should be a school of instruction for our navy as well as artillery; and I do not see why the same establishment might not suffice for both. Both require the same basis of general mathematics, adding projectiles and fortifications for the artillery exclusively, and astronomy and theory of navigation exclusively for the naval students. Berout conducted both schools in France, and has left us the best book extant for their joint and separate instruction. It ought not to require a separate professor.

A 4th of July oration delivered in the town of Milford, in your State, gives to Samuel Chase the credit of having "first started the cry of independence in the ears of his countrymen." Do you remember anything of this? I do not. I have no doubt it was uttered in Massachusetts even before it was by Thomas Paine. But certainly I never considered Samuel Chase as foremost, or even forward in that hallowed cry. I know that Maryland hung heavily on our backs, and that Chase, although first named, was not most in unison with us of that delegation, either in politics or morals, *et c'est ainsi que l'on ecrit l'histoire!* [16]

Your doubt of the legitimacy of the word *gloriola,* is resolved by Cicero, who, in his letter to Lucceius expresses a wish *"ut nos metipsi vivi gloriola nostra perfruamur."* [17] Affectionately adieu.

TO THOMAS JEFFERSON

Quincy, August 15, 1823.

Watchman, what of the night? Is darkness that may be felt, to prevail over the whole world? or can you perceive any rays of a returning dawn? Is the devil to be the "Lords' anointed" over the whole globe? or do you foresee the fulfilment of the prophecies according to Dr. Priestley's interpretation of them? I know not, but I have in some of my familiar, and frivolous letters to you, told the story four times over; but if I have, I never applied it so well as now.

Not long after the denouement of the tragedy of Louis XVI, when I was Vice-President, my friend the Doctor came to breakfast with me alone; he was very sociable, very learned and eloquent, on the subject of the French revolution. It was opening a new era in the world, and presenting a near view of the millennium. I listened; I heard with great attention and perfect *sang froid*. At last I asked the Doctor. Do you really believe the French will establish a free democratical government in France? He answered: I do firmly believe it. Will you give me leave to ask you upon what grounds you entertain this opinion? Is it from anything you ever read in history? Is there any instance of a Roman Catholic monarchy of five and twenty millions at once converted into a free and national people? No. I know of no instance like it. Is there anything in your knowledge of human nature, derived from books, or experience, that any nation, ancient or modern, consisting of such multitudes of ignorant people,

---

[16] "and this is the way history is written!"
[17] "that we might enjoy our little glory in our own lifetimes"

ever were, or ever can be converted suddenly into materials capable of conducting a free government, especially a democratical republic? No—I know nothing of the kind. Well then, Sir, what is the ground of your opinion? The answer was, my opinion is founded altogether upon revelation, and the prophecies. I take it that the ten horns of the great beast in revelations, mean the ten crowned heads of Europe; and that the execution of the King of France, is the falling off of the first of those horns; and the nine monarchies of Europe will fall one after another in the same way. Such was the enthusiasm of that great man, that reasoning machine. After all, however, he did recollect himself so far as to say: There is, however, a possibility of doubt; for I read yesterday a book put into my hands, by a gentleman, a volume of travels written by a French gentleman in 1659; in which he says he had been travelling a whole year in England; into every part of it, and conversed freely with all ranks of people; he found the whole nation earnestly engaged in discussing and contriving a form of government of their future regulations; there was but one point in which they all agreed, and in that they were unanimous: that monarchy, nobility, and prelacy never would exist in England again. The Doctor paused; and said: Yet, in the very next year, the whole nation called in the King and run mad with nobility, monarchy, and prelacy. I am no King killer; merely because they are Kings. Poor creatures; they know no better; they believe sincerely and conscientiously that God made them to rule the world. I would not, therefore, behead them, or send them to St. Helena, to be treated as Bonaparte was; but I would shut them up like the man in the iron mask; feed them well, give them as much finery as they pleased, until they could be converted to right reason and common sense. I have nothing to communicate from this part of the country, except that you must not be surprised if you hear something wonderful in Boston before long. With my profound respects for your family, and half a century's affection for yourself, I am your humble servant.

TO JOHN ADAMS

Monticello, March 25, 1826.

Dear Sir,—My grandson, Thomas J. Randolph, the bearer of this letter, being on a visit to Boston, would think he had seen nothing were he to leave without seeing you. Although I truly sympathize with you in the trouble these interruptions give, yet I must ask for him permission to pay to you his personal respects. Like other young people, he wishes to be able in the winter nights of old age, to recount to those around him, what he has heard and learnt of the heroic age preceding his birth, and which of the Argonauts individually he was in time to have seen.

It was the lot of our early years to witness nothing but the dull monotony of a colonial subservience; and of our riper years, to breast the labors and perils of working out of it. Theirs are the Halcyon calms succeeding the storm which our Argosy had so stoutly weathered. Gratify his ambition then, by receiving his best bow; and my solicitude for your health, by enabling him to bring me a favorable account of it. Mine is but indifferent, but not so my friendship and respect for you.

PATTERNS OF LIFE AND THOUGHT IN AMERICA

Literature sometimes shapes and determines the life of a people profoundly. Always it is a reflection of that life. The writer can produce nothing which has not come from his own experience, and his experience is largely determined by the life around him. To communicate at all, he must use the media, conventions and techniques which his audience is prepared to accept. And the kind of imaginative experience he creates must be recognizable, or he will draw a blank with his audience. Hence the literary records and the merely informative records of the patterns of outward behavior and inward reactions of people in an age are mutually supporting. By placing them side by side one can understand both kinds of records themselves *and* the age much better than by taking one kind of record alone.

The records of life and thought in the period of the early republic deal with a number of different kinds of people and their ways. There are regional types, city, sea-faring, rural, and frontier people. As the patterns of their outward lives are different so are the covert patterns of idea, religion, and value judgement. This variety gives rise to an equal diversity of content in their writing.

One of the most pervasive and insistent themes is the question of an American civilization. How shall it be American and what should be its relation to the European past and present, to the hope of American newness, and to the conditions of the wilderness? This involves problems of education and anti-intellectualism, of high-browism vs. low-browism in education itself. It gives special point to the opposition of the frontiersman and settled civilian. An adjustment had to be made between the jostling new ideals of democracy and a firm old tradition of society dominated by gentry.

With millions of acres stretching beyond the half-subdued wilderness of the settlements, one of the familiar themes was that of the farmer and his destiny—agrarianism. Timothy Dwight, hymning the beauties of the independent, upright, abundant life of the thrifty yeoman working his own soil within sound of the church and school-house bells, expressed an ideal which became official in the American pantheon. Crèvecoeur, as Rousseauist, waxed sentimental and almost mystical about the American farmer: the farmer and his land are perhaps the hope of humanity. John Taylor of Caroline began to suspect that agrarianism must become a fighting creed beset by urban and industrial opponents.

The alternate patterns of warfare and reconciliation between science and theology were troubling religious people in this era as later. To see the religious picture one needs to turn to the writers affected by deism as well as to the more evangelical ones. Franklin, Paine, and Jefferson became unchurched after being exposed to the deistic thinking which was focussed on the achievements of Sir Isaac Newton. Other equally knowledgeable men—like Adams and the scientist Rush—were comparatively orthodox. They kept both religion and intellectual respectability by deciding that reason and revelation were really the same, and that science explained, not contradicted, the basic Christian tradition.

All this was decidedly intellectual, however. It was vivid, simple, inhibition-releasing, and emotionally powerful evangelicism like that of Lorenzo Dow which captured the American people and made the nineteenth century both romantic and Victorian in its religion.

JOHN TRUMBULL
(1750-1831)

Legend tells us that Trumbull was so precocious that he passed the entrance examinations for Yale at the age of seven, sitting on the president's knee. Before the law took first place in his career, he promised for a time to vindicate the Connecticut Wits' faith in their power to evoke a genuine American poet from their ranks. As it was, he wrote a great deal of derivative but competent and occasionally sparkling satire modelled on Hudibras Butler, Le Sage, Pope, and others. But if the styles and themes were a bit old, the ideas were sharply modern. Trumbull advocates education shaped to immediate uses, taught in modern idiom, for women as well as men, and based on what was then contemporary literature. In his criticism of books as well as religion, he was relying upon the Scottish common sense philosophers just then beginning their long dominance of American education.

Bibliography: Alexander Cowie, *John Trumbull, Connecticut Wit*, Chapel Hill, 1936; Leon Howard, *The Connecticut Wits*, Chicago, 1943.

Text: *The Poetical Works of John Trumbull*, Hartford, 1820.

from THE PROGRESS OF DULNESS

PART I

OR THE ADVENTURES OF TOM BRAINLESS

"Our Tom has grown a sturdy boy;
His progress fills my heart with joy;
A steady soul, that yields to rule,
And quite ingenious too, at school.
Our master says, (I'm sure he's right,)
There's not a lad in town so bright.
He'll cypher bravely, write and read,
And say his catechism and creed,
And scorns to hesitate or falter
In Primer, Spelling-book or Psalter.
Hard work indeed, he does not love it;

His genius is too much above it.
Give him a good substantial teacher,
I'll lay he'd make a special preacher.
I've loved good learning all my life;
We'll send the lad to college, wife."

Thus sway'd by fond and sightless passion,
His parents hold a consultation;
If on their couch, or round their fire,
I need not tell, nor you enquire.

The point's agreed; the boy well pleased,
From country cares and labor eased;
No more to rise by break of day
To drive home cows, or deal out hay;
To work no more in snow or hail,
And blow his fingers o'er the flail,
Or mid the toils of harvest sweat
Beneath the summer's sultry heat,
Serene, he bids the farm, good-bye,
And quits the plough without a sigh.

Kind head-ache hail! thou blest disease,
The friend of idleness and ease;
Who mid the still and dreary bound
Where college walls her sons surround,
In spite of fears, in justice' spite,
Assumest o'er laws dispensing right,
Sett'st from his task the blunderer free,
Excused by dulness and by thee.
The vot'ries bid a bold defiance
To all the calls and threats of science,
Slight learning human and divine,
And hear no prayers, and fear no fine.

And yet how oft the studious gain,
The dulness of a letter'd brain;
Despising such low things the while,

As English grammar, phrase and style;
Despising ev'ry nicer art,
That aids the tongue, or mends the heart;
Read ancient authors o'er in vain,
Nor taste one beauty they contain;
Humbly on trust accept the sense,
But deal for words at vast expense;
Search well how every term must vary
From Lexicon to Dictionary;
And plodding on in one dull tone,
Gain ancient tongues and lose their own,
Bid every graceful charm defiance,
And woo the skeleton of science.

  Come ye, who finer arts despise,
And scoff at verse as heathen lies;
In all the pride of dulness rage
At Pope, or Milton's deathless page;
Or stung by truth's deep-searching line,
Rave ev'n at rhymes as low as mine;
Say ye, who boast the name of wise,
Wherein substantial learning lies.
Is it, superb in classic lore,
To speak what Homer spoke before,
To write the language Tully wrote,
The style, the cadence and the note?
Is there a charm in sounds of Greek,
No language else can learn to speak;
That cures distemper'd brains at once,
Like Pliny's rhymes for broken bones?
Is there a spirit found in Latin,
That must evap'rate in translating?
And say are sense and genius bound
To any vehicles of sound?
Can knowledge never reach the brains,
Unless convey'd in ancient strains?
While Homer sets before your eyes

Achilles' rage, Ulysses' lies,
Th' amours of Jove in masquerade,
And Mars entrapp'd by Phœbus' aid;
While Virgil sings, in verses grave,
His lovers meeting in a cave,
His ships turn'd nymphs, in pagan fables,
And how the Trojans eat their tables;
While half this learning but displays
The follies of the former days;
And for the linguists, fairly try them,
A tutor'd parrot might defy them.

. . . . .

Oh! might I live to see that day,
When sense shall point to youths their way;
Through every maze of science guide;
O'er education's laws preside;
The good retain, with just discerning
Explode the quackeries of learning;
Give ancient arts their real due,
Explain their faults, and beauties too;
Teach where to imitate, and mend,
And point their uses and their end.
Then bright philosophy would shine,
And ethics teach the laws divine;
Our youths might learn each nobler art,
That shews a passage to the heart;
From ancient languages well known
Transfuse new beauties to our own;
With taste and fancy well refin'd,
Where moral rapture warms the mind,
From schools dismiss'd, with lib'ral hand,
Spread useful learning o'er the land;
And bid the eastern world admire
Our rising worth, and bright'ning fire.

But while through fancy's realms we roam,
The main concern is left at home;
Return'd, our hero still we find
The same, as blundering, and as blind.
  Four years at college dozed away
In sleep, and slothfulness and play,
Too dull for vice, with clearest conscience,
Charged with no fault but that of nonsense,
And nonsense long, with serious air,
Has wander'd unmolested there,
He passes trial, fair and free,
And takes in form his first degree.
  A scholar see him now commence
Without the aid of books or sense;
For passing college cures the brain,
Like mills to grind men young again.
The scholar-dress, that once array'd him,
The charm, *Admitto te ad gradum*,[1]
With touch of parchment can refine,
And make the veriest coxcomb shine,
Confer the gift of tongues at once,
And fill with sense the vacant dunce.
So kingly crowns contain quintessence
Of worship, dignity and presence;
Give learning, genius, virtue, worth,
Wit, valor, wisdom, and so forth;
Hide the bald pate, and cover o'er
The cap of folly worn before.
  Our hero's wit and learning now may
Be proved by token of diploma,
Of that diploma, which with speed
He learns to construe and to read;
And stalks abroad with conscious stride,

---

[1] "I admit you to a degree"—part of the words used in conferring the honours of college.

In all the airs of pedant pride,
With passport sign'd for wit and knowledge,
And current under seal of college.

Next see our youth at school appear,
Procured for forty pounds a year;
His ragged regiment round assemble,
Taught, not to read, but fear and tremble.
Before him, rods prepare his way,
Those dreaded antidotes to play.
Then throned aloft in elbow chair,
With solemn face and awful air,
He tries, with ease and unconcern,
To teach what ne'er himself could learn;
Gives law and punishment alone,
Judge, jury, bailiff, all in one;
Holds all good learning must depend
Upon his rod's extremest end,
Whose great electric virtue's such,
Each genius brightens at the touch;
With threats and blows, incitements pressing,
Drives on his lads to learn each lesson;
Thinks flogging cures all moral ills,
And breaks their heads to break their wills.

The year is done; he takes his leave;
The children smile; the parents grieve;
And seek again, their school to keep,
One just as good and just as cheap.

Now to some priest, that's famed for teaching,
He goes to learn the art of preaching;
And settles down with earnest zeal
Sermons to study, and to steal.
Six months from all the world retires
To kindle up his cover'd fires;
Learns, with nice art, to make with ease

The scriptures speak whate'er he please;
With judgment, unperceived to quote
What Pool explain'd, or Henry wrote;
To give the gospel new editions,
Split doctrines into propositions,
Draw motives, uses, inferences,
And torture words in thousand senses;
Learn the grave style and goodly phrase,
Safe handed down from Cromwell's days,
And shun, with anxious care, the while,
The infection of a modern style;
Or on the wings of folly fly
Aloft in metaphysic sky;
The system of the world explain,
Till night and chaos come again;
Deride what old divines can say,
Point out to heaven a nearer way;
Explode all known establish'd rules,
Affirm our fathers all were fools;
The present age is growing wise,
But wisdom in her cradle lies;
Late, like Minerva, born and bred,
Not from a Jove's, but scribbler's head,
While thousand youths their homage lend her,
And nursing fathers rock and tend her.

  Round him much manuscript is spread,
Extracts from living works, and dead,
Themes, sermons, plans of controversy,
That hack and mangle without mercy,
And whence to glad the reader's eyes,
The future dialogue shall rise.

  At length, matured the grand design,
He stalks abroad, a grave divine.

  Mean while, from every distant seat,
At stated time the clergy meet,
Our hero comes, his sermons reads,

Explains the doctrine of his creeds,
A license gains to preach and pray,
And makes his bow, and goes his way.

What though his wits could ne'er dispense
One page of grammar, or of sense;
What though his learning be so slight,
He scarcely knows to spell or write;
What though his skull be cudgel-proof!
He's orthodox, and that's enough.

Perhaps with genius we'd dispense;
But sure we look at least for sense.

Ye fathers of our church attend
The serious counsels of a friend,
Whose utmost wish, in nobler ways,
Your sacred dignity to raise.
Though blunt the style, the truths set down
Ye can't deny—though some may frown.

Yes, there are men, nor these a few,
The foes of virtue and of you;
Who, nurtured in the scorner's school,
Make vice their trade, and sin by rule;
Who deem it courage heav'n to brave,
And wit, to scoff at all that's grave;
Vent stolen jests, with strange grimaces,
From folly's book of common-places;
While mid the simple throng around
Each kindred blockhead greets the sound,
And, like electric fire, at once,
The laugh is caught from dunce to dunce.

The deist's scoffs ye may despise;
Within yourselves your danger lies;
For who would wish, neglecting rule,
To aid the trumphs of a fool?
From heaven at first your order came,
From heaven received its sacred name,

Indulged to man, to point the way,
That leads from darkness up to day.
Your highborn dignity attend,
And view your origin and end.

  While human souls are all your care,
By warnings, counsels, preaching, prayer,
In bands of christian friendship join'd,
Where pure affection warms the mind,
While each performs the pious race,
Nor dulness e'er usurps a place;
No vice shall brave your awful test,
Nor folly dare to broach the jest,
Each waiting eye shall humbly bend,
And reverence on your steps attend.

  But when each point of serious weight
Is torn with wrangling and debate,
When truth, mid rage of dire divisions,
Is left, to fight for definitions,
And fools assume your sacred place,
It threats your order with disgrace;
Bids genius from your seats withdraw,
And seek the pert, loquacious law;
Or deign in physic's paths to rank,
With every quack and mountebank;
Or in the ways of trade content,
Plod ledgers o'er of cent. per cent.

  While in your seats so sacred, whence
We look for piety and sense,
Pert dulness raves in school-boy style,
Your friends must blush, your foes will smile;
While men, who teach the glorious way,
Where heaven unfolds celestial day,
Assume the task sublime, to bring
The message of th' Eternal King,
Disgrace those honours they receive,

And want that sense, they aim to give.
  Now in the desk, with solemn air,
Our hero makes his audience stare;
Asserts with all dogmatic boldness,
Where impudence is yoked to dulness;
Reads o'er his notes with halting pace,
Mask'd in the stiffness of his face;
With gestures such as might become
Those statues once that spoke at Rome,
Or Livy's ox, that to the state
Declared the oracles of fate,
In awkward tones, not said, nor sung,
Slow rumbling o'er the falt'ring tongue,
Two hours his drawling speech holds on,
And names it preaching, when he's done.
  With roving tired, he fixes down
For life, in some unsettled town.
People and priest full well agree,
For why—they know no more than he.
Vast tracts of unknown land he gains,
Better than those the moon contains;
There deals in preaching and in prayer,
And starves on sixty pounds a year,
And culls his texts, and tills his farms,
Does little good, and little harm;
On Sunday, in his best array,
Deals forth the dulness of the day,
And while above he spends his breath,
The yawning audience nod beneath.
  Thus glib-tongued Merc'ry in his hand
Stretch'd forth the sleep-compelling wand,
Each eye in endless doze to keep—
The God of speaking, and of sleep.

END OF PART FIRST

PART II

OR THE LIFE AND CHARACTER OF DICK HAIRBRAIN

'Twas in a town remote, the place
We leave the reader wise to guess,
(For readers wise can guess full well
What authors never meant to tell,)
There dwelt secure a country clown,
The wealthiest farmer of the town.
Though rich by villany and cheats,
He bought respect by frequent treats;
Gain'd offices by constant seeking,
'Squire, captain, deputy and deacon;
Great was his power, his pride as arrant;
One only son his heir apparent.
He thought the stripling's parts were quick,
And vow'd to make a man of DICK;
Bless'd the pert dunce, and praised his looks,
And put him early to his books.

 More oaths than words DICK learn'd to speak
And studied knavery more than Greek;
Three years at school, as usual, spent
Then all equipp'd to college went,

. . . . . .

But bred in distant woods, the clown
Brings all his country airs to town;
The old address with awkward grace,
That bows with all-averted face;
The half-heard compliments, whose note
Is swallowed in the trembling throat;
The stiffen'd gait, the drawling tone,
By which his native place is known;
The blush, that looks, by vast degrees,
Too much like modesty to please;

The proud displays of awkward dress,
That all the country fop express,
The suit right gay, though much belated,
Whose fashion's superannuated;
The watch, depending far in state,
Whose iron chain might form a grate;
The silver buckle, dread to view,
O'ershad'wing all the clumsy shoe;
The white-gloved hand, that tries to peep
From ruffle, full five inches deep;
With fifty odd affairs beside,
The foppishness of country pride.

   Poor DICK! though first thy airs provoke
Th' obstreperous laugh and scornful joke,
Doom'd all the ridicule to stand,
While each gay dunce shall lend a hand;
Yet let not scorn dismay thy hope
To shine a witling and a fop.
Blest impudence the prize shall gain,
And bid thee sigh no more in vain.
Thy varied dress shall quickly show
At once the spendthrift and the beau.
With pert address and noisy tongue,
That scorns the fear of prating wrong,
'Mongst list'ning coxcombs shalt thou shine,
And every voice shall echo thine.

   How blest the brainless fop, whose praise
Is doom'd to grace these happy days,
When well-bred vice can genius teach,
And fame is placed in folly's reach,
Impertinence all tastes can hit,
And every rascal is a wit.
The lowest dunce, without despairing,
May learn the true sublime of swearing;
Learn the nice art of jests obscene,
While ladies wonder what they mean;

The heroism of brazen lungs,
The rhetoric of eternal tongues;
While whim usurps the name of spirit,
And impudence takes place of merit,
And every money'd clown and dunce
Commences gentleman at once.

  For now, by easy rules of trade,
Mechanic gentlemen are made!
From handicrafts of fashion born;
Those very arts so much their scorn.
To taylors half themselves they owe,
Who make the clothes, that make the beau.

    . . . . .

  And who for beauty need repine,
That's sold at every barber's sign;
Nor lies in features or complexion,
But curls disposed in meet direction,
With strong pomatum's grateful odour,
And *quantum sufficit* of powder?
These charms can spread a sprightly grace,
O'er the dull eye and clumsy face;
While the trim dancing-master's art
Shall gestures, trips, and bows impart,
Give the gay piece its final touches,
And lend those airs, would lure a dutchess.

  Thus shines the form, not aught behind,
The gifts that deck the coxcomb's mind;
Then hear the daring muse disclose
The sense and piety of beaux.

  To grace his speech, let France bestow
A set of compliments for show.
Land of politeness! that affords
The treasure of new-fangled words,
And endless quantities disburses
Of bows and compliments and curses;

The soft address, with airs so sweet,
That cringes at the ladies' feet;
The pert, vivacious, play-house style,
That wakes the gay assembly's smile;
Jests that his brother beaux may hit,
And pass with young coquettes for wit,
And prized by fops of true discerning,
Outface the pedantry of learning.
Yet learning too shall lend its aid,
To fill the coxcomb's spongy head,
And studious oft he shall peruse
The labours of the modern muse.
From endless loads of novels gain
Soft, simp'ring tales of amorous pain,
With double meanings, neat and handy,
From Rochester and Tristram Shandy.
The blund'ring aid of weak reviews,
That forge the fetters of the muse,
Shall give him airs of criticising
On faults of books, he ne'er set eyes on.
The magazines shall teach the fashion,
And common-place of conversation,
And where his knowledge fails, afford
The aid of many a sounding word.

Then least religion he should need,
Of pious Hume he'll learn his creed,
By strongest demonstration shown,
Evince that nothing can be known;
Take arguments, unvex'd by doubt,
On Voltaire's trust, or go without;
'Gainst scripture rail in modern lore,
As thousand fools have rail'd before;
Or pleased a nicer art display
T'expound the doctrines all away,
Suit it to modern tastes and fashions
By various notes and emendations;

The rules the ten commands contain,
With new provisos well explain;
Prove all religion was but fashion,
Beneath the Jewish dispensation.

. . . . .

  Blest be his ashes! under ground
If any particles be found,
Who friendly to the coxcomb race,
First taught those arts of common-place,
Those topics fine, on which the beau
May all his little wits bestow,
Secure the simple laugh to raise,
And gain the dunce's palm of praise.
For where's the theme that beaux could hit
With least similitude of wit,
Did not religion and the priest
Supply materials for the jest?
The poor in purse, with metals vile
For current coins, the world beguile;
The poor in brain, for genuine wit
Pass off a viler counterfeit;
While various thus their doom appears,
These lose their souls, and those their ears;
The want of fancy, whim supplies,
And native humour, mad caprice;
Loud noise for argument goes off,
For mirth polite, the ribald's scoff;
For sense, lewd droll'ries entertain us,
And wit is mimick'd by profaneness.
  Thus 'twixt the taylor and the player,
And Hume, and Tristram, and Voltaire,
Complete in modern trim array'd,
The clockwork gentleman is made;
As thousand fops ere DICK have shown,
In airs, which DICK ere long shall own.

But not immediate from the clown,
He gains his zenith of renown;
Slow dawns the coxcomb's op'ning fray;
Rome was not finished in a day.
Perfection is the work of time;
Gradual he mounts the height sublime;
First shines abroad with bolder grace,
In suits of second-handed lace,
And learns by rote, like studious players,
The fop's infinity of airs;
Till merit, to full ripeness grown,
By constancy attains the crown.

Now should our tale at large proceed,
Here might I tell, and you might read
At college next how DICK went on,
And prated much and studied none;
Yet shone with fair, unborrow'd ray,
And steer'd where nature led the way.
What though each academic science
Bade all his efforts bold defiance!
What though in algebra his station
Was negative in each equation;
Though in astronomy survey'd,
His constant course was retrograde;
O'er Newton's system though he sleeps
And finds his wits in dark eclipse!
His talents proved of highest price
At all the arts of cards and dice;
His genius turn'd, with greatest skill,
To whist, loo, cribbage, and quadrille,
And taught, to every rival's shame,
Each nice distinction of the game.

As noon-day sun, the case is plain,
Nature has nothing made in vain.
The blind mole cannot fly; 'tis found
His genius leads him underground.

The man that was not made to think,
Was born to game, and swear, and drink.
Let fops defiance bid to satire,
Mind Tully's rule, and follow nature.

   Yet here the muse, of DICK, must tell
He shone in active scenes as well;
The foremost place in riots held,
In all the gifts of noise excell'd,
His tongue, the bell, whose rattling din would
Summon the rake's nocturnal synod;
Swore with a grace that seem'd design'd
To emulate the infernal kind,
Nor only make their realms his due,
But learn, betimes, their language too;
And well expert in arts polite,
Drank wine by quarts to mend his sight,
For he that drinks till all things reel,
Sees double, and that's twice as well;
And ere its force confined his feet,
Led out his mob to scour the street;
Made all authority his may-game,
And strain'd his little wits to plague 'em.
Then, every crime atoned with ease,
Pro meritis,[2] received degrees;
And soon, as fortune chanced to fall,
His father died, and left him all.
Then, bent to gain all modern fashions,
He sail'd to visit foreign nations,
Resolved, by toil unaw'd, to import
The follies of the British court;
But in his course o'er looked whate'er
Was learned or valued, rich or rare.

   As fire electric draws together
Each hair and straw and dust and feather,
The travell'd dunce collects betimes

---

[2] "For his merits"—the customary phrase in collegiate diplomas.

The levities of other climes;
And when long toil has given success,
Returns his native land to bless,
A patriot fop, that struts by rules,
A Knight of all the shire of fools.

The praise of other learning lost,
To know the world is all his boast,
By conduct teach our country widgeons,
How coxcombs shine in other regions,
Display his travell'd airs and fashions,
And scoff at college educations.

Whoe'er at college points his sneer,
Proves that himself learn'd nothing there,
And wisely makes his honest aim
To pay the mutual debt of shame.

Meanwhile our hero's anxious care
Was all employed to please the fair;
With vows of love and airs polite,
Oft sighing at some lady's feet;
Pleased, while he thus in form address'd her,
With his own gracefulness of gesture,
And gaudy flattery, that displays
A studied elegance of phrase
So gay at balls the coxcomb shone,
He thought the female world his own.
By beauty's charms he ne'er was fired;
He flatter'd where the world admired.
Himself, so well he prized desert,
Possest his own unrivall'd heart;
Nor charms, nor chance, nor change could move
The firm foundations of his love;
His heart, so constant and so wise,
Pursued what sages old advise,
Bade others seek for fame or pelf;
His only study was himself.

Yet DICK allow'd the fair, desert,

Nor wholly scorn'd them in his heart;
There was an end, as oft he said,
For which alone the sex were made,
Whereto, of nature's rules observant,
He strove to render them subservient;
And held the fair by inclination,
Were form'd exactly for their station,
That real virtue ne'er could find
Her lodging in a female mind;
Quoted from Pope, in phrase so smart,
That all the sex are 'rakes at heart,'
And praised Mahomet's sense, who holds
That women ne'er were born with souls.

  Thus blest, our hero saw his name
Rank'd in the foremost lists of fame.
What though the learn'd, the good, the wise,
His light affected airs despise!
What though the fair of higher mind,
With brighter thought and sense refined,
Whose fancy rose on nobler wing,
Scorn'd the vain, gilt, gay, noisy thing!
Each light coquette spread forth her charms,
And lured the hero to her arms.
For beaux and light coquettes, by fate
Were each designed the other's mate,
By instinct love, for each may find
Its likeness in the other's mind.

  Each gayer fop of modern days
Allow'd to DICK the foremost praise,
Borrow'd his style, his airs, grimace,
And aped his modish form of dress.
Even some, with sense endued, felt hopes
And warm ambition to be fops;
But men of sense, 'tis fix'd by fate,
Are coxcombs but of second rate.
The pert and lively dunce alone

Can steer the course that DICK has shown;
The lively dunce alone can climb
The summit, where he shines sublime.

But ah! how short the fairest name
Stands on the slippery steep of fame!
The noblest heights we're soonest giddy on;
The sun ne'er stays in his meridian;
The brightest stars must quickly set;
And DICK has deeply run in debt.
Not all his oaths can duns dismay,
Or deadly bailiffs fright away,
Not all his compliments can bail,
Or minuets dance him from the jail.
Law not the least respect can give
To the laced coat, or ruffled sleeve;
His splendid ornaments must fall,
And all is lost, for these were all.

What then remains? in health's decline,
By lewdness, luxury, and wine,
Worn by disease, with purse too shallow,
To lead in fashions, or to follow,
The meteor's gaudy light is gone;
Lone age with hasty step comes on.
How pale the palsied fop appears,
Low shivering in the vale of years;
The ghost of all his former days,
When folly lent the ear of praise,
And beaux with pleased attention hung
On accents of his chatt'ring tongue.
Now all those days of pleasure o'er,
That chatt'ring tongue must prate no more.
From every place, that bless'd his hopes,
He's elbow'd out by younger fops.
Each pleasing thought unknown, that cheers,
The sadness of declining years,

In lonely age he sinks forlorn,
Of all, and even himself, the scorn.
  The coxcomb's course was gay and clever,
Would health and money last for ever,
Did conscience never break the charm,
Nor fear of future worlds alarm.
But oh, since youth and years decay,
And life's vain follies fleet away,
Since age has no respect for beaux,
And death the gaudy scene must close,
Happy the man, whose early bloom
Provides for endless years to come;
That learning seeks, whose useful gain
Repays the course of studious pain,
Whose fame the thankful age shall raise,
And future times repeat its praise;
Attains that heart-felt peace of mind,
To all the will of heaven resign'd,
Which calms in youth, the blast of rage,
Adds sweetest hope to sinking age,
With valued use prolongs the breath,
And gives a placid smile to death.

END OF PART SECOND

PART III

OR THE ADVENTURES OF MISS HARRIET SIMPER

"Come hither, HARRIET, pretty Miss,
Come hither; give your aunt a kiss.
What, blushing? fye, hold up your head,
Full six years old and yet afraid!
With such a form, an air, a grace,
You're not ashamed to show your face!
Look like a lady—bold—my child!

Why ma'am, your HARRIET will be spoil'd.
What pity 'tis, a girl so sprightly
Should hang her head so unpolitely?
And sure there's nothing worth a rush in
That odd, unnatural trick of blushing;
It marks one ungenteelly bred,
And shows there's mischief in her head.
I've heard Dick Hairbrain prove from Paul,
Eve never blush'd before the fall.
'Tis said indeed, in latter days,
It gain'd our grandmothers some praise;
Perhaps it suited well enough
With hoop and farthingale and ruff;
But this politer generation
Holds ruffs and blushes out of fashion.

"And what can mean your simple whim here
To keep her poring on her primer?
'Tis quite enough for girls to know,
If she can read a billet-doux,
Or write a line you'd understand
Without a cypher of the hand.
Why need she learn to write, or spell?
A pothook scrawl is just as well;
Might rank her with the better sort,
For 'tis the reigning mode at court.
And why should girls be learn'd or wise?
Books only serve to spoil their eyes.
The studious eye but faintly twinkles,
And reading paves the way to wrinkles.
In vain may learning fill the head full;
'Tis beauty that's the one thing needful;
Beauty, our sex's sole pretence,
The best recipe for female sense,
The charm that turns all words to witty,

And makes the silliest speeches pretty.
Ev'n folly borrows killing graces
From ruby lips and roseate faces.
Give airs and beauty to your daughter,
And sense and wit will follow after."

  Thus round the infant Miss in state,
The council of the ladies meet,
And gay in modern style and fashion
Prescribe their rules of education.
The mother once herself a toast,
Prays for her child the self-same post;
The father hates the toil and pother,
And leaves his daughters to their mother;
From whom her faults, that never vary,
May come by right hereditary,
Follies be multiplied with quickness,
And whims keep up the family likeness.

  Thus HARRIET, rising on the stage,
Learns all the arts, that please the age,
And studies well, as fits her station,
The trade and politics of fashion:
A judge of modes in silks and satins,
From tassels down to clogs and patterns;
A genius, that can calculate
When modes of dress are out of date,
Cast the nativity with ease
Of gowns, and sacks and negligees,
And tell, exact to half a minute,
What's out of fashion and what's in it;
And scanning all with curious eye,
Minutest faults in dresses spy;
(So in nice points of sight, a flea
Sees atoms better far than we;)
A patriot too, she greatly labours,

To spread her arts among her neighbors,
Holds correspondences to learn
What facts the female world concern,
To gain authentic state-reports
Of varied modes in distant courts,
The present state and swift decays
Of tuckers, handkerchiefs, and stays,
The colour'd silk that beauty wraps,
And all the rise and fall of caps.
Then shines, a pattern to the fair,
Of mien, address and modish air,
Of every new, affected grace,
That plays the eye, or decks the face,
The artful smile, that beauty warms,
And all the hypocrisy of charms.

. . . . .

   Yet that we fairly may proceed,
We own that ladies sometimes read,
And grieve, that reading is confin'd
To books that poison all the mind;
Novels and plays, (where shines display'd
A world that nature never made,)
Which swell their hopes with airy fancies,
And amorous follies of romances;
Inspire with dreams the witless maiden
On flowery vales and fields Arcadian,
And constant hearts no chance can sever,
And mortal loves, that last for ever.
   For while she reads romance, the fair one
Fails not to think herself the heroine;
For every glance, or smile, or grace,
She finds resemblance in her face,
Expects the world to fall before her,
And every fop she meets adore her.

Thus HARRIET reads, and reading really
Believes herself a young Pamela,
The high-wrought whim, the tender strain
Elate her mind and turn her brain:
Before her glass, with smiling grace,
She views the wonders of her face;
There stands in admiration moveless,
And hopes a Grandison, or Lovelace.
  Then shines she forth, and round her hovers,
The powder'd swarm of bowing lovers;
By flames of love attracted thither,
Fops, scholars, dunces, cits, together.
No lamp exposed in nightly skies,
E'er gather'd such a swarm of flies;
Or flame in tube electric draws
Such thronging multitudes of straws.

. . . .

'Twould weary all the pow'rs of verse
Their amorous speeches to rehearse,
Their compliments, whose vain parade
Turns Venus to a kitchen-maid;
With high pretence of love and honour,
They vent their folly all upon her,
(Ev'n as the scripture precept saith,
More shall be given to him that hath;)
Tell her how wondrous fair they deem her,
How handsome all the world esteem her;
And while they flatter and adore,
She contradicts to call for more.
  "And did they say I was so handsome?
My looks—I'm sure no one can fancy 'em.
'Tis true we're all as we were framed,
And none have right to be ashamed;
But as for beauty—all can tell

I never fancied I look'd well;
I were a fright, had I a grain less.
You're only joking, Mr. Brainless."

Yet beauty still maintain'd her sway,
And bade the proudest hearts obey;
Ev'n sense her glances could beguile,
And vanquish'd wisdom with a smile;
While merit bow'd and found no arms,
To oppose the conquests of her charms,
Caught all those bashful fears, that place
The mask of folly on the face,
That awe, that robs our airs of ease,
And blunders, when it hopes to please;
For men of sense will always prove
The most forlorn of fools in love.
The fair esteem'd, admired, 'tis true,
And praised—'tis all coquettes can do.

And when deserving lovers came,
Believed her smiles and own'd their flame,
Her bosom thrill'd, with joy affected
T' increase the list, she had rejected;
While pleased to see her arts prevail,
To each she told the self-same tale.
She wish'd in truth they ne'er had seen her,
And feign'd what grief it oft had giv'n her,
And sad, of tender-hearted make,
Grieved they were ruin'd for her sake.
'Twas true, she own'd on recollection,
She'd shown them proofs of kind affection:
But they mistook her whole intent,
For friendship was the thing she meant.
She wonder'd how their hearts could move 'em
So strangely as to think she'd love 'em;
She thought her purity above
The low and sensual flames of love;
And yet they made such sad ado,

She wish'd she could have loved them too.
She pitied them, and as a friend
She prized them more than all mankind,
And begg'd them not their hearts to vex,
Or hang themselves, or break their necks,
Told them 'twould make her life uneasy,
If they should run forlorn, or crazy;
Objects of love she could not deem 'em;
But did most marv'lously esteem 'em.

  For 'tis esteem, coquettes dispense
Tow'rd learning, genius, worth and sense,
Sincere affection, truth refined,
And all the merit of the mind.

  But love's the passion they experience
For gold, and dress, and gay appearance.

. . . .

  But now the time was come, our fair
Should all the plagues of passion share,
And after ev'ry heart she'd won,
By sad disaster lose her own.
So true the ancient proverb sayeth,
'Edge-tools are dang'rous things to play with';
The fisher, ev'ry gudgeon hooking,
May chance himself to catch a ducking;
The child that plays with fire, in pain
Will burn its fingers now and then;
And from the dutchess to the laundress,
Coquettes are seldom salamanders.

  For lo! Dick Hairbrain heaves in sight,
From foreign climes returning bright;
He danced, he sung to admiration,
He swore to gen'ral acceptation,
In airs and dress so great his merit,
He shone—no lady's eyes could bear it.
Poor HARRIET saw; her heart was stouter;

She gather'd all her smiles about her;
Hoped by her eyes to gain the laurels,
And charm him down, as snakes do squirrels.
So prized his love and wish'd to win it,
That all her hopes were center'd in it;
And took such pains his heart to move,
Herself fell desp'rately in love;
Though great her skill in am'rous tricks,
She could not hope to equal Dick's;
Her fate she ventured on his trial,
And lost her birthright of denial.

And here her brightest hopes miscarry;
For Dick was too gallant to marry.
He own'd she'd charms for those who need 'em,
But he, be sure, was all for freedom;
So, left in hopeless flames to burn,
Gay Dick esteem'd her in her turn.
In love, a lady once given over
Is never fated to recover,
Doom'd to indulge her troubled fancies,
And feed her passion by romances;
And always amorous, always changing,
From coxcomb still to coxcomb ranging,
Finds in her heart a void, which still
Succeeding beaux can never fill:
As shadows vary o'er a glass,
Each holds in turn the vacant place;
She doats upon her earliest pain,
And following thousands loves in vain.

Poor HARRIET now hath had her day;
No more the beaux confess her sway;
New beauties push her from the stage;
She trembles at th' approach of age,
And starts to view the alter'd face,
That wrinkles at her in her glass:
So Satan, in the monk's tradition,

Fear'd, when he met his apparition.
  At length her name each coxcomb cancels
From standing lists of toasts and angels;
And slighted where she shone before,
A grace and goddess now no more,
Despised by all, and doom'd to meet
Her lovers at her rival's feet,
She flies assemblies, shuns the ball,
And cries out, vanity, on all;
Affects to scorn the tinsel-shows
Of glittering belles and gaudy beaux;
Nor longer hopes to hide by dress
The tracks of age upon her face.
Now careless grown of airs polite,
Her noonday nightcap meets the sight;
Her hair uncomb'd collects together,
With ornaments of many a feather;
Her stays for easiness thrown by,
Her rumpled handkerchief awry,
A careless figure half undress'd,
(The reader's wits may guess the rest;)
All points of dress and neatness carried,
As though she'd been a twelvemonth married;
She spends her breath, as years prevail,
At this sad wicked world to rail,
To slander all her sex *impromptu,*
And wonder what the times will come to.

  Tom Brainless, at the close of last year,
Had been six years a rev'rend Pastor,
And now resolved, to smooth his life,
To seek the blessing of a wife.
His brethren saw his amorous temper,
And recommended fair Miss Simper,
Who fond, they heard, of sacred truth,
Had left her levities of youth,
Grown fit for ministerial union,

And grave, as Christian's wife in Bunyan.
  On this he rigg'd him in his best,
And got his old grey wig new dress'd,
Fix'd on his suit of sable stuffs,
And brush'd the powder from his cuffs,
With black silk stockings, yet in being,
The same he took his first degree in;
Procured a horse of breed from Europe,
And learn'd to mount him by the stirrup,
And set forth fierce to court the maid;
His white-hair'd Deacon went for aid;
And on the right, in solemn mode,
The Reverend Mr. Brainless rode.
Thus grave, the courtly pair advance,
Like knight and squire in famed romance.
The priest then bow'd in sober gesture,
And all in scripture terms address'd her;
He'd found, for reasons amply known,
It was not good to be alone,
And thought his duty led to trying
The great command of multiplying;
So with submission, by her leave,
He'd come to look him out an Eve,
And hoped, in pilgrimage of life,
To find an helpmate in a wife,
A wife discreet and fair withal,
To make amends for Adam's fall.
  In short, the bargain finish'd soon
A reverend Doctor made them one.
  And now the joyful people rouse all
To celebrate their priest's espousal;
And first, by kind agreement set,
In case their priest a wife could get,
The parish vote him five pounds clear,
T' increase his salary every year.
Then swift the tag-rag gentry come

To welcome Madam Brainless home;
Wish their good Parson joy; with pride
In order round salute the bride;
At home, at visits and at meetings,
To Madam all allow precedence;
Greet her at church with rev'rence due,
And next the pulpit fix her pew.

 END OF PART THIRD

HUGH HENRY BRACKENRIDGE
(1748-1816)

A classmate of Freneau and Madison at Princeton, Brackenridge went into politics but drifted back to an early yen for authorship when his Pittsburgh frontier constituency disciplined him for his independence. He was left to the comparative quiet of his legal career and to his keen reflections on the life of the times. The result was *Modern Chivalry,* a book conceived in the mode of one of the most enduringly popular and elastic of the forms of fiction—the picaresque romance. It was written in six main installments, over a period of 23 years, and ran to a final length of more than 800 pages. The piecemeal composition fits the tradition of picaresque fiction, which is to create self-contained satiric units held together only by the reappearance of the central character in each. This structure, which makes it easy for the author to focus each segment on a special critical purpose, also, fortunately for the anthologist, makes it easy to extract portions without destroying the life of an artistic whole. The following selection is therefore thoroughly representative of the whole enormous work.

Bibliography: Claude M. Newlin, *The Life and Writings of Hugh Henry Brackenridge,* Princeton, 1932.

Text: *Modern Chivalry,* ed. Claude M. Newlin, New York, 1937.

from MODERN CHIVALRY

CHAPTER I

John Farrago, was a man of about fifty-three years of age, of good natural sense, and considerable reading; but in some things whimsical, owing perhaps to his greater knowledge of books than of the world; but, in some degree, also, to his having never married, being what they call an old bachelor, a characteristic of which is, usually, singularity and whim. He had the advantage of having had in early life, an academic education; but having never applied himself to any of the learned professions, he had lived the greater part of his life on a small farm, which he cultivated with servants or hired hands, as he could conveniently supply himself with either. The servant that he had at this time, was an Irishman, whose name was Teague Oregan. I shall say nothing of the character of this man, because the very name imports what he was.

A strange idea came into the head of Captain Farrago about this time; for, by the bye, I had forgot to mention that having been chosen captain of a company of militia in the neighbourhood, he had gone by the name of Captain ever since; for the rule is, once a captain, and always a captain; but, as I was observing, the idea had come in to his head, to saddle an old horse that he had, and ride about the world a little, with his man Teague at his heels, to see how things were going on here and there, and to observe human nature. For it is a mistake to suppose, that a man cannot learn man by reading him in a corner, as well as on the widest space of transaction. At any rate, it may yield amusement.

. . . .

CHAPTER III

The Captain rising early next morning, and setting out on his way, had now arrived at a place where a number of people were convened, for the purpose of electing persons to represent them in the legislature of the state. There was a weaver who was a candidate for this appointment, and seemed to have a good deal of interest among the people. But another, who was a man of education, was his competitor. Relying on some talent of speaking which he thought he possessed, he addressed the multitude.

Said he, Fellow citizens, I pretend not to any great abilities; but am conscious to myself that I have the best good will to serve you. But it is very astonishing to me, that this weaver should conceive himself qualified for the trust. For though my acquirements are not great, yet his are still less. The mechanical business which he pursues, must necessarily take up so much of his time, that he cannot apply himself to political studies. I should therefore think it would be more answerable to your dignity, and conducive to your interest, to be represented by a man at least of some letters, than by an illiterate handicraftsman like this. It will be more honourable for himself, to remain at his loom and knot threads, than to come forward in a legislative capacity: because, in the one case, he is in the sphere where God and nature has placed him; in the other, he is like a fish out of water, and must struggle for breath in a new element.

Is it possible he can understand the affairs of government, whose mind has been concentered to the small object of weaving webs; to the price by the yard, the grist of the thread, and such like matters as concern a manufacturer of cloths? The feet of him who weaves, are more occupied than the head, or at least as much; and therefore the whole man must be, at least, but in half accustomed to exercise his mental powers. For these reasons, all other things set aside, the chance is in my favour, with respect to information. However, you will decide, and give your suffrages to him or to me, as you shall judge expedient.

The Captain hearing these observations, and looking at the weaver, could not help advancing, and undertaking to subjoin something in support of what had been just said. Said he, I have no prejudice against a weaver more than another man. Nor do I know any harm in the trade; save that from the sedentary life in a damp place, there is usually a paleness of the countenance: but this is a physical, not a moral evil. Such usually occupy subterranean apartments; not for the purpose, like Demosthenes, of shaving their heads, and writing over eight times the history of Thucydides, and perfecting a stile of oratory; but rather to keep the thread moist; or because this is considered but as an inglorious sort of trade, and is frequently thrust away into cellars, and damp outhouses, which are not occupied for a better use.

But to rise from the cellar to the senate house, would be an unnatural hoist. To come from counting threads, and adjusting them to the splits of a reed, to regulate the finances of a government, would be preposterous; there being no congruity in the case. There is no analogy between knoting threads and framing laws. It would be a reversion of the order of things. Not that a manufacturer of linen or woolen, or other stuff, is an inferior character, but a different one, from that which ought to be employed in affairs of state. It is unnecessary to enlarge on this subject; for you must all be convinced of the truth and propriety of what I say. But if you will give me leave to take the manufacturer aside a little, I think I can explain to him my ideas on the subject; and very probably prevail with him to withdraw his pretensions. The people seeming to acquiesce, and beckoning to the weaver, they drew aside, and the Captain addressed him in the following words:

Mr. Traddle, said he, for that was the name of the manufacturer, I have not the smallest idea of wounding your sensibility; but it would seem to me, it would be more your interest to pursue your occupation, than to launch out into that of which you have no knowledge. When you go to the senate house, the application to you will not be to warp a web; but to make laws for the commonwealth. Now, suppose that the making these laws, requires a knowledge of commerce, or of the interests of agriculture, or those principles upon which the different manufactures depend, what service could you render. It is possible you might think justly enough; but could you speak? You are not in the habit of public speaking. You are not furnished with those common place ideas, with which even very ignorant men can pass for knowing something. There is nothing makes a man so ridiculous as to attempt what is above his sphere. You are no tumbler for instance; yet should you give out that you could vault upon a man's back; or turn head over heels, like the wheels of a cart; the stiffness of your joints would encumber you; and you would fall upon your backside to the ground. Such a squash as that would do you damage. The getting up to ride on the state is an unsafe thing to those who are not accustomed to such horsemanship. It is a disagreeable thing for a man to be laughed at, and there is no way of keeping ones self from it but by avoiding all affectation.

While they were thus discoursing, a bustle had taken place among the croud. Teague hearing so much about elections, and serving the government, took it into his head, that he could be a legislator himself. The thing was not displeasing to the people, who seemed to favour his pretensions; owing, in some degree, to there being several of his countrymen among the croud; but more especially to the fluctuation of the popular mind, and a disposition to what is new and ignoble. For though the weaver was not the most elevated object of choice, yet he was still preferable to this tatter-demalion, who was but a menial servant, and had so much of what is called the brogue on his tongue, as to fall far short of an elegant speaker.

The Captain coming up, and finding what was on the carpet, was greatly chagrined at not having been able to give the multitude a better idea of the importance of a legislative trust; alarmed also, from an apprehension of the loss of his servant. Under these impressions he resumed his address to the multitude. Said he, This is making the matter still worse, gentlemen: this servant of mine is but a bog-trotter; who can scarcely speak the dialect in which your laws ought to be written; but certainly has never read a single treatise on any political subject; for the truth is, he cannot read at all. The young people of the lower class, in Ireland, have seldom the advantage of a good education; especially the descendants of the ancient Irish, who have most of them a great assurance of countenance, but little information, or literature. This young man, whose family name is Oregan, has been my servant for several years. And, except a too great fondness for women, which now and then brings him into scrapes, he has demeaned himself in a manner tolerable enough. But he is totally ignorant of the great principles of legislation; and more especially, the particular interests of the government. A free government is a noble possession to a people: and this freedom consists in an equal right to make laws, and to have the benefit of the laws when made. Though doubtless, in such a government, the lowest citizen may become chief magistrate; yet it is sufficient to possess the right; not absolutely necessary to exercise it. Or even if you should think proper, now and then, to shew your privilege, and exert, in a signal manner, the democratic prerogative, yet is it not descending too low to filch away from me a hireling, which I cannot well spare, to serve your purpose. You are surely carrying the matter too far, in thinking to make a senator of this hostler; to take him away from an employment to which he has been bred, and put him to another, to which he has served no apprenticeship: to set those hands which have been lately employed in currying my horse, to the draughting bills, and preparing business for the house.

The people were tenacious of their choice, and insisted on giving Teague their suffrages; and by the frown upon their brows, seemed to indicate resentment at what has been said; as indirectly charging them with want of judgment; or calling in question their privilege to do what they thought proper. It is a very strange thing, said one of them, who was a speaker for the rest, that after having conquered Burgoyne and Cornwallis, and got a government of our own, we cannot put in it whom we please. This young man may be your servant, or another man's servant; but if we chuse to make him a delegate, what is that to you. He may not be yet skilled in the matter, but there is a good day a-coming. We will impower him; and it is better to trust a plain man like him, than one of your high flyers, that will make laws to suit their own purposes.

Said the Captain, I had much rather you would send the weaver, though I thought that improper, than to invade my household, and thus detract from me the very person that I have about me to brush my boots, and clean my spurs. The prolocutor of the people gave him to understand that his surmises were useless, for the people had determined on the choice, and Teague they would have, for a representative.

Finding it answered no end to expostulate with the multitude, he requested to speak a word with Teague by himself. Stepping aside, he said to him, composing his voice, and addressing him in a soft manner; Teague, you are quite wrong in this matter they have put into your head. Do you know what it is to be a member of a deliberate body? What qualifications are necessary? Do you understand any thing of geography? If a question should be, to make a law to dig a canal in some part of the state, can you describe the bearing of the mountains, and the course of the rivers? Or if commerce is to be pushed to some new quarter, by the force of regulations, are you competent to decide in such a case? There will be questions of law, and astronomy on the carpet. How you must gape and stare like a fool, when you come to be asked your opinion on these subjects? Are you acquainted with the abstract principles of finance; with the funding public securities; the ways and means of raising the revenue; providing for the discharge of the public debts, and all other things which respect the economy of the government? Even if you had knowledge, have you a facility of speaking. I would suppose you would have too much pride to go to the house just to say, Ay, or No. This is not the fault of your nature, but of your education; having been accustomed to dig turf in your early years, rather than instructing yourself in the classics, or common school books.

When a man becomes a member of a public body, he is like a racoon, or other beast that climbs up the fork of a tree; the boys pushing at him with pitch-forks, or throwing stones, or shooting at him with an arrow, the dogs barking in the mean time. One will find fault with your not speaking; another with your speaking, if you speak at all. They will have you in the newspapers, and ridicule you as a perfect beast. There is what they call the caricatura; that is, representing you with a dog's head, or a cat's claw. As you have a red head, they will very probably make a fox of you, or a sorrel horse, or a brindled cow. It is the devil in hell to be exposed to the squibs and crackers of the gazette wits and publications. You know no more about these matters than a goose; and yet you would undertake rashly, without advice, to enter on the office; nay, contrary to advice. For I would not for a thousand guineas, though I have not the half of it to spare, that the breed of the Oregans should come to this; bringing on them a worse stain than stealing sheep; to which they are addicted. You have nothing but your character, Teague, in a new country to depend upon. Let it never be said, that you quitted an honest livelihood, the taking care of my horse, to follow the new fangled whims of the times, and to be a statesman.

Teague was moved chiefly with the last part of the address, and consented to give up the object.

The Captain, glad of this, took him back to the people, and announced his disposition to decline the honour which they had intended him.

Teague acknowledged that he had changed his mind, and was willing to remain in a private station.

The people did not seem well pleased with the Captain; but as nothing more could be said about the matter, they turned their attention to the weaver, and gave him their suffrages.

CHAPTER IV

Captain Farrago leaving this place, proceeded on his way; and at the distance of a mile or two, met a man with a bridle in his hand; who had lost a horse, and had been at a conjurer's to make enquiry, and recover his property.

It struck the mind of the Captain to go to this conjuring person, and make a demand of him, what was the cause that the multitude were so disposed to elevate the low to the highest station. He had rode but about a mile, when the habitation of the conjurer, by the direction and description of the man who had lost the horse had given, began to be in view. Coming up to the door, and enquiring if that was not where conjurer Kolt lived, they were answered Yes. Accordingly alighting, and entering the domicile, all those things took place which usually happen, or are described in cases of this nature, *viz.* there was the conjurer's assistant, who gave the Captain to understand that master had withdrawn a little, but would be in shortly.

In the mean time, the assistant endeavoured to draw from him some account of the occasion of his journey; which the other readily communicated; and the conjurer, who was listening through a crack in the partition, overheard. Finding it was not a horse or a cow, or a piece of linen that was lost, but an abstract question of political philosophy which was to be put, he came from his lurking place, and entered, as if not knowing that any person had been waiting for him.

After mutual salutations, the Captain gave him to understand the object which he had in view by calling on him.

Said the conjurer, This lies not at all in my way. If it had been a dozen of spoons, or a stolen watch, that you had to look for, I could very readily, by the assistance of my art, have assisted you in the recovery; but as to this matter of man's imaginations and attachments in political affairs, I have no more understanding than another man.

It is very strange, said the Captain, that you who can tell by what means a thing is stolen, and the place where it is deposited, though at a thousand miles distance, should know so little of what is going on in the breast of man, as not to be able to develope his secret thoughts, and the motives of his actions.

It is not of our business, said the other; but should we undertake it, I do not see that it would be very difficult to explain all that puzzles you at present. There is no need of a conjurer to tell why it is that the common people are more disposed to trust one of their own class, than those who may affect to be superior. Besides, there is a certain pride in man, which leads him to elevate the low, and pull down the high. There is a kind of creating power exerted in making a senator of an unqualified person; which when the author has done, he exults over the work, and like the Creator himself when he made the world, sees that "it is very good." Moreover, there is in every government a patrician class, against whom the spirit of the multitude naturally militates: And hence a perpetual war; the aristocrats endeavouring to detrude the people, and the people contending to obtrude themselves. And it is right it should be so; for by this fermentation, the spirit of democracy is kept alive.

The Captain, thanking him for his information, asked him what was to pay; at the same time pulling out half a crown from a green silk purse which he had in his breeches pocket. The conjurer gave him to understand, that as the solution of these difficulties was not within his province, he took nothing for it. The Captain expressing his sense of his disinterested service, bade him adieu.

CHAPTER V

CONTAINING REFLECTIONS

A democracy is beyond all question the freest government: because under this, every man is equally protected by the laws, and has equally a voice in making them. But I do not say an equal voice; because some men have stronger lungs than others, and can express more forcibly their opinions of public affairs. Others, though they may not speak very loud, yet have a faculty of saying more in a short time; and even in the case of others, who speak little or none at all, yet what they do say containing good sense, comes with greater weight; so that all things considered, every citizen, has not, in this sense of the word, an equal voice. But the right being equal, what great harm if it is unequally exercised? is it necessary that every man should become a statesman? No more than that every man should become a poet or a painter. The sciences, are open to all; but let him only who has taste and genius pursue them. If any man covets the office of a bishop, says St. Paul, he covets a good work. But again, he adds this caution, Ordain not a novice, lest being lifted up with pride, he falls into the condemnation of the devil. It is indeed making a devil of a man to lift him up to a state to which he is not suited. A ditcher is a respectable character, with his over-alls on, and a spade in his hand; but put the same man to those offices which require the head whereas he has been accustomed to impress with his foot, and there appears a contrast between the individual and the occupation.

There are individuals in society, who prefer honour to wealth; or cultivate political studies as a branch of literary pursuits; and offer themselves to serve public bodies, in order to have an opportunity of discovering their knowledge, and exercising their judgment. It must be chagrining to these, and hurtful to the public, to see those who have no talent this way, and ought to have no taste, preposterously obtrude themselves upon the government. It is the same as if a brick-layer should usurp the office of a taylor, and come with his square and perpendicular, to take the measure of a pair of breeches.

It is proper that those who cultivate oratory, should go to the house of orators. But for an Ay and No man to be ambitious of that place, is to sacrifice his credit to his vanity.

I would not mean to insinuate that legislators are to be selected from the more wealthy of the citizens, yet a man's circumstances ought to be such as afford him leisure for study and reflection. There is often wealth without taste or talent. I have no idea, that because a man lives in a great house and has a cluster of bricks or stones about his backside, that he is therefore fit for a legislator. There is so much pride and arrogance with those who consider themselves the first in a government, that it deserves to be checked by the populace, and the evil most usually commences on this side. Men associate with their own persons, the adventitious circumstances of birth and fortune: So that a fellow blowing with fat and repletion, conceives himself superior to the poor lean man, that lodges in an inferior mansion. But as in all cases, so in this, there is a medium. Genius and virtue are independent of rank and fortune; and it is neither the opulent, nor the indigent, but the man of ability and integrity that ought to be called forth to serve his country: and while, on the one hand, the aristocratic part of the government, arrogates a right to represent; on the other hand, the democratic contends the point; and from this conjunction and opposition of forces, there is produced a compound resolution, which carries the object in an intermediate direction. When we see therefore, a Teague Oregan lifted up, the philosopher will reflect, that it is to balence some purse-proud fellow, equally as ignorant, that comes down from the sphere of aristocratic interest.

But every man ought to consider for himself, whether it is his use to be this draw-back, on either side. For as when good liquor is to be distilled, you throw in some material useless in itself to correct the effervescence of the spirit; so it may be his part to act as a sedative. For though we commend the effect, yet still the material retains but its original value.

But as the nature of things is such, let no man who means well to the commonwealth, and offers to serve it, be hurt in his mind when some one of meaner talents is preferred. The people are a sovereign, and greatly despotic; but, in the main, just.

I have a great mind, in order to elevate the composition, to make quotations from the Greek and Roman history. And I am conscious to myself, that I have read the writers on the government of Italy and Greece, in ancient, as well as in modern times. But I have drawn a great deal more from reflection on the nature of things, than from all the writings I have ever read. Nay, the history of the election, which I have just given, will afford a better lesson to the American mind, than all that is to be found in other examples. We have seen here, a weaver a favoured candidate, and in the next instance, a bog-trotter superseding him. Now it may be said, that this is fiction; but fiction, or no fiction, the nature of the thing will make it a reality. But I return to the adventures of the Captain, whom I have upon my hands; and who, as far as I can yet discover, is a good honest man; and means what is benevolent and useful; though his ideas may not comport with the ordinary manner of thinking, in every particular.

. . . . .

VOLUME II

BOOK IV

CHAPTER I

The insuing day, the Captain arrived in a certain city, and put up at the sign of the Indian Queen. Taking a day or two to refresh himself, and get a new pair of breeches made, and his coat mended, which was a little worn at the elbows, he went to look about the city. The fourth day, when he had proposed to set out to prerambulate this modern Babylon, and called for Teague to bring him his boots, there was no Teague there. The hostler being called, with whom he used to sleep, informed, that he had disappeared the day before. The Captain was alarmed: and, from the recollection of former incidents, began to enquire if there were any elections going on at that time. As it so happened, there was one that very day. Thinking it probable the bog-trotter, having still a hankering after an appointment, might offer himself on that occasion, he set out to the place where the people were convened, to see if he could discover Teague amongst the candidates. He could see nothing of him; and though he made enquiry, he could hear no account. But the circumstance of the election drawing his attention for some time, he forgot Teague.

The candidates were all remarkably pot-bellied; and waddled in their gait. The Captain enquiring what were the pretensions of these men to be elected; he was told, that they had all stock in the funds, and lived in large brick buildings; and some of them entertained fifty people at a time, and eat and drank abundantly; and, living an easy life, and pampering their appetites, they had swollen to this size.

It is a strange thing, said the Captain, that in the country, in my route, they would elect no one but a weaver, or a whiskey distiller; and here none but fat swabs, that guzzle wine, and smoke segars. It was not so in Greece, where Phocion came with his plain coat, from his humble dwelling, and directed the counsels of the people; or in Rome, where Cincinnatus was made dictator from the plough. Something must be wrong, where the inflate, and the pompous are the objects of choice. Though there is one good arising from it, that there is no danger of my Teague here. He could not afford to give a dinner; and as to funds, he has not a single shilling in them. They will make him neither mayor nor legislator in this city.

Na faith, said Mr. M'Donald, the Scotch gentleman who had been present at the embarrassment of the Captain, on the occasion of the former election; and having, a few days before, come to the city, and observing the Captain in the crowd, had come up to accost him, just as he was uttering these last words to himself: Na faith, said he, there is na danger of Teague here, unless he had his scores o' shares in the bank; and was in league with the brokers, and had a brick house at his hurdies, or a ship or twa on the stocks. A great deal used to be done, by employing advocates with the tradesmen, to listen to the news, and tell them fair stories; but all is now lost in substantial interest, and the funds command every thing. Besides, this city is swarming with Teagues, and O'Regans, and O'Brians, and O'Murphys, and O'Farrels; I see, that they cannot be at a loss without your bog-trotter.

The Captain having his fears eased, in this particular, returned home, greatly troubled, nevertheless, that he could not come up with the Irishman.

. . . . .

BOOK V

CHAPTER V

The next day, revolving everything in his mind, it occurred to the Captain, that the Irishman might have gone out of town, hearing of an election at a district, and have been elected to Congress. As that body was then sitting, he thought it could be no great trouble to go to the house, and cast an eye from the gallery, and see if the ragamuffin had got there. There was one that had a little of the brogue of Teague upon his tongue, but nothing of his physiognomy; others had a good deal of his manner; but there was none that came absolutely up to the physic of his person.

However, being here, the Captain tho't it not amiss to listen a while to the debates upon the carpet. A certain bill was depending, and made, it seems, the order of the day. Mr. Cogan being on the floor, spoke:—Sir, said he, addressing himself to the chair, the bill in contemplation, is, in my opinion, of a dangerous tendency. I will venture to foretel, that, if it goes into a law, the cows will have fewer calves, and the sheep less wool; hens will lay fewer eggs, and cocks forget to crow daylight. The horses will be worse shod, and stumble more; our watches go too slow; corns grow upon our toes; young women have the stomach ach; old men the gout; and middle aged persons fainting fits. The larks will fall dead in the field; the frogs croak till they burst their bags; and the leaves of the trees fall before the autumn. Snow will be found in the heat of harvest, and dog days in winter. The rivers will revert; and the shadows fall to the east in the morning. The moon will be eclipsed; and the equinoxes happen at a wrong season of the year. Was it not such a bill as this, that changed the old stile; that made the eclipse in the time of Julius Cesar; that produced an earthquake at Jamaica, and sunk Port Royal? All history, both ancient and modern, is full of the mischiefs of such a bill. I shall, therefore, vote against it.

Mr. Bogan was now on the floor, and advocated the good effects of the bill.

Sir, said he, addressing himself to the chair, I appear in support of the bill. I say, it will have a good effect on the physical world especially. The ducks will be fatter, the geese heavier, the swans whiter, the redbirds sing better, and partridges come more easily into traps. It will kill rats, muzzle calves, and cut colts; and multiply the breed of oysters, and pickle cod-fish. It will moderate the sun's heat, and the winter's cold; prevent fogs, and cure the ague. It will help the natural brain; brace the nerves, cure sore eyes, and the cholic, and remove rheumatisms. Consult experience, and it will be found, that provisions of the nature proposed by this bill, have an astonishing influence in this respect, where they have been tried. I must take the liberty to say, the gentleman's allegations are totally *unfounded;* and he has *committed* himself in the matter of his history; the earthquake in Jamaica, not happening in the time of Julius Cesar; and therefore could have nothing to do with the eclipse of the sun. I shall, therefore, vote in favour of the bill.

Mr. Cogan rose to explain; and said, that he did not say, that the earthquake at Jamaica was at the same time with the eclipse of the sun, which happened at the birth of Julius Cesar.

Mr. Bogan rose to correct the gentleman: it was not at the birth of Julius Cesar, but at his death, that the earthquake happened.

Mr. Hogan was on the floor: Said, he thought he could reconcile the gentlemen on that head. It was well known Julius Cesar lived about the time of the rebellion in Scotland, a little after Nebuchadnezzar, king of the Jews. As to the earthquake, he did not remember what year it happened; and therefore could say nothing about it.

At this period, the question being called, it was put, and carried by a majority of 25.

The Captain, satisfied with this sample of Congressional debates, retired, and came to his lodging.

. . . . .

PART II (1804)

CHAPTER I

. . . . .

We shall go no farther back upon the steps of the Captain, with the bog-trotter at his heels, than where we find them within a mile, or less of the village where his home was, and where he had resided some years, before he had set out on his peregrinations. Passing through a wood just as he approached the town, he saw at some distance before him the semblance of men suspended on the limbs of trees, or at least the exuviae of men, coats, waist-coats, breeches, and hats. What can this be, said the Captain? It is probable that hearing of your return, Teague, the wags of the village have been making what are called Padies, and have set them up on these trees, knowing that this way we should come along. By St. Patrick, said Teague, but I will Pady dem wid dis shalelah. I will tache dem to make Padies, and hang dem up for sign posts in de wood here. Dis is not St. Patrick's day in de morning neider: Bad luck to dem, it may be some poor fellows dat dey have hanged up in reality, for shape-stealing as dey do in Ireland.

I see nothing, said the Captain, drawing nearer, but the emptyings of ward-robes, jibbeted on these trees, through the grove: stretched on limbs, or suspended from them, a phenomenon, which I am unable to comprehend, or explain; For I see no corn growing underneath, or near about, from which, a priapus, or scarecrow might affright the birds; nor can they be the vestments of people at work, near hand, or stripped to bathe, as I see no water pond, or river, but a dry grove.

The fact is, these habiliments were of the people of the town, who had hung them up to take the dew, in order to take off the musk of a pole-cat which had affected them from the perfusions of one of these animals. The story is as follows.

Not long before this, a typographist had set up a paper in the village and having reference to the sharpness of his writing, the editor had chosen to assume the symbol, or hieroglyphic of the Porcupine, and in allusion to his quills called himself Peter Porcupine; whimsically Peter, because Peter, and Porcupine, begin with the same letter, and produces what is called an alliteration. Such respondence has been thought a beauty, in some languages, and at some periods. In the English language, it was a constituent of poetry a few centuries ago; and though now disused, yet is retained in appellations, where fiction is at liberty, and quaintness and humour is intended. Nor was the device or synonime of Porcupine, ill chosen. For the editor could dart his quills to some purpose. To drop the figure, a happy nature had fited him for a satyrist, and felicity of education was not wanting to qualify him for the office. He had not the pleasantry of Horace, nor the pungency of Juvenal, but an original stricture of his own that supplied the place of them. The truth is he had been bred in the barracks, and had at his finger ends, the familiar phrases of the common soldiery, with that peculiar species of wit, which is common with that occupation of men, and in that grade. Doubtless we see something like it among the plebeians of all classes and denominations; The women that sell fish at a certain stand in London, have a species of it, known by the name of Billingsgate, either because there is a gate of that name near the place, or formerly was one. The miners and coal heavers have a good deal of it. The scavengers and chimney sweepers are adepts, though without the least scholastic education, or knowledge of letters whatsoever. I have known even in our own country, where we are remote from the seats of the muses, a good deal of it possessed, by way travellers, or boat men on our rivers. It is a kind of unshackled dialect; fettered by no rule of delicacy, or feeling of humanity. I have been turning in my mind what word in our English language, best expresses it, and I have found it to be that which has been given it by Thomas Paine, *black-guardism*. The editor of the Porcupine had scored the village not a little. I do not say rubbed. For that is a translation of the phrase of Horace; *urbem defricuit;* and conveys the idea of tickling, and causing a sensation in part pleasant, yet hurting a little. That was not the case here. For what man without indignation and bitter resentment, can bear the touch of the slanderer, more especially if that slander is of a private, and domestic nature and alludes to what cannot be explained or defended. Not that it is true, but a man in the just pride of standing in society, would scorn to appeal to the public or bring it before a court!

There was in the village a man of understanding, and sensibility who had been the subject of caricature by Peter, and not chusing for reasons that weighed with himself, to take it in good part, thought of retaliation. But what could he do? The same language was unbecoming a gentleman. The like strictures of foibles or of faults on the part of an adversary, could only become the character of a subordinate. Nor was it so much his object to repress the licentiousness of this buffoon as to correct the taste and judgment of the public who did not all at once distinguish the impropriety of countenancing such ribaldry. This they continued to do by receiving his papers.

With a view to this having taken a pole-cat on the mountains, he had put it in a cage and hiring an office contiguous to that of Porcupine, he kept it, suffering the boys of the village to provoke it, and the dogs to bark at it through the bars. The consequence was, that Peter himself, and not unfrequently the female part of his family passing and repassing, were besprinkled with the effluvia and offended with the odour of the animal. The effusions were excited by the irritations of others; but friend and foe were indiscriminately the object of the vapour when they came in the way of its ascension. It was in vain to complain; the owner called himself Paul Pole-cat, and when Peter expostulated and justified his gall on the *freedom of the Press,* Paul fortified himself on the liberty of the *Express.*

But it was not Peter alone, nor his unoffending wife and family that had reason to complain of this nuisance. The children running home to their parents, and the dogs with them brought the perfume to the houses of the village. The wearing apparel of almost every one was affected with the musk; the women buried their dresses; the men in some instances did so, and in others, hung them up to the action of the air, and the dews of the adjoining wood.

The vestiges of these were the phenomena, which the Captain saw, in his approach to the town.

He had now got within sight of the main square, when a tumultuous assembly struck his eye; some with fists raised; others with sticks, and all in a menacing attitude. He could also hear tongues of people altercating with one another and using opprobrious epithets.

The fact was that the village had become divided. Those who had been the subjects of the obloquy of Porcupine, justified the emission of the cats, and were of opinion that the one had as good a right to be borne as the other. Counsel had been taken and learned opinions given. But this making the matter no better, the dissention had increased, and the people had come together in a rage.

Teague at a distance seeing this, stoped short; said he, what means all this paple in de street? It is as bad as dat of St. Anthony in Paris, or de place de greve where dey have de gillotine. The devil burn me if I go farther, 'till your honour goes on and sees what is de matter.

The Captain advancing to the populace was recognized by them, and his appearance contributed not a little to a longer suspension of hostilities.

Countrymen and fellow-citizens, said he, is this the satisfaction that I have, in returning amongst you after an absence of several years, to see man armed against man, and war waged not only in the very bosom of the republic, but in the village which I have instructed by many precepts? What can be the madness that possesses you? are not the evils of life sufficient? but you must increase them by the positive acts of your own violence. You cannot wholly preserve yourselves at all times free from the maladies of the body, or the distresses of the mind. But it is in your power greatly to assuage these, by the virtues of temperance and moderation. What fury can prompt you, to this degree of apparent resentment, and approaching tumult? Is it local or general politics? Is it any disagreement with regard to your corporate interests, or is religion the cause? Has any flagrant instance of moral turpitude, or exceeding knavery in an individual, roused you to this excess of violence, and exclamation?

Captain, said a middle aged man stepping forward, companion of his years, and who had long lived with him in the village; it is not only pleasing to see you return in apparent, good health, but more especially, at this particular moment when your interference cannot but be of the greatest use, to the citizens; not only on account of that confidence which they have in your judgment and discretion, of which they have a lively recollection; but as they must naturally think that your opportunities from travelling must have given you knowledge, and brought you home full fraught with learning and information. Your humanity is also, well remembered by them, that man, woman or child was never injured by you, in life, estate, or reputation; that on the contrary, it was always your study to do good, and compose differences. Now a misfortune has happened to the village; if I can call it a misfortune, which was at first thought a good; a printer came to this place and set up a paper, or gazette, by taking subscriptions from those that were willing to give them. His device was the Porcupine; and his motto, I forget what. Scarcely a month had gone over his head before he began to lampoon; searching into the secrets of families, and publishing matters of individuals, with which, whether true or false, the public had nothing to do; ridiculing virtue as if it was vice; and this in so low and disorderly a manner, that the more intelligent have disapproved of it; but the bulk read, and it seems to increase rather than curtail his subscribers. A young man on the other hand that has come to us since you went away, and has had an academic education, had given his opinion pretty freely in companies, that this Porcupine was not a gentleman, which drew upon himself the paragraphs of Porcupine, which he has resented in a manner, that has wrought much disturbance. Meaning to burlesque his manner of writing, having gone to the mountain with a dog, or a trap, or both, and having taken a pole-cat, he puts the beast in a cage; hires that frame building that you see, one story high, and but a room on a floor, and calls it his office. Here he places the pole-cat with a man to attend it. What a running of boys; what a barking of dogs we have had! and when the children run home, and the dogs after them; what a putting of the hand upon the nose, by the servant girls and the mistresses, at the smell that accompanies. The young man justifies himself under the pretence that it is but retaliation to the worse than animal odor that proceeds from the press of Porcupine; for, as this affects the organ of smelling, that disgusts the judgment of the mind. The people are divided, as will always be the case, if for no other cause, yet for the sake of division; because the pride of one man forbids him to think just as another does. But in this case, the cause is serious and solid, for the olfactory organ is offended by Paul, but the heart is wounded by Peter. The adversaries of the opposum, or what else it is, insist that it shall be put down as a nuisance, and have met with clubs, staves and knives, to carry the threat into execution. The advocates of the animal on the other hand have convened to oppose them.

But said the Captain, did I not leave you a regular corporation? Have you not power to make bye laws? and is not this done upon notice given by the chief or Assistant Burgesses? Why such hurry scurry as this? Moreover it is a weighty question that agitates the public mind; a question of right; and where the rights of the citizen come in question, I hold it a most delicate thing to decide; in a free government, more especially, where the essence of liberty is the preservation of right; and there are three rights, the right of concience, the right of property and the right of reputation. This is a right of property; for if this animal which is ferae naturae, has been reclaimed by the owner, he has a right to put it to such use as suits his trade, or accords with his whim, provided that it does not affect the rights of others. The limit, boundary, or demarkation of this use, is a question of wise discussion and examination; and not in a tumultuous assembly, heated not with wine, but with the ardency of their own spirits. I advise therefore, and so far as my weak judgment deserves to be regarded would recommend, that each man lay down his shalelah, baton, or walking-stick, and retire for the evening; and convene to-morrow in a regular town meeting, where the adversaries and advocates on both sides may have an opportunity of being heard. You have lawyers also amongst you, who on such an occasion owe their services to the public without fee or reward; for as when the matter respects the digging a trench, or building a bridge, the mechanics speak, and ask no peculiar douceur, or perquisite; so on this occasion, the gentlemen of the long robe will not be wanting to develope a case that involves in it a nice question of law and municipal regulation. To-morrow when ye meet with the chief Burgess regularly in the chair, to keep order, and preserve decorum assign the proper times of speaking, and call to order on a deviation from the subject, as is usual in deliberative assemblies, the business can be taken up and conducted as is proper in town meetings. Besides I am just from my journey; somewhat fatigued; but more moved by the consideration that I am on horseback, and it is not becoming that I take a part in your debates as if my horse were to speak also; for though it is true that some of you may speak with perhaps as little sense as he could, were he to open his mouth and attempt utterance; yet the decency of the thing forbids, and even the exercise of the right might be questioned; for the faculty might exist, yet he could not be considered as legitimately franchised to this privilege, at least not having a right to vote in town meetings. For though in the Congress of the United States, the representatives of the territories, not yet organized into independent states, and made regular and complete members of the Union, have a right to speak, but not to vote, this is not to be drawn into precedent in subordinate corporations; for that is a special provision of the constitution within which as a groove, the states move. And it is even indecorous for myself to sit here and speak, mounted, as occupying a more elevated station; and should I descend from my cavalry, my servant whom you see yonder, is kept at bay, by an apprehension of your swords, and refuses to come up, so that I am without an attendant to hold the beast; all things considered therefore, I move, if you will excuse the expression, a chairman not yet being appointed, who might put the question, that you adjourn, or dissolve until to-morrow about this time, when the matter may be taken up as we now have it, and the affair canvassed as becomes members of the same community, and inhabitants of the same village.

It cannot be difficult to conceive that these words had a favourable effect upon the audience; as oils compose a storm. For as the waves of the ocean rise and fall suddenly, so the passions of men; and in no instance more than where they are just coming to blows; for approaching anger disposes to peace, every one having felt half a blow already on his head; and the difficulty only is to get an excuse, for returning, or sheathing the weapon. They are much obliged to a man that councils concord; and advises the puting down the brick-bat, or puting on the coat. Even in dueling it holds the same, and the principal is a friend to the second ever after, that manages the matter so wisely that no blood is shed.

It was moved and seconded before the people should retire; for the mob had insensibly begun to assume the form of a regular assembly, it was moved that in the mean time, the keeper, or as he called himself the editor of the pole-cat, should keep his charge within the claustrum, or bars of his cage, and covered with a matting, so that access might not be had to him, by man or beast, or egress on his part, of that offensive odour, which had been the cause of the disturbance. This, the partizans of the skunk, were willing to admit and sanction with their acquiescence, on condition, nevertheless, that the Porcupine in the mean time, should also restrain his quills; in other words, suspend the effusions of his press, and cease to distribute papers for a day or two while the matter was depending. This was thought reasonable, and carried by the multitude holding up their hands.

CHAPTER II

CONTAINING PROCEEDINGS OF THE TOWN MEETING

The day following, a meeting being held, and the Chief Burgess in the chair, an advocate of Porcupine took the ground and spoke.

Gentlemen, said he, the press is the palladium of liberty. "The image that fell down from Jupiter." The freedom of the press is essential to liberty. Shackle the press, and you restrain freedom. The constitutions of the states have provided that the press shall be free. If you muzzle this, you may as well muzzle the mouth of man.

It is not the freedom of the press, said one interrupting him, it is the abuse of it that is in question.

The chief burgess called to order, and the speaker went on.

That is the point, said he, to which I meant to come. What shall be said to be the abuse of the press? In order to determine this, we must consider its use. This is,

1. The amusement of the editor. For as some men amuse themselves, shooting, fishing, or chacing with the hound, wild beasts, so men of literary taste, find their recreation in penning paragraphs for a paper, sometimes containing information, or observations on the state of empires, and the characters of great men; at other times by descending, or not rising at all, but confining themselves to the subordinate, affairs of individuals, and private persons.

2. The profit of the editor: and this depends on the number of subscribers. It is not every one that has a taste for refined writing. An editor must be "all things to all men, that he may gain some."

Guts and garbage delight bears; and swine swill the trough in preference to the running stream. Black-guardism is the gout of many. Nay it is the more prevailing taste;

> "The world is naturally averse
> To all the truth it sees or hears;
> But swallows nonsense and a lie,
> With greediness and gluttony."

In Britain, or some other countries, delicacy may succeed. But the coarse stomachs of the Americans crave rather indelicacy and indecency, at least a portion of it. Rough like their own woods, and wild beasts, they digest scurrility.

Well done Porcupine, said the pole-cat man, taking the ground in his turn: well said. But this furnishes a ground to justify the introduction of the pole-cat. You talk of the freedom of the press. Here is the freedom of the express. Nay the word *expression* which is common to both institutions, the artificial one of the types, and the natural one of the cat, shews the original to be similar, and the comparison to *run on all-fours*. If the ink cast into black letter, and carrying with it pain and pungency from the ideas communicated, is tolerated; much more the volatile alkali of the animal that is now set up, is to be born, as not more offensive to body or mind. Shall the bark of trees made into powder, and this powder into a liquid, impregnated with thought, and put upon paper, and carried to the press, be accounted harmless, notwithstanding the violence of the decoction, yet the wild cats that inhabit those trees, and are denizens of the forest, be prohibited the haunts of men, because of a bag under their tails which contains all unsavory distillation, and may occasionally be spurted upon men?

A lawyer took him up on the part of Porcupine. The principles of the common law embrace this case. It is unlawful to exercise trades in towns that occasion noisome smells; they are abateable as nuisances.

Grant it, said another on the pole-cat side; but when it is in retaliation, or in self-defence against an editor whose defamation is more offensive to the feelings of the mind, than the hogo of a civet to the sense of smelling; or when it is used in burlesque, and by way of analogy and symbol to explain the impropriety of encouraging personal abuse, by taking papers, it may correct by leading to reflection. The mind may be insensible to abstract lessons, but a paradigm, or object set before it may affect. As to this man exercising his trade by the smell of a cat, it is an occupation which can be carried on to advantage only in a town; for it is in towns chiefly that editors assemble; and it is by seting up under our noses, and affecting the readers, that the impression is made. For if the public will receive into their houses for the use of themselves and families gossip slander, let them take a little of this hartshorn with it and if they will have the one bear the other. A ground of the common law is general reason adapted to particular cases. I grant that it even goes so far as to make the keeping hogs in a pen so near my window, in towns, as to offend by the smell, a nuisance; but this is a borough incorporated, and can by a bye law regulate a new trade. I hold it to be a matter of vote whether this quadruped shall be tolerated or excluded.

The advocate for the press rejoined. The common law, said he, protects the press. It is the right of the tongue transfered to the hand: it ought to be as free as the air that we breathe: The privilege as unfettered as the organs of articulation. But what is there in the common law to protect from the aspersion of this animal?

The pole-cat man replied. It is on principle and by analogy, said he, that it is protected. Does not the law of water courses apply to this. If a man divert a stream from my meadow, or obstruct one running through it, so as to dam it up, and drown the grass, have not I a remedy; shall this man at much expence and charge bring a beast from the mountains, tame it, or reduce it under his dominion, and apply it to a purpose in civilized and domestic life, and shall we say that the common law does not protect him in the enjoyment of its musk?

The lawyer on the side of the Porcupine rejoined. So use your own said he, that you trespass not upon another mans. If you keep your smell, and hogs at home to your own nose, there is no objection. But in the nature of the thing it cannot be; for the air is the natural conductor; and therefore it cannot but exist a nuisance.

Surrejoinder by the other. But after all, is it more a nuisance than the press, which it has in view to correct?

At this instant a commotion was perceivable amongst the multitude; not on account of what was said, or meaning any disturbance like debate; but the rumour was that a fresh cat had been brought from the hills above the town, and was on its way to the college-man who had offered a reward for an additional puss to increase his stock; and as it was conjectured, meant to play it off under the pretext that the prohibition contained in the armistice extended only to the individual beast that he had before in his possession.

The Captain, at this, rising, said: young man, this is not fair. It is within the reason, if not the express words of the convention, that all annoyances by steam, vapour or effluviæ proceeding from a pole-cat shall be suspended during the pendency of this question; and it is an evasion to substitute another badger, and by that means attempt to elude the stipulation.

The young man got up to explain. It is far from me, said he, to elude or evade the performance of the stipulation. The fact is, that hearing, a day or two ago, that Porcupine, was about to enlarge his sheet, and for that purpose had employed a journeyman, or two more, I thought it not amiss to extend the scale of my vapour and employ two conduits instead of one. For that purpose had sent to the woods, for another cat, which is now on the way, but in a leathern bag by my directions, and not to have regress, or egress, until this assembly shall dissolve, nor for a reasonable time after, that eundo, and redeundo, or going as well as coming you may be safe let what will be the issue of the controversy; whether I am to break up stock, or be suffered to go on.

This explanation gave satisfaction, and composed the assembly.

Another speaker had now occupied the ground. I cannot say the floor, for there was no floor. I am, said he, for supporting the press. The objection is, that it is a blackguard press. But while there are blackguards to write, must they not have a press? Is it only men of polished education that have a right to express their sentiments? Let them write in magazines, or make books, or have gazettes of their own, but not restrict the right that people of a more uncultivated understanding have to amuse themselves and others by their lucubrations. You call us the Swinish Multitude, and yet refuse us the food that is natural to us. Are there not amongst us those that have no relish for disquisitions on the balance of power or form of governments, agricultural essays, or questions of finance; but can comprehend and relish a laugh raised at the expense of the master of a family; or a public character in high station; if for no other reason, but because it gratifies the self-love of those who cannot attain the same eminence? Take away from us this, and what have we more? What is the press to us, but as it amuses?

I think, said another rising, that the gentleman means irony. But let us take the matter seriously. I am on the same side with him, but not for the same reasons. I take it, that scurrility may be useful to those that bear it, and are the subjects of it. It may bring to a man's knowledge and serve to correct foibles that he would not otherwise have been conscious of, or amended. Men will hear from the buffoon or the jester, things they would not take from a friend, and scarcely from a confessor. It was on this principle that in the middle ages of Europe, a profession of men was indulged, and rewarded, in the houses of the great, called the Joculators, or Jesters. So late as the time of James I. we had one of these of the name of Archy. The Duke of Buckingham having taken offence at something that he said, had him whipped. It was thought beneath a man of honour to have taken notice of it; and inflicted punishment. I consider the bulk of our editors as succeeding to the joculators or fool-caps of the early periods; and as the knights or men of character and dignity of those time were not bound to notice the follies, however gross of jokers, so now a gentleman is not bound to notice the defamation of gazettes; nay, as in the former instance, it was deemed uncourteous, and unbecoming to resent what the fool said, so more what a printer chooses to publish. Selden in his table talk remarks, "That a gallant man, is above ill words. We have an example of this in the old Lord of Salsbury, who was a great wise man. Stone had called some Lord about the Court fool. The Lord complains and has Stone whipped. Stone cries, I might have called my Lord of Salsbury often enough, fool, before he would have had me whipped." As in the case of the Merry Andrew, even when there was no wit, it was taken for wit; so now, when an editor means to divert, however dull his abuse, it ought to be the mode to laugh, to keep those who know no better in countenance.

The Captain rising and putting himself in the attitude of speaking, seemed to claim the attention of the audience. I see here, said he, the Principal of the Academy, a man of letters and learning. I would wish to hear from him how the ancients managed these matters: in the republics of Greece and Rome especially. For since I have been abroad, and read and heard public speeches, I find that it is no unusual thing to draw similies, and illustrations from the sayings and doings of antiquity. In deliberative assemblies talking of governments, they tell you of the Amphictyonic Council; the Achean league, the Ionian confederacy. What was the freedom of the press at Athens, or at Rome?

The principal rising—— The fact is, said he, there was no press at these places, or in these times. The invention of printing is of a later date. But they had in lieu of pen and ink, what they called the style, hence our phrase style, vertere stylum, and they impressed their thoughts upon wax. They made use of ink in copying upon vellum and parchment. But notwithstanding the want of a press, they were not without satyric salt in their writings. Nor are we to suppose that they were altogether free from what we denominate scurrility. They could call a spade a spade. Aristophanes was a great blackguard. His Comedy of the Clouds is a sufficient specimen. Lucilius, amongst the Romans was a rough man. Cum lutulentus flueret, &c. Do we suppose that nature was not then the same as it is now? On board the Roman gallies was there no low humour? In the Roman camps none? In the Forum no occasional ribaldry? Would not this naturally get up into higher walks? Would not this creep into corporations? sometimes in verse; sometimes in prose: versis famosis. The poet speaks of the fesscenine verses. Amongst the Romans the Saturnalia, or days of Saturn became a festival, in which it was allowable to exercise their faculties in all intemperance of language.

This is all wide of the question, said an individual, holding his hand upon his nose; it is, shall we tolerate the pole-cat in this village?—For, maugre all the pains that may have been taken to restrain the pett, and confine it by a matting, I feel a portion of the fetor this very moment, come across my nose, by a puff of wind from that quarter, where it is. I move that the question be taken, whether, whatever becomes of the press, the nuisance of this beast, be suffered in the vicinity. For what can a news-paper do, compared with this? It is sent us and we read the publication. But this is involuntary, on our part, and there is no saving ourselves from the exhalation.

I move the previous question said a friend to the baboon; or rather an enemy to the Porcupine. I move that the press be put down, or that both go together.

There is hardship both ways, said an elderly inhabitant. In a community different interests will exist. Family interests; family attachments; party conceptions; and party interests. The passions of the heart will create differences. To have a printer all on one side, even though he be a dunce, is an inequality. What if we prevail upon the owner, or as he would call himself the publisher of the pole-cat, to give up or sell out his establishment, dismiss the wild beast, or return it to the mountains, and institute in its place, a counter press of types and black-ball that may be a match for Porcupine. O Jehu! Said a man laughing, where will you get a match for Porcupine? A man neither of conscience or shame, taught and educated as he is, with typography that is adequate? Who will be willing to be the ostensible vehicle of language becoming a scavenger? Can any one be found who will have front from insensibility of heart, or the forehead of brass, to bear the imputation? If we could get some Teague O'Regan now, that did not know what we were doing with him: that would think it an honour to be employed; that would not take amiss the proposition of making him the conduit of reproach, and dishonourable inuendo; in short, from whom it could be concealed on what account he was chosen; the project might be plausible.

The Captain, at this rising hastily; a thing unusual with him; for he was naturally grave and sedate; but suddenly feeling the impulse of the congruity, he started from his seat, and seconded the proposition of another press; for said he, the very Teague O'Regan that you want is at hand; a waiter of mine. A bog-trotter, taken, not on the Balagate, but, on the Irish mountains: an aboriginal of the island; not your Scotch-Irish, so called, a colony planted in Ulster, by king James the first of England, when he subdued the natives; but a real Paddy, with the brogue on his tongue, and none on his feet; brought up to sheep-stealing from his youth; for his ancestors inhabiting the hills, were a kind of freebooters, time immemorial, coming down to the low grounds, and plundering the more industrious inhabitants. Captured by traps set upon the hills, or surrounded in the bogs, attempting his escape, he had been tamed and employed, many years, digging Turf, before he came to my hands. I bought him from an Irish vessel, just as a curiosity, not that I expected much service from him; but to see what could be made of a rude man by care and patience. The rogue has a low humour, and a sharp tongue; unbounded impudence. And what may be a restraint upon the licentiousness of his press, should he set up one, he is a most abominable coward; the idea of cudgeling will keep him in bounds; should he over-match Porcupine, and turn upon his employers. He has all the low phrases, cant expressions, illiberal reflections, that could be collected from the company he has kept since he has had the care of my horse, and run after my heels in town and country for several years past. What is more, he has been in France, and has a spice of the language, and a tang of Jacobinism in his principles, and conversation, that will match the contrary learning carried to an exorbitant excess in Peter

Porcupine. I do not know that you can do better than contribute to a paper of his setting up. He may call it the Mully-Grub, or give it some such title as will bespeak the nature, of the matter it will usually contain.

The college-man at this came forward. I am far, said he, from a disposition to spoil sport; but when the useful is mixed with the jest, I count every point gained.

Yes, said the principal of the academy, Omne tulit punctum, qui miscuit utile dulci.

I never had intended, continued the other, more than to reach the sensations of the multitude, and bring them to their senses. It is only by an appeal to feeling that mind sometimes can be awakened. The public have now some idea of what I mean, that the licentiousness of the press, is not more a nuisance in the moral, than offensive smells are in the physical world. I agree that the cat be removed, and as a substitute, that we may taper off gradually, shall subscribe to the Mully-Grub.

The speech was applauded, and the vote taken.

TIMOTHY DWIGHT
(1752-1817)

One of the brilliant grandsons of Jonathan Edwards, Dwight was president of Yale, an important clerical leader of his day, and in one sense "the Pope of Federalism" in Connecticut. As one of the ablest of the Connecticut Wits, he was also devoted to producing an adequate national literature for America. Of his imaginative productions, *Greenfield Hill* is the most attractive. Frankly derivative in style and tone, even borrowing specific phrasings from the tradition of English georgic verse, it nevertheless manages to express Dwight's dearest convictions forcibly and freshly through its use of Yankee conditions. Coming from the pen of an agrarian Federalist and Calvinist minister, the poem is a hymn to the middle-class evangelical virtues. The firmness of its faith in the American people and the general sanity of its tone reveal one reason why, to the dismay of Hamiltonian Federalists like Ames and Dennie, agrarian Federalists like Adams and Dwight were able to join with the Jeffersonians to make the Constitution work.

Bibliography: Charles E. Cunningham, *Timothy Dwight,* New York, 1942; Leon Howard, *The Connecticut Wits,* Chicago, 1943.

Text: *Greenfield Hill: A Poem in Seven Parts,* Hartford, 1794.

from GREENFIELD HILL

PART II

THE FLOURISHING VILLAGE

Fair Verna! loveliest village of the west;
Of every joy, and every charm, possess'd;
How pleas'd amid thy varied walks I rove,
Sweet, cheerful walks of innocence, and love,
And o'er thy smiling prospects cast my eyes,
And see the seats of peace, and pleasure, rise,
And hear the voice of Industry resound,
And mark the smile of Competence, around!
Hail, happy village! O'er thy cheerful lawns,
With earliest beauty, spring delighted dawns;
The northward sun begins his vernal smile;

Kind Hospitality attends the door,
To welcome in the stranger and the poor;
Sweet Chastity, still blushing as she goes;
And Patience smiling at her train of woes;
And meek-eyed Innocence, and Truth refin'd,
And Fortitude, of bold, but gentle mind.

Thou pay'st the tax, the rich man will not pay;
Thou feed'st the poor, the rich man drives away.
Thy sons, for freedom, hazard limbs, and life,
While pride applauds, but shuns the manly strife:
Thou prop'st religion's cause, the world around,
And shew'st thy faith in works, and not in sound.

Say, child of passion! while, with idiot stare,
Thou seest proud grandeur wheel her sunny car;
While kings, and nobles, roll bespangled by,
And the tall palace lessens in the sky;
Say, while with pomp thy giddy brain runs round,
What joys, like these, in splendour can be found?
Ah, yonder turn thy wealth-inchanted eyes,
Where that poor, friendless wretch expiring lies!
Hear his sad partner shriek, beside his bed,
And call down curses on her landlord's head,
Who drove, from yon small cot, her household sweet,
To pine with want, and perish in the street.
See the pale tradesman toil, the live-long day,
To deck imperious lords, who never pay!
Who waste, at dice, their boundless breadth of soil,
But grudge the scanty meed of honest toil.
See hounds and horses riot on the store,
By HEAVEN created for the hapless poor!
See half a realm one tyrant scarce sustain,
While meagre thousands round him glean the plain!
See, for his mistress' robe, a village sold,
Whose matrons shrink from nakedness and cold!

And every charm, that rural nature yields;
And every joy, to Competence allied,
And every good, that Virtue gains from Pride!

No griping landlord here alarms the door,
To halve, for rent, the poor man's little store.
No haughty owner drives the humble swain
To some far refuge from his dread domain;
Nor wastes, upon his robe of useless pride,
The wealth, which shivering thousands want beside;
Nor in one palace sinks a hundred cots;
Nor in one manor drowns a thousand lots;
Nor, on one table, spread for death and pain,
Devours what would a village well sustain.
O Competence, thou bless'd by Heaven's decree,
How well exchang'd is empty pride for thee!
Oft to thy cot my feet delighted turn,
To meet thy chearful smile, at peep of morn;
To join thy toils, that bid the earth look gay;
To mark thy sports, that hail the eve of May;
To see thy ruddy children, at thy board,
And share thy temperate meal, and frugal hoard;
And every joy, by winning prattlers giv'n,
And every earnest of a future Heaven.

There the poor wanderer finds a table spread,
The fireside welcome, and the peaceful bed.
The needy neighbour, oft by wealth denied,
There finds the little aids of life supplied;
The horse, that bears to mill the hard-earn'd grain;
The day's work given, to reap the ripen'd plain;
The useful team, to house the precious food,
And all the offices of real good.

There too, divine Religion is a guest,
And all the Virtues join the daily feast.

And, many a month elaps'd, was pleas'd to view
How well the houshold far'd, the children grew;
While tales of sympathy deceiv'd the hour,
And Sleep, amus'd, resign'd his wonted power.

Yes! let the proud despise, the rich deride,
These humble joys, to Competence allied:
To me, they bloom, all fragrant to my heart,
Nor ask the pomp of wealth, nor gloss of art.
And as a bird, in prison long confin'd,
Springs from his open'd cage, and mounts the wind,
Thro' fields of flowers, and fragrance, gaily flies,
Or re-assumes his birth-right, in the skies:
Unprison'd thus from artificial joys,
Where pomp fatigues, and fussful fashion cloys,
The soul, reviving, loves to wander free
Thro' native scenes of sweet simplicity;
Thro' Peace' low vale, where Pleasure lingers long,
And every songster tunes his sweetest song,
And Zephyr hastes, to breathe his first perfume,
And Autumn stays, to drop his latest bloom:
'Till grown mature, and gathering strength to roam,
She lifts her lengthen'd wings, and seeks her home.

But now the wintery glooms are vanish'd all;
The lingering drift behind the shady wall;
The dark-brown spots, that patch'd the snowy field;
The surly frost, that every bud conceal'd;
The russet veil, the way with slime o'erspread,
And all the saddening scenes of March are fled.

Sweet-smiling village! loveliest of the hills!
How green thy groves! How pure thy glassy rills!
With what new joy, I walk thy verdant streets!
How often pause, to breathe thy gale of sweets;
To mark thy well-built walls! thy budding fields!

The spring-bird carols o'er the cressy rill:
The shower, that patters in the ruffled stream,
The ploughboy's voice, that chides the lingering team,
The bee, industrious, with his busy song,
The woodman's axe, the distant groves among,
The waggon, rattling down the rugged steep,
The light wind, lulling every care to sleep,
All these, with mingled music, from below,
Deceive intruding sorrow, as I go.

How pleas'd, fond Recollection, with a smile,
Surveys the varied round of wintery toil!
How pleas'd, amid the flowers, that scent the plain,
Recalls the vanish'd frost, and sleeted rain;
The chilling damp, the ice-endangering street,
And treacherous earth that slump'd beneath the feet.

Yet even stern winter's glooms could joy inspire:
Then social circles grac'd the nutwood fire;
The axe resounded, at the sunny door;
The swain, industrious, trimm'd his flaxen store;
Or thresh'd, with vigorous flail, the bounding wheat,
His poultry round him pilfering for their meat;
Or slid his firewood on the creaking snow;
Or bore his produce to the main below;
Or o'er his rich returns exulting laugh'd;
Or pledg'd the healthful orchard's sparkling draught:
While, on his board, for friends and neighbours spread,
The turkey smoak'd, his busy housewife fed;
And Hospitality look'd smiling round,
And Leisure told his tale, with gleeful sound.

Then too, the rough road hid beneath the sleigh,
The distant friend despis'd a length of way,
And join'd the warm embrace, and mingling smile,
And told of all his bliss, and all his toil;

See too the Farmer prowl around the shed,
To rob the starving houshold of their bread;
And seize, with cruel fangs, the helpless swain,
While wives, and daughters, plead, and weep, in vain;
Or yield to infamy themselves, to save
Their sire from prison, famine, and the grave.

There too foul luxury taints the putrid mind,
And slavery there imbrutes the reasoning kind:
There humble worth, in damps of deep despair,
Is bound by poverty's eternal bar:
No motives bright the etherial aim impart,
Nor one fair ray of hope allures the heart.

But, O sweet Competence! how chang'd the scene,
Where thy soft footsteps lightly print the green!
Where Freedom walks erect, with manly port,
And all the blessings to his side resort,
In every hamlet, Learning builds her schools,
And beggars' children gain her arts, and rules;
And mild Simplicity o'er manners reigns
And blameless morals Purity sustains.

From thee the rich enjoyments round me spring,
Where every farmer reigns a little king;
Where all to comfort, none to danger, rise;
Where pride finds few, but nature all supplies;
Where peace and sweet civility are seen,
And meek good-neighbourhood endears the green.
Here every class (if classes those we call,
Where one extended class embraces all,
All mingling, as the rainbow's beauty blends,
Unknown where every hue begins or ends)
Each following each, with uninvidious strife,
Wears every feature of improving life.
Each gains from other comeliness of dress,

And learns, with gentle mien to win and bless,
With welcome mild the stranger to receive,
And with plain, pleasing decency to live;
Refinement hence even humblest life improves;
Not the loose fair, that form and frippery loves;
But she, whose mansion is the gentle mind,
Is thought, and action, virtuously refin'd.
Hence, wives and husbands act a lovelier part,
More just the conduct, and more kind the heart;
Hence brother, sister, parent, child, and friend,
The harmony of life more sweetly blend;
Hence labour brightens every rural scene;
Hence cheerful plenty lives along the green;
Still Prudence eyes her hoard, with watchful care,
And robes of thrift and neatness, all things wear.

. . . . .

LORENZO DOW
(1777-1834)

While the deism of Tom Paine and the rationalism and humanism of Jefferson and Adams dominated the religious thought of intellectuals of the period, the religion of the people was increasingly evangelical. Particularly on the frontier, fanatically devoted men were bringing—to men and women whose lives were typically too hard, too dangerous, and culturally starved—vivid emotional and imaginative outlets, a gospel of simple choice, and a concern for individual souls. Some of the preachers were great builders and religious statesmen who established many of the major Protestant denominations in America. Others were wild, visionary men like Lorenzo, widely known as "Crazy Dow" or "the eccentric Cosmopolite." A dramatic, audience-wise man famous for his wit and powers of controversy, Dow was quite typically drawn in his later years into an abortive scheme for a Utopian venture in the wilderness. Eccentric or not, he fairly represents the forcefulness of the evangelism which determined the main religious direction of the early republic.

Bibliography: Charles C. Sellers, *Lorenzo Dow, The Bearer of the Word*, New York, 1928; W. W. Sweet, *Religion in Colonial America*, New York, 1942.

Text: *The Dealings of God, Man, and the Devil, as Exemplified in the Life, Experience, and Travels of Lorenzo Dow*, Norwich, 1833.

from EXEMPLIFIED EXPERIENCE,
OR, LORENZO'S JOURNAL

1. I was born, October 16, 1777, in Coventry (Tolland County) State of Connecticut, North-America. My parents were born in the same town and descended from English ancestors. They had a son, and then three daughters, older than myself, and one daughter younger; they were very tender towards their children, and endeavoured to educate them well, both in religion and common learning.

2. When I was two years old, I was taken sick, and my parents having been a long journey and returning homewards, heard of my dangerous illness, and that I was dead, and expected to meet

the people returning from my funeral. But to their joy I was living, and beyond the expectation of all, I recovered.

3. When I was between three and four years old, one day, whilst I was at play with my companion, I suddenly fell into a muse about God and those places called heaven and hell, which I heard people converse about, so that I forgot my play, which my companion observing, desired to know the cause; I asked him if he ever said his prayers, morning or night; to which he replied, no—then said I, you are wicked and I will not play with you, so I quit his company and went into the house.

4. My mind, frequently on observing the works of creation desired to know the cause of things, and I asked my parents many questions which they scarcely knew how to answer.

5. Being for a few weeks in an other neighbourhood, I associated with one who would both swear and lie, which proved some harm to me: but these serious impressions did not leave me until in my eighth year, when my parents removed to another vicinity, the youth of which were very corrupt; and on joining their company, I too soon learned their ways, grieved the tender feelings of my mind; and began to promise myself felicity, when I should arrive to manhood.

6. One day I was the means of killing a bird, and upon seeing it gasp, I was struck with horror; and upon seeing any beast struggle in death it made my heart beat hard, as it would cause the thoughts of my death to come into my mind. And death appeared such a terror to me, I sometimes wished that I might be translated as Enoch and Elijah were; and at other times I wished I had never been born.

7. About this time a query arose in my mind, whether God would answer prayer now as in primitive times, and there being a small lottery in the neighborhood, and I wishing for the greatest prize, promised within myself, that if it was my luck to obtain the prize, I would take it as an answer to prayer and afterwards would serve God. No sooner had I got the prize, which was nine shillings, than I broke my promise; my conscience condemned me, and I was very uneasy for some weeks.

8. After I had arrived at the age of twelve years, my hopes of worldly pleasure were greatly blasted by a sudden illness, occasioned by overheating myself with hard labor, and drinking a quantity of cold milk and water. I then murmured and complained, thinking my lot to be harder than my companions; for they enjoyed health, whilst I was troubled with an asthmatic disorder or stoppage of breath. Oh! the pain I endured!

9. Sometimes I could lie for several nights together and sleep sound; and at other times would be necessitated to sit up part or all the night—and sometimes I could not lie down at all for six or seven days together.—But as yet did not consider that the hand of God was in all this. About this time, I DREAMED THAT I SAW THE PROPHET NATHAN, in a large assembly of people, prophecying many things; I got an opportunity to ask him how long I should live? SAID HE, UNTIL YOU ARE TWO-AND-TWENTY; this dream was so imprinted in my mind, that it caused me many serious and painful hours at intervals.

10. When past the age of thirteen years, and about the time that JOHN WESLEY died, (1791) it pleased God to awaken my mind by a dream of the night, which was, that an old man came to me at mid-day, having a staff in his hand, and said to me, Do you ever pray? I told him, no—said he, you must, and then went away—he had not been long gone before he returned; and said again, Do you pray? I again said, no; and after his departure I went out of doors, and was taken up by a whirlwind and carried above the skies: at length I discovered, across a gulph as it were through a mist of darkness, a glorious place, in which was a throne of ivory overlaid with gold, and God sitting upon it, and Jesus Christ at his right hand, and angels, and glorified spirits, celebrating praise—Oh! the joyful music! I thought the angel Gabriel came to the edge of heaven, holding a golden trumpet in his right hand, and cried to me with a mighty voice to know if I desired to come there, I told him I did—Said he, You must go back to yonder world, and if you will be faithful to God, you shall come here in the end.

11. With reluctance I left the beautiful sight and came back

to the earth again; and then I thought the old man came to me the third time and asked me if I had prayed? I told him I had; then said he, BE FAITHFUL, AND I WILL COME AND LET YOU KNOW AGAIN. I thought that was to be when I should be blest; and when I awaked behold it was a dream. But it was strongly impressed on my mind, that this singular dream must be from God —and the way that I should know it, I should let my father know of it at such time and in such a place, viz. as he would be feeding the cattle in the morning, which I accordingly did; and no sooner had I done than keen conviction seized my heart—I knew I was unprepared to die; tears began to run down plentifully, and I again resolved to seek the salvation of my soul; I began that day to pray in secret, but how to pray or what to pray for, I scarcely knew.

12. I at once broke off from my old companions and evil practices, which some call innocent mirth, which I had never been told was wrong; and betook to the bible, *kneeling* in private, which example I had never seen. Soon I became like a speckled bird, among the birds of the forest, in the eyes of my friends:— I frequently felt for a few seconds, *cords of sweet love* to draw me on; but from whence it flowed, I could not tell: which I since believe was for an encouragement to hope in the mercy of God.

13. If now I had had any one to have instructed me in the way and plan of salvation, I doubt not but I should have found salvation: But, alas, I felt like one wandering and benighted in an unknown wilderness, who wants both light and a guide. The bible was like a sealed book; so mysterious I could not understand it, and in order to hear it explained, I applied to this person and that book; but got no satisfactory instruction. I frequently wished I had lived in the days of the prophets or apostles, that I could have had sure guides; for by the misconduct of professors, I thought there were no bible saints in the land: thus with sorrow, many months heavily rolled away.

14. But at length, not finding what my soul desired, I began to examine the cause more closely, if possible to find it out: and

immediately the doctrine of unconditional *reprobation* and particular *election,* was exhibited to my view; that the state of all was unalterably fixed by God's *"eternal decrees."* Here discouragements arose, and I began to slacken my hand by degrees, until I entirely left off secret prayer, and could not bear to read (or hear) the scriptures, saying, if God has fore-ordained whatever comes to pass, then all our labors are vain.

15. Feeling still condemnation in my breast, I concluded myself reprobated: despair of mercy arose, hope was fled: and I was resolved to end my wretched life; concluding the longer I live, the more sin I shall commit, and the greater my punishment will be; but the shorter my life, the less sin, and of course the less punishment, and the sooner I shall know the worst of my case; accordingly I loaded a gun, and withdrew to a wilderness.

16. As I was about to put my intention into execution, a sudden solemn thought darted into my mind, "stop and consider what you are about, if you end your life, you are undone for ever; but if you omit it a few days longer, it may be that something will turn up in your favor;" this was attended with a small degree of hope, that if I waited a little while, it should not be altogether in vain: and I thought I felt thankful that God prevented me from sending my soul to everlasting misery.

17. About this time, there was much talk about the people called *Methodists,* who were lately come into the western part of New England. There were various reports and opinions concerning them, some saying they were the deceivers that were to come in the last times; that such a delusive spirit attended them, that it was dangerous to hear them preach, lest they should lead people out of the good old way, which they had been brought up in: that they would deceive if possible the very elect; some on the other hand said they were a good sort of people.

18. A certain man invited *Hope Hull* to come to his own town, who appointed a time when he would endeavor, if possible, to comply with his request. The day arrived, and the people flocked out from every quarter to hear, as they supposed, a new gospel: and I went to the door and looked in to see a Methodist;

but to my surprise, he appeared like other men. I heard him preach from—"this is a faithful saying and worthy of all acceptation, that Christ Jesus came into the world to save sinners." And I thought he told me all that ever I did.

19. The next day he preached from these words: "Is there no balm in Gilead? Is there no Physician there? Why then is not the health of the daughter of my people recovered? Jer. viii. 22."

20. As he drew the analogy between a person sick of a consumption and a sin-sick soul, he endeavored also to show how the real balm of Gilead would heal the consumption; and to spiritualize it, in the blood of Christ healing the soul; in which he described the way to heaven, and pointed out the way marks; which I had never heard described so clearly before. By which means I was convinced that this man enjoyed something that I was destitute of, consequently that he was a servant of God.

21. He then got upon the application, and pointing his finger towards me, made this expression: "Sinner, there is a frowning providence above your head, and a burning hell beneath your feet; and nothing but the brittle thread of life prevents your soul from falling into endless perdition. But, says the sinner, What must I do? You must pray: But I can't pray: If you don't pray then you'll be damn'd;" and (as he brought out the last expression) he either stamped with his foot on the box on which he stood, or smote with his hand upon the bible, which both together came home like a dagger to my heart. I had like to have fallen backwards from my seat, but saved myself by catching hold of my cousin who sat by my side, and I durst not stir for some time for fear lest I should tumble into hell. My sins and the damnable nature of them, were in a moment exhibited to my view; and I was convinced that I was unprepared to die.

22. After the assembly was dismissed, I went out of doors; all nature seemed to wear a gloomy aspect; and every thing I cast my eyes upon seemed to bend itself against me, and wish me off the face of the earth.

23. I went to a funeral of one of my acquaintance the same day, but durst not look upon the corpse, for fear of becoming

one myself: I durst not go near the grave, fearing lest I should fall in, and the earth come in upon me; for if I then died, I knew I must be undone. So I went home with a heavy heart.

24. I durst not close my eyes in sleep, until I first attempted to supplicate the throne of grace for preservation through the night. The next morning, as I went out of doors, a woman passing by told me that my cousin the evening past, had found the pardoning love of God. This surprised me, to think that one of my companions was taken and I was left. I instantly came to a resolution to forsake my sins and seek the salvation of my soul. I made it my practice to pray thrice in a day for about the space of a week; when another of my cousins, brother to the former, was brought to cry for mercy in secret retirement in a garden, and his cries were so loud that he was *heard upwards of a mile*. The same evening he found comfort.

25. Shortly afterwards, several persons in the neighborhood, professed to have found the pardoning love of God, among whom was my brother-in-law FISH, and his brother.

26. Sorrows arose in my mind, to think that they were heavenward, whilst I, a guilty one, was in the downward road. I endeavored to double and treble my diligence in prayer, but found no comfort to my soul. Here the doctrine of unconditional reprobation was again presented to my view, with strong temptations to end this mortal life; but the thought again arose in my mind; if I comply, I am undone forever, and if I continue crying to God, I can but be damned at last.

27. One evening there being (by my desire) a prayer-meeting appointed by the young converts, I set out to go; and on my way by the side of a wood, I kneeled down and made a solemn promise to God, if he would pardon my sins and give me an evidence of my acceptance, that I would forsake all those things, wherein I had formerly thought to have taken my happiness, and lead a religious life devoted to him; and with this promise I went to meeting.

28. I believe that many present felt the power of God; saints were happy and sinners were weeping on every side: but I could

not shed a tear: then I thought within myself, if I could weep I would begin to take hope, but, oh! how hard is my heart. I went from one to another to know if there was any mercy for me. The young converts answered; "God is all love; he is all mercy;" I replied, "God is just too, and justice will cut me down:" I saw no way how God could be *just* and yet show me mercy.

29. A certain woman bound upon a journey, tarried at this house that night; discovering the distress of mind I was in, broke through the crowd with the hymn book in her hand, and after reading a part of a hymn, said to me; "My friend, I feel for you; my heart aches for you, but this I can tell you, that before I leave town in the morning, you will come down here praising God;" I told her no; I believed I should be in hell before morning.

30. After the meeting had concluded, which was about nine o'clock, and previous to the foregoing circumstance, I had, by the advice of my parents, set out for home, thrice, but by a strong impression, as it were a voice whispering to my heart, "you must not go yet; but go back and pray to God: I turned about and went into a wheat field, and kneeled down; and striving to pray, I felt as if the heavens were brass, and the earth iron; it seemed as though my prayers did not go higher than my head.

31. At length I durst not go home alone, fearing I should be carried away by the devil, for I saw destruction before me.

32. Several of the young converts accompanied me on my way; one of whom was Roger Searle; they since have told me that I fell down several times by the way; which I do not remember, as my distress was so great, that I scarcely knew what position I was in. When I got home, I went into my bed room, and kneeling down, strove to look to God for mercy again, but found no comfort. I then lay down to rest, but durst not close my eyes in sleep, for fear I should never awake, until I awaked in endless misery.

33. I strove to plead with God for mercy, for several hours, as a man would plead for his life; until at length being weary in body, as the night was far spent, I fell into a slumber; and in it

I dreamed that two devils entered the room, each with a chain in his hand; they laid hold on me, one at my head, the other at my feet, and bound me fast, and breaking out the window, carried me a distance form the house, and laid me on a spot of ice, and whilst the weaker devil flew off in flames of fire, the stronger one set out to drag me down to hell.—And when I got within sight of hell, to see the blue blazes ascending, and to hear the screeches and groans of devils and damned spirits, what a shock it gave me, I cannot describe: I thought that within a few moments, this must be my unhappy lot. I cannot bear the thought, I will struggle and strive to break these chains; and if I can, and get away, it will be gain, and if I cannot, there will be nothing lost, and in my struggle, I waked up, and, oh! how glad was I that it was only a dream. Still I thought, that within a few hours it would surely be my case. I again strove to lift my heart to God for mercy—and these words struck my mind; "In that day there shall a fountain be opened to the house of David, and to the inhabitants of Jerusalem; for sin and for uncleanness." A thought darted into my mind that the fountain was Christ; and if it were so deep and wide for the wicked numerous inhabitants of Jerusalem to wash in and be clean; why not for the WHOLE WORLD? why not for me?—Here hope sprang up, there was a Saviour offered to ALL instead of a certain few; and if so, possibly there might be mercy yet for me; but these words followed; "woe to them that are at ease in Zion;" here discouragements arose, concluding that if there had been a time when I might have obtained mercy, yet as I had omitted it so long, the day of grace is now passed, and the woe denounced against me. I thought myself to be the unprofitable servant, who had wrapped his talent in the napkin, and buried it in the earth: I had not on the wedding garment, but was unprepared to meet God.

34. I thought I heard the voice of God's justice saying, "take the unprofitable servant, and cast him into utter darkness." I put my hands together, and cried in my heart, the time has been, that I might have had religion; but now it is too late; mercy's gate is shut against me, and my condemnation for ever sealed:—Lord,

I give up; I submit; I yield; I yield; if there be mercy in heaven for me, let me know it; and if not, let me go down to hell and know the worst of my case. As these words flowed from my heart, I saw the Mediator step in, as it were, between the Father's justice and my soul, and these words were applied to my mind with great power; "Son! thy sins which are many, are forgiven thee; thy faith hath saved thee; go in peace."

35. The burden of sin and guilt and the fear of hell vanished from my mind, as perceptibly as an hundred pounds weight falling from a man's shoulder; my soul flowed out in love to God, to his ways and to his people; yea, and to ALL mankind.

36. As soon as I obtained deliverance, I said in my heart, I have now found Jesus and his religion, but I will keep it to myself; but instantly my soul was so filled with peace and love and joy, that I could no more keep it to myself, seemingly, than a city set on a hill could be hid.—At this time day-light dawned into the window; I arose and went out of doors, and behold, every thing I cast my eye upon, seemed to be speaking forth the praise and wonders of the Almighty: It appeared more like a new world than any thing else I can compare it to: this happiness is easier felt than described.

37. I set out to go down to the house where the meeting was held the preceding evening, but the family not being up, I being young, thought it not proper to go in and disturb them; and seeing a wicked swearer coming down the road, I wished to shun him, accordingly I went down to the barn, and as he drew near me I went round it and looked up towards the house, and saw the *woman who was bound on the journey,* coming out at the back door. I made to her with all the speed I could. It seemed to me that I scarcely touched the ground, for I felt so happy, that I scarcely knew whether I was in the body or out of it.

38. When I got to her, she said, "good morning!" Yes said I, it is the blessedest morning that ever I saw; and walking into the house, the first words that I said were, I am happy, happy, happy enough:—My voice penetrated almost every part of the

house, and a preacher coming down stairs, opened his hymn-book on these words,

> "O! for a thousand tongues to sing,
> My dear Redeemer's praise."

Indeed I did want a thousand tongues and ten thousand to the end of it; to praise God for what he had done for my soul.

39. About nine o'clock I set out for home; and to behold the beautiful sun rising in the east above the hills, although it was on the 12th of November, and the ground partly frozen, yet to me it was as pleasant as May.

. . . . .

[EDITOR'S NOTE: Dow's conversion was followed by an overwhelming urge to preach. He never obtained entire recognition by the disciplined Methodists, who thought him unstable. But traveling on the frontiers and operating on his own, he was a powerfully effective evangelist in an uninhibited tradition.]

632. Monday, January 9th, 1804. I rode 52 miles, and arrived at Charleston late in the evening; and put up with W. Turpin, Esq., who received me when I first was in this place; and procured me picked meetings at his house: I find Mr. Hamet has gone to a world of spirits, to answer for the deeds done in the body. As it respects his division it appears his motives were impure, arising from a desire of popularity; in consequence of which, there was a breach of confidence by him as respected the incorporation of the house: awful to relate, it appears he died drunk.

I spoke in his house called Trinity Church; also in the Methodist meeting house. Here I saw Dr. Coke; who informed me that he saw a recommendation for me at the house of Brother John Harper, signed by some of the members of the Legislature and the Governor of the state; which has not yet fallen into my hands; the cause I know not, though I have sent for it repeatedly.

Friday 13th, I left Charlestown, crossing a ferry; and rode thirty-three miles; keeping up with the mail stage.

633. 14th, I crossed a bad ferry of several miles; in consequence of a fresh in the river; which took three hours, with the stage. Hence we went on to Georgetown, where I held a few meetings; and then rode forty-three miles to Kingston; leaving brothers Mallard and Jones behind; the former was blessed in his labors here last year; and Hamet's conduct had done injury; Jones soon after was found drowned in a creek; supposed to have been seized with a fit of the epilepsy, which he was subject to: but the verdict of the Coroner's jury was that he had died drunk; though he was exemplary for temperance and piety.

634. I put up at a tavern, (though a Methodist preacher lived near,) hired a room for a meeting; and called in the neighbors. Next day I fell in with brother Russel, who was going to his station; so we crossed a ferry together, and continued on upwards of eighty miles, until we came to Wilmington, where I found religion low; and bigotry so prominent, particularly in the leading local preacher, that had not Mr. Russel been with me, who was stationed here, I should have been shut out. I held several meetings, and got some religious handbills on paper and silk printed, *Rules for holy living,* which I distributed to the people of the town; and took my departure for Newbern: But this being so far north, and near the sea board, at this cold season of the year, that I almost perished with the cold, frost and snow; having no outer garment and my clothing thin.

635. I held a few meetings in Newbern and proceeded to Washington; where I had like to have been chilled in crossing a ferry; but after getting somewhat warmed and refreshed with a cup of tea I proceeded to meeting; where God made it up to me.

636. 25th, I spoke at Tarborough, then at Prospect. 27th, at Sampson's meeting house: Jones's at night; being now in North Carolina, near Virginia. Hence to Raleigh, and spoke twice in the State house. Here the petty constable who took me up as a

horse stealer near this, did not meet me according to expectation: My appointments were not given out according to direction.

From hence I proceeded to Iredell county, to the house of a man, of whom I had bought an horse, when on my way from N. England to Georgia. Some people mocked him for giving me credit; saying, "you have lost your horse;" but now their mouth was shut; as I paid him his demand, although he only had my word.

637. I visited several places around, and took my departure for Tennessee; having a cloak and shirt given to me. My money is now almost out; my expenses have been so enormous, in consequence of the unusual floods, &c.

638. In crossing the Celuda mountains, the way was narrow; whilst precipices were on one side, the other arose perpendicular; which rendered it dangerous travelling in the night, had not the mountains been on fire, which illuminated the heavens to my convenience.

639. February 14th, I spoke in Buncomb to more than could get into the Presbyterian meeting house; and at night also; and good I trust was done. The minister was not an A-double-L-part[1] man; but pious. Next day I rode forty-five miles in company with Dr. Nelson, across the dismal Allegany mountains, by the warm springs; and on the way, a young man, a traveller, came in (where I breakfasted gratis at an inn) and said that he had but three sixteenths of a dollar left, having been robbed of seventy-one dollars on the way; and he being far from home, I gave him half of what I had with me.

640. My horse having a navel gall come on his back, I sold him, with the saddle, bridle, cloak and blanket, &c. on credit for about three-fourths of the value; with uncertainty whether I should ever be paid:[2] thus I crossed the river French broad in a

---

[1] "A-double-L-part" was Dow's ironic term for the Calvinists—whose doctrine of limited atonement restricted salvation to a *part* of mankind where, Dow held, it was for *all*.

[2] Lost it forever.—*Dow*.

canoe; and set out for my appointment; but fearing I should be behind the time, I hired a man, (whom I met on the road with two horses,) to carry me five miles in haste for three shillings; which left me but one sixteenth of a dollar. In our speed he observed, there was a nigh way, by which I could clamber the rocks, and cut off some miles: so we parted; he having not gone two-thirds of the way, yet insisted on the full sum.

641. I took to my feet the nigh way as fast as I could pull on, as intricate as it was, and came to a horrid ledge of rocks, on the bank of the river where there was no such thing as going round; and to clamber over would be at the risk of my life, as there was danger of slipping into the river; however, being unwilling to disappoint the people, I pulled off my shoes, and with my handkerchief fastened them about my neck; and creeping upon my hands and feet with my fingers and toes in the cracks of the rocks with difficulty I got safe over; and in about four miles I came to a house, and hired a woman to take me over the river in a canoe, for my remaining money and a pair of scissors; the latter of which was the chief object with her: so our extremities are other's opportunities: Thus with difficulty I got to my appointment in Newport in time.

642. I had heard about a singularity called the *jerks* or *jerking exercise* which appeared first near Knoxville, in August last, to the great alarm of the people; which reports at first I considered as vague and false; but at length, like the Queen of Sheba, I set out to go and see for myself; and sent over these appointments into this country accordingly.

When I arrived in sight of this town, I saw hundreds of people collected in little bodies; and observing no place appointed for meeting, before I spoke to any, I got on a log and gave out an hymn; which caused them to assemble round, in solemn attentive silence: I observed several involuntary motions in the course of the meeting, which I considered as a specimen of the jerks. I rode seven miles behind a man across streams of water; and held meeting in the evening; being ten miles on my way.

643. In the night I grew uneasy, being twenty-five miles from

my appointment for next morning at eleven o'clock, I prevailed on a young man to attempt carrying me with horses until day, which he thought was impracticable, considering the darkness of the night, and the thickness of the trees. Solitary shrieks were heard in these woods; which he told me were said to be the cries of murdered persons; at day we parted, being still seventeen miles from the spot; and the ground covered with a white frost. I had not proceeded far, before I came to a stream of water, from the springs of the mountain, which made it dreadful cold; in my heated state I had to wade this stream five times in the course of about an hour; which I perceived so affected my body, that my strength began to fail: Fears began to arise that I must disappoint the people; till I observed some fresh tracks of horses which caused me to exert every nerve to overtake them; in hopes of aid or assistance on my journey, and soon I saw them on an eminence. I shouted for them to stop, till I came up; they inquired what I wanted, I replied, I had heard there was meeting at Seversville by a stranger, and was going to it; they replied that they had heard that a crazy man was to hold forth there; and were going also; and perceiving that I was weary, they invited me to ride: and soon our company was increased to forty or fifty; who fell in with us on the road, from different plantations: at length I was interrogated, whether I knew any thing about the preacher: I replied, I have heard a good deal about him; and had heard him preach; but I had no great opinion of him: and thus the conversation continued for some miles before they found me out, which caused some color and smiles in the company: thus I got on to meeting; and after taking a cup of tea gratis, I began to speak to a vast audience; and I observed about thirty to have the *jerks;* though they strove to keep still as they could, these emotions were involuntary, and irresistible; as any unprejudiced eye might discern. Lawyer Porter, (who had come a considerable distance,) got his heart touched under the word, and being informed how I came to meeting, voluntarily lent me a horse to ride near one hundred miles and gave me a dollar, though he had never seen me before.

644. Hence to Mary's-ville, where I spoke to about one thousand five hundred; and many appeared to feel the word, but about fifty felt the jerks: at night I lodged with one of the Nicholites, a kind of Quakers who do not feel free to wear coloured clothes: I spoke to a number of people at his house that night. Whilst at tea I observed his daughter, (who sat opposite to me at the table) to have the jerks; and dropped the tea cup from her hand in the violent agitation: I said to her, "Young woman, what is the matter?" she replied, "I have got the jerks." I asked her how long she had it? she observed "a few days," and that it had been the means of the awakening and conversion of her soul, by stirring her up to serious consideration about her careless state, &c.

645. Sunday, February 19th, I spoke in Knoxville to hundreds more than could get into the court house, the Governor being present: about one hundred and fifty appeared to have jerking exercise, among whom was a circuit preacher, (Johnson) who had opposed them a little before, but he now had them powerfully; and I believe he would have fallen over three times had not the auditory been so crowded that he could not, unless he fell perpendicularly.

646. After meeting I rode eighteen miles to hold meeting at night: the people of this settlement were mostly Quakers; and they had said, (as I was informed) the Methodists and Presbyterians have the *jerks* because they *sing* and *pray* so much, but we are a still peaceable people, wherefore we do not have them: however, about twenty of them came to meeting, to hear one, as was said, somewhat in a Quaker line: but their usual stillness and silence was interrupted; for about a dozen of them had the jerks as keen and as powerful as any I had seen, so as to have occasioned a kind of grunt or groan when they would jerk. It appears that many have undervalued the great revival, and attempted to account for it altogether on natural principles; therefore it seems to me, (from the best judgment I can form,) that God hath seen proper to take this method, to convince people, that he will work in a way to show his power; and sent the *jerks*

as a sign of the times, partly in judgment for the people's unbelief, and yet as a mercy to convict people of divine realities.

647. I have seen Presbyterians, Methodists, Quakers, Baptists, Church of England, and independents, exercised with the *jerks;* Gentleman and Lady, black and white, the aged and the youth, rich and poor, without exception; from which I infer, as it cannot be accounted for on natural principles, and carries such marks of involuntary motion, that it is no trifling matter: I believe that those who are most pious and given up to God, are rarely touched with it; and also those naturalists, who wish and try to get it to philosophize upon it are excepted: but the lukewarm, lazy, half-hearted, indolent professor, is subject to it; and many of them I have seen, who when it came upon them, would be alarmed and stirred up to redouble their diligence with God; and after they would get happy, were thankful it ever came upon them. Again, the wicked are frequently more afraid of it than the small pox or yellow fever; these are subject to it: but the persecutors are more subject to it than any, and they sometimes have cursed, and swore, and damned it, whilst jerking: there is no pain attending the jerks except they resist it, which if they do it, it will weary them more in an hour, than a day's labor; which shows, that it requires the *consent* of the *will* to avoid suffering.

648. 20th I passed by a meeting house, where I observed the undergrowth had been cut up for a camp meeting, and from fifty to one hundred saplings, left breast high; which to me appeared so slovenish that I could not but ask my guide the cause, who observed they were topped so high, and left for the people to jerk by: this so excited my attention that I went over the ground, to view it; and found where the people had laid hold of them and jerked so powerfully, that they had kicked up the earth as a horse stamping flies: I observed some emotion, both this day and night among the people; a Presbyterian minister (with whom I stayed,) observed, "yesterday whilst I was preaching some had the jerks, and a young man from N. Carolina mimicked them out of derision and soon was seized with them himself, (which was the case with many others) he grew ashamed and on at-

tempting to mount his horse to go off, his foot jerked about so, that he could not put it into the stirrup; some youngsters seeing this, assisted him on, but he jerked so that he could not sit alone, and one got up to hold him on; which was done with difficulty: I observing this, went to him and asked him what he thought of it? said he, "I believe God sent it on me for my wickedness, and making so light of it in others;" and he requested me to pray for him.

I observed his wife had it; she said she was first attacked with it in bed. Dr. Nelson said, he had frequently strove to get it, (in order to philosophize upon it,) but could not; and observed they could not account for it on natural principles.

649. I called at a gentleman's house to get some breakfast, and enquired the road; the gentleman observing my tin case in my pocket (containing my credentials from the state of Georgia, and supposing me to be some vile character) took it out and examined the contents without asking my consent; when he had got half through, he looked at me, I observed he appeared pale: he gave me what I wanted, and treated me as a king.

I had not been long gone from the house before a runner on foot overtook me, and another servant on horseback, with a request that I should go back and preach: I did, (to many of the neighbors, who were called in;) the mistress deserted during the meeting; which to me, she denied, until the servants affirmed that she was in the negro house.

I observed to her, that I considered her absence a slight as they had called me back, and to make it up with me, desired she should let me know the cause of her absence. She replied, she was afraid of the jerks more than of the small pox or yellow fever.

650. Next day he gave me some money and sent a horse with me several miles; and then I took to my feet and went on to Greenville, and so on to Abingdon in Virginia: the last jerks that I saw was on a young woman, who was severely exercised during meeting. She followed me into the house, I observed to her the indecency and folly of such public gestures and grunts;

and requested (speaking sternly to make an impression on her mind) if she had any regard for her character, to leave it off; she replied, "I will if I can." I took her by the hand, looking her in the face and said, "do not tell lies." I perceived (by the emotion of her hand) that she exerted every nerve to restrain it, but instantly she jerked as if it would have jerked her out of her skin if it were possible; I did this to have an answer to others on the subject, which I told her, that my abruptness might leave no bad impression on her mind.

651. These appointments had been given out rising of six months, with the days and hours fixed; I replied in Abingdon, (as I was dismissing the auditory,) that on such a day thirteen months, such an hour, I should be in town to hold a meeting God willing: and steered westerly on a circuitous rout to Turswell; where I preached in sunk hole formed by nature, to a vast auditory; being accommodated thus far by an attorney's horse; here I saw a gentleman, a stranger, of whom I purchased a horse at a word; and proceeded across the mountains of Clinch, which were tremendously high, and covered with snow, and having no outer garment, I felt as if I should freeze; however all was made up at good meetings on the other side: so I came to With court house; hence to Grayson, and the Lead mines, thence to New river, so to Montgomery, to Salem, Fin-castle, Lexington; where I spoke in the Presbyterian meeting house; Woodstock Rocktown, so on to Newtown, where God was graciously with us: hence to Winchester, where I spoke in the Methodist chapel, and a champion bully of an A-double-L-part minister was present; for whom the Methodist preacher's heart did ache; next day he went from house to house amongst his friends, to represent me as crazy man, but three of his pillars were shaken, one of whom replied to him, "if a crazy man will talk so, what would he be if he was in his right mind?" which seemed to confound him. I preached at Frontroyal, and crossed the Blue Ridge in the night, in order to get on to my next day's appointment: a deist was present; on hearing me observe, "that no man was a deist who would not dare to take an oath to relinquish all favors from

God through Christ:" he began to examine whether he would be willing, and something replied "no not for ten thousand worlds." Thus his foundation shook and conviction ensued.

652. An A-double-L-part man (who had followed up my meetings,) perceiving the man to be shaken, appointed a time to answer my discourse; but whilst attempting to answer it, forgot one of the heads of the discourse; which so confounded him, that he complained of being unwell, and concluded his meeting; and so sunk into disgrace.

. . . . .

BENJAMIN RUSH
(1746-1813)

An enthusiastic innovator in politics, religion, social reforms and medicine, Benjamin Rush had a catalytic finger in almost every major American event of his lifetime. Beyond his historic importance as advisor to Paine on "Common Sense" and a signer of the Declaration, Rush was the foremost medical practitioner, educator, and theorist of America in his day. A keen interest in psychiatry and the operations of the mind give his theories a surprisingly modern cast. Especially interesting are his faith in physiological scientific investigation and his speculation on something like a modern behavioristic basis. Neither one lessened his unorthodox but pious Christianity or his broad humanitarian optimism. Both established points of view of the greatest importance to the future development of the psychological grounds of literary and critical theory in America.

Bibliography: Nathan G. Goodman, *Benjamin Rush, Physician and Citizen,* Philadelphia, 1934; George W. Corner, ed., *The Autobiography of Benjamin Rush,* Princeton, 1948.

Text: Dagobert D. Runes, ed., *The Writings of Benjamin Rush,* New York, 1947.

THE INFLUENCE OF PHYSICAL CAUSES UPON THE MORAL FACULTY

By the moral faculty I mean a capacity in the human mind of distinguishing and choosing good and evil, or, in other words, virtue and vice. It is a native principle, and though it be capable of improvement by experience and reflection, it is not derived from either of them. . . . The moral faculty is what the schoolmen call the "regula regulans;" the conscience is their "regula regulata;" or, to speak in more modern terms, the moral faculty performs the office of a lawgiver, while the business of conscience is to perform the duty of a judge. The moral faculty is to the conscience, what taste is to the judgment, and sensation to perception. It is quick in its operations, and like the sensitive plant, acts without reflection, while conscience follows with deliberate steps, and measures all her actions by the unerring square of right and wrong. The moral faculty exercises itself upon the actions of others. It approves, even in books, of the virtues of a Trajan, and disapproves of the vices of a Marius, while conscience confines its operations only to its own actions. These two capacities of the mind are generally in an exact ratio to each other, but they sometimes exist in different degrees in the same person. Hence we often find conscience in its full vigour, with a diminished tone, or total absence of the moral faculty. . . .

The moral faculty has received different names from different authors. It is the "moral sense" of Dr. Hutchison; "the sympathy" of Dr. Adam Smith; the "moral instinct" of Rousseau; and "the light that lighteth every man that cometh into the world" of St. John. I have adopted the term of moral faculty from Dr. Beattie, because I conceive it conveys, with the most perspicuity, the idea of a capacity in the mind of choosing good and evil.

Our books of medicine contain many records of the effects of physical causes upon the memory, the imagination, and the judgment. In some instances we behold their operation only on one, in others on two, and in many cases, upon the whole of these faculties. Their derangement has received different names, according to the number or nature of the faculties that are affected. The loss of memory has been called "amnesia;" false judgment upon one subject has been called "melancholia;" false judgment upon all subjects has been called "mania;" and a defect of all the three intellectual faculties that have been mentioned has received the name of "amentia." Persons who labour under the derangement, or want, of these faculties of the mind, are considered, very properly, as subjects of medicine; and there are many cases upon record, that prove that their diseases have yielded to the healing art.

I am aware, that in venturing upon this subject I step upon untrodden ground. I feel as Æneas did, when he was about to enter the gates of Avernus, but without a sybil to instruct me in the mysteries that are before me. I foresee, that men who have been educated in the mechanical habits of adopting popular or established opinions will revolt at the doctrine I am about to deliver, while men of sense and genius will hear my propositions with candour, and if they do not adopt them, will commend that boldness of inquiry, that prompted me to broach them.

I shall begin with an attempt to supply the defects of nosological writers, by naming the partial or weakened action of the moral faculty, MICRONOMIA. The total absence of this faculty I shall call ANOMIA. By the law, referred to in these new genera of vesaniæ, I mean the law of nature written in the human heart, and which I formerly quoted from the writings of St. Paul.

In treating of the effects of physical causes upon the moral faculty, it might help to extend our ideas upon this subject, to reduce virtues and vices to certain species, and to point out the effects of particular species of virtue and vice; but this would lead us into a field too extensive for the limits of the present inquiry. I shall only hint at a few cases, and have no doubt but the ingenuity of my auditors will supply my silence, by applying the rest.

It is immaterial, whether the physical causes that are to be enumerated act upon the moral faculty through the medium of the senses, the passions, the memory, or the imagination. Their influence is equally certain, whether they act as remote, predisposing, or occasional causes.

1. The effects of CLIMATE upon the moral faculty claim our first attention. Not only individuals, but nations, derive a considerable part of their moral, as well as intellectual character, from the different portions they enjoy of the rays of the sun. Irascibility, levity, timidity, and indolence, tempered with occasional emotions of benevolence, are the moral qualities of the inhabitants of warm climates, while selfishness, tempered with sincerity and integrity, form the moral character of the inhabitants of cold countries. The state of the weather, and the seasons of the year also, have a visible effect upon moral sensibility. The month of November, in Great Britain, rendered gloomy by constant fogs and rains, has been thought to favour the perpetration of the worst species of murder, while the vernal sun, in middle latitudes, has been as generally remarked for producing gentleness and benevolence.

2. The effects of DIET upon the moral faculty are more certain, though less attended to, than the effects of climate. "Fullness of bread," we are told, was one of the predisposing causes of the vices of the Cities of the Plain. The fasts so often inculcated among the Jews were intended to lessen the incentives to vice; for pride, cruelty, and sensuality, are as much the natural consequences of luxury, as apoplexies and palsies. But the *quality* as well as the quantity of aliment has an influence upon morals; hence we find the moral diseases that have been mentioned are most frequently the offspring of animal food. The prophet Isaiah seems to have been sensible of this, when he ascribes such salutary effects to a temperate and vegetable diet. "Butter and honey shall he eat," says he, "*that* he may know to refuse the evil, and to choose the good." But we have many facts which prove the efficacy of a vegetable diet upon the passions. Dr. Arbuthnot assures us, that he cured several patients of irascible tempers, by nothing but a prescription of this simple and temperate regimen.

3. The effects of CERTAIN DRINKS upon the moral faculty are not less observable, than upon the intellectual powers of the mind. Fermented liquors, of a good quality, and taken in a moderate quantity, are favourable to the virtues of candour, benevolence, and generosity; but when they are taken in excess, or when they are of a bad quality, and taken even in a moderate quantity, they seldom fail of rousing every latent spark of vice into action. The last of these facts is so notorious, that when a man is observed to be ill-natured or quarrelsome in Portugal, after drinking, it is common in that country to say, that "he has drunken bad wine." While occasional fits of intoxication produce ill-temper in many people, habitual drunkenness (which is generally produced by distilled spirits) never fails to eradicate veracity and integrity from the human mind. Perhaps this may be the reason why the Spaniards, in ancient times, never admitted a man's evidence in a court of justice, who had been convicted of drunkenness. Water is the universal sedative of turbulent passions; it not only promotes a general equanimity of temper, but it composes anger. I have heard several well-attested cases, of

a draught of cold water having suddenly composed this violent passion, after the usual remedies of reason had been applied to no purpose.

4. EXTREME HUNGER produces the most unfriendly effects upon moral sensibility. It is immaterial, whether it act by inducing a relaxation of the solids, or an acrimony of the fluids, or by the combined operations of both those physical causes. The Indians in this country whet their appetites for that savage species of war, which is peculiar to them, by the stimulus of hunger; hence, we are told, they always return meagre and emaciated from their military excursions. In civilized life we often behold this sensation to overbalance the restraints of moral feeling; and perhaps this may be the reason why poverty, which is the most frequent parent of hunger, disposes so generally to theft; for the character of hunger is taken from that vice; it belongs to it "to break through stone walls." So much does this sensation predominate over reason and moral feeling, that Cardinal de Retz suggests to politicians, never to risk a motion in a popular assembly, however wise or just it may be, immediately before dinner. That temper must be uncommonly guarded, which is not disturbed by long abstinence from food. One of the worthiest men I ever knew, who made his breakfast his principal meal, was peevish and disagreeable to his friends and family, from the time he left his bed till he sat down to his morning repast; after which, cheerfulness sparkled in his countenance, and he became the delight of all around him.

5. I hinted formerly, in proving the analogy between the effects of DISEASES upon the intellects, and upon the moral faculty, that the latter was frequently impaired by fevers and madness. I beg leave to add further upon this head, that not only madness, but the hysteria and hypochondriasis, as well as all those states of the body, whether idiopathic or symptomatic, which are accompanied with preternatural irritability—sensibility—torpor—stupor on mobility of the nervous system, dispose to vice, either of the body or of the mind. It is in vain to attack these vices with lectures upon the morality. They are only to be cured by medi-

cine,—particularly by exercise,—the cold bath,—and by a cold or warm atmosphere. The young woman, whose case I mentioned formerly, that lost her habit of veracity by a nervous fever, recovered this virtue, as soon as her system recovered its natural tone, from the cold weather which happily succeeded her fever.[1]

6. Idleness is the parent of every vice. It is mentioned in the Old Testament as another of the predisposing causes of the vices of the Cities of the Plain. Labor of all kinds favors and facilitates the practice of virtue. The country life is happy, chiefly because its laborious employments are favourable to virtue, and unfriendly to vice. It is a common practice, I have been told, for the planters in the southern states, to consign a house slave, who has become vicious from idleness, to the drudgery of the field, in order to reform him. The bridewells and workhouses of all civilized countries prove that LABOR is not only a very severe, but the most benevolent of all punishments, in as much as it is one of the most suitable means of reformation. Mr. Howard tells us in his History of Prisons, that in Holland it is a common saying, "Make men work and you will make them honest." And over the rasp and spin-house at Grœningen, this sentiment is expressed (he tells us) by a happy motto:

"Vitiorum semina—otium—labore exhauriendum."[2]

---

[1] There is a morbid state of excitability in the body during the convalescence from fever, which is intimately connected with an undue propensity to venereal pleasures. I have met with several instances of it. The marriage of the celebrated Mr. Howard to a woman who was twice as old as himself, and very sickly, has been ascribed by his biographer, Dr. Aiken, to *gratitude* for her great attention to him in a fit of sickness. I am disposed to ascribe it to a sudden paroxysm of another passion, which as a religious man, he could not gratify in any other, than in a lawful way. I have heard of two young clergymen who married the women who had nursed them in fits of sickness. In both cases there was great inequality in their years, and condition in life. Their motive was, probably, the same as that which I have attributed to Mr. Howard. Dr. Patrick Russel takes notice of an uncommon degree of venereal excitability which followed attacks of the plague at Messina, in 1743, in all ranks of people. Marriages, he says, were more frequent after it than usual, and virgins were, in some instances violated, who died of that disease, by persons who had just recovered from it.—*Rush*.

[2] "The seed of the vices is leisure—in work it is taken away."

The effects of steady labour in early life, in creating virtuous habits, is still more remarkable. The late Anthony Benezet of this city, whose benevolence was the sentinel of the virtue, as well as of the happiness of his country, made it a constant rule in binding out poor children, to avoid putting them into wealthy families, but always preferred masters for them who worked themselves, and who obliged these children to work in their presence. If the habits of virtue, contracted by means of this apprenticeship to labour, are purely mechanical, their effects are, nevertheless, the same upon the happiness of society, as if they flowed from principle. The mind, moreover, when preserved by these means from weeds, becomes a more mellow soil afterwards, for moral and rational improvement.

7. The effects of EXCESSIVE SLEEP are intimately connected with the effects of idleness upon the moral faculty; hence we find that moderate, and even scanty portions of sleep, in every part of the world, have been found to be friendly, not only to health and long life, but in many instances to morality. The practice of the monks, who often sleep upon a floor, and who generally rise with the sun, for the sake of mortifying their sensual appetites, is certainly founded in wisdom, and has often produced the most salutary moral effects.

8. The effects of BODILY PAIN upon the moral, are not less remarkable than upon the intellectual powers of the mind. The late Dr. Gregory, of the University of Edinburgh, used to tell his pupils, that he always found his perceptions quicker in a fit of the gout, than at any other time. The pangs which attend the dissolution of the body, are often accompanied with conceptions and expressions upon the most ordinary subjects, that discover an uncommon elevation of the intellectual powers. The effects of bodily pain are exactly the same in rousing and directing the moral faculty. Bodily pain, we find, was one of the remedies employed in the Old Testament, for extirpating vice and promoting virtue: and Mr. Howard tells us, that he saw it employed successfully as a means of reformation, in one of the prisons which he visited. If pain has a physical tendency to cure vice, I submit

it to the consideration of parents and legislators, whether moderate degrees of corporal punishments, inflicted for a great length of time, would not be more medicinal in their effects, than the violent degrees of them, which are of short duration.

9. Too much cannot be said in favour of CLEANLINESS, as a physical means of promoting virtue. The writings of Moses have been called, by military men, the best "orderly book" in the world. In every part of them we find cleanliness inculcated with as much zeal, as if it was part of the moral, instead of the Levitical law. Now, it is well-known, that the principal design of every precept and rite of the ceremonial parts of the Jewish religion, was to prevent vice, and to promote virtue. All writers upon the leprosy, take notice of its connection with a certain vice. To this disease gross animal food, particularly swine's flesh, and a dirty skin, have been thought to be predisposing causes—hence the reason, probably, why pork was forbidden, and why ablutions of the body and limbs were so frequently inculcated by the Jewish law. Sir John Pringle's remarks, in his oration upon Captain Cook's Voyage, delivered before the Royal Society in London, are very pertinent to this part of our subject:—"Cleanliness (says he) is conducive to health, but is it not obvious, that it also tends to good order and other virtues? Such (meaning the ship's crew) as were made more cleanly, became more sober, more orderly, and more attentive to duty." The benefit to be derived by parents and schoolmasters from attending to these facts, is too obvious to be mentioned.

10. I hope I shall be excused in placing SOLITUDE among the physical causes which influence the moral faculty, when I add, that I confine its effects to persons who are irreclaimable by rational or moral remedies. Mr. Howard informs us, that the chaplain of the prison at Liege in Germany assured him "that the most refractory and turbulent spirits, became tractable and submissive, by being closely confined for four or five days." In bodies that are predisposed to vice, the stimulus of cheerful, but much more of profane society and conversation, upon the animal spirits, becomes an exciting cause, and like the stroke of the flint upon the steel, renders the sparks of vice both active and visible. By

removing men out of the reach of this exciting cause, they are often reformed, especially if they are confined long enough to produce a sufficient chasm in their habits of vice. Where the benefit of reflection, and instruction from books, can be added to solitude and confinement, their good effects are still more certain. To this philosophers and poets in every age have assented, by describing the life of a hermit as a life of passive virtue.

11. Connected with solitude, as a mechanical means of promoting virtue, SILENCE deserves to be mentioned in this place. The late Dr. Fothergill, in his plan of education for that benevolent institution at Ackworth, which was the last care of his useful life, says every thing that can be said in favour of this necessary discipline, in the following words: "To habituate children from their early infancy, to silence and attention, is of the greatest advantage to them, not only as a preparative to their advancement in a religious life, but as the groundwork of a well-cultivated understanding. To have the active minds of children put under a kind of restraint—to be accustomed to turn their attention from external objects, and habituated to a degree of abstracted quiet, is a matter of great consequence, and lasting benefit to them. Although it cannot be supposed, that young and active minds are always engaged in silence as they ought to be, yet to be accustomed thus to quietness, is no small point gained towards fixing a habit of patience, and recollection, which seldom forsakes those who have been properly instructed in this entrance of the school of wisdom, during the residue of their days."

For the purpose of acquiring this branch of education, children cannot associate too early, nor too often with their parents, or with their superiors in age, rank, and wisdom.

12. The effects of music upon the moral faculty, have been felt and recorded in every country. Hence we are able to discover the virtues and vices of different nations, by their tunes, as certainly as by their laws. The effects of music, when simply mechanical, upon the passions, are powerful and extensive. But it remains yet to determine the degrees of moral ecstacy, that may be produced by an attack upon the ear, the reason, and the moral

principle, at the same time, by the combined powers of music and eloquence.

13. The ELOQUENCE of the PULPIT is nearly allied to music in its effects upon the moral faculty. It is true, there can be no permanent change in the temper and moral conduct of a man, that is not derived from the understanding and the will; but we must remember that these two powers of the mind are most assailable, when they are attacked through the avenue of the passions; and these, we know, when agitated by the powers of eloquence, exert a mechanical action upon every power of the soul. Hence we find, in every age and country where Christianity has been propagated, the most accomplished orators have generally been the most successful reformers of mankind. There must be a defect of eloquence in a preacher, who, with the resources for oratory which are contained in the Old and New Testaments, does not produce in every man who hears him at least a temporary love of virtue. I grant that the eloquence of the pulpit alone cannot change men into Christians, but it certainly possesses the power of changing brutes into men. Could the eloquence of the stage be properly directed, it is impossible to conceive the extent of its mechanical effects upon morals. The language and imagery of a Shakspeare, upon moral and religious subjects, poured upon the passions and the senses, in all the beauty and variety of dramatic representation; who could resist, or describe their effects?

14. ODOURS of various kinds have been observed to act in the most sensible manner upon the moral faculty. Brydone tells us, upon the authority of a celebrated philosopher in Italy, that the peculiar wickedness of the people who live in the neighbourhood of Ætna and Vesuvius is occasioned chiefly by the smell of the sulphur, and of the hot exhalations which are constantly discharging from those volcanoes. Agreeable odours seldom fail to inspire serenity, and to compose the angry spirits. Hence the pleasure, and one of the advantages, of a flower-garden. The smoke of tobacco is likewise of a composing nature, and tends not only to produce what is called a train in perception, but to hush the agitated passions into silence and order. Hence the practice of

connecting the pipe or cigar and the bottle together, in public company.

15. It will be sufficient only to mention LIGHT and DARKNESS, to suggest facts in favour of the influence of each of them upon moral sensibility. How often do the peevish complaints of the night, in sickness, give way to the composing rays of the light of the morning? Othello cannot murder Desdemona by candlelight, and who has not felt the effects of a blazing fire upon the gentle passions?[3]

16. It is to be lamented, that no experiments have as yet been made, to determine the effects of all the different species of AIRS, which chemistry has lately discovered, upon the moral faculty. I have authority, from actual experiments, only to declare, that dephlogisticated air, when taken into the lungs, produces cheerfulness, gentleness, and serenity of mind.

17. What shall we say of the effects of MEDICINES upon the moral faculty? That many substances in the materia medica act upon the intellects is well known to physicians. Why should it be thought impossible for medicines to act in like manner upon the moral faculty? May not the earth contain, in its bowels, or upon its surface, antidotes? But I will not blend facts with conjectures. Clouds and darkness still hang upon this part of my subject.

Let it not be suspected, from any thing that I have delivered, that I suppose the influence of physical causes upon the moral faculty renders the agency of divine influence unnecessary to our moral happiness. I only maintain, that the operations of the divine government are carried on in the moral, as in the natural world, by the instrumentality of second causes. I have only trodden in the footsteps of the inspired writers; for most of the physical causes I have enumerated are connected with moral precepts, or have been used as the means of reformation from vice, in the Old

---

[3] The temperature of the air has a considerable influence upon moral feeling. Henry the Third of France was always ill-humoured, and sometimes cruel, in cold weather. There is a damp air which comes from the sea in Northumberland county in England, which is known by the name of the *seafret,* from its inducing fretfulness in the temper.—*Rush.*

and New Testaments. To the cases that have been mentioned, I I shall only add, that Nebuchadnezzar was cured of his pride, by means of solitude and a vegetable diet. Saul was cured of his evil spirit, by means of David's harp, and St. Paul expressly says, "I keep my body under, and bring it into subjection, lest that by any means, when I have preached to others, I myself should be a castaway." But I will go one step further, and add, in favour of divine influence upon the moral principle, that in those extraordinary cases, where bad men are suddenly reformed, without the instrumentality of physical, moral or rational causes, I believe that the organization of those parts of the body, in which the faculties of the mind are seated, undergoes a physical change;[4] and hence the expression of a "new creature," which is made use of in the Scriptures to denote this change, is proper in a literal, as well as a figurative sense. It is probably the beginning of that perfect renovation of the human body, which is predicted by St. Paul in the following words: "For our conversation is in heaven, from whence we look for the Saviour, who shall change our vile bodies, that they may be fashioned according to his own glorious body." I shall not pause to defend myself against the charge of enthusiasm in this place; for the age is at length arrived, so devoutly wished for by Dr. Cheyne, in which men will not be deterred in their researches after truth, by the terror of odious or unpopular names.

I cannot help remarking under this head, that if the conditions of those parts of the human body which are connected with the human soul influence morals, the same reason may be given for a virtuous education, that has been admitted for teaching music, and the pronunciation of foreign languages, in the early and yielding state of those organs which form the voice and speech. Such is the effect of a moral education, that we often see its fruits in advanced stages of life, after the religious principles which were connected with it have been renounced; just as we

---

[4] St. Paul was suddenly transformed from a persecutor into a man of a gentle and amiable spirit. The manner in which this change was effected upon his mind, he tells us in the following words: "Neither circumcision availeth any thing, nor uncircumcision, but a new creature. From henceforth let no man trouble me; for I bear in *my body* the *marks* of our Lord Jesus." Galatians vi. 15, 17.—*Rush.*

perceive the same care in a surgeon in his attendance upon patients, after the sympathy which first produced this care has ceased to operate upon his mind. The boasted morality of the deists is, I believe, in most cases, the offspring of habits, produced originally by the principles and precepts of christianity. Hence appears the wisdom of Solomon's advice, "Train up a child in the way he should go, and when he is old he will not," I had almost said, he cannot, "depart from it."

Thus have I enumerated the principal causes which act mechanically upon morals. If, from the combined action of physical powers that are opposed to each other, the moral faculty should become stationary, or if the virtue or vice produced by them should form a neutral quality, composed of both of them, I hope it will not call in question the truth of our general propositions. I have only mentioned the effects of physical causes in a simple state.[5]

It might help to enlarge our ideas upon this subject, to take notice of the influence of the different stages of society, of agriculture and commerce, of soil and situation, of the different degrees of cultivation of taste, and of the intellectual powers, of the different forms of government, and lastly, of the different professions and occupations of mankind, upon the moral faculty; but as these act indirectly only, and by the intervention of causes that are unconnected with matter, I conceive they are foreign to the business of the present inquiry. If they should vary the action of the simple physical causes in any degree, I hope it will not call in question the truth of our general propositions, any more than the compound action of physical powers that are opposed to each other. There remain but a few more causes which are of a compound nature, but they are so nearly related to those which are purely mechanical, that I should beg leave to trespass upon your patience, by giving them a place in my oration.

The effects of imitation, habit, and association, upon morals,

---

[5] The doctrine of the influence of physical causes on morals is happily calculated to beget charity towards the failings of our fellow-creatures. Our duty to practise this virtue is enforced by motives drawn from science, as well as from the precepts of christianity.—*Rush*.

would furnish ample matter for investigation. Considering how much the shape, texture, and conditions of the human body influence morals, I submit it to the consideration of the ingenious, whether, in our endeavours to imitate moral examples, some advantage may not be derived, from our copying the features and external manners of the originals. What makes the success of this experiment probable is, that we generally find men, whose faces resemble each other, have the same manners and dispositions. I infer the possibility of success in an attempt to imitate originals in a manner that has been mentioned, from the facility with which domestics acquire a resemblance to their masters and mistresses, not only in manners, but in countenance, in those cases where they are tied to them by respect and affection. Husbands and wives also, where they possess the same species of face, under circumstances of mutual attachment often acquire a resemblance to each other.

From the general detestation in which hypocrisy is held, both by good and bad men, the mechanical effects of habit upon virtue have not been sufficiently explored. There are, I am persuaded, many instances, where virtues have been assumed by accident or necessity, which have become real from habit, and afterwards derived their nourishment from the heart. Hence the propriety of Hamlet's advice to his mother:

> "Assume a virtue, if you have it not.
> That monster, Custom, who all sense doth eat
> Of habits evil, is angel yet in this,
> That to the use of actions fair and good
> He likewise gives a frock or livery,
> That aptly is put on. Refrain to-night,
> And that shall lend a kind of easiness
> To the next abstinence; the next more easy:
> For use can almost change the stamp of nature,
> And master even the devil, or throw him out,
> With wondrous potency."

The influence of ASSOCIATION upon morals opens an ample field for inquiry. It is from this principle, that we explain the reformation from theft and drunkenness in servants, which we sometimes see produced by a draught of spirits, in which tartar emetic had been secretly dissolved. The recollection of the pain and sickness excited by the emetic, naturally associates itself with the spirits, so as to render them both equally the objects of aversion. It is by calling in this principle only, that we can account for the conduct of Moses, in grinding the golden calf into a powder, and afterwards dissolving it (probably by means of hepar sulphuris,) in water, and compelling the children of Israel to drink of it, as a punishment for their idolatry. This mixture is bitter and nauseating in the highest degree. An inclination to idolatry, therefore, could not be felt, without being associated with the remembrance of this disagreeable mixture, and of course being rejected, with equal abhorrence. The benefit of corporal punishments, when they are of a short duration, depends in part upon their being connected, by time and place, with the crimes for which they are inflicted. Quick as the thunder follows the lightning, if it were possible, should punishments follow the crimes, and the advantage of association would be more certain, if the spot where they were committed were made the theatre of their expiation. It is from the effects of this association, probably, that the change of place and company, produced by exile and transportation, has so often reclaimed bad men, after moral, rational, and physical means of reformation had been used to no purpose.

As SENSIBILITY is the avenue to the moral faculty, every thing which tends to diminish it tends also to injure morals. The Romans owed much of their corruption to the sights of the contests of their gladiators, and of criminals, with wild beasts. For these reasons, executions should never be public. Indeed, I believe there are no public punishments of any kind, that do not harden the hearts of spectators, and thereby lessen the natural horror which all crimes at first excite in the human mind.

CRUELTY to brute animals is another means of destroying

moral sensibility. The ferocity of savages has been ascribed in part to their peculiar mode of subsistence. Mr. Hogarth points out, in his ingenious prints, the connection between cruelty to brute animals in youth, and murder in manhood. The emperor Domitian prepared his mind, by the amusement of killing flies, for all those bloody crimes which afterwards disgraced his reign. I am so perfectly satisfied of the truth of a connection between morals and humanity to brutes, that I shall find it difficult to restrain my idolatry for that legislature, that shall first establish a system of laws to defend them from outrage and oppression.

In order to preserve the vigour of the moral faculty, it is of the utmost consequence to keep young people as ignorant as possible of those crimes that are generally thought most disgraceful to human nature. Suicide, I believe, is often propagated by means of newspapers. For this reason, I should be glad to see the proceedings of our courts kept from the public eye, when they expose or punish monstrous vices.

The last mechanical method of promoting morality that I shall mention, is to keep sensibility alive, by a familiarity with scenes of distress from poverty and disease. Compassion never awakens in the human bosom, without being accompanied by a train of sister virtues. Hence the wise man justly remarks, that "By the sadness of the countenance, the heart is made better."

A late French writer in his prediction of events that are to happen in the year 4000, says, "That mankind in that era shall be so far improved by religion and government, that the sick and the dying shall no longer be thrown, together with the dead, into splendid houses, but shall be relieved and protected in a connection with their families and society." For the honor of humanity, an institution,[6] destined for that distant period, has lately been founded in this city, that shall perpetuate the year 1786 in the history of Pennsylvania. Here the feeling heart, the tearful eye, and the charitable hand, may always be connected together, and the flame of sympathy, instead of being extinguished in taxes, or expiring in a solitary blaze by a single con-

---
[6] A public dispensary.—*Rush*.

tribution, may be kept alive by constant exercise. There is a necessary connection between animal sympathy and good morals. The priest and the Levite, in the New Testament, would probably have relieved the poor man who fell among thieves, had accident brought them near enough to his wounds. The unfortunate Mrs. Bellamy was rescued from the dreadful purpose of drowning herself, by nothing but the distress of a child, rending the air with its cries for bread. It is probably owing, in some measure, to the connection between good morals and sympathy, that the fair sex, in every age and country, have been more distinguished for virtue than men; for how seldom do we hear of a woman devoid of humanity?

Lastly, ATTRACTION, COMPOSITION, and DECOMPOSITION, belong to the passions as well as to matter. Vices of the same species attract each other with the most force—hence the bad consequences of crowding young men (whose propensities are generally the same) under one roof, in our modern plans of education. The effects of composition and decomposition upon vices, appear in the meanness of the school boy, being often cured by the prodigality of a military life, and by the precipitation of avarice, which is often produced by ambition and love.[7]

If physical causes influence morals in the manner we have described, may they not also influence religious principles and opinions?—I answer in the affirmative; and I have authority, from the records of physic, as well as from my own observations, to declare, that religious melancholy and madness, in all their variety of species, yield with more facility to medicine, than simply to polemical discourses, or to casuistical advice. But this subject is foreign to the business of the present inquiry.

From a review of our subject, we are led to contemplate with

---

[7] A citizen of Philadelphia had made many unsuccessful attempts to cure his wife of drinking ardent spirits. At length, despairing of her reformation, he purchased a hogshead of rum, and after tapping it, left the key in the door where he had placed it, as if he had forgotten it. His design was to give her an opportunity of destroying herself, by drinking as much as she pleased. The woman suspected this to be his design—and suddenly left off drinking. Anger here became the antidote of intemperance.—*Rush*.

admiration, the curious structure of the human mind. How distinct are the number, and yet how united! How subordinate and yet how coequal are all its faculties! How wonderful is the action of the mind upon the body! Of the body upon the mind!—And of the divine spirit upon both! What a mystery is the mind of man to itself!——O! nature!——Or to speak more properly, ——O! THOU GOD OF NATURE!——In vain do we attempt to scan THY immensity, or to comprehend THY various modes of existence, when a single particle of light issued from THYSELF, and kindled into intelligence in the bosom of man, thus dazzles and confounds our understandings!

The extent of the moral powers and habits in man is unknown. It is not improbable, but the human mind contains principles of virtue, which have never yet been excited into action. We behold with surprise the versatility of the human body in the exploits of tumblers and rope-dancers. Even the agility of a wild beast has been demonstrated in a girl of France, and an amphibious nature has been discovered in the human species, in a young man in Spain. We listen with astonishment to the accounts of the *memories* of Mithridates, Cyrus, and Servin. We feel a veneration bordering upon divine homage, in contemplating the stupendous *understandings* of Lord Verulam and Sir Isaac Newton; and our eyes grow dim, in attempting to pursue Shakspeare and Milton in their immeasurable flights of *imagination*. And if the history of mankind does not furnish similar instances of the versatility and perfection of our species in virtue, it is because the moral faculty has been the subject of less culture and fewer experiments than the body, and the intellectual powers of the mind. From what has been said, the reason of this is obvious. Hitherto the cultivation of the moral faculty has been the business of parents, schoolmasters and divines.[8] But if the principles, we have laid down, be just, the

---

[8] The people commonly called Quakers, and the Methodists, make use of the greatest number of physical remedies in their religious and moral discipline, of any sects of Christians; and hence we find them every where distinguished for their good morals. There are several excellent *physical* institutions in other churches; and if they do not produce the same moral effects that we observe from

improvement and extension of this principle should be equally the business of the legislator—the natural philosopher—and the physician; and a physical regimen should as necessarily accompany a moral precept, as directions with respect to the air—exercise—and diet, generally accompany prescriptions for the consumption and the gout. To encourage us to undertake experiments for the improvement of morals, let us recollect the successs of philosophy in lessening the number, and mitigating the violence of incurable diseases. The intermitting fever, which proved fatal to two of the monarchs of Britain, is now under absolute subjection to medicine. Continual fevers are much less fatal than formerly. The small-pox is disarmed of its mortality by inoculation, and even the tetanus and the cancer have lately received a check in their ravages upon mankind. But medicine has done more. It has penetrated the deep and gloomy abyss of death, and acquired fresh honours in his cold embraces.—Witness the many hundred people who have lately been brought back to life, by the successful efforts of the humane societies, which are now established in many parts of Europe, and in some parts of America. Should the same industry and ingenuity, which have produced these triumphs of medicine over diseases and death, be applied to the moral science, it is highly probable, that most of those baneful vices, which deform the human breast, and convulse the nations of the earth, might be banished from the world. I am not so sanguine as to suppose, that it is possible for man to acquire so much perfection from science, religion, liberty and good government, as to cease to be mortal; but I am fully persuaded, that from the combined action of causes, which operate at once upon the reason, the moral faculty, the passions, the senses, the brain, the nerves, the blood and the heart, it is possible to produce such a change in his moral character, as shall raise him to a resemblance of angels—nay more, to the likeness of GOD himself. The state of Pennsylvania still deplores the loss of a man, in whom not only reason and revela-

---

physical institutions among those two modern sects, it must be ascribed to their being more neglected by the members of those churches.—*Rush.*

tion, but many of the physical causes that have been enumerated, concurred to produce such attainments in moral excellency, as have seldom appeared in a human being. This amiable citizen, considered his fellow-creature, man, as God's extract, from his own works; and, whether this image of himself, was cut out from ebony or copper—whether he spoke his own or a foreign language—or whether he worshipped his Maker with ceremonies, or without them, he still considered him as a brother, and equally the object of his benevolence. Poets and historians, who are to live hereafter, to you I commit his panegyric; and when you hear of a law for abolishing slavery in each of the American states, such as was passed in Pennsylvania, in the year 1780—when you hear of the kings and queens of Europe, publishing edicts for abolishing the trade in human souls—and lastly, when you hear of schools and churches with all the arts of civilized life, being established among the nations of Africa, then remember and record, that this revolution in favour of human happiness, was the effect of the labours—the publications—the private letters—and the prayers of ANTHONY BENEZET.[9]

I return from this digression, to address myself in a particular manner to you, VENERABLE SAGES and FELLOW-CITIZENS in the REPUBLIC OF LETTERS. The influence of philosophy, we have been

---

[9] This worthy man was descended from an ancient and honourable family that flourished in the court of Louis XIV. With liberal prospects in life, he early devoted himself to teaching an English school; in which, for industry, capacity, and attention to the morals and principles of the youth committed to his care, he was without an equal. He published many excellent tracts against the African trade, against war, and the use of spirituous liquors, and one in favour of civilizing and christianizing the Indians. He wrote to the queen of Great Britain, and the queen of Portugal, to use their influence in their respective courts to abolish the African trade. He also wrote an affectionate letter to the king of Prussia, to dissuade him from making war. The history of his life affords a remarkable instance, how much it is possible for an individual to accomplish in the world; and that the most humble stations do not preclude good men from the most extensive usefulness. He bequeathed his estate (after the death of his widow), to the support of a school for the education of negro children, which he had founded and taught for several years before he died. He departed this life in May, 1784, in the seventy-first year of his age, in the meridian of his usefulness, universally lamented by persons of all ranks and denominations.—*Rush.*

told, has already been felt in course. To increase, and complete, this influence, there is nothing more necessary, than for the numerous literary societies in Europe and America to add the SCIENCE OF MORALS to their experiments and inquiries. The godlike scheme of Henry IV. of France, and of the illustrious queen Elizabeth, of England, for establishing a perpetual peace in Europe, may be accomplished without a system of jurisprudence, by a confederation of learned men and learned societies. It is in their power, by multiplying the objects of human reason, to bring the monarchs and rulers of the world under their subjection, and thereby to extirpate war, slavery, and capital punishments, from the list of human evils. Let it not be suspected that I detract, by this declaration, from the honour of the Christian religion. It is true, Christianity was propagated without the aid of human learning; but this was one of those miracles, which was necessary to establish it, and which, by repetition, would cease to be a miracle. They misrepresent the Christian religion, who suppose it to be wholly an internal revelation, and addressed only to the moral faculties of the mind. The truths of Christianity afford the greatest scope for the human understanding, and they will become intelligible to us, only in proportion as the human genius is stretched, by means of philosophy, to its utmost dimensions. Errors may be opposed to errors; but truths, upon all subjects, mutually support each other. And perhaps one reason why some parts of the Christian revelation are still involved in obscurity, may be occasioned by our imperfect knowledge of the phenomena and laws of nature. The truths of philosophy and Christianity dwell alike in the mind of the Deity, and reason and religion are equally the offspring of his goodness. They must, therefore, stand and fall together. By reason, in the present instance, I mean the power of judging of truth, as well as the power of comprehending it. Happy era! when the divine and the philosopher shall embrace each other, and unite their labours for the reformation and happiness of mankind!

JOHN TAYLOR OF CAROLINE
(1753-1824)

After any major figure has done his work, followers take it up and use it as they can or must. This was true of the movement by which Jefferson's career and writings were translated into varieties of Jeffersonianism. And John Taylor of Caroline County, Virginia, was one of the thinkers most important in creating the kind of Jeffersonianism which has lived on as Southern agrarianism. Taylor kept the older conviction of both the agrarian Federalists and the Jeffersonians that the good life is to be lived on the soil. Corollaries to this were that the backbone of the nation was the free holding farmer and that upon his welfare depended the health of democracy. The new factor in *Arator* (1813) was the sense of danger from the urban and capitalist elements rapidly rising in the country. Philosophically and emotionally this tended to estrange the farmer from the new powers, and, as the North became more industrial and the South more agrarian, to alienate the regions.

Bibliography: Parrington, *op. cit.;* Arthur M. Schlesinger, Jr., *The Age of Jackson,* New York, 1945.

Text: *Arator,* Baltimore, 1817.

from ARATOR

NUMBER 59

THE PLEASURES OF AGRICULTURE

In free countries, are more, and in enslaved, fewer, than the pleasures of most other employments. The reason of it is, that agriculture both from its nature, and also as being generally the employment of a great portion of a nation, cannot be united with power, considered as an exclusive interest. It must of course be enslaved, wherever despotism exists, and its masters will enjoy more pleasures in that case, than it can ever reach. On the contrary, where power is not an exclusive, but a general interest, agriculture can employ its own energies for the attainment of its own happiness.

Under a free government it has before it, the inexhaustible

sources of human pleasure, of fitting ideas to substances, and substances to ideas; and of a constant rotation of hope and fruition.

The novelty, frequency and exactness of accommodations between our ideas and operations, constitutes the most exquisite source of mental pleasure. Agriculture feeds it with endless supplies in the natures of soils, plants, climates, manures, instruments of culture and domestick animals. Their combinations are inexhaustible, the novelty of results is endless, discrimination and adaption are never idle, and an unsatiated interest receives gratifications in quick succession.

Benevolence is so closely associated with this interest, that its exertion in numberless instances, is necessary to foster it. Liberality in supplying its labourers with the comforts of life, is the best sponsor for the prosperity of agriculture, and the practice of almost every moral virtue is amply remunerated in this world, whilst it is also the best surety for attaining the blessings of the next. Poetry, in allowing more virtue to agriculture, then to any other profession, has abandoned her privilege of fiction, and yielded to the natural moral effect of the absence of temptation. The same fact is commemorated by religion, upon an occasion the most solemn, within the scope of the human imagination. At the awful day of judgment, the discrimination of the good from the wicked, is not made by the criterion of sects or of dogmas, but by one which constitutes the daily employment and the great end of agriculture. The judge upon this occasion has anticipation pronounced, that to feed the hungry, clothe the naked, and give drink to the thirsty, are the passports to future happiness; and the divine intelligence which selected an agricultural state as a paradise for its first favourites, has here again prescribed the agricultural virtues as the means for the admission of their posterity into heaven.

With the pleasures of religion, agriculture unites those of patriotism, and among the worthy competitors for pre-eminence in the practice of this cardinal virtue, a profound author assigns a high station to him who has made two blades of grass grow instead of one; an idea capable of a signal amplification, by a comparison between a system of agriculture which doubles the fertility of a country, and a successful war which doubles its territory. By the first the territory itself is also substantially doubled, without wasting the lives, the wealth, or the liberty of the nation which has thus subdued sterility, and drawn prosperity from a willing source. By the second, the blood pretended to be enriched, is spilt; the wealth pretended to be increased, is wasted; the liberty said to be secured, is immolated to the patriotism of a victorious army; and desolation in every form is made to stalk in the glittering garb of false glory, throughout some neighbouring country. Moral law decides the preference with undeviating consistency, in assigning to the nation, which elects true patriotism, the recompense of truth, and to the electors of the false, the expiation of errour. To the respective agents, the same law assigns the remorses of a conqueror, and the quiet conscience of the agriculturist.

The capacity of agriculture for affording luxuries to the body, is not less conspicuous than its capacity for affording luxuries to the mind; it being a science singularly possessing the double qualities of feeding with unbounded liberality, both the moral appetites of the one, and the physical wants of the other. It can even feed a morbid love of money, whilst it is habituating us to the practice of virtue; and whilst it provides for the wants of the philosopher, it affords him ample room for the most curious and yet useful researches. In short, by the exercise it gives both to the body and to the mind, it secures health and vigour to both; and by combining a thorough knowledge of the real affairs of life, with a necessity for investigating the arcana of nature, and the strongest invitations to the practice of morality, it becomes the best architect of a complete man.

If this eulogy should succeed in awakening the attention of men of science to a skilful practice of agriculture, they will become models for individuals, and guardians for national happiness. The discoveries of the learned will be practised by the ignorant; and a system which sheds happiness, plenty and virtue all around, will be gradually substituted for one, which fosters vice, breeds want, and begets misery.

Politicians (who ought to know the most, and generally know the least, of a science in which the United States are more deeply interested than in any other) will appear, of more practical knowledge, or at least of better theoretical instruction; and the hopeless habit of confiding our greatest interest to people most ignorant of it, will be abandoned.

The errours of politicians ignorant of agriculture, or their projects designed to oppress it, can only rob it of its pleasures, and consign it to contempt and misery. This revolution of its natural state, is invariably affected by war, armies, heavy taxes, or exclusive privileges. In two cases alone, have nations ever gained any thing by war. Those of repelling invasion and emigrating into a more fruitful territory. In every other case, the industrious of all professions suffer by war, the effects of which in its modern form, are precisely the same to the victorious and the vanquished nation. The least evil to be apprehended from victorious armies, is a permanent system of heavy taxation, than which, nothing can more vitally wound or kill the pleasures of agriculture. Of the same stamp, are exclusive privileges in every form; and to pillage or steal under the sanction of the statute books, is no less fatal to the happiness of agriculture, than the hierarchical tyranny over the soul, under the pretended sanction of God, or the feudal tyranny over the body, under the equally fraudulent pretence of defending the nation. In a climate and soil, where good culture never fails to beget plenty, where bad cannot produce famine, begirt by nature against the risque of invasion, and favoured by the accident with the power of self government, agriculture can only lose its happiness by the folly or fraud of statesmen, or by its own ignorance.

NUMBER 60

THE RIGHTS OF AGRICULTURE

It is lamentable to confess, that this, to be a true, must be almost a negative number.—This most useful and virtuous interest, enjoys no rights, except in the United States; and there it enjoys no exclusive rights, whilst the few in which it shares are daily contracted by the various arts of ambition and avarice. Every where else, agriculture is a slave; here she is only a dupe. Abroad she is condemned by avowed force to feed voluptuousness, avarice and ambition; here, she is deluded by flattery and craft, during fits of joy or of fury, to squander her property, to mortgage her labourers, and to shackle her freedom. Abroad, she suffers contempt, and is sensible of her degradation; here, she is a blind Quixote, mounted on a wooden horse, and persuaded by the acclamations of her foes, that she is soaring to the stars, whilst she is ready to tumble into the dust.

Privileges are rearing by laws all around at her expense, and whilst she is taught to believe that they will only take from her a few inconsiderable slips, they will at length draw a spacious circumvallation, within which will gradually grow up a power, beyond her control. Tricks, as well as inventions, are daily fortified with legal bulwarks, called charters, to transfer her wealth, and to secure frauds against her efforts. Capital in every form, save that of agriculture, is fed by taxes and by bounties, which she must pay; whilst not a single bounty is paid to her by capital in any form; and instead of being favoured with some prizes in the lottery of society, she pays most, and is rewarded herself by the blanks of underwriting the projects of statesmen, and bearing the burthens of government.

The use of society, is to secure the fruits of his own industry and talents to each associator. Its abuse consists in artifice or force, for transferring those fruits from some partners to others. Of this abuse, that interest covering the majority of partners is the victim. And the difficulty of discriminating laws, transferring such fruits for the benefit of society, from those having in view the gratification of avarice and ambition, produces a sympathy and combination between these distinct kinds of law. As the members of the government, and members of legal frauds, both extract power and income from the majority, they are apt to coalesce; and each party to favour the designs of its ally, in their operations upon the common enemy. Hence governments love to create exclusive rights, and exclusive rights cling to governments. The ligament of parent and child, binds them together, and the power creating these abuses, must make them props for its support, or instruments for its subversion. Its election between these alternatives is certain, and society is thus unavoidably thrown into two divisions. One containing all those who pay, and the other those who receive contributions, required either for publick use, or to foster private avarice or ambition. Good government is graduated by this latter kind of contribution thus unfortunately allied to the former. The highest amount constitutes the worst, and the lowest, the best possible species of government. But as both are drawn from the majority of every society, whenever the agricultural interest covers that majority, this interest is the victim of the coalition; and as it almost universally does cover this majority, the agricultural interest is almost universally its slaves.

The consequences to agriculture will be demonstrated by converting this coalition between government and its creatures, or of all who receive tolls given by law, into a political pope, and placing in his mouth an address to agriculture, in a parody of Ernulphus's form of excommunication.

"May you be taxed in your lands, your slaves, your houses, your carriages, your horses, your clothing, your liquors, your coffee, your tea, and your salt. May you be taxed by banks, by protecting duties, by embargoes, and by charters of a thousand different forms. May the exemption of your exports from taxation be removed, and may you then be taxed through your wheat, your corn, your tobacco, your cotton, your rice, your indigo, your sugar, your hemp, your live stock, your beef, your pork, your tar, pitch and turpentine, your onions, your cheese, and your potatoes. May you be taxed for the support of government, or to enrich exclusive or chartered interests, through every article you import, and through every article you export, by duties called protecting, but intended to take away your constitutional protection against taxation for the benefit of capitalists. May you be taxed through every article produced by your labour or necessary to your subsistence, comfort and pleasure, by exercises. And whilst every species of your products, and of your consumptions are thus taxed, may your capital, being visible, be moreover taxed in various modes. May all these taxes whether plain or intricate, (after deducting the small sum necessary to produce the genuine end of society) be employed in enriching capitalists, and buying soldiers, placemen and contractors, to make you submissive to usurpations, and as quiet under your burthens, as a martyr tied to the stake, under the flames. After you have been taxed as far as you can pay, may you by the bounty of God Almighty be moreover mortgaged up to your value or credit, for the benefit of the said coalition of capitalists. And finally, may none of this good and useful coalition, to whom is given the wealth of this world, as the kingdom of heaven is to the pope and his clergy, be taxed in their stock or principal held under any law or charter whatsoever; nor in their capital employed in any manufacture or speculation, nor in any profit drawn from such principal stock or capital; nor thro' any of their sinecures, salaries, contracts or incomes; but on the contrary, may such stock, principal, capital, profits, salaries, contracts, and sinecures, be constantly fostered by bounties in various injurious forms, to be paid by you, you damned dirty working, productive bitch, agriculture." Throughout the world, agriculture, like one of Ernulphus's contrite excommunicants, responds, amen, to this pious invocation.

Throughout the world, agriculture has enjoyed, and in England, continues to enjoy, one of the rights in which she has a share in the United States; that of a voice in elections.—And throughout the world, this right has been unable to shield her against an anathema, which prescribes for her as perfect a hell, as the formula of Ernulphus prescribes for his heretick. Let the agricultural interest of the United States, pause here and look around. Is a blind confidence in a right so universally ineffectual, a sufficient safeguard for its freedom and happiness? To me it seems, that an interest can never be long free, which blindly confides in a coalition, whose object it is to draw from that interest, power and wealth. That the major interest must be as cunning, as wise and as watchful, as the minor, or that the minor interest will enslave it. And that agriculture must as attentively keep her eyes upon the coalition, to avoid its operations upon her, as the coalition does upon agriculture, for the purpose of transferring to its members portions of her power and wealth, whenever she slumbers.

Hence have arisen the political suggestions to be found in these essays. I cannot discern much good in an improvement of agriculture, to get luxury, voluptuousness and tyranny for a few, and wretchedness for a multitude.—The best cultivated country in the world, abounds most in paupers and thieves. Agriculture must be a politician to avoid this fate; and those who ridicule her pretensions to knowledge in this science, intend by persuading her to repose in a blind confidence, built upon the frail right of election, to expose her to it. How can she even judiciously elect, if she cannot or will not judge of publick measures, by the light of her own interest?

The moral consequence of this supineness or ignorance, is, that social happiness gradually becomes the dependant of a minority, and of course it is provided for, by continually subtracting from the happiness of a majority. The visible immorality of this, demonstrates the virtue, as well as wisdom of suggestions designed to obstruct it.

The remaining right in which agriculture participates, in common with all other interests, having any thing to export, is bestowed by the constitutional prohibition of duties upon exports. This right originated in state jealousies, and not from a disposition to favour agriculture, but yet it is her best security, for the preservation of that portion of our government, which will longest be sensible of her elective influence; and its relinquishment will be the most fatal wound which can be inflicted on her. The coalition I have described will try every art in her most unguarded moments, to snatch it from her, and it will be the last relinquishment it will need. To determine whether her elective influence can bear further wounds, let agriculture re-survey the legislation of our whole term of independence, and compare the catalogues she may select, of laws for creating or fostering privileges and exclusive interests, with those for fostering herself; and let this comparison form the criterion for ascertaining her legislative influence. Thus only can she judiciously increase this influence, if it has settled too low, or diminish it, if it has raised too high. There is no fair mode of judging, except by these legislative acts. To infer, that the agricultural interest influences legislatures, because it chiefly elects them, would be like inferring, that the French nation influences the tribunate, because they wholly elect it. Let agriculture therefore hold fast the solitary security she enjoys in common with her industrious associates, against the ambition of usurpers, and the avarice of capitalists, nor be deluded into the absurd notion, that it is wise to relinquish the peculium of industry, for the sake of some temporary operation upon foreign nations, inevitably resulting upon herself in the form of retaliation, whilst the protection of exports against taxation, will be gone forever.

TWO FRENCH VIEWS OF AMERICA

I MOREAU de ST. MÉRY
(1750-1819)

Born in Martinique of French colonial parents, Moreau had become a distinguished Parisian lawyer and colonial historian before the French Revolution. A key figure in early phases of the Revolution, he fled to America in 1793 one jump ahead of Robespierre's order for his arrest, which would have brought him to the guillotine. In Philadelphia, where his bookshop became an important center of *emigré* life, he used his enforced leisure to turn out the basic histories of San Domingo and the American diary upon which his reputation rests.

The hangover from colonialism which long made Americans too sensitive to European opinions has begun to disappear only in the mid-twentieth century. That sensitivity tended to give the foreign observer's word peculiar weight for Americans, even when it merely infuriated them. In Moreau's account the inaccuracies which justly annoyed them and the home truths they rejected with equal annoyance are interestingly mingled. Moreau's observations are scattered and sometimes contradictory; often they are based on hearsay or snap-judgement. Nevertheless they are often penetrating, always refreshingly frank. The sense they give of human immediacy is hard to come by in most of the writings of travellers who have committed to paper their estimates of the American new world.

Bibliography and Text: *Moreau de St. Méry's American Journey, 1793-1798,* trans. and ed. Kenneth and Anna M. Roberts; biographical introduction by Stewart L. Mims, New York, 1947.

from MOREAU de ST. MÉRY'S AMERICAN JOURNEY, 1793-1798

The houses of Philadelphia, more than nine thousand in number, seldom have more than two stories. Usually they have a ground floor, a first floor and an attic. They are covered with clapboards, or painted or tarred shingles. Each house is numbered. In streets which go from north to south, the numbering starts with number 1 on the north side; and then for the south side of Market Street too. That is, on one side of Market Street going north, number 1 is on one side followed by number 3, whereas on the other side of the street it begins 2, 4 and so on through all the even numbers. Going from Market Street south, there is the same system. For the streets going from the Delaware to Broad Street, number 1 is at the left, followed by 3, 5, 7, and so on, whereas the numbers 2, 4, 6, are on the right.

I adopted this system when the houses in the States of Parma had to be numbered. It has since been used in Paris, too.

In Philadelphia one finds the ridiculous custom of using guillotine windows. The result is that they cannot be tightly closed in winter, nor widely opened in summer. Only occasionally are there shutters on the first floor, though they are usual on the ground floor.

A little Greek portico, or one with a triangular top or with a cornice, spoils their appearance. The doors are too narrow. Only stables and coach houses have porte-cocheres.

The houses have a gloomy appearance because of the bricks of which they are built. These bricks are eight inches in depth. An attempt is made to enliven the façades by painting them brick-color, then painting symmetrical white lines in squares, thus seemingly outlining the divisions between the bricks. The window trim is also painted white in imitation of cut stone.

A custom that might be termed extravagant is that of washing doors, sidewalks and window ledges every Wednesday and Saturday morning, even in winter when it's freezing. This lunacy exposes the passers-by to the danger of breaking their necks; and as a matter of fact, falls on the sidewalk are not rare.

The water used by the inhabitants of Philadelphia is taken from the Schuylkill. It is distributed by wooden pumps placed forty toises apart on the outside edge of the sidewalk, as well as forty toises apart, but alternately, on the other side of the street; thus, on one or the other side of each street, there is one of these pumps every twenty toises.

The water from these pumps is used for everything, but especially for drinking. At a convenient height the pumps have an iron piston that serves to draw up the water.

None of the water is particularly good, and it cannot be kept pure for a twenty-four-hour period. Some of the pumps have a better reputation than others, but that is only relative, and in only a few cases.

Everybody is free to use these pumps.

Several streets have trees, usually elms, planted on the outer edge of the sidewalk.

This use of trees was not common, and the streets were not particularly beautified by them. Some persons considered them helpful in hot weather; others believed they prevented the free circulation of air and attracted insects, especially mosquitoes. Since then Italian poplars have been put at both ends of each street, as well as on all sides of the city's principal square on Market Street between the Delaware and the Schuylkill.

. . . . .

The Schuylkill bridge has three arches, is covered, and has windows like portholes. Carriages pass to the right, following the custom of the United States, to avoid collisions. Each side has a sidewalk for pedestrians. The Schuylkill bridge, at the point where High Street ends, is of stone.

The canal which furnishes water to Philadelphia has its intake between Middle Alley and Gray's.

The canal is vaulted in all parts with a double vault of freestone. A steam machine has been constructed to pump the water so that it flows to all the streets.

It is carried by a subterranean canal running beneath the sidewalks on both sides of each street; and whenever one wishes, the turn of a knob makes it flow from the end of a faucet about two and a half feet high.

This water is excellent for drinking.

It is piped into the homes of private persons who have bought the right of using it.

The wooden bridge at the Gray's Ferry crossing remains unchanged.

The water stored for city use is pumped to a reservoir fifty feet high. This advantage cannot be overestimated. Starting July 12, 1795, Front Street was watered at ten o'clock every morning by watering carts like those which serve the Paris boulevards. But now that the waters of the Schuylkill are collected in a reservoir, it is made to flow in every street. And words cannot express how much good is accomplished by the manner in which it renews and refreshes the air during the extreme heat of summer.

Trees have been planted on both sides of every street, the Italian poplar being the one most in favor.

. . . . .

American men, generally speaking, are tall and thin, especially the Quakers, but they seem to have no strength. They are listless, those in the towns even more than the others. Neither sex can boast a complexion. They are brave, but they lack drive. Indifferent toward almost everything, they sometimes behave in a manner that suggests real energy; then follow it with a "Oh-to-hell-with-it" attitude which shows that they seldom feel genuine enthusiasm.

Their manner of living is always the same. They breakfast at nine o'clock on ham or salt fish, herring, for example, which is accompanied by coffee or tea, and slices of toasted or untoasted bread spread with butter.

At about two o'clock they dine without soup. Their dinner consists of broth, with a main dish of an English roast surrounded by potatoes. Following that are boiled green peas, on which they put butter which the heat melts, or a spicy sauce; then baked or fried eggs, boiled or fried fish, salad which may be thinly sliced cabbage seasoned to each man's taste on his own plate, pastries, sweets to which they are excessively partial and which are insufficiently cooked.

For dessert, they have a little fruit, some cheese and a pudding. The entire meal is washed down with cider, weak or strong beer, then white wine. The entrée is accompanied by Bordeaux or

Madeira, which they keep drinking right through dessert, toward the end of which any ladies who are at the dinner leave the table and withdraw by themselves, leaving the men free to drink as much as they please, because then bottles go the round continuously, each man pouring for himself. Toasts are drunk, cigars are lighted, diners run to the corners of the room hunting night tables and vases which will enable them to hold a greater amount of liquor.

Sometimes dinner is prolonged in this manner far into the night, but finally the dinner table is deserted because of boredom, fatigue or drunkenness.

Before dinner and all during dinner, as is the English custom, all the silver one owns is displayed on the sideboard in the dining room.

In the evening, around seven or eight o'clock (on such ordinary days as have not been set aside for formal dinners), tea is served in the evening as in the morning, but without meat. The whole family is united at tea, to which friends, acquaintances and even strangers are invited.

There you have the three meals of the day, because there is no supper. Evening tea is a boring and monotonous ceremony. The mistress of the house serves it and passes it around, and as long as a person has not turned his cup upside down and placed his spoon upon it, just so often will he be brought another cup. You hear a thousand true and false accounts of Frenchmen who, in their ignorance of this peculiar custom, have been so inundated by tea that they have suffered intensely.

Americans have almost a passion for oysters, which they eat at all hours, even in the streets. They are exposed in open containers in their own liquor, and are sold by dozens and hundreds up to ten o'clock at night in the streets, where they are peddled on barrows to the accompaniment of mournful cries.

. . . . .

The population of Philadelphia is, as we have noted, fifty-five or sixty thousand souls, made up of three different classes,

1. Whites
2. People of Color } of two sexes.
3. And Slaves

Let us examine them in turn.

I. The Whites, as everyone knows, are the dominant class, but they are subdivided, nonetheless, into five classes—1. white men; 2. white women; 3. white children; 4. white servants; 5. indentured white servants. II. Colored People are divided into men, women and children. III. Slaves into men, women and children.

We shall not speak of the Indians, who are red men and aborigines. Moreover, they inhabit only such places as are set apart for them; and if they appear in cities, even in Philadelphia, it is always for some political reason.

I *The Whites*

I. White Men.—Everything I have said about the general character of the Americans refers to them. They are made up of English, Scotch, Irish and all the nationalities of Europe; and Americans born in different provinces of the United States have extremely diversified European ancestors.

. . . . .

Americans, indifferent in love and friendship, cling to nothing, attach themselves to nothing. There is plenty of evidence of this among country dwellers. Four times running they will break land for a new home, abandoning without a thought the house in which they were born, the church where they learned about God, the tombs of their fathers, the friends of their childhood, the companions of their youth, and all the pleasures of their first society. They emigrate, especially from north to south, or toward the outermost western boundary of the United States on the Ohio. Everywhere, even in Philadelphia, which is America's outstanding city, everything is for sale, provided the owner is offered a tempting price. He will part with his house, his carriage, his horse, his dog—anything at all.

Americans are not only smokers, but they chew too. Sometimes they indulge in both, that custom so dear to sailors. But an American of either sex who uses snuff is a sort of phenomenon, and the women never deform or dirty their noses by using this powder so cherished by Europeans.

And in spite of all the pretenses invented by those who have the habit, it is far more contrary to cleanliness than useful to health.

In Philadelphia, as elsewhere in the United States, three meals are eaten each day, as I have already told in detail. Hot drinks are also used immoderately, and tea is served boiling hot. In summer everyone drinks cold and iced water, and makes frequent use of liqueurs, rum, brandy, whiskey. Brandy is mixed with water and called grog.

People consume green fruits, eat seven or eight times as much meat as bread, and lie far too long in feather beds.

Even when houses are repainted, which is usually done at the beginning of autumn almost every year, the Americans continue to live in their apartments without interruption.

. . . . .

Now let us speak of white women:

2. White Women.—We will begin our observations concerning this beautiful sex with a flattering and happy statement. An American woman, no matter what her rank or where she was born, never—except as a result of an accident—displays one of those faces so common among the lower orders of Europe and even of France: repulsive faces with bloodshot or bleary eyes and offensively deformed features. If one encounters such a face in America, he can safely jump to the conclusion that it was imported from another land: never the product of a soil so favorable to womankind.

American women are pretty, and those of Philadelphia are prettiest of all, and generally acknowledged to be superior to any others on the continent. Philadelphia has thousands of them between the ages of fourteen and eighteen; and proof of this can be had on any fine winter day on the north sidewalk of

Market Street between Third and Fifth streets. There one can see four hundred young persons, each of whom would certainly be followed on any Paris promenade. This tempting state of affairs is one which no other city in the world could offer in like degree.

But they soon grow pale, and suffer almost universally from an inconvenience which is known to be highly destructive to the preservation of a woman's freshness and youth. Their hair is scanty, their teeth bad; and all the little details which adorn beauty, or rather which join to create it, soon fail most of them. In short, while charming and adorable at fifteen, they are faded at twenty-three, old at thirty-five, decrepit at forty or forty-five. They are subject to nervous illnesses. . . .

Young girls never appear at social gatherings until they have reached puberty.

As they are usually large for their age, one is struck by the tall and pretty young girls one sees in the streets, going and coming from school. They wear their hair long, and skirts with closed seams. But when nubility has arrived they put up their hair with a comb, and the back of the skirt has a placket. At this time they meet everybody at tea, become their own mistresses, and can go walking alone and have suitors.

They invariably make their own choice of a suitor, and the parents raise no objection because that's the custom of the country. The suitor comes into the house when he wishes; goes on walks with his loved one whenever he desires. On Sunday he often takes her out in a cabriolet, and brings her back in the evening without anyone wanting to know where they went.

Philadelphia women are markedly extravagant in their purchase of ribbons, shoes and negligees of lawn and muslin. However, they still have no gauze or lace, and almost no artificial flowers. They have a habit, which they think is stylish, of letting the men pay for what they buy in the shops, and of forgetting to pay them back.

They are greatly addicted to finery and have a strong desire to display themselves—a desire resulting from and inflamed by their love of adornment. They cannot, however, imitate that elegance of style possessed by French women. All except those of the highest position go to market Tuesday and Friday evenings (the evenings before market days) dressed for dancing.

After eighteen years old they lose their charms, and fade. Their breasts, never large, already have vanished. It is true that many of them, because of a notion as harmful as it is ridiculous, flatten and compress those female charms with which the sex has been endowed by Nature.

The women of the Lutheran religion may be distinguished from the others because they wear untrimmed hats with a fold in the back, like those of Quakeresses.

Although in general one is conscious of widespread modesty in Philadelphia, the customs are not particularly pure, and the disregard on the part of some parents for the manner in which their daughters form relationships to which they, the parents, have not given their approval is an encouragement of indiscretions which, however, are not the result of love, since American women are not affectionate.

But they are very ridiculous in their aversion to hearing certain words pronounced; and this scruple is frequently a confession of too much knowledge, rather than of ignorance.

A woman made her brother leave the room while she changed the diaper of her own son, aged five weeks, although women and young girls were present.

The adoption in this city of French styles in dress and manner does not, however, indicate that it has any marked affection for the French nation, and its residents have no hesitation in charging the French higher prices and higher rents than anyone else.

The young ladies commonly stick to their first suitor unless circumstances more or less unavoidable necessitate the absence of the first, which may then result in their making a second choice. The same situation may arise several times, always with the same result.

If the suitor continues to reside in the same place, he is always bound by the same chains unless he is criminally inconstant and, having drained the delights of happiness, flees and laughs at the tears of the loved one he has betrayed.

But if the dastardly deceiver should seduce a married woman, he is universally execrated and watched wherever he may go in the United States; and never, never will he ever be able to obtain in this vast country any situation, any position, not even that of watchman or patroller of the streets.

It is true that virtue is the result of habit or of disposition. A young woman trusts in her suitor's delicacy and charges him with maintaining for her a respect which she is not always able to command. Each day both of them are entrusted to no one but each other. Since the young lady must wait for her servant, who leaves the house as soon as night has arrived and cannot be persuaded to return until eleven-thirty or midnight, her only protection is her suitor. Her father, her mother, her entire family have gone to bed. The suitor and his mistress remain alone; and sometimes, when the servant returns, she finds them asleep and the candle out, such is the frigidity of love in this country.

When a young lady notices that her chosen one is growing cold, she reproaches him most outrageously in public; and if another young lady, either through ignorance or by desire, seeks to supplant her, she tells the latter that she has rights which she has no intention of giving up.

They are cold and without passion, however, and—a thing that is unpermissible except in an uncontrollable delirium—they endure the company of their lovers for whole hours without being sufficiently moved to change their expression. They always act as though everything they do is done for a purpose.

When one considers the unlimited liberty which young ladies enjoy, one is astonished by their universal eagerness to be married, to become wives who will for the most part be nothing but housekeepers of their husbands' homes. But this eagerness is just another exhibition of self-love, inspired by the fear that she who does not marry will be thought to have some fault that disgusted her suitors.

They think, too, that French women have some peculiar talent because of the way in which men of their own nation make efforts to please them, especially by their politeness.

Marriages are all the more easy as sometimes they are made in a hurry, and many of them are secret.

I am going to say something that is almost unbelievable. These women, without real love and without passions, give themselves up at an early age to the enjoyment of themselves; and they are not at all strangers to being willing to seek unnatural pleasures with persons of their own sex.

Among common people, at a tavern-keeper's, for example, or at a small shopkeeper's, the daughter of the house, when no longer a child, sleeps with the servant. That is to say, from her eighth to her tenth year she may have shared the bed of fifty or sixty creatures of whom nothing is known except their names. They may be dirty, unhealthy, subject to a communicable disease of more or less seriousness, and possessors of habits that could be disastrous to young persons.

When a young woman marries, she enters a wholly different existence. She is no longer a giddy young person, a butterfly who denies herself nothing and whose only laws are her whims and her suitor's wish. She now lives only for her husband, and to devote herself without surcease to the care of her household and her home. In short, she is no more than a housekeeper. To put it more correctly, she is often the one and only servant.

American women carve meat with a great deal of elegance, and carving skill that would seem astounding in a French woman is commonplace to them. They also prepare pastries with great success.

At Philadelphia, starting the day after their marriage, a bride serves punch and cold meats for three successive mornings to all her friends and all those who wish to give themselves that title. Then, on the three following days, the bride serves tea in the evening, and her friends and acquaintances attend, each one trying to outdo the other in the elegance of their apparel. The honors are done by her young relatives, or by friends of the bride, who are called bridesmaids. So go the outward rejoicings of the marriage feast. The mistress of the house busies herself with all the details, carving and serving at table.

If she has had the misfortune to lose her chastity, her already altered health finds new dangers in the very pleasures of matrimony. The more her husband is capable of multiplying them, the more her health may suffer, most of all when she has a child; for sometimes while still nursing it, or as soon as it is weaned, she has already conceived another.

The women don't dress warmly, their food is bad, and they make too much use of over-hot tea. On the other hand, false modesty prevents them from admitting infirmities of which the husband has never been told and which become serious.

They also have bad teeth, weak stomachs, minor illnesses which wither or at least tarnish their beauty; sometimes a neglected fault results in skin eruptions.

Women wash their feet with cold water during menstruation, and mothers do not like to teach children why this imprudence is dangerous, because they do not wish, they say, to discuss such things with them.

They take no precaution against changes of climate, not even those which cleanliness seems to require. They wear only one colored skirt which they put on during menstruation, and which serves always in the same capacity until it must be thrown away. Men have given them a disgusting name. They consider French women most reprehensible for having a different custom, and washing the linen thus used.

The American women divide their whole body in two parts; from the top to the waist is stomach; from there to the foot is ankles.

Let us imagine the embarrassment of the doctor who must guess from such a description the nature and especially the location of an illness! He is forbidden the slightest touch; his patient, even at the risk of her life, leaves him in the vaguest doubt.

Here is an example: A young woman was nursing her first child. One of her breasts had a crack. She was suffering dreadfully from it, but only complained to her doctor that she had pains in her stomach, and her trouble continued to grow.

A woman neighbor, seeing this woman fading away, questioned her. She told her the truth, and even went so far as to show her the ailing breast. But when her friend urged her to let the doctor see it, she was refused.

Frightened by the danger, she spoke to me about it. I determined to speak to this woman about her condition, using all the discretion demanded by the most violent prejudice, and tell her of the risk she was running, and of the death with which her condition threatened her much-loved little boy. I argued that she was failing in the most sacred duties of nature and religion; and finally I told her that her obstinacy was truly suicide.

Speaking as a husband and father, I used such eloquence that the patient was convinced, and promised to entrust herself to the enlightened care of the doctor.

She did it and, after long treatment, recovered her health; but with this result: although she knew that she owed me the saving of her life and that of her child, this young mother never spoke to me again and didn't even wish to acknowledge my existence.

. . . . .

One very remarkable and very important thing is the respect in which married women are held, and the virtuous conduct of almost all.

This respect is demonstrated in one particularly praiseworthy manner. I have spoken of the unrestrained life of the young girls. Before their marriage several suitors may possibly have enjoyed a dangerous freedom in their company. But once they have pledged their faith to a husband, no matter how many times they may meet one or all of their former suitors, never will a word which might wound the ears of the wife or make her blush escape from the mouth of one of them. This is perhaps a unique state of affairs: a country in which love is silent where marriage exists.

II CRÈVECOEUR
(1735-1813)

Hector St. John de Crèvecoeur was a member of the minor nobility of Normandy who came to New France to fight under Montcalm. He wandered extensively from wilderness Ohio to Nantucket and down into the South before marrying an American girl and settling on a farm in Orange County, New York. When the Revolution came he adhered to the Loyalist side, was persecuted and impoverished and returned to Europe in 1780. In 1782 *Letters from an American Farmer* was printed in London. Perhaps the most significant feature of Crèvecoeur's volume and its long popularity is the evidence it offers to show that much American thought about America itself has been made in Europe. Crèvecoeur's own selection from among his manuscripts of those to be printed shows a determination to make American life and ideals conform to the patterns of agrarianism and humanitarianism most usually associated with Rousseau. It was to be expected that Crèvecoeur would see America with a French eye. The special emphasis and fore-shortening given that scene by that angle of vision was intensified when he edited the book which has kept his name alive. The enduring paradox is that this preconceived and thoroughly foreign picture of America has come to be regarded as a classic statement of the American dream.

Bibliography: *Sketches of Eighteenth Century America by St. John de Crèvecoeur,* eds. (with a special introduction by each editor) H. L. Bourdin, Ralph H. Gabriel, Stanley Williams, New Haven, 1925; Chester E. Eisinger, "The Freehold Concept in Eighteenth-Century American Letters," *William and Mary Quarterly,* IV (January, 1947).

Text: *Letters from an American Farmer,* London, 1793.

from LETTERS FROM AN AMERICAN FARMER

LETTER II

ON THE SITUATION, FEELINGS, AND PLEASURES, OF AN
AMERICAN FARMER

. . . . .

When my first son was born, the whole train of my ideas were suddenly altered; never was there a charm that acted so quickly and powerfully; I ceased to ramble in imagination through the wide world; my excursions since have not exceeded the bounds of my farm, and all my principal pleasures are now centred within its scanty limits: but at the same time there is not an operation belonging to it in which I do not find some food for useful reflections. This is the reason, I suppose, that when you was here, you used, in your refined style, to denominate me the farmer of feelings; how rude must those feelings be in him who daily holds the axe or the plough, how much more refined on the contrary those of the European, whose mind is improved by education, example, books, and by every acquired advantage! Those feelings, however, I will delineate as well as I can, agreeably to your earnest request.

When I contemplate my wife, by my fire-side, while she either spins, knits, darns, or suckles our child, I cannot describe the various emotions of love, of gratitude, of conscious pride, which thrill in my heart and often overflow in involuntary tears. I feel the necessity, the sweet pleasure of acting my part, the part of an husband and father, with an attention and propriety which may entitle me to my good fortune. It is true these pleasing images vanish with the smoke of my pipe, but though they disappear from my mind, the impression they have made on my heart is indelible. When I play with the infant, my warm imagination runs forward, and eagerly anticipates his future temper and constitution. I would willingly open the book of fate, and know in which page his destiny is delineated; alas! where is the father who in those moments of paternal ecstasy can delineate one half of the thoughts which dilate his heart? I am sure I cannot; then again I fear for the health of those who are become so dear to me, and in their sicknesses I severely pay for the joys I experienced while they were well. Whenever I go abroad it is always involuntary. I never return home without feeling some pleasing emotion, which I often suppress as useless and foolish. The instant I enter on my own land, the bright idea of property, of exclusive right, of independence exalt my mind. Precious soil, I say to myself, by what singular custom of law is it that thou wast made to constitute the riches of the freeholder? What should we American farmers be without the distinct possession of that soil? It feeds, it clothes us, from it we draw even a great exuberancy, our best meat, our richest drink, the very honey of our bees comes from this privileged spot. No wonder we should thus cherish its possession, no wonder that so many Europeans who have never been able to say that such portion of land was theirs, cross the Atlantic to realise that happiness. This formerly rude soil has been converted by my father into a pleasant farm, and in return it has established all our rights; on it is founded our rank, our freedom, our power as citizens, our importance as inhabitants of such a district. These images I must confess I always behold with pleasure, and extend them as far as my imagination can reach: for this is what may be called the true and the only philosophy of an American farmer.

Pray do not laugh in thus seeing an artless countryman tracing himself through the simple modifications of his life; remember that you have required it, therefore with candour, though with diffidence, I endeavour to follow the thread of my feelings, but I cannot tell you all. Often when I plough my low ground, I place my little boy on a chair which screws to the beam of the plough—its motion and that of the horses please him, he is perfectly happy and begins to chat. As I lean over the handle, various are the thoughts which crowd into my mind. I am now doing for him, I say, what my father formerly did for me, may God enable him to live that he may perform the same operations for the same purposes when I am worn out and old! I relieve his mother of some trouble while I have him with me, the odoriferous furrow exhilarates his spirits, and seems to do the child a great deal of good, for he looks more blooming since I have adopted that practice; can more pleasure, more dignity be added to that primary occupation? The father thus ploughing with his child, and to feed his family, is inferior only to the emperor of China ploughing as an example to his kingdom. In the evening when I return home through my low grounds, I am astonished at the myriads of insects which I perceive dancing in the beams of the setting sun. I was before scarcely acquainted with their existence, they are so small that it is difficult to distinguish them; they are carefully improving this short evening space, not daring to expose themselves to the blaze of our meridian sun. I never see an egg brought on my table but I feel penetrated with the wonderful change it would have undergone but for my gluttony; it might have been a gentle useful hen leading her chickens with a care and vigilance which speaks shame to many women. A cock perhaps, arrayed with the most majestic plumes, tender to its mate, bold, courageous, endowed with an astonishing instinct, with thoughts, with memory, and every distinguishing characteristic of the reason of man. I never see my trees drop their leaves and their fruit in the autumn, and bud again in the spring, without wonder; the sagacity of those animals which have long been the tenants of my farm astonish me: some of them seem to surpass even men in memory and sagacity. . . .

LETTER III

WHAT IS AN AMERICAN

. . . . .

In this great American asylum, the poor of Europe have by some means met together, and in consequence of various causes; to what purpose should they ask one another what countrymen they are? Alas, two thirds of them had no country. Can a wretch who wanders about, who works and starves, whose life is a continual scene of sore affliction or pinching penury; can that man call England or any other kingdom his country? A country that had no bread for him, whose fields procured him no harvest, who met with nothing but the frowns of the rich, the severity of the laws, with jails and punishments; who owned not a single foot of the extensive surface of this planet? No! urged by a variety of motives, here they came. Every thing has tended to regenerate them; new laws, a new mode of living, a new social system; here they are become men: in Europe they were as so many useless plants, wanting vegetative mould, and refreshing showers; they withered, and were mowed down by want, hunger, and war; but now by the power of transplantation, like all other plants they have taken root and flourished! Formerly they were not numbered in any civil lists of their country, except in those of the poor; here they rank as citizens. By what invisible power has this surprising metamorphosis been performed? By that of the laws and that of their industry. The laws, the indulgent laws, protect them as they arrive, stamping on them the symbol of adoption; they receive ample rewards for their labours; these accumulated rewards procure them lands; those lands confer on them the title of freemen, and to that title every benefit is affixed which men can possibly require. This is the great operation daily performed by our laws. From whence proceed these laws? From our government. Whence the government? It is derived from the original genius and strong desire of the people ratified and confirmed by the crown. . . .

What attachment can a poor European emigrant have for a country where he had nothing? The knowledge of the language, the love of a few kindred as poor as himself, were the only cords that tied him: his country is now that which gives him land, bread, protection, and consequence: *Ubi panis ibi patria,* is the motto of all emigrants. What then is the American, this new man? He is either an European, or the descendant of an European, hence that strange mixture of blood, which you will find in no other country. I could point out to you a family whose grandfather was an Englishman, whose wife was Dutch, whose son married a French woman, and whose present four sons have now four wives of different nations. *He* is an American, who, leaving behind him all his ancient prejudices and manners, receives new ones from the new mode of life he has embraced, the new government he obeys, and the new rank he holds. He becomes an American by being received in the broad lap of our great *Alma Mater*. Here individuals of all nations are melted into a new race of men, whose labours and posterity will one day cause great changes in the world. Americans are the western pilgrims, who are carrying along with them that great mass of arts, sciences, vigour, and industry which began long since in the east; they will finish the great circle. The Americans were once scattered all over Europe; here they are incorporated into one of the finest systems of population which has ever appeared, and which will hereafter become distinct by the power of the different climates they inhabit. The American ought therefore to love this country much better than that wherein either he or his forefathers were born. Here the rewards of his industry follow with equal steps the progress of his labour; his labour is founded on the basis of nature, *self-interest;* can it want a stronger allurement? Wives and children, who before in vain demanded of him a morsel of bread, now, fat and frolicsome, gladly help their father to clear those fields whence exuberant crops are to arise to feed and to clothe them all; without any part being claimed, either by a despotic prince, a rich abbot, or a mighty lord. Here religion demands but little of him; a small voluntary salary to the minister, and gratitude to God; can he refuse these? The American is a new man, who acts upon new principles; he must therefore entertain new ideas, and form new opinions. From involuntary idleness, servile dependence, penury, and useless labour, he has passed to toils of a very different nature, rewarded by ample subsistence.—This is an American.

. . . . .

Men are like plants; the goodness and flavour of the fruit proceeds from the peculiar soil and exposition in which they grow. We are nothing but what we derive from the air we breathe, the climate we inhabit, the government we obey, the system of religion we profess, and the nature of our employment. Here you will find but few crimes; these have acquired as yet no root among us. I wish I was able to trace all my ideas; if my ignorance prevents me from describing them properly, I hope I shall be able to delineate a few of the outlines, which are all I propose.

Those who live near the sea, feed more on fish than on flesh, and often encounter that boisterous element. This renders them more bold and enterprising; this leads them to neglect the confined occupations of the land. They see and converse with a variety of people; their intercourse with mankind becomes extensive. The sea inspires them with a love of traffic, a desire of transporting produce from one place to another; and leads them to a variety of resources which supply the place of labour. Those who inhabit the middle settlements, by far the most numerous, must be very different; the simple cultivation of the earth purifies them, but the indulgences of the government, the soft remonstrances of religion, the rank of independent freeholders, must necessarily inspire them with sentiments, very little known in Europe among people of the same class. What do I say? Europe has no such class of men; the early knowledge they acquire, the early bargains they make, give them a great degree of sagacity. As freemen they will be litigious; pride and obstinacy are often the cause of law suits; the nature of our laws and governments may be another. As citizens it is easy to imagine, that they will carefully read the newspapers, enter into every political disquisition, freely blame or censure governors and others. As farmers they will be careful and anxious to get as much as they can, because what they get is their own. As northern men they will love the cheerful cup. As Christians, religion curbs them not in their opinions; the general indulgence leaves every one to think for themselves in spiritual matters; the laws inspect our actions, our thoughts are left to God. Industry, good living, selfishness, litigiousness, country politics, the pride of freemen, religious indifference, are their characteristics. If you recede still farther from the sea, you will come into more modern settlements; they exhibit the same strong lineaments, in a ruder appearance. Religion seems to have still less influence, and their manners are less improved.

Now we arrive near the great woods, near the last inhabited districts; there men seem to be placed still farther beyond the reach of government, which in some measure leaves them to themselves. How can it pervade every corner; as they were driven there by misfortunes, necessity of beginnings, desire of acquiring large tracts of land, idleness, frequent want of economy, ancient debts; the re-union of such people does not afford a very pleasing spectacle. When discord, want of unity and friendship; when either drunkenness or idleness prevail in such remote districts; contention, inactivity, and wretchedness must ensue. There are not the same remedies to these evils as in a long established community. The few magistrates they have, are in general little better than the rest; they are often in a perfect state of war; that of man against man, sometimes decided by blows, sometimes by means of the law; that of man against every wild inhabitant of these venerable woods, of which they are come to dispossess them. There men appear to be no better than carnivorous animals of a superior rank, living on the flesh of wild animals when they can catch them, and when they are not able, they subsist on grain. He who would wish to see America in its proper light, and have a true idea of its feeble beginnings and barbarous rudiments, must visit our extended line of frontiers where the last settlers dwell, and where he may see the first labours of settlement, the mode of clearing the earth, in all their different appearances; where men are wholly left dependent on their native tempers, and on the spur of uncertain industry, which often fails when not sanctified by the efficacy of a few moral rules. There, remote from the power of example and check of shame, many families exhibit the most hideous parts of our society. They are a kind of forlorn hope, preceding by ten or twelve years the most respectable army of veterans which come after them. In that space, prosperity will polish some, vice and the law will drive off the rest, who uniting again with others like themselves will recede still farther; making room for more industrious people, who will finish their improvements, convert the loghouse into a convenient habitation, and rejoicing that the first heavy labours are finished, will change in a few years that hitherto barbarous country into a fine fertile, well regulated district. Such is our progress, such is the march of the Europeans toward the interior parts of this continent. In all societies there are off-casts; this impure part serves as our precursors or pioneers; my father himself was one of that class, but he came upon honest principles, and was therefore one of the few who held fast; by good conduct and temperance, he transmitted to me his fair inheritance, when not above one in fourteen of his contemporaries had the same good fortune.

Forty years ago this smiling country was thus inhabited; it is now purged, a general decency of manners prevails throughout, and such has been the fate of our best countries. . . .

I must tell you, that there is something in the proximity of the woods, which is very singular. It is with men as it is with the plants and animals that grow and live in the forests; they are entirely different from those that live in the plains. I will candidly tell you all my thoughts but you are not to expect that I shall advance any reasons. By living in or near the woods, their actions are regulated by the wilderness of the neighbourhood. The deer often come to eat their grain, the wolves to destroy their sheep, the bears to kill their hogs, the foxes to catch their poultry. This surrounding hostility immediately puts the gun into their hands; they watch these animals, they kill some; and thus by defending their property, they soon become professed hunters; this is the progress; once hunters, farewell to the plough. The chase renders them ferocious, gloomy, and unsociable; a hunter wants no neighbour, he rather hates them, because he dreads the competition. In a little time their success in the woods makes them neglect their tillage. They trust to the natural fecundity of the earth, and therefore do little; carelessness in fencing often exposes what little they sow to destruction; they are not at home to watch; in order therefore to make up the deficiency, they go oftener to the woods. That new mode of life brings along with it a new set of manners, which I cannot easily describe. These new manners being grafted on the old stock, produce a strange sort of lawless profligacy, the impressions of which are indelible. The manners of the Indian natives are respectable, compared with this European medley. Their wives and children live in sloth and inactivity; and having no proper pursuits, you may judge what education the latter receive. Their tender minds have nothing else to contemplate but the example of their parents;

like them they grow up a mongrel breed, half civilised, half savage, except nature stamps on them some constitutional propensities. That rich, that voluptuous sentiment is gone that struck them so forcibly; the possession of their freeholds no longer conveys to their minds the same pleasure and pride. To all these reasons you must add, their lonely situation, and you cannot imagine what an effect on manners the great distances they live from each other has! Consider one of the last settlements in its first view: of what is it composed? Europeans who have not that sufficient share of knowledge they ought to have, in order to prosper; people who have suddenly passed from oppression, dread of government, and fear of laws, into the unlimited freedom of the woods. This sudden change must have a very great effect on most men, and on that class particularly. Eating of wild meat, whatever you may think, tends to alter their temper: though all the proof I can adduce, is, that I have seen it: and having no place of worship to resort to, what little society this might afford is denied them. The Sunday meetings, exclusive of religious benefits, were the only social bonds that might have inspired them with some degree of emulation in neatness. Is it then surprising to see men thus situated, immersed in great and heavy labours, degenerate a little? It is rather a wonder the effect is not more diffusive. The Moravians and the Quakers are the only instances in exception to what I have advanced. The first never settle singly, it is a colony of the society which emigrates; they carry with them their forms, worship, rules, and decency: the others never begin so hard, they are always able to buy improvements, in which there is a great advantage, for by that time the country is recovered from its first barbarity. Thus our bad people are those who are half cultivators and half hunters; and the worst of them are those who have degenerated altogether into the hunting state. As old ploughmen and new men of the woods, as Europeans and new made Indians, they contract the vices of both; they adopt the moroseness and ferocity of a native, without his mildness, or even his industry at home. If manners are not refined, at least they are rendered simple and inoffensive by tilling the earth; all our wants are supplied by it, our time is divided between labour and rest, and leaves none for the commission of great misdeeds. As hunters it is divided between the toil of the chase, the idleness of repose, or the indulgence of inebriation. Hunting is but a licentious idle life, and if it does not always pervert good dispositions; yet, when it is united with bad luck, it leads to want: want stimulates that propensity to rapacity and injustice, too natural to needy men, which is the fatal gradation. After this explanation of the effects which follow by living in the woods, shall we yet vainly flatter ourselves with the hope of converting the Indians? We should rather begin with converting our back-settlers; and now if I dare mention the name of religion, its sweet accents would be lost in the immensity of these woods. Men thus placed are not fit either to receive or remember its mild instructions; they want temples and ministers, but as soon as men cease to remain at home, and begin to lead an erratic life, let them be either tawny or white, they cease to be its disciples.

Thus have I faintly and imperfectly endeavoured to trace our society from the sea to our woods! yet you must not imagine that every person who moves back, acts upon the same principles, or falls into the same degeneracy. Many families carry with them all their decency of conduct, purity of morals, and respect of religion; but these are scarce, the power of example is sometimes irresistible. Even among these back-settlers, their depravity is greater or less, according to what nation or province they belong. Were I to adduce proofs of this, I might be accused of partiality. If there happens to be some rich intervals, some fertile bottoms, in those remote districts, the people will there prefer tilling the land to hunting, and will attach themselves to it; but even on these fertile spots you may plainly perceive the inhabitants to acquire a great degree of rusticity and selfishness.

It is in consequence of this straggling situation, and the astonishing power it has on manners, that the back-settlers of both the Carolinas, Virginia, and many other parts, have been long a set of lawless people; it has been even dangerous to travel among them. Government can do nothing in so extensive a country, better it should wink at these irregularities, than that it should use means inconsistent with its usual mildness. Time will efface those stains: in proportion as the great body of population approaches them they will reform, and become polished and subordinate. Whatever has been said of the four New England provinces, no such degeneracy of manners has ever tarnished their annals; their back-settlers have been kept within the bounds of decency, and government, by means of wise laws, and by the influence of religion. What a detestable idea such people must have given to the natives of the Europeans! They trade with them, the worst of people are permitted to do that which none but persons of the best characters should be employed in. They get drunk with them, and often defraud the Indians. Their avarice, removed from the eyes of their superiors, knows no bounds; and aided by the little superiority of knowledge, these traders deceive them, and even sometimes shed blood. Hence those shocking violations, those sudden devastations which have so often stained our frontiers, when hundreds of innocent people have been sacrificed for the crimes of a few. It was in consequence of such behaviour, that the Indians took the hatchet against the Virginians in 1774. Thus are our first steps trod, thus are our first trees felled, in general, by the most vicious of our people; and thus the path is opened for the arrival of a second and better class, the true American freeholders; the most respectable set of people in this part of the world: respectable for their industry, their happy independence, the great share of freedom they possess, the good regulation of their families, and for extending the trade and the dominion of our mother country. . . .

An European, when he first arrives, seems limited in his intentions, as well as in his views; but he very suddenly alters his scale; two hundred miles formerly appeared a very great distance, it is now but a trifle; he no sooner breathes our air than he forms schemes, and embarks in designs he never would have thought of in his own country. There the plenitude of society confines many useful ideas, and often extinguishes the most laudable schemes which here ripen into maturity. Thus Europeans become Americans.

But how is this accomplished in that crowd of low, indigent people, who flock here every year from all parts of Europe? I will tell you; they no sooner arrive than they immediately feel the good effects of that plenty of provisions we possess: they fare on our best food, and they are kindly entertained; their talents, character, and peculiar industry are immediately inquired into; they find countrymen everywhere disseminated, let them come from whatever part of Europe. Let me select one as an epitome of the rest; he is hired, he goes to work, and works moderately; instead of being employed by a haughty person, he finds himself with his equal, placed at the substantial table of the farmer, or else at an inferior one as good; his wages are high, his bed is not like that bed of sorrow on which he used to lie: if he behaves with propriety, and is faithful, he is caressed, and becomes as it were a member of the family. He begins to feel the effects of a sort of resurrection; hitherto he had not lived, but simply vegetated; he now feels himself a man, because he is treated as such; the laws of his own country had overlooked him in his insignificancy; the laws of this cover him with their mantle. Judge what an alteration there must arise in the mind and thoughts of this man; he begins to forget his former servitude and dependence, his heart involuntarily swells and glows; this first swell inspires him with those new thoughts which constitute an American. What love can he entertain for a country where his existence was a burthen to him; if he is a generous good man, the love of this new adoptive parent will sink deep into his heart. He looks around, and sees many a prosperous person, who but a few years before was as poor as himself. This encourages him much, he begins to form some little scheme, the first, alas, he ever formed in his life. If he is wise he thus spends two or three years, in which time he acquires knowledge, the use of tools, the modes of working the lands, felling trees, etc. This prepares the foundation of a good name, the most useful acquisition he can make. He is encouraged, he has gained friends; he is advised and directed, he feels bold, he purchases some land; he gives all the money he has brought over, as well as what he has earned, and trusts to the God of harvests for the discharge of the rest. His good name procures him credit. He is now possessed of the deed, conveying to him and his posterity the fee simple and absolute property of two hundred acres of land, situated on such a river. What an epocha in this man's life! He is become a freeholder, from perhaps a German boor—he is now an American, a Pennsylvanian, an English subject. He is naturalised, his name is enrolled with those of the other citizens of the province. Instead of being a vagrant, he has a place of residence; he is called the inhabitant of such a county, or of such a district, and for the first time in his life counts for something; for hitherto he has been a cypher. I only repeat what I have heard many say, and no wonder their hearts should glow, and be agitated with a multitude of feelings, not easy to describe. From nothing to start into being; from a servant to the rank of a master; from being the slave of some despotic prince, to become a freeman, invested with lands, to which every municipal blessing is annexed! What a change indeed! It is in consequence of that change that he becomes an American. This great metamorphosis has a double effect, it extinguishes all his European prejudices, he forgets that mechanism of subordination, that servility of disposition which poverty had taught him; and sometimes he is apt to forget too much, often passing from one extreme to the other. If he is a good man, he forms schemes of future prosperity, he proposes to educate his children better than he has been educated himself; he thinks of future modes of conduct, feels an ardour to labour he never felt before. Pride steps in and leads him to everything that the laws do not forbid: he respects them; with a heart-felt gratitude he looks toward the east, toward that insular government from whose wisdom all his new felicity is derived, and under whose wings and protection he now lives. These reflections constitute him the good man and the good subject. Ye poor Europeans, ye, who sweat, and work for the great—ye, who are obliged to give so many sheaves to the church, so many to your lords, so many to your government, and have hardly any left for yourselves—ye, who are held in less estimation than favourite hunters or useless lap-dogs—ye, who only breathe the air of nature, because it cannot be withheld from you; it is here that ye can conceive the possibility of those feelings I have been describing; it is here the laws of naturalisation invite every one to partake of our great labours and felicity, to till unrented, untaxed lands!

. . . . .

After a foreigner from any part of Europe is arrived, and become a citizen; let him devoutly listen to the voice of our great parent, which says to him, "Welcome to my shores, distressed European; bless the hour in which thou didst see my verdant fields, my fair navigable rivers, and my green mountains!—If thou wilt work, I have bread for thee; if thou wilt be honest, sober, and industrious, I have greater rewards to confer on thee—ease and independence. I will give thee fields to feed and clothe thee; a comfortable fireside to sit by, and tell thy children by what means thou hast prospered; and a decent bed to repose on. I shall endow thee beside with the immunities of a freeman. If thou wilt carefully educate thy children, teach them gratitude to God, and reverence to that government, that philanthropic government, which has collected here so many men and made them happy. I will also provide for thy progeny; and to every good man this ought to be the most holy, the most powerful, the most earnest wish he can possibly form, as well as the most consolatory prospect when he dies. Go thou and work and till; thou shalt prosper, provided thou be just, grateful, and industrious."

A NATIONAL LITERARY CULTURE

In the pre-revolutionary years, when Americans were beginning to think of national identity, they also began to think in terms of cultural nationalism. There was ample precedent for this in Europe, where the chauvinism of the coming century had already begun to set in. The one art in which Americans could then hope to make good was literature. Consequently, the press on both sides of the Atlantic rang with theories, resolutions, manifestoes, analyses, attacks, and protests on the question of a national American literature. When the Romantic concerns for uniqueness, originality, exoticism and genius began to take hold, the question of the possibility of a characteristically American literature was doubly intensified. It is still being asked in the mid-twentieth century.

From the beginning the question of originality has remained central to this issue. What do we mean when we demand originality in literature? Do we mean that there shall be no major debts to other men's writings and thought? If so, are we talking sense—are the works generally admired as "great" free from debts of this sort? Is the literature of any nation in the pattern of Western Civilization unique, original, exotic, really different in kind from the rest? Is special subject-matter what counts? And should Americans then confine themselves to writing about Indians, bison, the frontier, Niagara Falls, or other special American phenomena? Is American writing to be judged in terms of its Americanism or in terms of its artistry?

These are queries applicable to the analysis of any nation's literature, but with reference to America they took on particular force from circumstances. To the European observer the question of American culture was given strong interest by his sense of the *difference* of America: it was new, conglomerate, experimental. For the American there were the problems of colonialism, provincialism, and the cultural lag. How could he simultaneously be himself, do his own work, participate equally and creatively in the general movement of Western culture, and almost overnight contrive a genuine, adequate, and distinctive culture from crude beginnings? There is no reason to wonder at the degree of bad temper and confusion which American thinkers and writers sometimes exhibited.

In spite of all the confusion and the woefully small support they received, writers in America drove ahead to produce as best they could. They produced in this period a few things which stand the tests of time and familiarity. Even more important, they made the future of American literature possible. And they established conventions and forms in writing so successfully that one is considerably helped in understanding the major writers educated before the Civil War when he understands what those men took from the literary founding fathers of the period of the early republic. What was handed down was partly a set of conventions and techniques for which audiences had been prepared, and partly a set of subject-matter themes which had been proved of interest to an American audience.

Since every author has to depend on reading to learn his art, inevitably these writers used the conventions, genres, and techniques of Europe, mainly of England. The most popular conventions were those stemming from the work of Samuel Richardson. A formula which is still successful, Richardsonianism was a blend of the seduction motif, sentimental exploitation of irresponsible emotion, and sententious moralism. It asserted the special merits of the Sir Charles Grandison type of Christian gentleman over what it regarded as the false glitter of the Chesterfieldian, "fine" gentleman. Richardsonianism was the principal ingredient of the novel of the period, but its flavor is also strong in Trumbull's "The Progress of Dulness" and in Tyler's *The Contrast*.

Humor of one variety or another appeared often. In the established traditions of critical humor—satire, irony, and the bagatelle—Franklin was particularly expert, with most of the other writers trying their hands with varying success. Brackenridge adopted the picaresque formula to frontier conditions excellently. With Franklin's creation in Poor Richard of the philosopher-humorist type usually labelled "cracker-barrel," an original and American touch was added. Similarly, Royall Tyler invented Jonathan, the original stage Yankee. Aside from his satires, Freneau achieved a genuine lyricism in some of his nature poetry. But his most striking innovation was "The House of Night." Truly Gothic in its use of the motifs and apparatus of vicarious horror and terror, the poem anticipated the full vogue of Gothicism in England and struck a note which has continued in American writing.

Many of the themes and subjects treated by these authors became standard. The bourgeois success-story—the achievement of financial independence and material comfort through thrift, perseverance, hard work, and shrewdness—was immortalized by Franklin. Domestic joys about the prosperous hearth have been continuously celebrated since Dwight. Critiques of the middle-class ideal, both from the sophisticated upper-class and from the anti-materialistic points of view began at once: in Franklin himself and in young men-about-town like Tyler. And themes such as Nature, the primitive, Indians, adventure, and science were permanently launched into the much greater future of literature in America

BENJAMIN FRANKLIN
(1706-1790)

Benjamin Franklin's literary achievement has never been systematically or adequately evaluated. His reputation for many-sided virtuosity and his historical importance have tended to overshadow his writings as such. His Frankensteinian success in imagining and characterizing Poor Richard has boomeranged when incautious readers have assumed that he himself was that plain-minded symbol of acquisitiveness and incapable of artistry. Patrician prejudice, such as that in Joseph Dennie's critique printed below, has tended to deny him any un-Philistine virtues. Actually, Franklin is one of the great practitioners of the plain style, gifted with fine control of the standard literary techniques of irony, satire, humor, and narration, and of such various delicate effects as pathos, urbanity, and cogency. In an age of gifted letter-writers he was a recognized master. Franklin is a true and major artist. The enduring vitality of his writings stands as objective witness to that fact.

Bibliography: Carl Van Doren, *Benjamin Franklin,* New York, 1938; Carl Van Doren, ed., *Benjamin Franklin's Autobiographical Writings,* New York, 1945; F. L. Mott and Chester E. Jorgenson, *Benjamin Franklin,* New York, 1936.

Text: Albert H. Smyth, ed., *The Writings of Benjamin Franklin,* New York, 1905-1907.

TO MRS. ABIAH FRANKLIN

Phil[a] April 12, 1750

Honoured Mother,

We received your kind Letter of the 2d Instant, and we are glad to hear you still enjoy such a Measure of Health, notwithstanding your great Age. We read your Writing very easily. I never met with a Word in your Letters but what I could readily understand; for, tho' the Hand is not always the best, the Sense makes every thing plain. My Leg, which you inquire after, is now quite well. I shall keep those Servants; but the Man not in my own house. I have hired him out to the Man, that takes care of my Dutch Printing-Office, who agrees to keep him in Victuals and Clothes, and to pay me a Dollar a Week for his Work. His wife, since that Affair, behaves exceeding well; but we conclude to sell them both the first good Opportunity, for we do not like Negro Servants. We got again about half what we lost.

As to your Grandchildren, Will is now nineteen years of age, a tall proper Youth, and much of a Beau. He acquired a Habit of Idleness on the Expedition, but begins of late to apply himself to Business, and I hope will become an industrious Man. He imagin'd his Father had got enough for him, but I have assured him that I intend to spend what little I have myself, if it pleases God that I live long enough; and, as he by no means wants Sense, he can see by my going on, that I am like to be as good as my Word.

Sally grows a fine Girl, and is extreamly industrious with her Needle, and delights in her Book. She is of a most affectionate Temper, and perfectly dutiful and obliging to her Parents, and to all. Perhaps I flatter myself too much, but I have Hopes that she will prove an ingenious, sensible, notable, and worthy Woman, like her aunt Jenny. She goes now to the Dancing-School.

For my own Part, at present, I pass my Time agreably enough. I enjoy, thro' Mercy, a tolerable Share of Health. I read a great deal, ride a little, do a little Business for myself, more for others, retire when I can, and go into Company when I please; so the Years roll round, and the last will come; when I would rather have it said, *He lived Usefully,* than *He died Rich.*

Cousins Josiah and Sally are well, and I believe will do well, for they are an industrious saving young Couple; but they want a little more Stock to go on smoothly with their Business.

My Love to Brother and Sister Mecom, and their Children, and to all my Relations in general. I am your dutiful Son,

B. FRANKLIN

THE WAY TO WEALTH

COURTEOUS READER,

I have heard that nothing gives an Author so great Pleasure, as to find his Works respectfully quoted by other learned Authors. This Pleasure I have seldom enjoyed; for tho' I have been, if I may say it without Vanity, an *eminent Author* of Almanacks annually now a full Quarter of a Century, my Brother Authors in the same Way, for what Reason I know not, have ever been very sparing in their Applauses; and no other Author has taken the least Notice of me, so that did not my Writings produce me some solid *Pudding,* the great Deficiency of *Praise* would have quite discouraged me.

I concluded at length, that the People were the best Judges of my Merit; for they buy my Works; and besides, in my Rambles, where I am not personally known, I have frequently heard one or other of my Adages repeated, with, *as Poor Richard says,* at the End on't; this gave me some Satisfaction, as it showed not only that my Instructions were regarded, but discovered likewise some Respect for my Authority; and I own, that to encourage the Practice of remembering and repeating those wise Sentences, I have sometimes *quoted myself* with great Gravity.

Judge then how much I must have been gratified by an Incident I am going to relate to you. I stopt my Horse lately where a great Number of People were collected at a Vendue of Merchant Goods. The Hour of Sale not being come, they were conversing on the Badness of the Times, and one of the Company call'd to a plain clean old Man, with white Locks, *Pray, Father* Abraham, *what think you of the Times? Won't these heavy Taxes quite ruin the Country? How shall we ever be able to pay them? What would you advise us to?*——Father *Abraham* stood up, and reply'd, if you'd have my Advice, I'll give it you in short, for a *Word to the Wise is enough,* and *many Words won't fill a Bushel,* as *Poor Richard says.* They join'd in desiring him to speak his Mind, and gathering round him, he proceeded as follows;

"Friends, says he, and Neighbours, the Taxes are indeed very heavy, and if those laid on by the Government were the only Ones we had to pay, we might more easily discharge them; but we have many others, and much more grievous to some of us. We are taxed twice as much by our *Idleness,* three times as much by our *Pride,* and four times as much by our *Folly,* and from these Taxes the Commissioners cannot ease or deliver us by allowing an Abatement. However let us hearken to good Advice, and something may be done for us; *God helps them that help themselves,* as *Poor Richard* says, in his Almanack of 1733.

It would be thought a hard Government that should tax its People one tenth Part of their *Time,* to be employed in its Service. But *Idleness* taxes many of us much more, if we reckon all that is spent in absolute *Sloth,* or doing of nothing, with that which is spent in idle Employments or Amusements, that amount to nothing. *Sloth,* by bringing on Diseases, absolutely shortens Life. *Sloth, like Rust, consumes faster than Labour wears, while the used Key is always bright,* as *Poor Richard* says. But *dost thou love Life, then do not squander Time, for that's the Stuff Life is made of,* as *Poor Richard* says.—How much more than is necessary do we spend in Sleep! forgetting that *The sleeping Fox catches no Poultry,* and that *there will be sleeping enough in the Grave,* as *Poor Richard* says. If Time be of all Things the most precious, *wasting Time* must be, as *Poor Richard* says, *the greatest Prodigality,* since, as he elsewhere tells us, *Lost Time is never found again;* and what we call *Time-enough always proves little enough:* Let us then up and be doing, and doing to the Purpose; so by Diligence shall we do more with less Perplexity. *Sloth makes all Things difficult, but Industry all easy,* as *Poor Richard* says; and *He that riseth late, must trot all Day, and shall scarce overtake his Business at Night.* While *Laziness travels so slowly, that Poverty soon overtakes him,* as we read in *Poor Richard,* who adds, *Drive thy Business, let not that drive thee;* and *Early to Bed, and early to rise, makes a Man healthy, wealthy and wise.*

So what signifies *wishing* and *hoping* for better Times. We may make these Times better if we bestir ourselves. *Industry need not wish,* as *Poor Richard* says, and *He that lives upon Hope will die fasting. There are no Gains, without Pains;* then *Help Hands, for I have no Lands,* or if I have, they are smartly taxed. And, as *Poor Richard* likewise observes, *He that hath a Trade hath an Estate,* and *He that hath a Calling, hath an Office of Profit and*

Honour; but then the *Trade* must be worked at, and the *Calling* well followed, or neither the *Estate,* nor the *Office,* will enable us to pay our Taxes.—If we are industrious we shall never starve; for, as *Poor Richard* says, *At the working Man's House* Hunger *looks in, but dares not enter.* Nor will the Bailiff or the Constable enter, for *Industry pays Debts, while Despair encreaseth them,* says *Poor Richard.*—What though you have found no Treasure, nor has any rich Relation left you a Legacy, *Diligence is the Mother of Good luck,* as *Poor Richard* says, *and God gives all Things to Industry.* Then *plough deep, while Sluggards sleep, and you shall have Corn to sell and to keep,* says *Poor Dick.* Work while it is called To-day, for you know not how much you may be hindered To-morrow, which makes *Poor Richard* say, *One To-day is worth two To-morrows;* and farther, *Have you somewhat to do To-morrow, do it To-day.* If you were a Servant, would you not be ashamed that a good Master should catch you idle? Are you then your own Master, *be ashamed to catch yourself idle,* as *Poor Dick* says. When there is so much to be done for yourself, your Family, your Country, and your gracious King, be up by Peep of Day; *Let not the Sun look down and say, Inglorious here he lies.* Handle your Tools without Mittens; remember that *the Cat in Gloves catches no Mice,* as *Poor Richard* says. 'Tis true there is much to be done, and perhaps you are weak handed, but stick to it steadily, and you will see great Effects, for *constant Dropping wears away Stones,* and by *Diligence and Patience the Mouse ate in two the Cable;* and *little Strokes fell great Oaks,* as *Poor Richard* says in his Almanack, the Year I cannot just now remember.

Methinks I hear some of you say, *Must a Man afford himself no Leisure?*—I will tell thee, my Friend, what *Poor Richard* says, *Employ thy Time well if thou meanest to gain Leisure; and since thou art not sure of a Minute, throw not away an Hour.* Leisure, is Time for doing something useful; this Leisure the diligent Man will obtain, but the lazy Man never; so that, as *Poor Richard* says, a *Life of Leisure and a Life of Laziness are two Things.* Do you imagine that Sloth will afford you more Comfort than

Labour? No, for as *Poor Richard* says, *Trouble springs from Idleness, and grievous Toil from needless Ease. Many without Labour, would live by their* WITS *only, but they break for want of Stock.* Whereas Industry gives Comfort, and Plenty, and Respect: *Fly Pleasures, and they'll follow you. The diligent Spinner has a large Shift;* and *now I have a Sheep and a Cow, every Body bids me Good morrow;* all which is well said by *Poor Richard.*

But with our Industry, we must likewise be *steady, settled* and *careful,* and oversee our own Affairs *with our own Eyes,* and not trust too much to others; for, as *Poor Richard* says,

> *I never saw an oft removed Tree,*
> *Nor yet an oft removed Family,*
> *That throve so well as those that settled be.*

And again,*Three Removes is as bad as a Fire;* and again, *Keep thy Shop, and thy Shop will keep thee;* and again, *If you would have your Business done, go; If not, send.* And again,

> *He that by the Plough would thrive,*
> *Himself must either hold or drive.*

And again, *The Eye of a Master will do more Work than both his Hands;* and again, *Want of Care does us more Damage than Want of Knowledge;* and again, *Not to oversee Workmen, is to leave them your Purse open.* Trusting too much to others Care is the Ruin of many; for, as the *Almanack* says, *In the Affairs of this World, Men are saved, not by Faith, but by the Want of it;* but a Man's own Care is profitable; for, saith *Poor Dick, Learning is to the Studious,* and *Riches to the Careful,* as well as *Power to the Bold,* and *Heaven to the Virtuous.* And farther, *If you would have a faithful Servant, and one that you like, serve yourself.* And again, he adviseth to Circumspection and Care, even in the smallest Matters, because sometimes *a little Neglect may breed great Mischief;* adding, *For want of a Nail the Shoe was lost; for want of a Shoe the Horse was lost; and for want of a Horse the Rider was lost,* being overtaken and slain by the Enemy, all for want of Care about a Horse shoe Nail.

So much for Industry, my Friends, and Attention to one's own Business; but to these we must add *Frugality,* if we would make our *Industry* more certainly successful. A Man may, if he knows not how to save as he gets, *keep his Nose all his Life to the Grindstone,* and die not worth a *Groat* at last. *A fat Kitchen makes a lean Will,* as *Poor Richard* says; and,

> *Many Estates are spent in the Getting,*
> *Since Women for Tea forsook Spinning and Knitting,*
> *And Men for Punch forsook Hewing and Splitting.*

If you would be wealthy, says he, in another Almanack, *think of Saving as well as of Getting: The* Indies *have not made* Spain *rich, because her* Outgoes *are greater than her* Incomes. Away then with your expensive Follies, and you will not have so much Cause to complain of hard Times, heavy Taxes, and chargeable Families; for, as *Poor Dick* says,

> *Women and Wine, Game and Deceit,*
> *Make the Wealth small, and the Wants great.*

And farther, *What maintains one Vice, would bring up two Children.* You may think perhaps, That a *little* Tea, or a *little* Punch now and then, Diet a *little* more costly, Clothes a *little* finer, and a *little* Entertainment now and then, can be no *great* Matter; but remember what *Poor Richard* says, *Many* a Little *makes a Mickle;* and farther, *Beware of little Expences; a small Leak will sink a great Ship;* and again, *Who Dainties love, shall Beggars prove;* and moreover, *Fools make Feasts, and wise Men eat them.*

Here you are all got together at this Vendue of *Fineries* and *Knicknacks.* You call them *Goods,* but if you do not take Care, they will prove *Evils* to some of you. You expect they will be sold *cheap,* and perhaps they may for less than they cost; but if you have no Occasion for them, they must be *dear* to you. Remember what *Poor Richard* says, *Buy what thou hast no Need of, and ere long thou shalt sell thy Necessaries*. And again, *At a great Pennyworth pause a while:* He means, that perhaps the Cheapness is *apparent* only, and not *real;* or the Bargain, by straitning thee in thy Business, may do thee more Harm than Good. For in another Place he says, *Many have been ruined by buying good Pennyworths*. Again, *Poor Richard* says, *'Tis foolish to lay out Money in a Purchase of Repentance;* and yet this Folly is practised every Day at Vendues, for want of minding the Almanack. *Wise Men,* as *Poor Dick* says, *learn by others Harms, Fools scarcely by their own;* but *Felix quem faciunt aliena Pericula cautum.*[1] Many a one, for the Sake of Finery on the Back, have gone with a hungry Belly, and half starved their Families; *Silks and Sattins, Scarlet and Velvets,* as *Poor Richard* says, *put out the Kitchen Fire.* These are not the *Necessaries* of Life; they can scarcely be called the *Conveniencies,* and yet only because they look pretty, how many *want* to *have* them. The *artificial* Wants of Mankind thus become more numerous than the *natural;* and, as *Poor Dick* says, *For one* poor *Person, there are an hundred* indigent. By these, and other Extravagancies, the Genteel are reduced to Poverty, and forced to borrow of those whom they formerly despised, but who through *Industry* and *Frugality* have maintained their Standing; in which Case it appears plainly, that a *Ploughman on his Legs is higher than a Gentleman on his Knees, as Poor Richard* says. Perhaps they have had a small Estate left them which they knew not the Getting of; they think *'tis Day, and will never be Night;* that a little to be spent out of *so much,* is not worth minding; (*a Child and a Fool,* as *Poor Richard* says, *imagine* Twenty Shillings *and Twenty Years can never be spent*) but, *always taking out of, the Meal-tub, and never putting in, soon comes to the Bottom;* then, as *Poor Dick* says, *When the Well's dry, they know the Worth of Water.* But this they might have known before, if they had taken his Advice; *If you would know the Value of Money, go and try to borrow some;*

---
[1] "Happy is he whom other people's dangers make cautious."

for, *he that goes a borrowing goes a sorrowing;* and indeed so does he that lends to such People, when he goes *to get it in again.—Poor Dick* farther advises, and says,

> *Fond* Pride of Dress *is sure a very Curse;*
> *E'er* Fancy *you consult, consult your Purse.*

And again, *Pride is as loud a Beggar as Want, and a great deal more saucy.* When you have bought one fine Thing you must buy ten more, that your Appearance may be all of a Piece; but *Poor Dick* says, *'Tis easier to suppress the first Desire, than to satisfy all that follow it.* And 'tis as truly Folly for the Poor to ape the Rich, as for the Frog to swell, in order to equal the Ox.

> *Great Estates may venture more,*
> *But little Boats should keep near Shore.*

'Tis however a Folly soon punished; for *Pride that dines on Vanity sups on Contempt,* as *Poor Richard* says. And in another Place, *Pride breakfasted with Plenty, dined with Poverty, and supped with Infamy.* And after all, of what Use is this *Pride of Appearance,* for which so much is risked, so much is suffered? It cannot promote Health, or ease Pain; it makes no Increase of Merit in the Person, it creates Envy, it hastens Misfortune.

> *What is a Butterfly? At best*
> *He's but a Caterpillar drest.*
> *The gaudy Fop's his Picture just,*

as *Poor Richard* says.

But what Madness must it be to *run in Debt* for these Superfluities! We are offered, by the Terms of this Vendue, *Six Months Credit;* and that perhaps has induced some of us to attend it, because we cannot spare the ready Money, and hope now to be fine without it. But, ah, think what you do when you run in Debt;

You give to another, Power over your Liberty. If you cannot pay at the Time, you will be ashamed to see your Creditor; you will be in Fear when you speak to him; you will make poor pitiful sneaking Excuses, and by Degrees come to lose your Varacity, and sink into base downright lying; for, as *Poor Richard* says, *The second Vice is Lying, the first is running in Debt.* And again, to the same Purpose, *Lying rides upon Debt's Back.* Whereas a freeborn *Englishman* ought not to be ashamed or afraid to see or speak to any Man living. But Poverty often deprives a Man of all Spirit and Virtue: *'Tis hard for an empty Bag to stand upright,* as *Poor Richard* truly says. What would you think of that Prince, or that Government, who should issue an Edict forbidding you to dress like a Gentleman or a Gentlewoman, on Pain of Imprisonment or Servitude? Would you not say, that you are free, have a Right to dress as you please, and that such an Edict would be a Breach of your Privileges, and such a Government tyrannical? And yet you are about to put yourself under that Tyranny when you run in Debt for such Dress! Your Creditor has Authority at his Pleasure to deprive you of your Liberty, by confining you in Goal [sic] for Life, or to sell you for a Servant, if you should not be able to pay him! When you have got your Bargain, you may, perhaps, think little of Payment; but *Creditors, Poor Richard* tells us, *have better Memories than Debtors;* and in another Place says, *Creditors are a superstitious Sect, great Observers of set Days and Times.* The Day comes round before you are aware, and the Demand is made before you are prepared to satisfy it. Or if you bear your Debt in Mind, the Term which at first seemed so long, will, as it lessens, appear extreamly short. *Time* will seem to have added Wings to his Heels as well as Shoulders. *Those have a short Lent,* saith *Poor Richard, who owe Money to be paid at Easter.* Then since, as he says, *The Borrower is a Slave to the Lender, and the Debtor to the Creditor,* disdain the Chain, preserve your Freedom; and maintain your Independency: Be *industrious* and *free;* be *frugal* and *free.* At present, perhaps, you may think yourself in thriving Circumstances, and that you can bear a little Extravagance without Injury; but,

For Age and Want, save while you may;
No Morning Sun lasts a whole Day,

as *Poor Richard* says—Gain may be temporary and uncertain, but ever while you live, Expence is constant and certain; and *'tis easier to build two Chimnies than to keep one in Fuel,* as *Poor Richard* says. So *rather go to Bed supperless than rise in Debt.*

Get what you can, and what you get hold;
'Tis the Stone that will turn all your Lead into Gold,

as *Poor Richard* says. And when you have got the Philosopher's Stone, sure you will no longer complain of bad Times, or the Difficulty of paying Taxes.

This Doctrine, my Friends, is *Reason* and *Wisdom;* but after all, do not depend too much upon your own *Industry,* and *Frugality,* and *Prudence,* though excellent Things, for they may all be blasted without the Blessing of Heaven; and therefore ask that Blessing humbly, and be not uncharitable to those that at present seem to want it, but comfort and help them. Remember *Job* suffered, and was afterwards prosperous.

And now to conclude, *Experience keeps a dear School, but Fools will learn in no other, and scarce in that;* for it is true, *we may give Advice, but we cannot give Conduct,* as *Poor Richard* says: However, remember this, *They that won't be counselled, can't be helped,* as *Poor Richard* says: And farther, That *if you will not hear Reason, she'll surely rap your Knuckles.*

Thus the old Gentleman ended his Harangue. The People heard it, and approved the Doctrine and immediately practised the contrary, just as if it had been a common Sermon; for the Vendue opened, and they began to buy extravagantly, notwithstanding all his Cautions, and their own Fear of Taxes.—I found the good Man had thoroughly studied my Almanacks, and digested all I had dropt on those Topicks during the Course of Five-and-twenty Years. The frequent Mention he made of me must have tired any one else, but my Vanity was wonderfully delighted with it, though I was conscious that not a tenth Part of the Wisdom was my own which he ascribed to me, but rather the *Gleanings* I had made of the Sense of all Ages and Nations. However, I resolved to be the better for the Echo of it; and though I had at first determined to buy Stuff for a new Coat, I went away resolved to wear my old One a little longer. *Reader,* if thou wilt do the same, thy Profit will be as great as mine.

I am, as ever,
Thine to serve thee,

July 7, 1757. RICHARD SAUNDERS.

TO MISS MARY STEVENSON

Craven Street, June 11, 1760.

DEAR POLLY:

'Tis a very sensible Question you ask, how the Air can affect the Barometer, when its Opening appears covered with Wood? If indeed it was so closely covered as to admit of no Communication of the outward Air to the Surface of the Mercury, the Change of Weight in the Air could not possibly affect it. But the least Crevice is sufficient for the Purpose; a Pinhole will do the Business. And if you could look behind the Frame to which your Barometer is fixed, you would certainly find some small Opening.

There are indeed some Barometers in which the Body of Mercury at the lower End is contain'd in a close Leather Bag, and so the Air cannot come into immediate Contact with the Mercury; yet the same Effect is produc'd. For, the Leather being flexible, when the Bag is press'd by any additional Weight of Air, it contracts, and the Mercury is forced up into the Tube; when the Air becomes lighter, and its Pressure less, the Weight of the Mercury prevails, and it descends again into the Bag.

Your Observation on what you have lately read concerning Insects is very just and solid. Superficial Minds are apt to despise those who make that Part of the Creation their Study, as mere Triflers; but certainly the World has been much oblig'd to them. Under the Care and Management of Man, the Labours of the little Silkworm afford Employment and Subsistence to Thousands of Families, and become an immense Article of Commerce. The Bee, too, yields us its delicious Honey, and its Wax useful to a Multitude of Purposes. Another Insect, it is said, produces the Cochineal, from whence we have our rich Scarlet Dye. The Usefulness of the Cantharides, or Spanish Flies, in Medicine, is known to all, and Thousands owe their Lives to that Knowledge. By human Industry and Observation, other Properties of other Insects may possibly be hereafter discovered, and of equal Utility. A thorough Acquaintance with the Nature of these little Creatures may also enable Mankind to prevent the Increase of such as are noxious, or secure us against the Mischiefs they occasion. These Things doubtless your Books make mention of: I can only add a particular late Instance which I had from a Swedish Gentleman of good Credit. In the green Timber, intended for Shipbuilding at the King's Yards in that Country, a kind of Worms were found, which every year became more numerous and more pernicious, so that the Ships were greatly damag'd before they came into Use. The King sent Linnæus, the great Naturalist, from Stockholm, to enquire into the Affair, and see if the Mischief was capable of any Remedy. He found, on Examination, that the Worm was produced from a small Egg, deposited in the little Roughnesses on the Surface of the Wood, by a particular kind of Fly or Beetle; from whence the Worm, as soon as it was hatched, began to eat into the Substance of the Wood, and after some time came out again a Fly of the Parent kind, and so the Species increased. The season in which this Fly laid its Eggs, Linnæus knew to be about a Fortnight (I think) in the Month of May, and at no other time of the Year. He therefore advis'd, that, some Days before that Season, all the green Timber should be thrown into the Water, and kept under Water till the Season was over. Which being done by the King's Order, the Flies missing their usual Nest, could not increase; and the Species was either destroy'd or went elsewhere; and the Wood was effectually preserved; for, after the first Year, it became too dry and hard for their purpose.

There is, however, a prudent Moderation to be used in Studies of this kind. The Knowledge of Nature may be ornamental, and it may be useful; but if, to attain an Eminence in that, we neglect the Knowledge and Practice of essential Duties, we deserve Reprehension. For there is no Rank in Natural Knowledge of equal Dignity and Importance with that of being a good Parent, a good Child, a good Subject or Citizen, that is, in short, a good Christian. Nicholas Gimcrack, therefore, who neglected the Care of his Family, to pursue Butterflies, was a just Object of Ridicule, and we must give him up as fair Game to the satyrist.

Adieu, my dear Friend, and believe me ever

Yours affectionately,

B. FRANKLIN.

TO PETER COLLINSON

Oct. 19, 1752.

SIR,

As frequent mention is made in public papers from *Europe* of the success of the *Philadelphia* experiment for drawing the electric fire from clouds by means of pointed rods of iron erected on high buildings, &c., it may be agreeable to the curious to be informed, that the same experiment has succeeded in *Philadelphia*, though made in a different and more easy manner, which is as follows:

Make a small cross of two light strips of cedar, the arms so long as to reach to the four corners of a large thin silk handkerchief when extended; tie the corners of the handkerchief to the extremities of the cross, so you have the body of a kite; which being properly accommodated with a tail, loop, and string, will rise in the air, like those made of paper; but this being made of silk, is fitter to bear the wet and wind of a thunder-gust without tearing. To the top of the upright stick of the cross is to be fixed a very sharp-pointed wire, rising a foot or more above the wood. To the end of the twine, next the hand, is to be tied a silk ribbon, and where the silk and twine join, a key may be fastened. This kite is to be raised when a thunder-gust appears to be coming on, and the person who holds the string must stand within a door or window, or under some cover, so that the silk ribbon may not be wet; and care must be taken that the twine does not touch the frame of the door or window. As soon as any of the thunderclouds come over the kite, the pointed wire will draw the electric fire from them, and the kite, with all the twine, will be electrified, and the loose filaments of the twine will stand out every way, and be attracted by an approaching finger. And when the rain has wet the kite and twine, so that it can conduct the electric fire freely, you will find it stream out plentifully from the key on the approach of your knuckle. At this key the phial may be charged; and from electric fire thus obtained, spirits may be kindled, and all other electric experiments be performed, which are usually done by the help of a rubbed glass globe or tube, and thereby the sameness of the electric matter with that of lighting completely demonstrated.

B. FRANKLIN

TO JOSEPH PRIESTLEY

Passy, February 8, 1780.

DEAR SIR,

Your kind Letter of September 27 came to hand but very lately, the Bearer having staied long in Holland. I always rejoice to hear of your being still employ'd in experimental Researches into Nature, and of the Success you meet with. The rapid Progress *true* Science now makes, occasions my regretting sometimes that I was born so soon. It is impossible to imagine the Height to which may be carried, in a thousand years, the Power of Man over Matter. We may perhaps learn to deprive large Masses of their Gravity, and give them absolute Levity, for the sake of easy Transport. Agriculture may diminish its Labour and double its Produce; all Diseases may by sure means be prevented or cured, not expecting even that of Old Age, and our Lives lengthened at pleasure even beyond the antediluvian Standard. O that moral Science were in as fair a way of Improvement, that Men would cease to be Wolves to one another, and that human Beings would at length learn what they now improperly call Humanity!

I am glad my little Paper on the *Aurora Borealis* pleased. If it should occasion further Enquiry, and so produce a better Hypothesis, it will not be wholly useless. I am ever, with the greatest and most sincere Esteem, dear Sir, yours very affectionately

B. FRANKLIN.

AN EDICT BY THE KING OF PRUSSIA

Dantzic, September 5, 1773.

We have long wondered here at the supineness of the English nation, under the Prussian impositions upon its trade entering our port. We did not, till lately, know the claims, ancient and modern, that hang over that nation; and therefore could not suspect that it might submit to those impositions from a sense of duty or from principles of equity. The following Edict, just made publick, may, if serious, throw some light upon this matter.

"FREDERIC, by the grace of God, King of Prussia, &c. &c. &c., to all present and to come, (*à tous présens et á venir,*) Health. The peace now enjoyed throughout our dominions, having afforded us leisure to apply ourselves to the regulation of commerce, the improvement of our finances, and at the same time the easing our domestic subjects in their taxes: For these causes, and other good considerations us thereunto moving, we hereby make known, that, after having deliberated these affairs in our council, present our dear brothers, and other great officers of the state, members of the same, we, of our certain knowledge, full power, and authority royal, have made and issued this present Edict, viz.

"Whereas it is well known to all the world, that the first German settlements made in the Island of Britain, were by colonies of people, subject to our renowned ducal ancestors, and drawn from their dominions, under the conduct of Hengist, Horsa, Hella, Uff, Cerdicus, Ida, and others; and that the said colonies have flourished under the protection of our august house for ages past; have never been emancipated therefrom; and yet have hitherto yielded little profit to the same: And whereas we ourself have in the last war fought for and defended the said colonies, against the power of France, and thereby enabled them to make conquests from the said power in America, for which we have not yet received adequate compensation: And whereas it is just and expedient that a revenue should be raised from the said colonies in Britain, towards our indemnification; and that those who are descendants of our ancient subjects, and thence still owe us due obedience, should contribute to the replenishing of our royal coffers as they must have done, had their ancestors remained in the territories now to us appertaining: We do therefore hereby ordain and command, that, from and after the date of these presents, there shall be levied and paid to our officers of the *customs,* on all goods, wares, and merchandizes, and on all grain and other produce of the earth, exported from the said Island of Britain, and on all goods of whatever kind imported into the same, a duty of four and a half per cent *ad valorem,* for the use of us and our successors. And that the said duty may more effectually be collected, we do hereby ordain, that all ships or vessels bound from Great Britain to any other part of the world, or from any other part of the world to Great Britain, shall in their respective voyages touch at our port of Koningsberg, there to be unladen, searched, and charged with the said duties.

"And whereas there hath been from time to time discovered in the said island of Great Britain, by our colonists there, many mines or beds of iron-stone; and sundry subjects, of our ancient dominion, skilful in converting the said stone into metal, have in time past transported themselves thither, carrying with them and communicating that art; and the inhabitants of the said island, presuming that they had a natural right to make the best use they could of the natural productions of their country for their own benefit, have not only built furnaces for smelting the said stone into iron, but have erected plating-forges, slitting-mills, and steel-furnaces, for the more convenient manufacturing of the same; thereby endangering a diminution of the said manufacture in our ancient dominion;—we do therefore hereby farther ordain, that, from and after the date hereof, no mill or other engine for slitting or rolling of iron, or any plating-forge to work with a tilt-hammer, or any furnace for making steel, shall be erected or continued in the said island of Great Britain: And the Lord Lieutenant of every county in the said island is hereby commanded, on information of any such erection within his county, to order and by force to cause the same to be abated and destroyed; as he shall answer the neglect thereof to us at his peril. But we are nevertheless graciously pleased to permit the inhabitants of the said island to transport their iron into Prussia, there to be manufactured, and to them returned; they paying our Prussian subjects for the workmanship, with all the costs of commission, freight, and risk, coming and returning; any thing herein contained to the contrary notwithstanding.

"We do not, however, think fit to extend this our indulgence to the article of wool; but, meaning to encourage, not only the manufacturing of woollen cloth, but also the raising of wool, in our ancient dominions, and to prevent both, as much as may be, in our said island, we do hereby absolutely forbid the transportation of wool from thence, even to the mother country, Prussia; and that those islanders may be farther and more effectually restrained in making any advantage of their own wool in the way of manufacture, we command that none shall be carried out of one country into another; nor shall any worsted, bay, or woollen yarn, cloth, says, bays, kerseys, serges, frizes, druggets, cloth-serges, shalloons, or any other drapery stuffs, or woollen manufactures whatsoever, made up or mixed with wool in any of the said counties, be carried into any other county, or be water-borne even across the smallest river or creek, on penalty of forfeiture of the same, together with the boats, carriages, horses, &c., that shall be employed in removing them. Nevertheless, our loving subjects there are hereby permitted (if they think proper) to use all their wool as manure for the improvement of their lands.

"And whereas the art and mystery of making hats hath arrived at great perfection in Prussia, and the making of hats by our remoter subjects ought to be as much as possible restrained: And forasmuch as the islanders before mentioned, being in possession of wool, beaver and other furs, have presumptuously conceived they had a right to make some advantage thereof, by manufacturing the same into hats, to the prejudice of our domestic manufacture: We do therefore hereby strictly command and ordain, that no hats or felts whatsoever, dyed or undyed, finished or unfinished, shall be loaded or put into or upon any vessel, cart, carriage, or horse, to be transported or conveyed out of one county in the said island into another county, or to any other place whatsoever, by any person or persons whatsoever; on pain of forfeiting the same, with a penalty of five hundred pounds sterling for every offence. Nor shall any hat-maker, in any of the said counties, employ more than two apprentices, on penalty of five pounds sterling per month; we intending hereby, that such hatmakers, being so restrained, both in the production and sale of their commodity, may find no advantage in continuing their business. But, lest the said islanders should suffer inconveniency by the want of hats, we are farther graciously pleased to permit them to send their beaver furs to Prussia; and we also permit hats made thereof to be exported from Prussia to Britain; the people thus favoured to pay all costs and charges of manufacturing, interest, commission to our merchants, insurance and freight going and returning, as in the case of iron.

"And, lastly, being willing farther to favour our said colonies in Britain, we do hereby also ordain and command, that all the *thieves,* highway and street robbers, house-breakers, forgerers, murderers, s—d—tes, and villains of every denomination, who have forfeited their lives to the law in Prussia; but whom we, in our great clemency, do not think fit here to hang, shall be emptied out of our gaols into the said island of Great Britain, for the better peopling of that country.

"We flatter ourselves, that these our royal regulations and commands will be thought just and reasonable by our much-favoured colonists in England; the said regulations being copied from their statutes of 10 and 11 William III. c. 10, 5 Geo. II. c. 22, 23, Geo. II. c. 29, 4 Geo. I. c. 11, and from other equitable laws made by their parliaments; or from instructions given by their Princes; or from resolutions of both Houses, entered into for the good government of their *own colonies in Ireland and America.*

"And all persons in the said island are hereby cautioned not to oppose in any wise the execution of this our Edict, or any part thereof, such opposition being high treason; of which all who are suspected shall be transported in fetters from Britain to Prussia, there to be tried and executed according to the Prussian law.

"Such is our pleasure.

"Given at Potsdam, this twenty-fifth day of the month of August, one thousand seven hundred and seventy-three, and in the thirty-third year of our reign.

"By the King, in his Council.

"RECHTMAESSIG, *Sec.*"

Some take this Edict to be merely one of the King's *Jeux d'Esprit:* others suppose it serious, and that he means a quarrel with England; but all here think the assertion it concludes with, "that these regulations are copied from acts of the English parliament respecting their colonies," a very injurious one; it being impossible to believe, that a people distinguished for their love of liberty, a nation so wise, so liberal in its sentiments, so just and equitable towards its neighbours, should, from mean and injudicious views of petty immediate profit, treat its own children in a manner so arbitrary and tyrannical!

THE SALE OF THE HESSIANS

FROM THE COUNT DE SCHAUMBERGH TO THE BARON HOHENDORF, COMMANDING THE HESSIAN TROOPS IN AMERICA

Rome, February 18, 1777.

MONSIEUR LE BARON:—

On my return from Naples, I received at Rome your letter of the 27th December of last year. I have learned with unspeakable pleasure the courage our troops exhibited at Trenton, and you cannot imagine my joy on being told that of the 1,950 Hessians engaged in the fight, but 345 escaped. There were just 1,605 men killed, and I cannot sufficiently commend your prudence in sending an exact list of the dead to my minister in London. This precaution was the more necessary, as the report sent to the English ministry does not give but 1,455 dead. This would make 483,450 florins instead of 643,500 which I am entitled to demand under our convention. You will comprehend the prejudice which such an error would work in my finances, and I do not doubt you will take the necessary pains to prove that Lord North's list is false and yours correct.

The court of London objects that there were a hundred wounded who ought not to be included in the list, nor paid for as dead; but I trust you will not overlook my instructions to you on quitting Cassel, and that you will not have tried by human succor to recall the life of the unfortunates whose days could not be lengthened but by the loss of a leg or an arm. That would be making them a pernicious present, and I am sure they would rather die than live in a condition no longer fit for my service. I do not mean by this that you should assassinate them; we should be humane, my dear Baron, but you may insinuate to the surgeons with entire propriety that a crippled man is a reproach to their profession, and that there is no wiser course than to let every one of them die when he ceases to be fit to fight.

I am about to send to you some new recruits. Don't economize them. Remember glory before all things. Glory is true wealth. There is nothing degrades the soldier like the love of money. He must care only for honour and reputation, but this reputation must be acquired in the midst of dangers. A battle gained without costing the conqueror any blood is an inglorious success, while the conquered cover themselves with glory by perishing with their arms in their hands. Do you remember that of the 300 Lacedæmonians who defended the defile of Thermopylæ, not one returned? How happy should I be could I say the same of my brave Hessians!

It is true that their king, Leonidas, perished with them: but things have changed, and it is no longer the custom for princes of the empire to go and fight in America for a cause with which they have no concern. And besides, to whom should they pay the thirty guineas per man if I did not stay in Europe to receive them? Then, it is necessary also that I be ready to send recruits to replace the men you lose. For this purpose I must return to Hesse. It is true, grown men are becoming scarce there, but I will send you boys. Besides, the scarcer the commodity the higher the price. I am assured that the women and little girls have begun to till our lands, and they get on not badly. You did right to send back to Europe that Dr. Crumerus who was so successful in curing dysentery. Don't bother with a man who is subject to looseness of the bowels. That disease makes bad soldiers. One coward will do more mischief in an engagement than ten brave men will do good. Better that they burst in their barracks than fly in a battle, and tarnish the glory of our arms. Besides, you know that they pay me as killed for all who die from disease, and I don't get a farthing for runaways. My trip to Italy, which has cost me enormously, makes it desirable that there should be a great mortality among them. You will therefore promise promotion to all who expose themselves; you will exhort them to seek glory in the midst of dangers; you will say to Major Maundorff that I am not at all content with his saving the 345 men who escaped the massacre of Trenton. Through the whole campaign he has not had ten men killed in consequence of his orders. Finally, let it be your principal object to prolong the war and avoid a decisive engagement on either side, for I have made arrangements for a grand Italian opera, and I do not wish to be obliged to give it up. Meantime I pray God, my dear Baron de Hohendorf, to have you in his holy and gracious keeping.

THE EPHEMERA

AN EMBLEM OF HUMAN LIFE

1778

You may remember, my dear friend, that when we lately spent that happy day in the delightful garden and sweet society of the Moulin Joly, I stopt a little in one of our walks, and staid some time behind the company. We had been shown numberless skeletons of a kind of little fly, called an ephemera, whose successive generations, we were told, were bred and expired within the day. I happened to see a living company of them on a leaf, who appeared to be engaged in conversation. You know I understand all the inferior animal tongues: my too great application to the study of them is the best excuse I can give for the little progress I have made in your charming language. I listened through curiosity to the discourse of these little creatures; but as they, in their national vivacity, spoke three or four together, I could make but little of their conversation. I found, however, by some broken expressions that I heard now and then, they were disputing warmly on the merit of two foreign musicians, one a *cousin,* the other a *moscheto;* in which dispute they spent their time, seemingly as regardless of the shortness of life as if they had been sure of living a month. Happy people! thought I, you live certainly under a wise, just, and mild government, since you have no public grievances to complain of, nor any subject of contention but the perfections and imperfections of foreign music. I turned my head from them to an old grey-headed one, who was single on another leaf, and talking to himself. Being amused with his soliloquy, I put it down in writing, in hopes it will likewise amuse her to whom I am so much indebted for the most pleasing of all amusements, her delicious company and heavenly harmony.

"It was," said he, "the opinion of learned philosophers of our race, who lived and flourished long before my time, that this vast world, the Moulin Joly, could not itself subsist more than eighteen hours; and I think there was some foundation for that opinion, since, by the apparent motion of the great luminary that gives life to all nature, and which in my time has evidently declined considerably towards the ocean at the end of our earth, it must then finish its course, be extinguished in the waters that surround us, and leave the world in cold and darkness, necessarily producing universal death and destruction. I have lived seven of those hours, a great age, being no less than four hundred and twenty minutes of time. How very few of us continue so long! I have seen generations born, flourish, and expire. My present friends are the children and grandchildren of the friends of my youth, who are now, alas, no more! And I must soon follow them; for, by the course of nature, though still in health, I cannot expect to live above seven or eight minutes longer. What now avails all my toil and labor, in amassing honey-dew on this leaf, which I cannot live to enjoy! What the political struggles I have been engaged in, for the good of my compatriot inhabitants of this bush, or my philosophical studies for the benefit of our race in general! for, in politics, what can laws do without morals? Our present race of ephemeræ will in a course of minutes become corrupt, like those of other and older bushes, and consequently as wretched. And in philosophy how small our progress! Alas! art is long, and life is short! My friends would comfort me with the idea of a name, they say, I shall leave behind me; and they tell me I have lived long enough to nature and to glory. But what will fame be to an ephemera who no longer exists? And what will become of all history in the eighteenth hour, when the world itself, even the whole Moulin Joly, shall come to its end, and be buried in universal ruin?"

To me, after all my eager pursuits, no solid pleasures now remain, but the reflection of a long life spent in meaning well, the sensible conversation of a few good lady ephemeræ, and now and then a kind smile and a tune from the ever amiable *Brillante*.

B. FRANKLIN.

THE WHISTLE

TO MADAME BRILLON

Passy, November 10, 1779.

I received my dear friend's two letters, one for Wednesday and one for Saturday. This is again Wednesday. I do not deserve one for to-day, because I have not answered the former. But, indolent as I am, and averse to writing, the fear of having no more of your pleasing epistles, if I do not contribute to the correspondence, obliges me to take up my pen; and as Mr. B. has kindly sent me word, that he sets out to-morrow to see you, instead of spending this Wednesday evening as I have done its namesakes, in your delightful company, I sit down to spend it in thinking of you, in writing to you, and in reading over and over again your letters.

I am charmed with your description of Paradise, and with your plan of living there; and I approve much of your conclusion, that, in the mean time, we should draw all the good we can from this world. In my opinion, we might all draw more good from it than we do, and suffer less evil, if we would take care not to give too much for *whistles*. For to me it seems, that most of the unhappy people we meet with, are become so by neglect of that caution.

You ask what I mean? You love stories, and will excuse my telling one of myself.

When I was a child of seven years old, my friends, on a holiday, filled my pocket with coppers. I went directly to a shop where they sold toys for children; and, being charmed with the sound of a *whistle,* that I met by the way in the hands of another boy, I voluntarily offered and gave all my money for one. I then came home, and went whistling all over the house, much pleased with my *whistle,* but disturbing all the family. My brothers, and sisters, and cousins, understanding the bargain I had made, told me I had given four times as much for it as it was worth; put me in mind what good things I might have bought with the rest of the money; and laughed at me so much for my folly, that I cried with vexation; and the reflection gave me more chagrin than the *whistle* gave me pleasure.

This however was afterwards of use to me, the impression continuing on my mind; so that often, when I was tempted to buy some unnecessary thing, I said to myself, *Don't give too much for the whistle;* and I saved my money.

As I grew up, came into the world, and observed the actions of men, I thought I met with many, very many, who *gave too much for the whistle.*

When I saw one too ambitious of court favour, sacrificing his time in attendance on levees, his repose, his liberty, his virtue, and perhaps his friends, to attain it, I have said to myself, *This man gives too much for his whistle.*

When I saw another fond of popularity, constantly employing himself in political bustles, neglecting his own affairs, and ruining them by that neglect, *He pays, indeed,* said I, *too much for his whistle.*

If I knew a miser, who gave up every kind of comfortable living, all the pleasure of doing good to others, all the esteem of his fellow-citizens, and the joys of benevolent friendship, for the sake of accumulating wealth, *Poor man,* said I, *you pay too much for your whistle.*

When I met with a man of pleasure, sacrificing every laudable improvement of the mind, or of his fortune, to mere corporeal sensations, and ruining his health in their pursuit, *Mistaken man,* said I, *you are providing pain for yourself, instead of pleasure; you give too much for your whistle.*

If I see one fond of appearance, or fine clothes, fine houses, fine furniture, fine equipages, all above his fortune, for which he contracts debts, and ends his career in a prison, *Alas!* say I, *he has paid dear, very dear, for his whistle.*

When I see a beautiful, sweet-tempered girl married to an ill-natured brute of a husband, *What a pity,* say I, *that she should pay so much for a whistle!*

In short, I conceive that great part of the miseries of mankind are brought upon them by the false estimates they have made of the value of things, and by their *giving too much for their whistles.*

Yet I ought to have charity for these unhappy people, when I consider, that, with all this wisdom of which I am boasting, there are certain things in the world so tempting, for example, the apples of King John, which happily are not to be bought; for if they were put to sale by auction, I might very easily be led to ruin myself in the purchase, and find that I had once more given too much for the *whistle.*

Adieu, my dear friend, and believe me ever yours very sincerely and with unalterable affection,

B. FRANKLIN.

ARTICLES OF BELIEF AND ACTS OF RELIGION

> Here will I hold. If there is a Pow'r above us,
> (And that there is, all Nature cries aloud,
> Thro' all her Works) He must delight in Virtue;
> And that which he delights in must be Happy.
>
> —CATO.

Philadelphia, November 20: 1728

FIRST PRINCIPLES

I believe there is one supreme, most perfect Being, Author and Father of the Gods themselves. For I believe that Man is not the most perfect Being but one, rather that as there are many Degrees of Beings his Inferiors, so there are many Degrees of Beings superior to him.

Also, when I stretch my Imagination thro' and beyond our System of Planets, beyond the visible fix'd Stars themselves, into that Space that is every Way infinite, and conceive it fill'd with Suns like ours, each with a Chorus of Worlds forever moving round him, then this little Ball on which we move, seems, even in my narrow Imagination, to be almost Nothing, and myself less than nothing, and of no sort of Consequence.

When I think thus, I imagine it great Vanity in me to suppose, that the *Supremely Perfect* does in the least regard such an inconsiderable Nothing as Man. More especially, since it is impossible for me to have any positive clear idea of that which is infinite and incomprehensible, I cannot conceive otherwise than that he *the Infinite Father* expects or requires no Worship or Praise from us, but that he is even infinitely above it.

But, since there is in all Men something like a natural principle, which inclines them to DEVOTION, or the Worship of some unseen Power;

And since Men are endued with Reason superior to all other Animals, that we are in our World acquainted with;

Therefore I think it seems required of me, and my Duty as a Man, to pay Divine Regards to SOMETHING.

I conceive then, that the INFINITE has created many beings or Gods, vastly superior to Man, who can better conceive his Perfections than we, and return him a more rational and glorious Praise.

As, among Men, the Praise of the Ignorant or of Children is not regarded by the ingenious Painter or Architect, who is rather honour'd and pleas'd with the approbation of Wise Men & Artists.

It may be that these created Gods are immortal; or it may be that after many Ages, they are changed, and others Supply their Places.

Howbeit, I conceive that each of these is exceeding wise and good, and very powerful; and that Each has made for himself one glorious Sun, attended with a beautiful and admirable System of Planets.

It is that particular Wise and good God, who is the author and owner of our System, that I propose for the object of my praise and adoration.

For I conceive that he has in himself some of those Passions he has planted in us, and that, since he has given us Reason whereby we are capable of observing his Wisdom in the Creation, he is not above caring for us, being pleas'd with our Praise, and offended when we slight Him, or neglect his Glory.

I conceive for many Reasons, that he is a *good Being;* and as I should be happy to have so wise, good, and powerful a Being my Friend, let me consider in what manner I shall make myself most acceptable to him.

Next to the Praise resulting from and due to his Wisdom, I believe he is pleas'd and delights in the Happiness of those he has created; and since without Virtue Man can have no Happiness in this World, I firmly believe he delights to see me Virtuous, because he is pleased when he sees Me Happy.

And since he has created many Things, which seem purely design'd for the Delight of Man, I believe he is not offended, when he sees his Children solace themselves in any manner of pleasant exercises and Innocent Delights; and I think no Pleasure innocent, that is to Man hurtful.

I *love* him therefore for his Goodness, and I *adore* him for his Wisdom.

Let me then not fail to praise my God continually, for it is his Due, and it is all I can return for his many Favours and great Goodness to me; and let me resolve to be virtuous, that I may be happy, that I may please Him, who is delighted to see me happy. Amen!

ADORATION

PREL. Being mindful that before I address the Deity, my soul ought to be calm and serene, free from Passion and Perturbation, or otherwise elevated with Rational Joy and Pleasure, I ought to use a Countenance that expresses a filial Respect, mixed wth a kind of Smiling, that Signifies inward Joy, and Satisfaction, and Admiration.

O wise God, my good Father!

Thou beholdest the sincerity of my Heart and of my Devotion; Grant me a Continuance of thy Favour!

1. O Creator, O Father! I believe that thou art Good, and that thou are *pleas'd with the pleasure* of thy children.—Praised be thy name for Ever!

2. By thy Power hast thou made the glorious Sun, with his attending Worlds; from the energy of thy mighty Will, they first received [their prodigious] motion, and by thy Wisdom hast thou prescribed the wondrous Laws, by which they move. —Praised be thy name for Ever!

3. By thy Wisdom hast thou formed all Things. Thou hast created Man, bestowing Life and Reason, and placed him in Dignity superior to thy other earthly Creatures.—Praised be thy name for Ever!

4. Thy Wisdom, thy Power, and thy Goodness are everywhere

clearly seen; in the air and in the water, in the Heaven and on the Earth; Thou providest for the various winged Fowl, and the innumerable Inhabitants of the Water; thou givest Cold and Heat, Rain and Sunshine, in their Season, & to the Fruits of the Earth Increase.—Praised be thy name for Ever!

5. Thou abhorrest in thy Creatures Treachery and Deceit, Malice, Revenge, [*Intemperance,*] and every other hurtful Vice; but Thou art a Lover of Justice and Sincerity, of Friendship and Benevolence, and every Virtue. Thou art my Friend, my Father, and my Benefactor.—Praised be thy name, O God, for Ever! Amen!

[After this, it will not be improper to read part of some such Book as Ray's *Wisdom of God in the Creation,* or *Blackmore on the Creation,* or the Archbishop of Cambray's *Demonstration of the Being of a God,* &c., or else spend some Minutes in a serious Silence, contemplating on those Subjects.]

Then sing

MILTON'S HYMN TO THE CREATOR

"These are thy Glorious Works, Parent of Good!
Almighty, Thine this Universal Frame,
Thus wondrous fair! Thyself how wondrous then!
Speak ye who best can tell, Ye Sons of Light,
Angels, for ye behold him, and with Songs
And Choral Symphonies, Day without Night,
Circle his Throne rejoicing you in Heav'n,
On Earth join all ye creatures to extol
Him first, him last, him midst, and without End.

"Fairest of Stars, last in the Train of Night,
If rather Thou belongst not to the Dawn,
Sure Pledge of Day! thou crown'st the smiling Morn
With thy bright Circlet, Praise him in thy Sphere
While Day arises, that sweet Hour of Prime.
Thou Sun, of this great World, both Eye and Soul,
Acknowledge him thy greater; Sound his Praise

In thy eternal Course; both when thou climb'st,
And when high Noon hast gain'd, and when thou fall'st.
Moon! that now meet's the orient sun, now fly'st,
With the fixed Stars, fixed in their orb that flies,
And ye five other wandering Fires, that move
In mystic Dance not without Song; resound
His Praise, that out of Darkness called up Light.
Air! and ye Elements! the eldest Birth
Of Nature's womb, that in Quaternion run
Perpetual Circle, multiform, and mix
And nourish all things, let your ceaseless Change
Vary to our great Maker still new Praise.
Ye mists and Exhalations, that now rise
From Hill or steaming lake, dusky or grey,
Till the Sun paint your fleecy skirts with Gold,
In honour to the World's Great Author rise;
Whether to deck with Clouds the uncolor'd sky,
Or wet the thirsty Earth with falling show'rs,
Rising or falling still advance his Praise.
His Praise, ye Winds! that from 4 quarters blow,
Breathe soft or Loud; and wave your Tops, ye Pines!
With every Plant, in sign of worship wave.
Fountains! and ye that warble, as ye flow
Melodious Murmurs, warbling tune his Praise.
Join voices all ye living souls, ye Birds!
That singing, up to Heaven's high gate ascend,
Bear on your wings, & in your Note his Praise;
Ye that in Waters glide! and ye that walk
The Earth! and stately tread or lowly creep;
Witness *if I be silent,* Ev'n or Morn,
To Hill, or Valley, Fountain, or Fresh Shade,
Made Vocal by my Song, and taught his Praise."

[Here follows the Reading of some Book, or part of a Book, Discoursing on and exciting to Moral Virtue.]

PETITION

Inasmuch as by Reason of our Ignorance We cannot be certain that many Things, which we often hear mentioned in the Petitions of Men to the Deity, would prove real Goods, if they were in our Possession, and as I have reason to hope and believe that the Goodness of my Heavenly Father will not withhold from me a suitable share of Temporal Blessings, if by a Virtuous and holy Life I conciliate his Favour and Kindness, Therefore I presume not to ask such things, but rather humbly and with a Sincere Heart, express my earnest desires that he would graciously assist my Continual Endeavours and Resolutions of eschewing Vice and embracing Virtue; which Kind of Supplications will *at least be thus far beneficial, as they remind me* in a solemn manner of my Extensive duty.

That I may be preserved from Atheism & Infidelity, Impiety, and Profaneness, and, in my Addresses to Thee, carefully avoid Irreverence and ostentation, Formality and odious Hypocrisy,—Help me, O Father!

That I may be loyal to my Prince, and faithful to my country, careful for its good, valiant in its defence, and obedient to its Laws, abhorring Treason as much as Tyranny,—Help me, O Father!

That I may to those above me be dutiful, humble, and submissive; avoiding Pride, Disrespect, and Contumacy,—Help me, O Father!

That I may to those below me be gracious, Condescending, and Forgiving, using Clemency, protecting *innocent Distress,* avoiding Cruelty, Harshness, and oppression, Insolence, and unreasonable Severity,—Help me, O Father!

That I may refrain from Censure, Calumny and Detraction; that I may avoid and abhor Deceit and Envy, Fraud, Flattery, and Hatred, Malice, Lying, and Ingratitude,—Help me, O Father!

That I may be sincere in Friendship, faithful in trust, and Impartial in Judgment, watchful against Pride, and against Anger (that momentary Madness),—Help me, O Father!

That I may be just in all my Dealings, temperate in my Pleasures, full of Candour and Ingenuity, Humanity and Benevolence,—Help me, O Father!

That I may be grateful to my Benefactors, and generous to my Friends, exercising Charity and Liberality to the Poor, and Pity to the Miserable,—Help me, O Father!

That I may avoid Avarice and Ambition, Jealousie, and Intemperance, Falsehood, Luxury, and Lasciviousness,—Help me, O Father!

That I may possess Integrity and Evenness of Mind, Resolution in Difficulties, and Fortitude under Affliction; that I may be punctual in performing my promises, Peaceable and prudent in my Behaviour,—Help me, O Father!

That I may have Tenderness for the Weak, and reverent Respect for the Ancient; that I may be Kind to my Neighbours, good-natured to my Companions, and hospitable to Strangers,—Help me, O Father!

That I may be averse to Talebearing, Backbiting, Detraction, Slander, & Craft, and overreaching, abhor Extortion, Perjury, and every Kind of wickedness,—Help me, O Father!

That I may be honest and open-hearted, gentle, merciful, and good, cheerful in spirit, rejoicing in the Good of others,—Help me, O Father!

That I may have a constant Regard to Honour and Probity, that I may possess a perfect innocence and a good Conscience, and at length become truly Virtuous and Magnanimous,—Help me, good God; help me, O Father!

And, forasmuch as ingratitude is one of the most odious of vices, let me not be unmindful gratefully to acknowledge the favours I receive from Heaven.

THANKS

For peace and liberty, for food and raiment, for corn, and wine, and milk, and every kind of healthful nourishment,—Good God, I thank thee!

For the common benefits of air and light; for useful fire and delicious water,—Good God, I thank thee!

For knowledge, and literature, and every useful art, for my friends and their prosperity, and for the fewness of my enemies, —Good God, I thank thee!

For all thy innumerable benefits; for life, and reason, and the use of speech; for health, and joy, and every pleasant hour,— My good God, I thank thee!

A PARABLE AGAINST PERSECUTION

1. And it came to pass after these things, that Abraham sat in the door of his tent, about the going down of the sun.

2. And behold a man, bent with age, coming from the way of the wilderness, leaning on a staff.

3. And Abraham arose and met him, and said unto him, Turn in, I pray thee, and wash thy feet, and tarry all night, and thou shalt arise early in the morning, and go on thy way.

4. But the man said, Nay, for I will abide under this tree.

5. And Abraham pressed him greatly; so he turned, and they went into the tent; and Abraham baked unleavened bread, and they did eat.

6. And when Abraham saw that the man blessed not God, he said unto him, Wherefore dost thou not worship the most high God, Creator of heaven and earth?

7. And the man answered and said, I do not worship thy God, neither do I call upon his name; for I have made to myself a god, which abideth always in mine house, and provideth me with all things.

8. And Abraham's zeal was kindled against the man, and he arose and fell upon him, and drove him forth with blows into the wilderness.

9. And God called unto Abraham, saying, Abraham, where is the stranger?

10. And Abraham answered and said, Lord, he would not worship thee, neither would he call upon thy name; therefore have I driven him out from before my face into the wilderness.

11. And God said, Have I borne with him these hundred and

ninety and eight years, and nourished him, and cloathed him, notwithstanding his rebellion against me; and couldst not thou, who art thyself a sinner, bear with him one night?

12. And Abraham said, Let not the anger of the Lord wax hot against his servant; lo, I have sinned; lo, I have sinned; forgive me, I pray thee.

13. And Abraham arose, and went forth into the wilderness, and sought diligently for the man, and found him, and returned with him to the tent; and when he had entreated him kindly, he sent him away on the morrow with gifts.

14. And God spake again unto Abraham, saying, For this thy sin shall thy seed be afflicted four hundred years in a strange land;

15. But for thy repentance will I deliver them; and they shall come forth with power, and with gladness of heart, and with much substance.

A PARABLE ON BROTHERLY LOVE

1. In those days there was no worker of iron in all the land. And the merchants of Midian passed by with their camels, bearing spices, and myrrh, and balm, and wares of iron.

2. And Reuben bought an axe of the Ishmaelite merchants, which he prized highly, for there was none in his father's house.

3. And Simeon said unto Reuben his brother, "Lend me, I pray thee, thine axe." But he refused, and would not.

4. And Levi also said unto him, "My brother, lend me, I pray thee, thine axe;" and he refused him also.

5. Then came Judah unto Reuben, and entreated him, saying, "Lo, thou lovest me, and I have always loved thee; do not refuse me the use of thine axe."

6. But Reuben turned from him, and refused him likewise.

7. Now it came to pass, that Reuben hewed timber on the bank of the river, and his axe fell therein, and he could by no means find it.

8. But Simeon, Levi, and Judah had sent a messenger after the Ishmaelites with money, and had bought for themselves each an axe.

9. Then came Reuben unto Simeon, and said, "Lo, I have lost mine axe, and my work is unfinished; lend me thine, I pray thee."

10. And Simeon answered him, saying, "Thou wouldest not lend me thine axe, therefore will I not lend thee mine."

11. Then went he unto Levi, and said unto him, "My brother, thou knowest my loss and my necessity; lend me, I pray thee, thine axe."

12. And Levi reproached him, saying, "Thou wouldest not lend me thine axe when I desired it, but I will be better than thou, and will lend thee mine."

13. And Reuben was grieved at the rebuke of Levi and being ashamed, turned from him, and took not the axe, but sought his brother Judah.

14. And as he drew near, Judah beheld his countenance as it were covered with grief and shame; and he prevented him, saying, "My brother, I know thy loss; but why should it trouble thee? Lo, have I not an axe that will serve both thee and me? Take it, I pray thee, and use it as thine own."

15. And Reuben fell on his neck, and kissed him, with tears, saying, "Thy kindness is great, but thy goodness in forgiving me is greater. Thou are indeed my brother, and whilst I live, will I surely love thee."

16. And Judah said, "Let us also love our other brethren; behold, are we not all of one blood?"

17. And Joseph saw these things, and reported them to his father Jacob.

18. And Jacob said, "Reuben did wrong, but he repented. Simeon also did wrong; and Levi was not altogether blameless.

19. "But the heart of Judah is princely. Judah hath the soul of a king. His father's children shall bow down before him, and he shall rule over his brethren."

PHILIP FRENEAU
(1752-1832)

Regarded simply as a poet, Freneau has often been taken as a primary example of the way in which circumstances in the era of the early republic combined to thwart writers. Such early productions as "The House of Night" and "Beauties of Santa Cruz" show talent and a promising poetic temperament in a young man still serving as apprentice to his art. But the war, the duties and attractions of newspaper political warfare, the lack of an adequate audience for poetry, the fact that most of the other writers and virtually all the organs of literary opinion were on the other political side, conspired together to stifle Freneau the poet. In his maturity he produced a few impressive lyrics, some abrasive satire, and some cogent discursive verse. But he appears to have burned himself out in political warfare, and perhaps in unresolved metaphysical tension. He turned out verse in the last thirty years of his life which ran ever more thinly in the vein of the country-newspaper poet. Nevertheless, he was the first really significant American poet published in his own lifetime, and produced a few poems which retain their music and imaginative force still.

Bibliography: Lewis Leary, *That Rascal Freneau*, New Brunswick, 1941; Harry Hayden Clark, ed., *Poems of Freneau*, New York, 1929; Lewis Leary, ed., *The Last Poems of Philip Freneau*, New Brunswick, 1946.

Text: H. H. Clark, ed., *Poems of Freneau*, New York, 1929; and *Poems . . . By Philip Freneau*, Philadelphia, 1809.

TO AN AUTHOR

Your leaves bound up compact and fair,
In neat array at length prepare,
To pass their hour on learning's stage,
To meet the surly critic's rage;
The statesman's slight, the smatterer's sneer—
Were these, indeed, your only fear,
You might be tranquil and resigned:
What most should touch your fluttering mind;
Is that, few critics will be found
To sift your works, and deal the wound.

Thus, when one fleeting year is past
On some bye-shelf your book is cast—
Another comes, with something new,
And drives you fairly out of view:

With some to praise, but more to blame,
The mind returns to—whence it came;
And some alive, who scarce could read
Will publish satires on the dead.

    Thrice happy Dryden, who could meet
Some rival bard in every street!
When all were bent on writing well
It was some credit to excel:—

Thrice happy Dryden, who could find
A Milbourne for his sport designed—
And Pope, who saw the harmless rage
Of Dennis bursting o'er his page
Might justly spurn the critic's aim,
Who only helped to swell his fame.

    On these bleak climes by Fortune thrown,
Where rigid Reason reigns alone,
Where lovely Fancy has no sway,
Nor magic forms about us play—
Nor nature takes her summer hue
Tell me, what has the muse to do?—

An age employed in edging steel
Can no poetic raptures feel;
No solitude's attracting power,
No leisure of the noon day hour,
No shaded stream, no quiet grove
Can this fantastic century move,

The muse of love in no request—
Go—try your fortune with the rest,
One of the nine you should engage,
To meet the follies of the age:—

On one, we fear, your choice must fall—
The least engaging of them all—
Her visage stern—an angry style—
A clouded brow—malicious smile—
A mind on murdered victims placed—
She, only she, can please the taste!

1788

from PICTURES OF COLUMBUS

PICTURE XIV

COLUMBUS AT CAT ISLAND

Columbus, solus

Hail, beauteous land! the first that greets mine eye
Since, bold, we left the cloud capp'd Teneriffe,
The world's last limit long suppos'd by men.—
Tir'd with dull prospects of the wat'ry waste
And midnight dangers that around us grew,
Faint hearts and feeble hands and traitors vile,
Thee, Holy Saviour, on this foreign land
We still adore, and name this coast from thee![1]
In these green groves who would not wish to stay
Where guardian nature holds her quiet reign,
Where beardless men speak other languages,
Unknown to us, ourselves unknown to them.

---

[1] He called the island San Salvador (Holy Saviour). It lies about 90 miles S. E. from Providence.—*Freneau.*

Antonio

In tracing o'er the isle no gold I find—
Nought else but barren trees and craggy rocks
Where screaming sea-fowl mix their odious loves,
And fields of burning marle, where devils play
And men with copper skins talk barbarously—
What merit has our chief in sailing hither
Discovering countries of no real worth!
Spain has enough of barren sands, no doubt,
And savages in crowds are found at home;—
Why then surmount the world's circumference
Merely to stock us with this Indian breed?

Hernando

Soft!—or Columbus will detect your murmuring—
This new found isle has re-instated him
In all our favors—see you yonder sands?—
Why, if you see them, swear that they are gold,
And gold like this shall be our homeward freight,
Gladding the heart of Ferdinand the great,
Who, when he sees it, shall say smilingly,
"Well done, advent'rous fellows, you have brought
The treasure we expected and deserv'd!"—
Hold!—I am wrong—there goes a savage man
With gold suspended from his ragged ears:
I'll brain the monster for the sake of gold;
There, savage, try the power of Spanish steel—
'Tis of Toledo[2]—true and trusty stuff!
He falls! he falls! the gold, the gold is mine!
First acquisition in this golden isle!—

Columbus, solus

Sweet sylvan scenes of innocence and ease,
How calm and joyous pass the seasons here!

---
[2] The best steel-blades in Spain are manufactured at Toledo and Bilboa.—*Freneau.*

No splendid towns or spiry turrets rise,
No lordly palaces—no tyrant kings
Enact hard laws to crush fair freedom here;
No gloomy jails to shut up wretched men;
All, all are free!—here God and nature reign;
Their works unsullied by the hands of men—
Ha! what is this—a murder'd wretch I see,
His blood yet warm—O hapless islander,
Who could have thus so basely mangled thee,
Who never offer'd insult to our shore—
Was it for those poor trinkets in your ears
Which by the custom of your tribe you wore,—
Now seiz'd away—and which would not have weigh'd
One poor piastre!
Is this the fruit of my discovery!
If the first scene is murder, what shall follow
But havoc, slaughter, chains and devastation
In every dress and form of cruelty!
O injur'd Nature, whelm me in the deep,
And let not Europe hope for my return,
Or guess at worlds upon whose threshold now
So black a deed has just been perpetrated!—
We must away—enjoy your woods in peace,
Poor, wretched, injur'd, harmless islanders;—
On Hayti's[3] isle you say vast stores are found
Of this destructive gold—which without murder
Perhaps, we may possess!—away, away!
And southward, pilots, seek another isle,
Fertile they say, and of immense extent:
There we may fortune find without a crime.

PICTURE XV

COLUMBUS IN A TEMPEST, ON HIS RETURN TO SPAIN

The storm hangs low; the angry lightning glares

---

[3] This island is now called Hispaniola.—*Freneau.*

And menaces destruction to our masts;
The Corposant[4] is busy on the decks,
The soul, perhaps, of some lost admiral
Taking his walks about most leisurely,
Foreboding we shall be with him to-night:
See, now he mounts the shrouds—as he ascends
The gale grows bolder!—all is violence!
Seas, mounting from the bottom of their depths,
Hang o'er our heads with all their horrid curls
Threatening perdition to our feeble barques,
Which three hours longer cannot bear their fury,
Such heavy strokes already shatter them;
Who can endure such dreadful company!—
Then, must we die with our discovery!
Must all my labors, all my pains, be lost,
And my new world in old oblivion sleep?—
My name forgot, or if it be remember'd,
Only to have it said, "He was a madman
Who perish'd as he ought—deservedly—
In seeking what was never to be found!"—
Let's obviate what we can this horrid sentence,
And, lost ourselves, perhaps, preserve our name.
'Tis easy to contrive this painted casket,
(Caulk'd, pitch'd, secur'd with canvas round and round)
That it may float for months upon the main,
Bearing the freight within secure and dry:
In this will I an abstract of our voyage,
And islands found, in little space enclose:
The western winds in time may bear it home
To Europe's coasts: or some wide wandering ship
By accident may meet it toss'd about,
Charg'd with the story of another world.

---

[4] A vapor common at sea in bad weather, something larger and rather paler than the light of a candle; which, seeming to rise out of the sea, first moves about the decks, and then ascends or descends the rigging in proportion to the increase or decrease of the storm. Superstition formerly imagined them to be the souls of drowned men.—*Freneau.*

PICTURE XVI

COLUMBUS VISITS THE COURT AT BARCELONA

Ferdinand

Let him be honor'd like a God, who brings
Tidings of islands at the ocean's end!
In royal robes let him be straight attir'd,
And seated next ourselves, the noblest peer.

Isabella

The merit of this gallant deed is mine:
Had not my jewels furnish'd out the fleet
Still had this world been latent in the main—
Since on this project every man look'd cold,
A woman, as his patroness, shall shine;
And through the world the story shall be told,
A woman gave new continents to Spain.

Columbus

A world, great prince, bright queen and royal lady,
Discover'd now, has well repaid our toils;
We to your bounty owe all that we are;
Men of renown and to be fam'd in story.
Islands of vast extent we have discover'd
With gold abounding: see a sample here
Of those most precious metals we admire;
And Indian men, natives of other climes,
Whom we have brought to do you princely homage,
Owning they hold their diadems from you.

Ferdinand

To fifteen sail your charge shall be augmented:
Hasten to Palos, and prepare again
To sail in quest of this fine golden country,
The Ophir, never known to Solomon;

Which shall be held the brightest gem we have,
The richest diamond in the crown of Spain.

PICTURE XVII

COLUMBUS IN CHAINS[5]

Are these the honors they reserve for me,
Chains for the man that gave new worlds to Spain!
Rest here, my swelling heart!—O kings, O queens,
Patrons of monsters, and their progeny,
Authors of wrong, and slaves to fortune merely!
Why was I seated by my prince's side,
Honor'd, caress'd like some first peer of Spain?
Was it that I might fall most suddenly
From honor's summit to the sink of scandal!
'Tis done, 'tis done!—what madness is ambition!
What is there in that little breath of men,
Which they call Fame, that should induce the brave
To forfeit ease and that domestic bliss
Which is the lot of happy ignorance,
Less glorious aims, and dull humility.—
Whoe'er thou art that shalt aspire to honor,
And on the strength and vigor of the mind
Vainly depending, court a monarch's favor,
Pointing the way to vast extended empire;
First count your pay to be ingratitude,
Then chains and prisons, and disgrace like mine!
Each wretched pilot now shall spread his sails,
And treading in my footsteps, hail new worlds,
Which, but for me, had still been empty visions.

---

[5] During his third voyage, while in San Domingo, such unjust representations were made of his conduct to the Court of Spain, that a new admiral, Bovadilla, was appointed to supersede him, who sent Columbus home in irons.—*Freneau.*

PICTURE XVIII

COLUMBUS AT VALLADOLID[6]

1

How sweet is sleep, when gain'd by length of toil!
No dreams disturb the slumbers of the dead—
To snatch existence from this scanty soil,
Were these the hopes deceitful fancy bred;
And were her painted pageants nothing more
Than this life's phantoms by delusion led?

2

The winds blow high: one other world remains;
Once more without a guide I find the way;
In the dark tomb to slumber with my chains—
Prais'd by no poet on my funeral day,
Nor even allow'd one dearly purchas'd claim—
My new found world not honor'd with my name.

3

Yet, in this joyless gloom while I repose,
Some comfort will attend my pensive shade,
When memory paints, and golden fancy shows
My toils rewarded, and my woes repaid;
When empires rise where lonely forests grew,
Where Freedom shall her generous plans pursue.

4

To shadowy forms, and ghosts and sleepy things,
Columbus, now with dauntless heart repair;
You liv'd to find new worlds for thankless kings,

---

[6] After he found himself in disgrace with the Court of Spain, he retired to Valladolid, a town of Old Castile, where he died, it is said, more of a broken heart than of any other disease, on the 20th of May, 1506.—*Freneau.*

Write this upon my tomb—yes—tell it there—
Tell of those chains that sullied all my glory—
Not mine, but their's—ah, tell the shameful story.
1774   1788

THE HOUSE OF NIGHT

A VISION

ADVERTISEMENT—This Poem is founded upon the authority of Scripture, inasmuch as these sacred books assert, that *the last enemy that shall be conquered is Death.* For the purposes of poetry he is here personified, and represented as on his dying bed. The scene is laid at a solitary palace, (the time midnight) which, tho' before beautiful and joyous, is now become sad and gloomy, as being the abode and receptacle of Death. Its owner, an amiable, majestic youth, who had lately lost a beloved consort, nevertheless with a noble philosophical fortitude and humanity, entertains him in a friendly manner, and by employing Physicians, endeavours to restore him to health, altho' an enemy; convinced of the excellence and propriety of that divine precept, *If thine enemy hunger, feed him; if he thirst, give him drink.* He nevertheless, as if by a spirit of prophecy, informs this (fictitiously) wicked being of the certainty of his doom, and represents to him in a pathetic manner the vanity of his expectations, either of a reception into the abodes of the just, or continuing longer to make havoc of mankind upon earth. The patient finding his end approaching, composes his epitaph, and orders it to be engraved on his tombstone, hinting to us thereby, that even Death and Distress have vanity; and would be remembered with honor after he is no more, altho' his whole life has been spent in deeds of devastation and murder. He dies at last in the utmost agonies of despair, after agreeing with the avaricious Undertaker to intomb his bones. This reflects upon the inhumanity of those men, who, not to mention an enemy, would scarcely cover a departed friend with a little dust, without the certainty of a reward for so doing. The circumstances of his funeral are then recited, and the visionary and fabulous part of the poem disappears. It concludes with a few reflections on the impropriety of a too great attachment to the present life, and incentives to such moral virtue as may assist in conducting us to a better.

1

Trembling I write my dream, and recollect
A fearful vision at the midnight hour;
So late, Death o'er me spread his sable wings,
Painted with fancies of malignant power!

2

Such was the dream the sage Chaldean saw
Disclos'd to him that felt heav'n's vengeful rod,
Such was the ghost, who through deep silence cry'd,
Shall mortal man—be juster than his God.

6

By some sad means, when Reason holds no sway,
Lonely I rov'd at midnight o'er a plain
Where murmuring streams and mingling rivers flow,
Far to their springs, or seek the sea again.

8

Dark was the sky, and not one friendly star
Shone from the zenith or horizon, clear,
Mist sate upon the woods, and darkness rode
In her black chariot, with a wild career.

9

And from the woods the late resounding note
Issued of the loquacious Whip-poor-will,[7]
Hoarse, howling dogs, and nightly roving wolves
Clamor'd from far off cliffs invisible.

10

Rude, from the wide extended *Chesapeke*
I heard the winds the dashing waves assail,

---

[7] A Bird peculiar to America, of a solitary nature, who sings but in the night. Her note resembles the name given to her by the country people.—*Freneau.*

And saw from far, by pictures fancy form'd,
The black ship travelling through the noisy gale.

11

At last, by chance and guardian fancy led,
I reach'd a noble dome, rais'd fair and high,
And saw the light from upper windows flame,
Presage of mirth and hospitality.

12

And by that light around the dome appear'd
A mournful garden of autumnal hue,
Its lately pleasing flowers all drooping stood
Amidst high weeds that in rank plenty grew.

14

No pleasant fruit or blossom gaily smil'd.
Nought but unhappy plants and trees were seen,
The yew, the myrtle, and the church-yard elm,
The cypress, with its melancholy green.

17

And here and there with laurel shrubs between
A tombstone lay, inscrib'd with strains of woe,
And stanzas sad, throughout the dismal green,
Lamented for the dead that slept below.

18

Peace to this awful dome!—when straight I heard
The voice of men in a secluded room,
Much did they talk of death, and much of life,
Of coffins, shrouds, and horrors of a tomb.

23

Then up three winding stairs my feet were brought
To a high chamber, hung with mourning sad,

The unsnuff'd candles glar'd with visage dim,
'Midst grief, in ecstasy of woe run mad.

24

A wide leaf'd table stood on either side,
Well fraught with phials, half their liquids spent,
And from a couch, behind the curtain's veil,
I heard a hollow voice of loud lament.

25

Turning to view the object whence it came,
My frighted eyes a horrid form survey'd;
Fancy, I own thy power—Death on the couch,
With fleshless limbs, at rueful length, was laid.

26

And o'er his head flew jealousies and cares,
Ghosts, imps, and half the black Tartarian crew,
Arch-angels damn'd, nor was their Prince remote,
Borne on the vaporous wings of Stygian dew.

27

Around his bed, by the dull flambeaux' glare,
I saw pale phantoms—Rage to madness vext,
Wan, wasting grief, and ever musing care,
Distressful pain, and poverty perplext.

28

Sad was his countenance, if we can call
That countenance, where only bones were seen
And eyes sunk in their sockets, dark and low,
And teeth, that only show'd themselves to grin.

29

Reft was his skull of hair, and no fresh bloom
Of cheerful mirth sate on his visage hoar:

Sometimes he rais'd his head, while deep-drawn groans
Were mixt with words that did his fate deplore.

30

Oft did he wish to see the daylight spring,
And often toward the window lean'd to hear,
Fore-runner of the scarlet-mantled morn,
The early note of wakeful Chanticleer.

47

But now this man of hell toward me turn'd,
And straight, in hideous tone, began to speak,
Long held he sage discourse, but I forbore
To answer him, much less his news to seek.

48

He talk'd of tomb-stones and of monuments,
Of Equinoxial climes and India shores,
He talk'd of stars that shed their influence,
Fevers and plagues, and all their noxious stores.

52

Then with a hollow voice thus went he on,
"Get up, and search, and bring, when found, to me,
Some cordial, potion, or some pleasant draught,
Sweet, slumb'rous poppy, or the mild Bohea.

53

"But hark, my pitying friend!—and, if you can,
Deceive the grim physician at the door—
Bring half the mountain springs—ah! hither bring
The cold rock water from the shady bower.

54

"For till this night such thirst did ne'er invade,
A thirst provok'd by heav'n's avenging hand;

Hence bear me, friends, to quaff, and quaff again
The cool wave bubbling from the yellow sand.

55

"To these dark walls with stately step I came,
Prepar'd your drugs and doses to defy;
Smit with the love of never dying fame,
I came, alas! to conquer—not to die!"

56

Glad, from his side I sprang, and fetch'd the draught,
Which down his greedy throat he quickly swills,
Then on a second errand sent me straight,
To search in some dark corner for his pills.

57

Quoth he, "These pills have long compounded been,
Of dead men's bones and bitter roots, I trow;
But that I may to wonted health return,
Throughout my lank veins shall their substance go."

58

So down they went—He rais'd his fainting head
And oft in feeble tone essay'd to talk;
Quoth he, "Since remedies have small avail,
Assist unhappy Death once more to walk."

59

Then slowly rising from his loathsome bed,
On wasted legs the meagre monster stood,
Gap'd wide, and foam'd, and hungry seem'd to ask,
Tho' sick, an endless quantity of food.

108

Yet, mindful of his dread command, I part
Glad from the magic dome—nor found relief;

Damps from the dead hung heavier round my heart,
While sad remembrance rous'd her stores of grief.

109

O'er a dark field I held my dubious way
Where Jack-a-lanthorn walk'd his lonely round,
Beneath my feet substantial darkness lay,
And screams were heard from the distemper'd ground.

110

Nor look'd I back, till to a far off wood
Trembling with fear, my weary feet had sped—
Dark was the night, but at the inchanted dome
I saw the infernal windows flaming red.

111

And from within the howls of Death I heard,
Cursing the dismal night that gave him birth,
Damning his ancient sire, and mother sin,
Who at the gates of hell, accursed, brought him forth.

112

[For fancy gave to my enraptur'd soul
An eagle's eye, with keenest glance to see,
And bade those distant sounds distinctly roll,
Which, waking, never had affected me.]

113

Oft his pale breast with cruel hand he smote,
And tearing from his limbs a winding sheet,
Roar'd to the black skies, while the woods around,
As wicked as himself, his words repeat.

114

Thrice tow'rd the skies his meagre arms he rear'd,
Invok'd all hell, and thunders on his head,

Bid light'nings fly, earth yawn, and tempests roar,
And the sea wrap him in its oozy bed.

115

"My life for one cool draught!—O, fetch your springs,
Can one unfeeling to my woes be found!
No friendly visage comes to my relief,
But ghosts impend, and spectres hover round.

116

"Though humbled now, dishearten'd and distrest,
Yet, when admitted to the peaceful ground,
With heroes, kings, and conquerors I shall rest,
Shall sleep as safely, and perhaps as sound."

117

Dim burnt the lamp, and now the phantom Death
Gave his last groans in horror and despair—
"All hell demands me hence,"—he said, and threw
The red lamp hissing through the midnight air.

118

Trembling, across the plain my course I held,
And found the grave-yard, loitering through the gloom,
And, in the midst, a hell-red, wandering light,
Walking in fiery circles round the tomb.

119

Among the graves a spiry building stood,
Whose tolling bell, resounding through the wood,
Sung doleful ditties to the adjacent wood,
And many a dismal drowsy thing it said.

120

This fabric tall, with towers and chancels grac'd,
Was rais'd by sinners' hands, in ages fled;

The roof they painted, and the beams they brac'd,
And texts from scripture o'er the walls they spread:

121

But wicked were their hearts, for they refus'd
To aid the helpless orphan, when distrest,
The shivering, naked stranger they mis-us'd,
And banish'd from their doors the starving guest.

122

By laws protected, cruel and profane,
The poor man's ox these monsters drove away;—
And left Distress to attend her infant train,
No friend to comfort, and no bread to stay.

123

But heaven look'd on with keen, resentful eye,
And doom'd them to perdition and the grave,
That as they felt not for the wretch distrest,
So heaven no pity on their souls would have.

124

In pride they rais'd this building tall and fair,
Their hearts were on perpetual mischief bent,
With pride they preach'd, and pride was in their prayer,
With pride they were deceiv'd, and so to hell they went.

125

At distance far approaching to the tomb,
By lamps and lanthorns guided through the shade,
A coal-black chariot hurried through the gloom,
Spectres attending, in black weeds array'd,

126

Whose woeful forms yet chill my soul with dread,
Each wore a vest in Stygian chambers wove,

Death's kindred all—Death's horses they bestrode,
And gallop'd fiercely, as the chariot drove.

127

Each horrid face a grisly mask conceal'd,
Their busy eyes shot terror to my soul
As now and then, by the pale lanthorn's glare,
I saw them for their parted friend condole.

128

Before the hearse Death's chaplain seem'd to go,
Who strove to comfort, what he could, the dead;
Talk'd much of Satan, and the land of woe,
And many a chapter from the scriptures read.

129

At last he rais'd the swelling anthem high,
In dismal numbers seem'd he to complain;
The captive tribes that by Euphrates wept,
Their song was jovial to his dreary strain.

130

That done, they plac'd the carcass in the tomb,
To dust and dull oblivion now resign'd,
Then turn'd the chariot tow'rd the House of Night,
Which soon flew off, and left no trace behind.

131

But as I stoop'd to write the appointed verse,
Swifter than thought the airy scene decay'd;
Blushing the morn arose, and from the east
With her gay streams of light dispell'd the shade.

132

What is this Death, ye deep read sophists, say?—
Death is no more than one unceasing change;

New forms arise, while other forms decay,
Yet all is Life throughout creation's range.

133

The towering *Alps,* the haughty *Appenine,*
The *Andes,* wrapt in everlasting snow,
The *Apalachian* and the *Ararat*
Sooner or later must to ruin go.

134

Hills sink to plains, and man returns to dust,
That dust supports a reptile or a flower;
Each changeful atom by some other nurs'd
Takes some new form, to perish in an hour.

135

Too nearly join'd to sickness, toils, and pains,
(Perhaps for former crimes imprison'd here)
True to itself the immortal soul remains,
And seeks new mansions in the starry sphere.

136

When Nature bids thee from the world retire,
With joy thy lodging leave, a fated guest;
In Paradise, the land of thy desire,
Existing always, always to be blest.

1779
                                                                        1786

THE BEAUTIES OF SANTA CRUZ [8]

1776

Sweet orange grove, the fairest of the isle,
  In thy soft shade luxuriously reclined,

---

[8] Or St. Croix, a Danish island (in the American Archipelago), commonly, tho' erroneously, included in the cluster of the Virgin Islands; belonging to the crown of Denmark.—*Freneau.*

*Where, round my fragrant bed, the flowrets smile,
  In sweet delusions I deceive my mind.*

*But Melancholy's glooms assail my breast,
  For potent nature reigns despotic there;—
A nation ruined, and a world oppressed,
  Might rob the boldest Stoic of a tear.*

Sick of thy nothern glooms, come, shepherd, seek
More equal climes, and a serener sky:
Why shouldst thou toil amid thy frozen ground,
Where half years' snows, a barren prospect, lie,

When thou mayst go where never frost was seen,
Or north-west winds with cutting fury blow,
Where never ice congealed the limpid stream,
Where never mountain tipt its head with snow?

Twice ten days prosperous gales thy barque shall bear
To isles that flourish in perpetual green,
Where richest herbage glads each fertile vale,
And ever verdant plants on every hill are seen.

Nor dread the dangers of the billowy deep,
Autumnal winds shall safely waft thee o'er;
Put off the timid heart, or, man unblest,
Ne'er shalt thou reach this gay enchanting shore.

Thus Judah's tribes beheld the promised land,
While Jordan's angry waters swelled between;
Thus trembling on the brink I see them stand,
Heav'n's type in view, the Canaanitish green.

Thus, some mean souls, in spite of age and care,
Are held so firmly to this earth below,

They never wish to cross fate's dusky main,
That parting them and happiness, doth flow.

Though Reason's voice might whisper to the soul
That nobler climes for man the heavens design—
Come, shepherd, haste—the northern breezes blow,
No more the slumbering winds thy barque confine.

Sweet orange grove, the fairest of the isle,
In thy soft shade luxuriously reclined,
Where, round my fragrant bed, the flowrets smile,
In sweet delusions I deceive my mind.

But Melancholy's glooms assail my breast,
For potent nature reigns despotic there;—
A nation ruined, and a world oppressed,
Might rob the boldest Stoic of a tear.

From the vast caverns of old Ocean's bed,
Fair Santa Cruz arising, laves her waist,
The threatening waters roar on every side,
For every side by ocean is embraced.

Sharp, craggy rocks repel the surging brine,
Whose caverned sides by restless billows wore,
Resemblance claim to that remoter isle
Where once the winds' proud lord the sceptre bore.

Betwixt old Cancer and the mid-way line,
In happiest climate, lies this envied isle:
Trees bloom throughout the year, soft breezes blow,
And fragrant Flora wears a lasting smile.

Cool, woodland streams from shaded cliffs descend,
The dripping rock no want of moisture knows,

Supplied by springs that on the skies depend,
That fountain feeding as the current flows.

Such were the isles which happy Flaccus sung,
Where one tree blossoms while another bears,
Where spring forever gay, and ever young,
Walks her gay round through her unceasing years.

Such were the climes which youthful Eden saw
Ere crossing fates destroyed her golden reign—
Reflect upon thy loss, unhappy man,
And seek the vales of Paradise again.

No lowering skies are here—the neighboring sun
Clear and unveiled, his brilliant journey goes,
Each morn emerging from the ambient main,
And sinking there, each evening, to repose.

In June's fair month the spangled traveller gains
The utmost limits of his northern way,
And blesses with his beams cold lands remote,
Sad Greenland's coast, and Hudson's frozen bay.

The shivering swains of those unhappy climes
Behold the side-way monarch through the trees,
Here glows his fiercer heat, his vertic beams,
Tempered with cooling gales and trade-wind breeze.

The native here, in golden plenty blest,
Bids from the soil the verdant harvests spring;
Feasts in the abundant dome, the joyous guest;
Time short,—life easy,—pleasure on the wing.

Here, fixt today in plenty's smiling vales,
Just as the year revolves, they laugh or groan;

September comes, seas swell with horrid gales,
And old Port-Royal's fate is found their own!

And, though so near heaven's blazing lamp doth run
They court the beam that sheds the golden day,
And hence are called the children of the sun,
Who, without fainting, bear his downward ray.

No threatening tides upon their island rise,
Gay Cynthia scarce disturbs the ocean here,
No waves approach her orb, and she, as kind,
Attracts no ocean to her silver sphere.

The happy waters boast, of various kinds,
Unnumbered myriads of the scaly race,
Sportive they glide above the deluged sand,
Gay as their clime, in ocean's ample vase.

Some streaked with burnished gold, resplendent, glare,
Some cleave the limpid deep, all silvered o'er,
Some, clad in living green, delight the eye,
Some red, some blue; of mingled colors more.

Here glides the spangled dolphin through the deep,
The giant carcased whales at distance stray,
The huge green turtles wallow through the wave,
Well pleas'd alike with land or water, they.

The Rainbow cuts the deep, of varied green,
The well-fed Grouper lurks remote, below,
The swift Bonetta coasts the watery scene,
The diamond-coated Angels kindle as they go,

Delicious to the taste, salubrious food,
Which might some temperate, studious sage allure

To curse the fare of his abstemious cell
And turn, for once, a cheerful epicure.

Unhurt mayest thou this luscious food enjoy,
To fulness feast upon the scaly kind;
These, well selected from a thousand more,
Delight the taste, and leave no bane behind.

Nor think Hygeia[9] is a stranger here—
To sensual souls the climate may fatal prove,
Anguish and death attend, and pain severe,
The midnight revel, and licentious love.

Full many a swain, in youth's serenest bloom,
Is borne untimely to this alien clay,
Constrained to slumber in a foreign tomb,
Far from his friends, his country far away.

Yet, if devoted to a sensual soul,
If fondly their own ruin they create,
These victims to the banquet and the bowl
Must blame their folly, only, not their fate.

But thou who first drew breath in northern air,
At early dawn ascend the sloping hills:
And oft, at noon, to lime-tree shades repair,
Where some soft stream from neighboring groves distills.

And with it mix the liquid of the lime,
The old-aged essence of the generous cane,
And sweetest syrups of this liquorish clime,
And drink, to cool thy thirst, and drink again.

This happy beverage, joy-inspiring bowl,
Dispelling far the shades of mental night,

---

[9] The goddess of health, in the Grecian mythology.—*Freneau*.

Beams bright ideas on the awakened soul,
And sorrow turns to pleasure and delight.

  Sweet verdant isle! through thy dark woods I rove,
And learn the nature of each native tree,
The fustic hard, the poisonous manchineel,
Which for its fragrant apple pleaseth thee;

Alluring to the smell, fair to the eye,
But deadliest poison in the taste is found—
O shun the dangerous tree, nor touch, like Eve,
This interdicted fruit, in Eden's ground.

The lowly mangrove fond of watery soil,
The white-barked gregory, rising high in air,
The mastic in the woods you may descry,
Tamarind, and lofty bay-trees flourish there.

Sweet orange groves in lonely valleys rise
And drop their fruits, unnoticed and unknown,
And cooling acid limes in hedges grow,
The juicy lemons swell in shades their own.

Sweet, spungy plums on trees wide spreading hang,
Bell-apples here, suspended, shade the ground,
Plump grenadilloes and güavas grey,
With melons in each plain and vale abound.

The conic-formed cashew, of juicy kind,
That bears at once an apple and a nut;
Whose poisonous coat, indignant to the lip,
Doth in its cell a wholesome kernel shut.

The prince of fruits, whom some jayama call,
Anana some, the happy flavoured pine;

In which unite the tastes and juices all
Of apple, quince, peach, grape, and nectarine,

Grows to perfection here, and spreads his crest,
His diadem toward the parent sun;
His diadem, in fiery blossoms drest,
Stands armed with swords, from potent Nature won.

Yon' cotton shrubs with bursting knobs behold,
Their snow white locks these humbler groves array;
On slender trees the blushing coffee hangs,
Like thy fair cherry, and would tempt thy stay.

Safe from the winds, in deep retreats, they rise;
Their utmost summit may thy arm attain;
Taste the moist fruit, and from thy closing eyes
Sleep shall retire, with all his drowsy train.

The spicy berry, they güava call,
Swells in the mountains on a stripling tree;
These some admire, and value more than all,
My humble verse, besides, unfolds to thee.

The smooth white cedar, here, delights the eye,
The bay-tree, with its aromatic green,
The sea-side grapes, sweet natives of the sand,
And pulse, of various kinds, on trees are seen.

Here mingled vines, their downward shadows cast,
Here, clustered grapes from loaded boughs depend,
Their leaves no frosts, their fruits no cold winds blast,
But, reared by suns, to time alone they bend.

The plantane and banana flourish here,
Of hasty growth, and love to fix their root

Where some soft stream of ambling water flows,
To yield full moisture to their clustered fruit.

No other trees so vast a leaf can boast,
So broad, so long—through these, refreshed, we stray,
And though the noon-sun all his radiance shed,
These friendly leaves shall shade me all the way,

And tempt the cooling breeze to hasten there,
With its sweet odorous breath to charm the grove;
High shades and verdant seats, while underneath
A little stream by mossy banks doth rove,

Where once the Indian dames slept with their swains,
Or fondly kissed the moon-light eves away;—
The lovers fled, the tearful stream remains,
And only I console it with my lay!

Among the shades of yonder whispering grove
The green palmettoes mingle, tall and fair,
That ever murmur, and forever move,
Fanning with wavy bough the ambient air.

Pomegranates grace the wild, and sweet-sops there
Ready to fall, require the helping hand,
Nor yet neglect the papaw or mamee,
Whose slighted trees with fruits unheeded stand.

Those shaddocks juicy shall thy taste delight,
And yon' high fruits, the noblest of the wood,
That cling in clusters to the mother tree,
The cocoa-nut; rich, milky, healthful food.

O grant me, gods, if yet condemned to stray,
At least to spend life's sober evening here,

To plant a grove where winds yon' sheltered bay,
And pluck these fruits, that frost nor winter fear.

Cassada shrubs abound—transplanted here
From every clime, exotic blossoms blow;
Here Asia plants her flowers, here Europe trees,
And hyperborean herbs, unwintered, grow.

Here, a new herbage glads the generous steed,
Mules, goats, and sheep, enjoy these pastures fair,
And for thy hedges, Nature has decreed,
Guards of thy toils, the date and prickly pear.

But chief the glory of these Indian isles
Springs from the sweet, uncloying sugar-cane:
Hence comes the planter's wealth, hence commerce sends
Such floating piles, to traverse half the main.

Whoe'er thou art that leavest thy native shore
And shalt to fair West-India climates come,
Taste not the enchanting plant—to taste forbear,
If ever thou wouldst reach thy much-loved home.

Ne'er through the isle permit thy feet to rove,
Or, if thou dost, let prudence lead the way,
Forbear to taste the virtues of the cane,
Forbear to taste what will complete your stay.

Whoever sips of this enchanting juice,
Delicious nectar, fit for Jove's own hall,
Returns no more from his loved Santa Cruz,
But quits his friends, his country, and his all.

And thinks no more of home—Ulysses so
Dragged off by force his sailors from that shore

Where lotos grew, and, had not strength prevailed,
They never would have sought their country more.

No annual toil inters this thrifty plant,
The stalk lopt off, the freshening showers prolong
To future years, unfading and secure,
The root so vigorous, and the juice so strong.

Unnumbered plants, besides, these climates yield,
And grass peculiar to the soil that bears:
Ten thousand varied herbs array the field,
This glads thy palate, that thy health repairs.

Along the shore a wondrous flower is seen,
Where rocky ponds receive the surging wave,
Some drest in yellow, some attired in green,
Beneath the water their gay branches lave.

This mystic plant, with its bewitching charms,
Too surely springs from some enchanted bower,
Fearful it is, and dreads impending harms,
And animal, the natives call the flower.

From the smooth rock its little branches rise,
The object of thy view, and that alone,
Feast on its beauties with thy ravished eyes,
But aim to touch it, and—the flower is gone.

Nay, if thy shade but intercept the beam
That gilds their boughs beneath the briny lake,
Swift they retire, like a deluding dream,
And even a shadow for destruction take.

Warned by experience, hope not thou to gain
The magic plant thy curious hand invades;

Returning to the light, it mocks thy pain,
Deceives all grasp, and seeks its native shades!

On yonder blue-browed hill, fresh harvests rise,
Where the dark tribe from Afric's sunburnt plain,
Oft o'er the ocean turn their wishful eyes
To isles remote high looming o'er the main.

And view soft seats of ease and fancied rest,
Their native groves new painted on the eye,
Where no proud misers their gay hours molest,
No lordly despots pass, unsocial, by.

See, yonder slave that slowly bends this way,
With years, and pain, and ceaseless toil opprest,
Though no complaining words his woes betray,
The eye dejected proves the heart distrest.

Perhaps in chains he left his native shore,
Perhaps he left a helpless offspring there,
Perhaps a wife, that he must see no more,
Perhaps a father, who his love did share.

Cursed be the ship, that brought him o'er the main,
And cursed the men, who from his country tore;
May she be stranded, ne'er to float again,
May they be shipwrecked on some hostile shore—

O gold accurst, of every ill the spring,
For thee compassion flies the darkened mind,
Reason's plain dictates no conviction bring,
And madness only sways all human kind.

O gold accurst! for thee we madly run,
With murderous hearts across the briny flood,

Seek foreign climes beneath a foreign sun,
And, there, exult to shed a brother's blood.

But thou, who ownest this sugar-bearing soil,
To whom no good the great First Cause denies,
Let free-born hands attend thy sultry toil,
And fairer harvests to thy view shall rise,

The teeming earth will mightier stores disclose
Than ever struck the longing eye before,
And late content shall shed a soft repose—
Repose, so long a stranger at thy door.

Give me some clime, the favorite of the sky,
Where cruel slavery never sought to reign—
But shun the theme, sad muse, and tell me why
These abject trees lie scattered o'er the plain?

These isles, lest Nature should have proved too kind,
Or man have sought his happiest heaven below,
Are torn with mighty winds, fierce hurricanes,
Nature convulsed in every shape of woe.

Nor scorn yon' lonely vale of trees so reft:
There plantane groves late grew of liveliest green,
The orange flourished, and the lemon bore,
The genius of the isle dwelt there, unseen.

Wild were the skies, affrighted Nature groaned
As though approached her last decisive day.
Skies blazed around and bellowing winds had nigh
Dislodged these cliffs, and tore yon' hills away.

O'er the wild main, dejected and afraid,
The trembling pilot lashed his helm a-lee

Or swiftly scudding, asked thy potent aid,
Dear Pilot of the Galilean sea.

Low hung the glooms, distended with the gale
The clouds, dark brooding, winged their circling flight,
Tremendous thunders joined the hurricane,
Daughter of chaos, and eternal night!

And how, alas! could these fair trees withstand
The wasteful madness of so fierce a blast,
That stormed along the plain, seized every grove,
And deluged with a sea this mournful waste.

That plantane grove, where oft I fondly strayed,
Thy darts, dread Phoebus, in those glooms to shun,
Is now no more a refuge or a shade,
Is now with rocks and deep sands over-run.

Those late proud domes of splendor, pomp, and ease
No longer strike the view, in grand attire;
But, torn by winds, flew piece-meal to the seas,
Nor left one nook to lodge the astonished 'squire.

But other groves the hand of Time shall raise,
Again shall Nature smile, serenely gay:
So soon each scene revives, why haste I leave
These green retreats, o'er the dark seas to stray.

For I must go where the mad pirate roves,
A stranger on the inhospitable main,
Lost to the scenes of Hudson's sweetest groves,
Cesarea's forests, and my native plain.

There endless waves deject the wearied eye,
And hostile winds incessant toil prepare;

But should loud bellowing storms all art defy,
The manly heart alone must conquer there.—

There wakes my fears, the guileful Calenture
Tempting the wanderer on the deep-sea main,
That paints gay groves upon the ocean floor,
Beckoning her victim to the faithless scene!

  On these blue hills, to cull bright Fancy's flowers,
Might yet awhile the unwelcome work delay,
Might yet beguile the few remaining hours—
Ere to those waves I take my destined way.

Thy vales, Bermuda, and thy sea-girt groves
Can never like these southern forests please;
And, lashed by stormy waves, you court in vain
The northern shepherd to your cedar trees.

Not o'er those isles such equal planets rule.
All, but the cedar, dread the wintry blast;
Too well thy charms the banished Waller sung;
Too near the pilot's star thy doom is cast.

Far o'er the waste of yonder surgy field
My native climes in fancied prospect lie,
Now hid in shades, and now by clouds concealed,
And now by tempests ravished from the eye.

There, triumphs to enjoy, are, Britain, thine,
There, thy proud navy awes the pillaged shore;
Nor sees the day when nations shall combine
That pride to humble, and our rights restore.

Yet o'er the globe shouldst thou extend thy reign,
Here may thy conquering arms one grotto spare;

Here—though thy conquests vex—in spite of pain,
We sip the enlivening glass, in spite of care.

What though we bend to a tyrannic crown;
Still Nature's charms in varied beauty shine—
What though we own the rude imperious Dane,
Gold is his sordid care, the Muses mine.

Winter, and winter's glooms are far removed,
Eternal spring with smiling summer joined:—
Absence, and death, and heart-corroding care,
Why should they cloud the sun-shine of the mind?

   But, shepherd, haste, and leave behind thee far
Thy bloody plains, and iron glooms above;
Quit the cold northern star, and here enjoy,
Beneath the smiling skies, this land of love.

The drowsy pelican wings home his way,
The misty eve sits heavy on the sea,
And though yon' storm hangs brooding o'er the main,
Say, shall a moment's gloom discourage thee?

To-morrow's sun new paints the faded scene:
Though deep in ocean sink his western beams,
His spangled chariot shall ascend more clear,
More radiant from the drowsy land of dreams.

   Of all the isles the neighboring ocean bears,
None can with this their equal landscapes boast,
What could we do on Saba's cloudy height;
Or what could please on 'Statia's barren coast?

Couldst thou content on rough Tortola stray,
Confest the fairest of the Virgin train;

Or couldst thou on those rocky summits play
Where high St. John stands frowning o'er the main?

Haste, shepherd, haste—Hesperian fruits for thee
And clustered grapes from mingled boughs depend—
What pleasure in thy forests can there be
That, leafless now, to every tempest bend?

To milder stars, and skies of clearer blue,
Sworn foe to tyrants, for a time repair:
And, till to mightier force proud Britain bends—
Despise her triumphs, and forget your care.

Soon shall the genius of the fertile soil
A new creation to thy view unfold—
Admire the works of Nature's magic hand,
But scorn that vulgar bait—the thirst for gold.—

 Yet, if persuaded by no verse of mine,
You still admire your lands of frost and snow,
And pleased, prefer above these southern groves,
The darksome forests that around you grow:

Still there remain—your native air enjoy,
Repel the Tyrant, who thy peace invades:
While charmed, we trace the vales of Santa Cruz,
And paint with rapture, her inspiring shades.
1776   1779

THE HURRICANE

Happy the man who, safe on shore,
Now trims, at home, his evening fire;
Unmoved, he hears the tempests roar,
That on the tufted groves expire:
Alas! on us they doubly fall,
Our feeble barque must bear them all.

Now to their haunts the birds retreat,
The squirrel seeks his hollow tree,
Wolves in their shaded caverns meet,
All, all are blest but wretched we—
Foredoomed a stranger to repose,
No rest the unsettled ocean knows.

While o'er the dark abyss we roam,
Perhaps, with last departing gleam,
We saw the sun descend in gloom,
No more to see his morning beam;
But buried low, by far too deep,
On coral beds, unpitied, sleep!

But what a strange, uncoasted strand
Is that, where fate permits no day—
No charts have we to mark that land,
No compass to direct that way—
What Pilot shall explore that realm,
What new Columbus take the helm!

While death and darkness both surround,
And tempests rage with lawless power,
Of friendship's voice I hear no sound,
No comfort in this dreadful hour—
What friendship can in tempests be,
What comforts on this raging sea?

The barque, accustomed to obey,
No more the trembling pilots guide:
Alone she gropes her trackless way,
While mountains burst on either side—
Thus, skill and science both must fall;
And ruin is the lot of all.

1785

PHILIP FRENEAU

TO THE MEMORY OF THE BRAVE AMERICANS

UNDER GENERAL GREENE, IN SOUTH CAROLINA, WHO FELL IN THE ACTION OF SEPTEMBER 8, 1781

At Eutaw Springs the valiant died;
  Their limbs with dust are covered o'er—
Weep on, ye springs, your tearful tide;
  How many heroes are no more!

If in this wreck of ruin, they
  Can yet be thought to claim a tear,
O smite your gentle breast, and say
  The friends of freedom slumber here!

Thou, who shalt trace this bloody plain,
  If goodness rules thy generous breast,
Sigh for the wasted rural reign;
  Sigh for the shepherds, sunk to rest!

Stranger, their humble graves adorn;
  You too may fall, and ask a tear;
'Tis not the beauty of the morn
  That proves the evening shall be clear.—

They saw their injured country's woe;
  The flaming town, the wasted field;
Then rushed to meet the insulting foe;
  They took the spear—but left the shield.

Led by thy conquering genius, Greene,
  The Britons they compelled to fly;
None distant viewed the fatal plain,
  None grieved, in such a cause to die—

But, like the Parthian, famed of old,
   Who, flying, still their arrows threw,
These routed Britons, full as bold,
   Retreated, and retreating slew.

Now rest in peace, our patriot band;
   Though far from nature's limits thrown,
We trust they find a happier land,
   A brighter sunshine of their own.
1781   1781

THE WILD HONEY SUCKLE

Fair flower, that dost so comely grow,
Hid in this silent, dull retreat,
Untouched thy honied blossoms blow,
Unseen thy little branches greet:
   No roving foot shall crush thee here,
   No busy hand provoke a tear.

By Nature's self in white arrayed,
She bade thee shun the vulgar eye,
And planted here the guardian shade,
And sent soft waters murmuring by;
   Thus quietly thy summer goes,
   Thy days declining to repose.

Smit with those charms, that must decay,
I grieve to see your future doom;
They died—nor were those flowers more gay,
The flowers that did in Eden bloom;
   Unpitying frosts, and Autumn's power
   Shall leave no vestige of this flower.

From morning suns and evening dews
At first thy little being came:

If nothing once, you nothing lose,
For when you die you are the same;
  The space between, is but an hour,
  The frail duration of a flower.

1786

THE INDIAN BURYING GROUND

In spite of all the learned have said,
I still my old opinion keep;
The posture, that we give the dead,
Points out the soul's eternal sleep.

Not so the ancients of these lands—
The Indian, when from life released,
Again is seated with his friends,
And shares again the joyous feast.

His imaged birds, and painted bowl,
And venison, for a journey dressed,
Bespeak the nature of the soul,
Activity, that knows no rest.

His bow, for action ready bent,
And arrows, with a head of stone,
Can only mean that life is spent,
And not the old ideas gone.

Thou, stranger, that shalt come this way,
No fraud upon the dead commit—
Observe the swelling turf, and say
They do not lie, but here they sit.

Here still a lofty rock remains,
On which the curious eye may trace
(Now wasted, half, by wearing rains)
The fancies of a ruder race.

Here still an aged elm aspires,
Beneath whose far-projecting shade
(And which the shepherd still admires)
The children of the forest played!

There oft a restless Indian queen
(Pale Shebah, with her braided hair)
And many a barbarous form is seen
To chide the man that lingers there.

By midnight moons, o'er moistening dews,
In habit for the chase arrayed,
The hunter still the deer pursues,
The hunter and the deer, a shade!

And long shall timorous fancy see
The painted chief, and pointed spear,
And Reason's self shall bow the knee
To shadows and delusions here.

1788

THE VANITY OF EXISTENCE

TO THYRSIS

In youth, gay scenes attract our eyes,
    And not suspecting their decay
Life's flowery fields before us rise,
    Regardless of its winter day.

But vain pursuits, and joys as vain,
    Convince us life is but a dream.
Death is to wake, to rise again
    To that true life you best esteem.

So nightly on some shallow tide,
    Oft have I seen a splendid show;

Reflected stars on either side,
    And glittering moons were seen below.

But when the tide had ebbed away,
    The scene fantastic with it fled,
A bank of mud around me lay,
    And sea-weed on the river's bed.

1781

from POLITICAL BIOGRAPHY: HUGH GAINE'S LIFE

. . . . .

I printed some treason for Philip Freneau,
Some damnable poems reflecting on Gage,
The King and his Council, and writ with such rage,
So full of invective, and loaded with spleen,
So sneeringly smart, and so hellishly keen,
That, at least in the judgment of half our wise men,
Alecto herself put the nib to his pen.

. . . . .

A POLITICAL LITANY

Libera Nos, Domine.—Deliver us, O Lord, not only from British Dependence, but also,

From a junto that labor with absolute power,
Whose schemes disappointed have made them look sour,
From the lords of the council, who fight against freedom,
Who still follow on where delusion shall lead them.

From the group at St. James's who slight our petitions,
And fools that are waiting for further submissions—
From a nation whose manners are rough and severe,
From scoundrels and rascals,—do keep us all clear.

From pirates sent out by command of the king
To murder and plunder, but never to swing;
From Wallace and Greaves, and *Vipers* and *Roses*,[10]
Whom, if heaven pleases, we'll give bloody noses.

From the valiant Dunmore, with his crew of banditti,
Who plunder Virginians at Williamsburg city,
From hot-headed Montague, mighty to swear,
The little fat man, with his pretty white hair.

From bishops in Britain, who butchers are grown,
From slaves, that would die for a smile from the throne,
From assemblies, that vote against Congress proceedings,
(Who now see the fruit of their stupid misleadings.)

From Tryon the mighty, who flies from our city,
And swelled with importance disdains the committee:
(But since he is pleased to proclaim us his foes,
What the devil care we where the devil he goes.)

From the caitiff, lord North, who would bind us in chains,
From a royal king Log, with his tooth-full of brains,
Who dreams, and is certain (when taking a nap)
He has conquered our lands, as they lay on his map.

From a kingdom that bullies, and hectors, and swears,
We send up to heaven our wishes and prayers
That we, disunited, may freemen be still,
And Britain go on—to be damned if she will.

New-York, June 1775

---

[10] Captains and ships in the British navy, then employed on the American coast.—*Freneau.*

EPIGRAM

OCCASIONED BY THE TITLE OF MR. RIVINGTON'S[11] NEW-YORK ROYAL GAZETTE BEING SCARCELY LEGIBLE

Says Satan to Jemmy, "I hold you a bet
"That you mean to abandon our Royal Gazette,
"Or, between you and me, you would manage things better
"Than the title to print on so sneaking a letter.

"Now being connected so long in the art,
"It would not be prudent at present to part;
"And people, perhaps, would be frightened, and fret
"If the devil alone carried on the Gazette."

Says Jemmy to Satan (by way of a wipe)
"Who gives me the matter should furnish the type;
"And why you find fault, I can scarcely divine,
"For the types, like the printer, are certainly thine.

" 'Tis yours to deceive with the semblance of truth,
"Thou friend of my age, and thou guide of my youth!
"But, to prosper, pray send me some further supplies,
"A set of new types, and a set of new lies."

1809

LINES

OCCASIONED BY MR. RIVINGTON'S NEW TITULAR TYPES TO HIS ROYAL GAZETTE

Well—now (said the devil) it looks something better!
Your title is struck on a *charming* new *letter:*
Last night in the dark, as I gave it a squint,
I saw my dear partner had taken the hint.

---

[11] Royal printer to his Britannic majesty, while his forces held the city of New York, from 1776 to November 25, 1783.—*Freneau.*

I ever surmised (though 'twas doubted by some)
That the old types were shadows of substance to come;
But if the NEW LETTER is pregnant with charms
It grieves me to think of those cursed King's Arms.
The *Dieu et mon droit* (his God and his right)
Is so dim, that I scarcely know what is meant by it;
The paws of the Lion can scarcely be seen,
And the Unicorn's guts are most shamefully lean!
The *Crown* is so worn of your master the despot,
That I hardly know which 'tis (a crown or a pisspot)
When I rub up my day-lights, and look very sharp
I just can distinguish the Irishman's harp,
Another device appears rather silly,
Alas! it is only the shade of the LILLY!
For the honour of George, and the fame of our nation,
Pray, give his escutcheons a rectification—
Or I know what I know (and I'm a queer shaver)
Of him and his arms I'll be the In-graver.

1809

TO A NOISY POLITICIAN

Since *Shylock's* book has walk'd the circles *here,*
What numerous blessings to our country flow!
Whales on our shores have run aground,
Sturgeons are in our rivers found;
Nay, ships have on the Delaware sail'd,
A sight most new!
Wheat has been sown, harvests have grown,
And *Shylock* held strange dialogues with *Sue.*

On coaches, now, gay coats of arms are wore
By *some,* who hardly had a coat before:
Silk gowns instead of homespun, now, are seen,
And, sir, 'tis true ('twixt me and you)

That some have grown prodigious fat,
That were prodigious lean!

1795

STANZAS

ON THE DECEASE OF THOMAS PAINE, WHO DIED AT NEW YORK, ON THE 8TH OF JUNE, 1809

Princes and kings decay and die
   And, instant, rise again:
But this is not the case, trust me,
   With men like THOMAS PAINE.

In vain the democratic host
   His *equal* would attain:
For years to come they will not boast
   A second Thomas Paine.

Though many may his name assume;
   Assumption is in vain;
For every man has not his plume—
   Whose name is *Thomas Paine*.

Though heaven bestow'd on all its sons
   Their *proper* share of brain,
It gives to few, ye simple ones,
   The mind of Thomas Paine.

To tyrants and the tyrant crew,
   Indeed, he was the bane;
He writ, and gave them all their due,
   And signed it,—THOMAS PAINE.

Oh! how we loved to see him write
   And curb the race of Cain!

They hope and wish that Thomas P——
   May never rise again.

What idle hopes!—yes—such a man
   May yet appear again,—
When *they* are dead they die for aye:
   —Not so with Thomas Paine.

1809

ODE

God save the Rights of Man!
Give us a heart to scan
Blessings so dear:
Let them be spread around
Wherever man is found,
And with the welcome sound
Ravish his ear.

Let us with France agree,
And bid the world be free,
While tyrants fall!
Let the rude savage host
Of their vast numbers boast—
Freedom's almighty trust
Laughs at them all!

Though hosts of slaves conspire
To quench fair Gallia's fire,
Still shall they fail:
Though traitors round her rise,
Leagu'd with her enemies,
To war each patriot flies,
And will prevail.

No more is valor's flame
Devoted to a name,

Taught to adore—
Soldiers of Liberty
Disdain to bow the knee,
But teach Equality
To every shore.

The world at last will join
To aid thy grand design,
Dear Liberty!
To Russia's frozen lands
The generous flame expands:
On Afric's burning sands
Shall man be free!

In this our western world
Be Freedom's flag unfurl'd
Through all its shores!
May no destructive blast
Our heaven of joy o'ercast,
May Freedom's fabric last
While time endures.

If e'er her cause require!—
Should tyrants e'er aspire
To aim their stroke,
May no proud despot daunt—
Should he his standard plant,
Freedom will never want
Her hearts of oak!

1793   1795

REFLECTIONS

ON THE GRADUAL PROGRESS OF NATIONS FROM DEMOCRATICAL STATES TO DESPOTIC EMPIRES

Mantua vae miserae nimium vicina Cremonae![12]
—Virgil

Oh fatal day! when to the Atlantic shore,
European despots sent the doctrine o'er,
That man's vast race was born to lick the dust;
Feed on the Winds, or toil through life accurst;
Poor and despised, that rulers might be great
And swell to monarchs, to devour the state.

Whence came these ills, or from what causes grew,
This vortex vast, that only spares the few,
Despotic sway, where every plague combined,
Distracts, degrades, and swallows up mankind;
Takes from the intellectual sun its light,
And shrouds the world in universal night?

Accuse not nature for the dreary scene,
That glooms her stage or hides her heaven serene,
She, equal still in all her varied ways,
An equal blessing to the world displays.
The suns that now on northern climates glow,
Will soon retire to melt Antarctic snow,
The seas she robb'd to form her clouds and rain,
Return in rivers to that source again;
But man, wrong'd man, borne down, deceived and vex'd,
Groans on through life, bewilder'd and perplex'd;
No suns on him but suns of misery shine,
Now march'd to war, now grovelling in the mine.
Chain'd, fetter'd, prostrate, sent from earth a slave,
To seek rewards in worlds beyond the grave.

---

[12] "Mantua, alas, too close to wretched Cremona!"

If in her general system, just to all,
We nature an impartial parent call,
Why did she not on man's whole race bestow,
Those fine sensations angels only know;
Who, sway'd by reason, with superior mind
In nature's state all nature's blessings find,
Which shed through all, does all their race pervade,
In streams not niggard by a despot made?

Leave this a secret in great nature's breast,
Confess that all her works tend to the best,
Or own that man's neglected culture here
Breeds all the mischiefs that we feel or fear.
In all, except the skill to rule her race,
Man, wise and skillful, gives each part its place:
Each nice machine he plans, to reason true,
Adapting all things to the end in view,
But taught in this, the art himself to rule
His sense is folly, and himself a fool.

Where social strength resides, there rests, 'tis plain,
The power, mankind to govern and restrain:
This strength is not but in the social plan
Controling all, the common good of man,
That power concentred by the general voice,
In honest men, an honest people's choice,
With frequent change, to keep the patriot pure,
And from vain views of power the heart secure:
Here lies the secret, hid from Rome or Greece,
That holds a state in awe, yet holds in peace.

See through the world, in ages now retired,
Man foe to man, as policy required:
At some proud tyrant's nod what millions rose,
To extend their sway, and make a world their foes.
View Asia ravaged, Europe drench'd with blood,

In feuds whose cause no nation understood.
The cause we fear, of so much misery sown,
Known at the helm of state, and there alone.

  Left to himself, wherever man is found,
In peace he aims to walk life's little round;
In peace to sail, in peace to till the soil,
Nor force false grandeur from a brother's toil.
All but the base, designing, scheming, few,
Who seize on nations with a robber's view,
With crowns and sceptres awe his dazzled eye,
And priests that hold the artillery of the sky;
These, these, with armies, navies, potent grown,
Impoverish man and bid the nations groan.
These with pretended balances of states
Keep worlds at variance, breed eternal hates,
Make man the poor base slave of low design,
Degrade his nature to its last decline,
Shed hell's worse blots on his exalted race,
And make them poor and mean, to make them base.

  Shall views like these assail our happy land,
Where embryo monarchs thirst for wide command,
Shall a whole nation's strength and fair renown
Be sacrificed, to prop a tottering throne,
That, ages past, the world's great curse has stood,
Has throve on plunder, and been fed on blood.—
Americans! will you control such views?
Speak—for you must—you have no hour to lose.

1815

ON THE UNIVERSALITY AND OTHER ATTRIBUTES
OF THE GOD OF NATURE

    All that we see, about, abroad,
    What is it all, but nature's God?
    In meaner works discover'd here

No less than in the starry sphere.

In seas, on earth, this God is seen;
All that exist, upon him lean;
He lives in all, and never stray'd
A moment from the works he made:

His system fix'd on general laws
Bespeaks a wise creating cause;
Impartially he rules mankind
And all that on this globe we find.

Unchanged in all that seems to change,
Unbounded space is his great range;
To one vast purpose always true,
No time, with him, is old or new.

In all the attributes divine
Unlimited perfectings shine;
In these enwrapt, in these complete,
All virtues in that centre meet.

This power who doth all powers transcend,
To all intelligence a friend,
Exists, the greatest and the best
Throughout all worlds, to make them blest.

All that he did he first approved,
He all things into *being* loved;
O'er all he made he still presides,
For them in life, or death provides.

1815

ON THE UNIFORMITY AND PERFECTION OF NATURE

On one fix'd point all nature moves,
Nor deviates from the track she loves;

Her system, drawn from reason's source,
She scorns to change her wonted course.

Could she descend from that great plan
To work unusual things for man,
To suit the insect of an hour—
This would betray a want of power,

Unsettled in its first design
And erring, when it did combine
The parts that form the vast machine,
The figures sketch'd on nature's scene.

Perfections of the great first cause
Submit to no contracted laws,
But all-sufficient, all-supreme,
Include no trivial views in them.

Who looks through nature with an eye
That would the scheme of heaven descry,
Observes her constant, still the same,
In all her laws, through all her frame.

No imperfection can be found
In all that is, above, around,—
All, nature made, in reason's sight
Is order all and all is right.

1815

ON THE RELIGION OF NATURE

The power, that gives with liberal hand
  The blessings man enjoys, while here,
And scatters through a smiling land
  The abundant products of the year;
    That power of nature, ever bless'd,
    Bestow'd religion with the rest.

Born with ourselves, her early sway
  Inclines the tender mind to take
The path of right, fair virtue's way
  Its own felicity to make.
    This universally extends
    And leads to no mysterious ends.

Religion, such as nature taught,
  With all divine perfection suits;
Had all mankind this system sought
  Sophists would cease their vain disputes,
    And from this source would nations know
    All that can make their heaven below.

This deals not curses on mankind,
  Or dooms them to perpetual grief,
If from its aid no joys they find,
  It damns them not for unbelief;
    Upon a more exalted plan
    Creatress nature dealt with man—

Joy to the day, when all agree
  On such grand systems to proceed,
From fraud, design, and error free,
  And which to truth and goodness lead:
    Then persecution will retreat
    And man's religion be complete.

1815

ROYALL TYLER
(1757-1826)

One of a group of sprightly young lawyer-wits who indulged literary leanings they dared not center their careers upon, Royall Tyler was a novelist and an associate of Dennie in his early adventures in criticism. But it is as author of the first American comedy that he is now remembered. *The Contrast* was so skilfully modelled on the plays of Richard Sheridan that it has proved thoroughly playable and stageworthy in several modern revivals. It also employs or reflects practically all of the dominant literary conventions of the day and many if not most of its intellectual concerns.

Bibliography: Arthur H. Quinn, *A History of American Drama from the Beginning to the Civil War*, New York, 1943.

Text: Arthur H. Quinn, ed., *Representative American Plays*, New York, 1938.

THE CONTRAST

PROLOGUE

Written by a Young Gentleman of New-York, and Spoken by Mr. Wignell

> Exult each patriot heart!—this night is shewn
> A piece, which we may fairly call our own;
> Where the proud titles of "My Lord! Your Grace!"
> To humble Mr. and plain Sir give place.
> Our Author pictures not from foreign climes
> The fashions, or the follies of the times;
> But has confin'd the subject of his work
> To the gay scenes—the circles of New-York.
> On native themes his Muse displays her pow'rs;
> If ours the faults, the virtues too are ours.
> Why should our thoughts to distant countries roam,
> When each refinement may be found at home?
> Who travels now to ape the rich or great,
> To deck an equipage and roll in state;
> To court the graces, or to dance with ease,
> Or by hypocrisy to strive to please?
> Our free-born ancestors such arts despis'd;
> Genuine sincerity alone they priz'd;

Their minds, with honest emulation fir'd,
To solid good—not ornament—aspir'd;
Or, if ambition rous'd a bolder flame,
Stern virtue throve, where indolence was shame.

But modern youths, with imitative sense,
Deem taste in dress the proof of excellence;
And spurn the meanness of your homespun arts,
Since homespun habits would obscure their parts;
Whilst all, which aims at splendour and parade,
Must come from Europe, and be ready made.
Strange! we should thus our native worth disclaim,
And check the progress of our rising fame.
Yet one, whilst imitation bears the sway,
Aspires to nobler heights, and points the way,
Be rous'd, my friends! his bold example view;
Let your own Bards be proud to copy you!
Should rigid critics reprobate our play,
At least the patriotic heart will say,
"Glorious our fall, since in a noble cause.
"The bold attempt alone demands applause."
Still may the wisdom of the Comic Muse
Exalt your merits, or your faults accuse.
But think not, 't is her aim to be severe;—
We all are mortals, and as mortals err.
If candour pleases, we are truly blest;
Vice trembles, when compell'd to stand confess'd.
Let not light Censure on your faults, offend,
Which aims not to expose them, but amend.
Thus does our Author to your candour trust;
Conscious, the free are generous, as just.

CHARACTERS

Col. Manly	Jessamy	Maria
Dimple	Jonathan	Letitia
Vanrough	Charlotte	Jenny
	Servants	

Scene, New York

ACT FIRST

SCENE I. *An Apartment at* CHARLOTTE'S. CHARLOTTE *and* LETITIA *discovered*.

LETITIA And so, Charlotte, you really think the pocket-hoop unbecoming.

CHARLOTTE No, I don't say so: It may be very becoming to saunter round the house of a rainy day; to visit my grandmamma, or go to Quakers' meeting: but to swim in a minuet, with the eyes of fifty well-dressed beaux upon me, to trip it in the Mall, or walk on the battery, give me the luxurious, jaunty, flowing, bell-hoop. It would have delighted you to have seen me the last evening, my charming girl! I was dangling o'er the battery with Billy Dimple; a knot of young fellows were upon the platform; as I passed them I faultered with one of the most bewitching false steps you ever saw, and then recovered myself with such a pretty confusion, flirting my hoop to discover a jet black shoe and brilliant buckle. Gad! how my little heart thrilled to hear the confused raptures of—*"Demme, Jack, what a delicate foot!" "Ha! General, what a well-turn'd—"*

LETITIA Fie! fie! Charlotte, (*stopping her mouth*) I protest you are quite a libertine.

CHARLOTTE Why, my dear little prude, are we not all such libertines? Do you think, when I sat tortured two hours under the hands of my friseur, and an hour more at my toilet, that I had any thoughts of my aunt Susan, or my cousin Betsey? though they are both allowed to be critical judges of dress.

LETITIA Why, who should we dress to please, but those who are judges of its merit?

CHARLOTTE Why a creature who does not know *Buffon* from *Souflee*—Man!—my Letitia—Man! for whom we dress, walk, dance, talk, lisp, languish, and smile. Does not the grave Spectator assure us, that even our much bepraised diffidence, modesty, and blushes, are all directed to make ourselves good wives and mothers as fast as we can. Why, I'll undertake with one flirt of this hoop to bring more beaux to my feet in one week, than the grave Maria, and her sentimental circle, can do, by sighing sentiment till their hairs are grey.

LETITIA Well, I won't argue with you; you always out talk me; let us change the subject. I hear that Mr. Dimple and Maria are soon to be married.

CHARLOTTE You hear true. I was consulted in the choice of the wedding clothes. She is to be married in a delicate white sattin, and has a monstrous pretty brocaded lutestring for the second day. It would have done you good to have seen with what an affected indifference the dear sentimentalist turned over a thousand pretty things, just as if her heart did not palpitate with her approaching happiness, and at last made her choice, and arranged her dress with such apathy, as if she did not know that plain white satin, and a simple blond lace, would shew her clear skin, and dark hair, to the greatest advantage.

LETITIA But they say her indifference to dress, and even to the gentleman himself, is not entirely affected.

CHARLOTTE How?

LETITIA It is whispered, that if Maria gives her hand to Mr. Dimple, it will be without her heart.

CHARLOTTE Though the giving the heart is one of the last of all laughable considerations in the marriage of a girl of spirit, yet I should like to hear what antiquated notions the dear little piece of old fashioned prudery has got in her head.

LETITIA Why you know that old Mr. John-Richard-Robert-Jacob-Isaac-Abraham-Cornelius Van Dumpling, Billy Dimple's father, (for he has thought fit to soften his name, as well as manners, during his English tour) was the most intimate friend of Maria's father. The old folks, about a year before Mr. Van Dumpling's death, proposed this match: the young folks were accordingly introduced, and told they must love one another. Billy was then a good natured, decent, dressing young fellow, with a little dash of the coxcomb, such as our young fellows of fortune usually have. At this time, I really believe she thought she loved him; and had they then been married, I doubt not, they might have jogged on, to the end of the chapter, a good kind of a sing-song lack-a-daysaical life, as other honest married folks do.

CHARLOTTE   Why did they not then marry?

LETITIA   Upon the death of his father, Billy went to England to see the world, and rub off a little of the patroon rust. During his absence, Maria like a good girl, to keep herself constant to her *nown true-love,* avoided company, and betook herself, for her amusement, to her books, and her dear Billy's letters. But, alas! how many ways has the mischievous demon of inconstancy of stealing into a woman's heart! Her love was destroyed by the very means she took to support it.

CHARLOTTE   How?—Oh! I have it—some likely young beau found the way to her study.

LETITIA   Be patient, Charlotte—your head so runs upon beaux. —Why she read Sir Charles Grandison, Clarissa Harlow, Shenstone, and the Sentimental Journey; and between whiles, as I said, Billy's letters. But as her taste improved, her love declined. The contrast was so striking betwixt the good sense of her books, and the flimsiness of her love-letters, that she discovered she had unthinkingly engaged her hand without her heart; and then the whole transaction managed by the old folks, now appeared so unsentimental, and looked so like bargaining for a bale of goods, that she found she ought to have rejected, according to every rule of romance, even the man of her choice, if imposed upon her in that manner—Clary Harlow would have scorned such a match.

CHARLOTTE   Well, how was it on Mr. Dimple's return? Did he meet a more favourable reception than his letters?

LETITIA   Much the same. She spoke of him with respect abroad, and with contempt in her closet. She watched his conduct and conversation, and found that he had by travelling acquired the wickedness of Lovelace without his wit, and the politeness of Sir Charles Grandison without his generosity. The ruddy youth who washed his face at the cistern every morning, and swore and looked eternal love and constancy, was now metamorphosed into a flippant, palid, polite beau, who devotes the morning to his toilet, reads a few pages of Chesterfield's letters, and then minces out, to put the infamous principles in practice upon every woman he meets.

CHARLOTTE But, if she is so apt at conjuring up these sentimental bugbears, why does she not discard him at once?

LETITIA Why, she thinks her word too sacred to be trifled with. Besides, her father, who has a great respect for the memory of his deceased friend, is ever telling her how he shall renew his years in their union, and repeating the dying injunctions of old Van Dumpling.

CHARLOTTE A mighty pretty story! And so you would make me believe, that the sensible Maria would give up Dumpling manor, and the all-accomplished Dimple as a husband, for the absurd, ridiculous reason, forsooth, because she despises and abhors him. Just as if a lady could not be privileged to spend a man's fortune, ride in his carriage, be called after his name, and call him her *nown dear lovee* when she wants money, without loving and respecting the great he-creature. Oh! my dear girl, you are a monstrous prude.

LETITIA I don't say what I would do; I only intimate how I suppose she wishes to act.

CHARLOTTE No, no, no! A fig for sentiment. If she breaks, or wishes to break, with Mr. Dimple, depend upon it, she has some other man in her eye. A woman rarely discards one lover, until she is sure of another.— Letitia little thinks what a clue I have to Dimple's conduct. The generous man submits to render himself disgusting to Maria, in order that she may leave him at liberty to address me. I must change the subject. (*Aside, and rings a bell.*)

(*Enter* SERVANT.)

Frank, order the horses to.— Talking of marriage—did you hear that Sally Bloomsbury is going to be married next week to Mr. Indigo, the rich Carolinian?

LETITIA Sally Bloomsbury married!— Why, she is not yet in her teens.

CHARLOTTE I do not know how that is, but, you may depend upon it, 't is a done affair. I have it from the best authority. There is my aunt Wyerley's Hannah (you know Hannah— though a black, she is a wench that was never caught in a lie in her life); now Hannah has a brother who courts Sarah, Mrs. Catgut the milliner's girl, and she told Hannah's brother, and Hannah, who, as I said before, is a girl of undoubted veracity, told it directly to me, that Mrs. Catgut was making a new cap for Miss Bloomsbury, which, as it was very dressy, it is very probable is designed for a wedding cap: now, as she is to be married, who can it be to, but to Mr. Indigo? Why, there is no other gentleman that visits at her papa's.

LETITIA Say not a word more, Charlotte. Your intelligence is so direct and well grounded, it is almost a pity that it is not a piece of scandal.

CHARLOTTE Oh! I am the pink of prudence. Though I cannot charge myself with ever having discredited a tea-party by my silence, yet I take care never to report any thing of my acquaintance, especially if it is to their credit,—*discredit,* I mean—until I have searched to the bottom of it. It is true, there is infinite pleasure in this charitable pursuit. Oh! how delicious to go and condole with the friends of some backsliding sister, or to retire with some old dowager or maiden aunt of the family, who love scandal so well, that they cannot forbear gratifying their appetite at the expence of the reputation of their nearest relations! And then to return full fraught with a rich collection of circumstances, to retail to the next circle of our acquaintance under the strongest injunctions of secrecy,—ha, ha, ha!—interlarding the melancholy tale with so many doleful shakes of the head, and more doleful, "Ah! who would have thought it! so amiable, so prudent a young lady, as we all thought her, what a monstrous pity! well, I have nothing to charge myself with; I acted the part of a friend, I warned her of the principles of that rake, I told her what would be the consequence; I told her so, I told her so."— Ha, ha, ha!

LETITIA Ha, ha, ha! Well, but Charlotte, you don't tell me what you think of Miss Bloomsbury's match.

CHARLOTTE Think! why I think it is probable she cried for a plaything, and they have given her a husband. Well, well, well, the puling chit shall not be deprived of her plaything: 't is only exchanging London dolls for American babies— Apropos, of babies, have you heard what Mrs. Affable's high-flying notions of delicacy have come to?

LETITIA Who, she that was Miss Lovely?

CHARLOTTE The same; she married Bob Affable of Schenectady. Don't you remember?

(*Enter* SERVANT.)

SERVANT Madam, the carriage is ready.

LETITIA Shall we go to the stores first, or visiting?

CHARLOTTE I should think it rather too early to visit; especially Mrs. Prim: you know she is so particular.

LETITIA Well, but what of Mrs. Affable?

CHARLOTTE Oh, I'll tell you as we go; come, come, let us hasten. I hear Mrs. Catgut has some of the prettiest caps arrived, you ever saw. I shall die if I have not the first sight of them.

(*Exeunt.*)

SCENE 2. *A Room in* VAN ROUGH's *House.* MARIA *sitting disconsolate at a Table, with Books, etc.*

Song

I

The sun sets in night, and the stars shun the day;
But glory remains when their lights fade away!
Begin, ye tormentors! your threats are in vain,
For the son of Alknomook shall never complain.

II

Remember the arrows he shot from his bow;
Remember your chiefs by his hatchet laid low:

Why so slow?—do you wait till I shrink from the pain?
No—the son of Alknomook will never complain.

III

Remember the wood where in ambush we lay;
And the scalps which we bore from your nation away:
Now the flame rises fast, you exult in my pain;
But the son of Alknomook can never complain.

IV

I go to the land where my father is gone;
His ghost shall rejoice in the fame of his son:
Death comes like a friend, he relieves me from pain;
And thy son, Oh Alknomook! has scorn'd to complain.

There is something in this song which ever calls forth my affections. The manly virtue of courage, that fortitude which steels the heart against the keenest misfortunes, which interweaves the laurel of glory amidst the instruments of torture and death, displays something so noble, so exalted, that in despite of the prejudices of education, I cannot but admire it, even in a savage. The prepossession which our sex is supposed to entertain for the character of a soldier, is, I know, a standing piece of raillery among the wits. A cockade, a lapell'd coat, and a feather, they will tell you, are irresistible by a female heart. Let it be so.— Who is it that considers the helpless situation of our sex, that does not see we each moment stand in need of a protector, and that a brave one too. Formed of the more delicate materials of nature, endowed only with the softer passions, incapable, from our ignorance of the world, to guard against the wiles of mankind, our security for happiness often depends upon their generosity and courage:— Alas! how little of the former do we find. How inconsistent! that man should be leagued to destroy that honour, upon which, solely rests his respect and esteem. Ten thousand temptations allure us, ten thousand passions betray us; yet the smallest deviation from the path of rectitude is followed by the contempt and insult of man, and the more remorseless pity of woman: years of penitence and tears cannot wash away the stain, nor a life of virtue obliterate its remembrance. Reputation is the life of woman; yet courage to protect it, is masculine and disgusting; and the only safe asylum a woman of delicacy can find, is in the arms of a man of honour. How naturally then, should we love the brave, and the generous; how gratefully should we bless the arm raised for our protection, when nerv'd by virtue, and directed by honour! Heaven grant that the man with whom I may be connected—may be connected!— Whither has my imagination transported me—whither does it now lead me?— Am I not indissolubly engaged by every obligation of honour, which my own consent, and my father's approbation can give, to a man who can never share my affections, and whom a few days hence, it will be criminal for me to disapprove—to disapprove! would to heaven that were all—to despise. For, can the most frivolous manners, actuated by the most depraved heart, meet, or merit, anything but contempt from every woman of delicacy and sentiment?

(VAN ROUGH, *without*. Mary!)

Ha, my father's voice— Sir!—

(*Enter* VAN ROUGH.)

VAN ROUGH What, Mary, always singing doleful ditties, and moping over these plaguy books.

MARIA I hope, Sir, that it is not criminal to improve my mind with books; or to divert my melancholy with singing at my leisure hours.

VAN ROUGH Why, I don't know that, child; I don't know that. They us'd to say when I was a young man, that if a woman knew how to make a pudding, and to keep herself out of fire and water, she knew enough for a wife. Now, what good have these books done you? have they not made you melancholy? as you call it. Pray, what right has a girl of your age to be in the dumps? haven't you every thing your heart can wish; an't you going to be married to a young man of great fortune; an't you going to have the quit-rent of twenty miles square?

MARIA One hundredth part of the land, and a lease for life of the heart of a man I could love, would satisfy me.

VAN·ROUGH Pho, pho, pho! child; nonsense, downright nonsense, child. This comes of your reading your story-books; your Charles Grandisons, your Sentimental Journals, and your Robinson Crusoes, and such other trumpery. No, no, no! child, it is money makes the mare go; keep your eye upon the main chance, Mary.

MARIA Marriage, Sir, is, indeed, a very serious affair.

VAN ROUGH You are right, child; you are right. I am sure I found it so to my cost.

MARIA I mean, Sir, that as marriage is a portion for life, and so intimately involves our happiness, we cannot be too considerate in the choice of our companion.

VAN ROUGH Right, child; very right. A young woman should be very sober when she is making her choice, but when she has once made it, as you have done, I don't see why she should not be as merry as a grig; I am sure she has reason enough to be so— Solomon says, that "there is a time to laugh, and a time to weep"; now a time for a young woman to laugh is when she has made sure of a good rich husband. Now a time to cry, according to you, Mary, is when she is making choice of him: but, I should think, that a young woman's time to cry was, when she despaired of *getting* one.— Why, there was your mother now; to be sure when I popp'd the question to her, she did look a little silly; but when she had once looked down on her apron-strings, as all modest young women us'd to do, and drawled out ye-s, she was as brisk and as merry as a bee.

MARIA My honoured mother, Sir, had no motive to melancholy; she married the man of her choice.

VAN ROUGH The man of her choice! And pray, Mary, an't you going to marry the man of your choice—what trumpery notion is this?— It is these vile books (throwing them away). I'd have you to know, Mary, if you won't make young Van Dumpling the man of *your* choice, you shall marry him as the man of *my* choice.

MARIA You terrify me, Sir. Indeed, Sir, I am all submission. My will is yours.

VAN ROUGH Why, that is the way your mother us'd to talk. "My will is yours, my dear Mr. Van Rough, my will is yours": but she took special care to have her own way though for all that.

MARIA Do not reflect upon my mother's memory, Sir—

VAN ROUGH Why not, Mary, why not? She kept me from speaking my mind all her *life,* and do you think she shall henpeck me now she is *dead* too? Come, come; don't go to sniveling: be a good girl, and mind the main chance. I'll see you well settled in the world.

MARIA I do not doubt your love, Sir; and it is my duty to obey you.— I will endeavour to make my duty and inclination go hand in hand.

VAN ROUGH Well, well, Mary; do you be a good girl, mind the main chance, and never mind inclination.— Why, do you know that I have been down in the cellar this very morning to examine a pipe of Madeira which I purchased the week you were born, and mean to tap on your wedding day.— That pipe cost me fifty pounds sterling. It was well worth sixty pounds; but I overreached Ben Bulkhead, the supercargo: I'll tell you the whole story. You must know that—

(*Enter* SERVANT.)

SERVANT Sir, Mr. Transfer, the broker, is below.   (*Exit.*)

VAN ROUGH Well, Mary, I must go.— Remember, and be a good girl, and mind the main chance.   (*Exit.*)

MARIA (*Alone.*) How deplorable is my situation! How distressing for a daughter to find her heart militating with her filial duty! I know my father loves me tenderly, why then do I reluctantly obey him? Heaven knows! with what reluctance I should oppose the will of a parent, or set an example of filial disobedience; at a parent's command I could wed aukwardness and deformity. Were the heart of my husband good, I would so magnify his good qualities with the eye of conjugal affection, that the defects of his person and manners should be lost in the emanation of his virtues. At a father's command, I could embrace poverty. Were the poor man my husband, I would learn resignation to my lot; I would enliven our frugal meal with good humour, and chase away misfortune from our cottage with a smile. At a father's command, I could almost submit, to what every female heart knows to be the most mortifying, to marry a weak man, and blush at my husband's folly in every company I visited.— But to marry a depraved wretch, whose only virtue is a polished exterior; who is actuated by the unmanly ambition of conquering the defenceless; whose heart, insensible to the emotions of patriotism, dilates at the plaudits of every unthinking girl: whose laurels are the sighs and tears of the miserable victims of his specious behaviour.— Can he, who has no regard for the peace and happiness of other families, ever have a due regard for the peace and happiness of his own? Would to heaven that my father were not so hasty in his temper! Surely, if I were to state my reasons for declining this match, he would not compel me to marry a man—whom, though my lips may solemnly promise to honour, I find my heart must ever despise. (*Exit.*)

END OF THE FIRST ACT

ACT SECOND

SCENE I

(*Enter* CHARLOTTE *and* LETITIA)

CHARLOTTE (*At entering.*) Betty, take those things out of the carriage and carry them to my chamber; see that you don't tumble them.— My dear, I protest, I think it was the homeliest of the whole. I declare I was almost tempted to return and change it.

LETITIA Why would you take it?

CHARLOTTE Didn't Mrs. Catgut say it was the most fashionable?

LETITIA But, my dear, it will never sit becomingly on you.

CHARLOTTE I know that; but did not you hear Mrs. Catgut say it was fashionable?

LETITIA Did you see that sweet airy cap with the white sprig?

CHARLOTTE Yes and I longed to take it; but, my dear, what could I do?— Did not Mrs. Catgut say it was the most fashionable; and if I had not taken it, was not that aukward gawky, Sally Slender, ready to purchase it immediately?

LETITIA Did you observe how she tumbled over the things at the next shop, and then went off without purchasing any thing, nor even thanking the poor man for his trouble?— But of all the aukward creatures, did you see Miss Blouze, endeavouring to thrust her unmerciful arm into those small kid gloves?

CHARLOTTE Ha, ha, ha, ha!

LETITIA Then did you take notice, with what an affected warmth of friendship she and Miss Wasp met? when all their acquaintances know how much pleasure they take in abusing each other in every company?

CHARLOTTE Lud! Letitia, is that so extraordinary? Why, my dear, I hope you are not going to turn sentimentalist.— Scandal, you know, is but amusing ourselves with the faults, foibles, follies and reputations of our friends;—indeed, I don't know why we should have friends, if we are not at liberty to make use of them. But no person is so ignorant of the world as to suppose, because I amuse myself with a lady's faults, that I am obliged to quarrel with her person, every time we meet; believe me, my dear, we should have very few acquaintances at that rate.

(SERVANT *enters and delivers a letter to* CHARLOTTE, *and Exit.*)

CHARLOTTE You'll excuse me, my dear. (*Opens and reads to herself.*)

LETITIA Oh, quite excusable.

CHARLOTTE As I hope to be married, my brother Henry is in the city.

LETITIA What, your brother, Colonel Manly?

CHARLOTTE Yes, my dear; the only brother I have in the world.

LETITIA Was he never in this city?

CHARLOTTE Never nearer than Harlem Heights, where he lay with his regiment.

LETITIA   What sort of a being is this brother of yours? If he is as chatty, as pretty, as sprightly as you, half the belles in the city will be pulling caps for him.

CHARLOTTE   My brother is the very counterpart and reverse of me: I am gay, he is grave; I am airy, he is solid; I am ever selecting the most pleasing objects for my laughter, he has a tear for every pitiful one. And thus, whilst he is plucking the briars and thorns from the path of the unfortunate, I am strewing my own path with roses.

LETITIA   My sweet friend, not quite so poetical, and little more particular.

CHARLOTTE   Hands off, Letitia. I feel the rage of simile upon me; I can't talk to you in any other way. My brother has a heart replete with the noblest sentiments, but then, it is like—it is like—Oh! you provoking girl, you have deranged all my ideas—it is like—Oh! I have it—his heart is like an old maiden lady's bandbox; it contains many costly things, arranged with the most scrupulous nicety, yet the misfortune is, that they are too delicate, costly, and antiquated, for common use.

LETITIA   By what I can pick out of your flowery description, your brother is no beau.

CHARLOTTE   No, indeed; he makes no pretension to the character. He'd ride, or rather fly, an hundred miles to relieve a distressed object, or to do a gallant act in the service of his country: but, should you drop your fan or bouquet in his presence, it is ten to one that some beau at the farther end of the room would have the honour of presenting it to you, before he had observed that it fell. I'll tell you one of his antiquated, anti-gallant notions.—He said once in my presence, in a room full of company—would you believe it—in a large circle of ladies, that the best evidence a gentleman could give a young lady of his respect and affection, was, to endeavour in a friendly manner to rectify her foibles. I protest I was crimson to the eyes, upon reflecting that I was known as his sister.

LETITIA   Insupportable creature! tell a lady of her faults! If he is so grave, I fear I have no chance of captivating him.

CHARLOTTE His conversation is like a rich old fashioned brocade, it will stand alone; every sentence is a sentiment. Now you may judge what a time I had with him, in my twelve months' visit to my father. He read me such lectures, out of pure brotherly affection, against the extremes of fashion, dress, flirting, and coquetry, and all the other dear things which he knows I doat upon, that, I protest, his conversation made me as melancholy as if I had been at church; and heaven knows, though I never prayed to go there but on one occasion, yet I would have exchanged his conversation for a psalm and a sermon. Church is rather melancholy, to be sure; but then I can ogle the beaux, and be regaled with "here endeth the first lesson"; but his brotherly *here,* you would think had no end. You captivate him! Why, my dear, he would as soon fall in love with a box of Italian flowers. There is Maria now, if she were not engaged, she might do something.— Oh! how I should like to see that pair of penserosos together, looking as grave as two sailors' wives of a stormy night, with a flow of sentiment meandering through their conversation like purling streams in modern poetry.

LETITIA Oh! my dear fanciful—

CHARLOTTE Hush! I hear some person coming through the entry.

(*Enter* SERVANT.)

SERVANT Madam, there's a gentleman below who calls himself Colonel Manly; do you chuse to be at home?

CHARLOTTE Shew him in. (*Exit* SERVANT.) Now for a sober face.

(*Enter* COLONEL MANLY.)

MANLY My dear Charlotte, I am happy that I once more enfold you within the arms of fraternal affection. I know you are going to ask (amiable impatience!) how our parents do,—the venerable pair transmit you their blessing by me—they totter on the verge of a well-spent life, and wish only to see their children settled in the world, to depart in peace.

CHARLOTTE I am very happy to hear that they are well. (*Coolly*.) Brother, will you give me leave to introduce you to our uncle's ward, one of my most intimate friends.

MANLY (*Saluting* LETITIA.) I ought to regard your friends as my own.

CHARLOTTE Come, Letitia, do give us a little dash of your vivacity; my brother is so sentimental, and so grave, that I protest he'll give us the vapours.

MANLY Though sentiment and gravity, I know, are banished the polite world, yet, I hoped, they might find some countenance in the meeting of such near connections as brother and sister.

CHARLOTTE Positively, brother, if you go one step further in this strain, you will set me crying, and that, you know, would spoil my eyes; and then I should never get the husband which our good papa and mamma have so kindly wished me—never be established in the world.

MANLY Forgive me, my sister—I am no enemy to mirth; I love your sprightliness; and I hope it will one day enliven the hours of some worthy man; but when I mention the respectable authors of my existence,—the cherishers and protectors of my helpless infancy, whose hearts glow with such fondness and attachment, that they would willingly lay down their lives for my welfare, you will excuse me, if I am so unfashionable as to speak of them with some degree of respect and reverence.

CHARLOTTE Well, well, brother; if you won't be gay, we'll not differ; I will be as grave as you wish. (*Affects gravity*.) And so, brother, you have come to the city to exchange some of your commutation notes for a little pleasure.

MANLY Indeed, you are mistaken; my errand is not of amusement, but business; and as I neither drink nor game, my expences will be so trivial, I shall have no occasion to sell my notes.

CHARLOTTE Then you won't have occasion to do a very good thing. Why, there was the Vermont General—he came down some time since, sold all his musty notes at one stroke, and then laid the cash out in trinkets for his dear Fanny. I want a dozen pretty things myself; have you got the notes with you?

MANLY I shall be ever willing to contribute as far as it is in my power, to adorn, or in any way to please my sister; yet, I hope, I shall never be obliged for this, to sell my notes. I may be romantic, but I preserve them as a sacred deposit. Their full amount is justly due to me, but as embarrassments, the natural consequences of a long war, disable my country from supporting its credit, I shall wait with patience until it is rich enough to discharge them. If that is not in my day, they shall be transmitted as an honourable certificate to posterity, that I have humbly imitated our illustrious WASHINGTON, in having exposed my health and life in the service of my country, without reaping any other reward than the glory of conquering in so arduous a contest.

CHARLOTTE Well said heroics. Why, my dear Henry, you have such a lofty way of saying things, that I protest I almost tremble at the thought of introducing you to the polite circles in the city. The belles would think you were a player run mad, with your head filled with old scraps of tragedy: and, as to the beaux, they might admire, because they would not understand you.— But, however, I must, I believe, venture to introduce you to two or three ladies of my acquaintance.

LETITIA And that will make him acquainted with thirty or forty beaux.

CHARLOTTE Oh! brother, you don't know what a fund of happiness you have in store.

MANLY I fear, sister, I have not refinement sufficient to enjoy it.

CHARLOTTE Oh! you cannot fail being pleased.

LETITIA Our ladies are so delicate and dressy.

CHARLOTTE And our beaux so dressy and delicate.

LETITIA Our ladies chat and flirt so agreeably.

CHARLOTTE And our beaux simper and bow so gracefully.

LETITIA With their hair so trim and neat.

CHARLOTTE And their faces so soft and sleek.

LETITIA Their buckles so tonish and bright.

CHARLOTTE And their hands so slender and white.

LETITIA I vow, Charlotte, we are quite poetical.

CHARLOTTE And then, brother, the faces of the beaux are of such a lily white hue! None of that horrid robustness of constitution, that vulgar corn-fed glow of health, which can only serve to alarm an unmarried lady with apprehensions, and prove a melancholy memento to a married one, that she can never hope for the happiness of being a widow. I will say this to the credit of our city beaux, that such is the delicacy of their complexion, dress, and address, that, even had I no reliance upon the honour of the dear Adonises, I would trust myself in any possible situation with them, without the least apprehensions of rudeness.

MANLY Sister Charlotte!

CHARLOTTE Now, now, now brother (*interrupting him*), now don't go to spoil my mirth with a dash of your gravity; I am so glad to see you, I am in tip-top spirits. Oh! that you could be with us at a little snug party. There is Billy Simper, Jack Chassé, and Colonel Van Titter, Miss Promonade, and the two Miss Tambours, sometimes make a party, with some other ladies, in a side-box at the play. Everything is conducted with such decorum,— first we bow round to the company in general, then to each one in particular, then we have so many inquiries after each other's health, and we are so happy to meet each other, and it is so many ages since we last had that pleasure, and, if a married lady is in company, we have such a sweet dissertation upon her son Bobby's chin-cough then the curtain rises, then our sensibility is all awake, and then by the mere force of apprehension, we torture some harmless expression into a double meaning, which the poor author never dreamt of, and then we have recourse to our fans, and then we blush, and then the gentlemen jog one another, peep under the fan, and make the prettiest remarks; and then we giggle and they simper, and they giggle and we simper, and then the curtain drops, and then for nuts and oranges, and then we bow, and it's pray Ma'am take it, and pray Sir keep it, and oh! not for the world, Sir: and then the curtain rises again, and then we blush, and giggle, and simper, and bow, all over again. Oh! the sentimental charms of a side-box conversation!

(*All laugh.*)

MANLY Well, sister, I join heartily with you in the laugh; for, in my opinion, it is as justifiable to laugh at folly, as it is reprehensible to ridicule misfortune.

CHARLOTTE Well, but brother, positively, I can't introduce you in these clothes: why, your coat looks as if it were calculated for the vulgar purpose of keeping yourself comfortable.

MANLY This coat was my regimental coat in the late war. The public tumults of our state have induced me to buckle on the sword in support of that government which I once fought to establish. I can only say, sister, that there was a time when this coat was respectable, and some people even thought that those men who had endured so many winter campaigns in the service of their country, without bread, clothing, or pay, at least deserved that the poverty of their appearance should not be ridiculed.

CHARLOTTE We agree in opinion entirely, brother, though it would not have done for me to have said it: it is the coat makes the man respectable. In the time of the war, when we were almost frightened to death, why, your coat was respectable, that is, fashionable; now another kind of coat is fashionable, that is, respectable. And pray direct the taylor to make yours the height of the fashion.

MANLY Though it is of little consequence to me of what shape my coat is, yet, as to the height of the fashion, there you will please to excuse me, sister. You know my sentiments on that subject. I have often lamented the advantage which the French have over us in that particular. In Paris, the fashions have their dawnings, their routine and declensions, and depend as much upon the caprice of the day as in other countries; but there every lady assumes a right to deviate from the general *ton,* as far as will be of advantage to her own appearance. In America, the cry is, what is the fashion? and we follow it, indiscriminately, because it is so.

CHARLOTTE Therefore it is, that when large hoops are in fashion, we often see many a plump girl lost in the immensity of a hoop petticoat, whose want of height and *em-bon-point* would never have been remarked in any other dress. When the high head-dress is the mode, how then do we see a lofty cushion, with a profusion of gauze, feathers, and ribband, supported by a face no bigger than an apple; whilst a broad full-faced lady, who really would have appeared tolerably handsome in a large head-dress, looks with her smart chapeau as masculine as a soldier.

MANLY But remember, my dear sister, and I wish all my fair country-women would recollect, that the only excuse a young lady can have for going extravagantly into a fashion, is, because it makes her look extravagantly handsome.— Ladies, I must wish you a good morning.

CHARLOTTE But, brother, you are going to make home with us.

MANLY Indeed, I cannot. I have seen my uncle, and explained that matter.

CHARLOTTE Come and dine with us, then. We have a family dinner about half past four o'clock.

MANLY I am engaged to dine with the Spanish ambassador. I was introduced to him by an old brother officer; and instead of freezing me with a cold card of compliment to dine with him ten days hence, he, with the true old Castilian frankness, in a friendly manner, asked me to dine with him to-day—an honour I could not refuse. Sister, adieu— Madam, your most obedient—
(*Exit.*)

CHARLOTTE I will wait upon you to the door, brother; I have something particular to say to you. (*Exit.*)

LETITIA (*alone*) What a pair!— She the pink of flirtation, he the essence of everything that is *outré* and gloomy.— I think I have completely deceived Charlotte by my manner of speaking of Mr. Dimple; she's too much the friend of Maria to be confided in. He is certainly rendering himself disagreeable to Maria, in order to break with her and proffer his hand to me. This is what the delicate fellow hinted in our last conversation.

(*Exit.*)

SCENE 2. *The Mall.*

(*Enter* JESSAMY.)

Positively this Mall is a very pretty place. I hope the city won't ruin it by repairs. To be sure, it won't do to speak of in the same day with Ranelagh or Vauxhall; however, it's a fine place for a young fellow to display his person to advantage. Indeed, nothing is lost here; the girls have taste, and I am very happy to find they have adopted the elegant London fashion of looking back, after a genteel fellow like me has passed them. Ah! who comes here? This, by his aukwardness, must be the Yankee colonel's servant. I'll accost him.

(*Enter* JONATHAN.)

Votre très—humble serviteur, Monsieur. I understand Colonel Manly, the Yankee officer, has the honour of your services.

JONATHAN Sir!—

JESSAMY I say, Sir, I understand that Colonel Manly has the honour of having you for a servant.

JONATHAN Servant! Sir, do you take me for a neger,—I am Colonel Manly's waiter.

JESSAMY A true Yankee distinction, egad, without a difference. Why, Sir, do you not perform all the offices of a servant? Do you not even blacken his boots?

JONATHAN Yes; I do grease them a bit sometimes; but I am a true blue son of liberty, for all that. Father said I should come as Colonel Manly's waiter to see the world, and all that; but no man shall master me: my father has as good a farm as the colonel.

JESSAMY Well, Sir, we will not quarrel about terms upon the eve of an acquaintance, from which I promise myself so much satisfaction,—therefore sans ceremonie—

JONATHAN What?—

JESSAMY I say, I am extremely happy to see Colonel Manly's waiter.

JONATHAN Well, and I vow, too, I am pretty considerably

glad to see you—but what the dogs need of all this outlandish lingo? Who may you be, Sir, if I may be so bold?

JESSAMY   I have the honour to be Mr. Dimple's servant, or, if you please, waiter. We lodge under the same roof, and should be glad of the honour of your acquaintance.

JONATHAN   You a waiter! By the living jingo, you look so topping, I took you for one of the agents to Congress.

JESSAMY   The brute has discernment notwithstanding his appearance.— Give me leave to say I wonder then at your familiarity.

JONATHAN   Why, as to the matter of that, Mr.—pray, what's your name?

JESSAMY   Jessamy, at your service.

JONATHAN   Why, I swear we don't make any great matter of distinction in our state, between quality and other folks.

JESSAMY   This is, indeed, a levelling principle. I hope, Mr. Jonathan, you have not taken part with the insurgents.

JONATHAN   Why, since General Shays has sneaked off, and given us the bag to hold, I don't care to give my opinion; but you'll promise not to tell—put your ear this way—you won't tell? — I vow, I did think the sturgeons were right.

JESSAMY   I thought, Mr. Jonathan, you Massachusetts men always argued with a gun in your hand.— Why didn't you join them?

JONATHAN   Why, the colonel is one of those folks called the Shin—shin—dang it all, I can't speak them lignum vitæ words— you know who I mean—there is a company of them—they wear a China goose at their button-hole—a kind of gilt thing.— Now the colonel told father and brother,—you must know there are, let me see—there is Elnathan, Silas, and Barnabas, Tabitha—no, no, she's a she—tarnation, now I have it—there's Elnathan, Silas, Barnabas, Jonathan, that's I—seven of us, six went into the wars, and I staid at home to take care of mother. Colonel said that it was a burning shame for the true blue Bunker-hill sons of liberty, who had fought Governor Hutchinson, Lord North, and the Devil, to have any hand in kicking up a cursed dust against a government, which we had every mother's son of us a hand in making.

JESSAMY   Bravo!— Well, have you been abroad in the city since your arrival? What have you seen that is curious and entertaining?

JONATHAN   Oh! I have seen a power of fine sights. I went to see two marble-stone men and a leaden horse, that stands out in doors in all weathers; and when I came where they was, one had got no head, and t' other wer'nt there. They said as how the leaden man was a damn'd tory, and that he took wit in his anger and rode off in the time of the troubles.

JESSAMY   But this was not the end of your excursion.

JONATHAN   Oh, no; I went to a place they call Holy Ground. Now I counted this was a place where folks go to meeting; so I put my hymn-book in my pocket, and walked softly and grave as a minister; and when I came there, the dogs a bit of a meeting-house could I see. At last I spied a young gentlewoman standing by one of the seats, which they have here at the doors—I took her to be the deacon's daughter, and she looked so kind, and so obliging, that I thought I would go and ask her the way to lecture, and would you think it—she called me dear, and sweeting, and honey, just as if we were married; by the living jingo, I had a month's mind to buss her.

JESSAMY   Well, but how did it end?

JONATHAN   Why, as I was standing talking with her, a parcel of sailor men and boys got round me, the snarl headed curs fell a-kicking and cursing of me at such a tarnal rate, that, I vow, I was glad to take to my heels and split home, right off, tail on end like a stream of chalk.

JESSAMY   Why, my dear friend, you are not acquainted with the city; that girl you saw was a— (*Whispers.*)

JONATHAN   Mercy on my soul! was that young woman a harlot!— Well, if this is New York Holy Ground, what must the Holy-day Ground be!

JESSAMY   Well, you should not judge of the city too rashly. We have a number of elegant fine girls here, that make a man's leisure hours pass very agreeably. I would esteem it an honour to announce you to some of them.— Gad! that announce is a select word; I wonder where I picked it up.

JONATHAN I don't want to know them.

JESSAMY Come, come, my dear friend, I see that I must assume the honour of being the director of your amusements. Nature has give us passions, and youth and opportunity stimulate to gratify them. It is no shame, my dear Blueskin, for a man to amuse himself with a little gallantry.

JONATHAN Girl huntry! I don't altogether understand. I never played at that game. I know how to play hunt the squirrel, but I can't play anything with the girls; I am as good as married.

JESSAMY Vulgar, horrid brute! Married, and above a hundred miles from his wife, and think that an objection to his making love to every woman he meets! He never can have read, no, he never can have been in a room with a volume of the divine Chesterfield.— So you are married?

JONATHAN No, I don't say so; I said I was as good as married, a kind of promise.

JESSAMY As good as married!—

JONATHAN Why, yes; there's Tabitha Wymen, the deacon's daughter, at home, she and I have been courting a great while, and folks say as how we are to be married; and so I broke a piece of money with her when we parted, and she promised not to spark it with Solomon Dyer while I am gone. You wouldn't have me false to my true love, would you?

JESSAMY May be you have another reason for constancy; possibly the young lady has a fortune? Ha! Mr. Jonathan, the solid charms; the chains of love are never so binding as when the links are made of gold.

JONATHAN Why, as to fortune, I must needs say her father is pretty dumb rich; he went representative for our town last year. He will give her—let me see—four times seven is—seven times four—nought and carry one;—he will give her twenty acres of land—somewhat rocky though—a bible, and a cow.

JESSAMY Twenty acres of rock, a bible, and a cow! Why, my dear Mr. Jonathan, we have servant maids, or, as you would more elegantly express it, wait'resses, in this city, who collect more in one year from their mistresses' cast clothes.

JONATHAN You don't say so!—

JESSAMY Yes, and I'll introduce you to one of them. There is a little lump of flesh and delicacy that lives at next door, wait'ress to Miss Maria; we often see her on the stoop.

JONATHAN But are you sure she would be courted by me?

JESSAMY Never doubt it; remember a faint heart never— blisters on my tongue—I was going to be guilty of a vile proverb; flat against the authority of Chesterfield.— I say there can be no doubt, that the brilliancy of your merit will secure you a favourable reception.

JONATHAN Well, but what must I say to her?

JESSAMY Say to her! why, my dear friend, though I admire your profound knowledge on every other subject, yet, you will pardon my saying, that your want of opportunity has made the female heart escape the poignancy of your penetration. Say to her!— Why, when a man goes a-courting, and hopes for success, he must begin with doing, and not saying.

JONATHAN Well, what must I do?

JESSAMY Why, when you are introduced you must make five or six elegant bows.

JONATHAN Six elegant bows! I understand that; six, you say? Well—

JESSAMY Then you must press and kiss her hand; then press and kiss, and so on to her lips and cheeks; then talk as much as you can about hearts, darts, flames, nectar and ambrosia—the more incoherent the better.

JONATHAN Well, but suppose she should be angry with I?

JESSAMY Why, if she should pretend—please to observe, Mr. Jonathan—if she should pretend to be offended, you must— But I'll tell you how my master acted in such a case: He was seated by a young lady of eighteen upon a sopha, plucking with a wanton hand the blooming sweets of youth and beauty. When the lady thought it necessary to check his ardour, she called up a frown upon her lovely face, so irresistibly alluring, that it would have warmed the frozen bosom of age: remember, said she, putting her delicate arm upon his, remember your character and my honour. My master instantly dropped upon his knees, with eyes swimming with love, cheeks glowing with desire, and in the gentlest modulation of voice, he said— My dear Caroline, in a few months our hands will be indissolubly united at the altar; our hearts I feel are already so—the favours you now grant as evidence of your affection, are favours indeed; yet when the ceremony is once past, what will now be received with rapture, will then be attributed to duty.

JONATHAN   Well, and what was the consequence?

JESSAMY   The consequence!— Ah! forgive me, my dear friend, but you New England gentlemen have such a laudable curiosity of seeing the bottom of every thing;—why, to be honest, I confess I saw the blooming cherub of a consequence smiling in its angelic mother's arms, about ten months afterwards.

JONATHAN   Well, if I follow all your plans, make them six bows, and all that; shall I have such little cherubim consequences?

JESSAMY   Undoubtedly.— What are you musing upon?

JONATHAN   You say you'll certainly make me acquainted?— Why, I was thinking then how I should contrive to pass this broken piece of silver—won't it buy a sugar-dram?

JESSAMY   What is that, the love-token from the deacon's daughter?— You come on bravely. But I must hasten to my master. Adieu, my dear friend.

JONATHAN   Stay, Mr. Jessamy—must I buss her when I am introduced to her?

JESSAMY   I told you, you must kiss her.

JONATHAN   Well, but must I buss her?

JESSAMY   Why, kiss and buss, and buss and kiss, is all one.

JONATHAN   Oh! my dear friend, though you have a profound knowledge of all, a pugnancy[1] of tribulation, you don't know everything.   (*Exit.*)

JESSAMY (*alone*)   Well, certainly I improve; my master could

---

[1] There is an obsolete word "pugnancy" meaning "opposition" but this is probably an attempt to imitate Jessamy's "poignancy."

not have insinuated himself with more address into the heart of a man he despised.— Now will this blundering dog sicken Jenny with his nauseous pawings, until she flies into my arms for very ease. How sweet will the contrast be, between the blundering Jonathan, and the courtly and accomplished Jessamy!

END OF THE SECOND ACT.

ACT THIRD

SCENE I. DIMPLE'S *Room.* DIMPLE *discovered at a Toilet, Reading.*

"Women have in general but one object, which is their beauty." Very true, my lord; positively very true. "Nature has hardly formed a woman ugly enough to be insensible to flattery upon her person." Extremely just, my lord; every day's delightful experience confirms this. "If her face is so shocking, that she must, in some degree, be conscious of it, her figure and air, she thinks, make ample amends for it." The sallow Miss Wan is a proof of this.— Upon my telling the distasteful wretch, the other day, that her countenance spoke the pensive language of sentiment, and that Lady Wortley Montague declared, that if the ladies were arrayed in the garb of innocence, the face would be the last part which would be admired as Monsieur Milton expresses it, she grin'd horribly a ghastly smile. "If her figure is deformed, she thinks her face counterbalances it."

(*Enter* JESSAMY *with letters.*)

DIMPLE Where got you these, Jessamy?
JESSAMY Sir, the English packet is arrived.

(DIMPLE *opens and reads a letter enclosing notes.*)
"Sir,
"I have drawn bills on you in favour of Messrs. Van Cash and Co. as per margin. I have taken up your note to Col. Piquet, and discharged your debts to my Lord Lurcher and Sir Harry Rook. I herewith enclose you copies of the bills, which I have no doubt

will be immediately honoured. On failure, I shall empower some lawyer in your country to recover the amounts.

"I am, Sir,
"Your most humble servant,
"JOHN HAZARD."

Now, did not my lord expressly say, that it was unbecoming a well-bred man to be in a passion, I confess I should be ruffled. (*Reads.*) "There is no accident so unfortunate, which a wise man may not turn to his advantage; nor any accident so fortunate, which a fool will not turn to his disadvantage." True, my lord: but how advantage can be derived from this, I can't see. Chesterfield himself, who made, however, the worst practice of the most excellent precepts, was never in so embarrassing a situation. I love the person of Charlotte, and it is necessary I should command the fortune of Letitia. As to Maria!—I doubt not by my *sang-froid* behavior I shall compel her to decline the match; but the blame must not fall upon me. A prudent man, as my lord says, should take all the credit of a good action to himself, and throw the discredit of a bad one upon others. I must break with Maria, marry Letitia, and as for Charlotte—why, Charlotte must be a companion to my wife.— Here, Jessamy!

(*Enter* JESSAMY.)

(DIMPLE *folds and seals two letters.*)

DIMPLE Here, Jessamy, take this letter to my love.
(*Gives one.*)

JESSAMY To which of your honour's loves?— Oh! (*reading*) to Miss Letitia, your honour's rich love.

DIMPLE And this (*delivers another*) to Miss Charlotte Manly. See that you deliver them privately.

JESSAMY Yes, your honour. (*Going.*)

DIMPLE Jessamy, who are these strange lodgers that came to the house last night?

JESSAMY Why, the master is a Yankee colonel; I have not seen much of him; but the man is the most unpolished animal your honour ever disgraced your eyes by looking upon. I have had one of the most *outré* conversations with him!— He really has a most prodigious effect upon my risibility.

DIMPLE I ought, according to every rule of Chesterfield, to wait on him and insinuate myself into his good graces.— Jessamy, wait on the colonel with my compliments, and if he is disengaged, I will do myself the honour of paying him my respects.— Some ignorant unpolished boor—

(JESSAMY *goes off and returns.*)

JESSAMY Sir, the colonel is gone out, and Jonathan, his servant, says that he is gone to stretch his legs upon the Mall— Stretch his legs! what an indelicacy of diction!

DIMPLE Very well. Reach me my hat and sword. I'll accost him there, in my way to Letitia's, as by accident; pretend to be struck with his person and address, and endeavour to steal into his confidence. Jessamy, I have no business for you at present.   (*Exit.*)

JESSAMY (*Taking up the book*) My master and I obtain our knowledge from the same source;—though, gad! I think myself much the prettier fellow of the two. (*Surveying himself in the glass.*) That was a brilliant thought, to insinuate that I folded my master's letters for him; the folding is so neat, that it does honour to the operator. I once intended to have insinuated that I wrote his letters too; but that was before I saw them; it won't do now; no honour there, positively.— "Nothing looks more vulgar (*reading affectedly*), ordinary, and illiberal, than ugly, uneven, and ragged nails; the ends of which should be kept even and clean, not tipped with black, and cut in small segments of circles"— Segments of circles! surely my lord did not consider that he wrote for the beaux. Segments of circles! what a crabbed term! Now I dare answer, that my master, with all his learning, does not know that this means, according to the present mode, to let the nails grow long, and then cut them off even at top. (*Laughing without.*) Ha! that's Jenny's titter. I protest I despair of ever teaching that girl to laugh; she has something so execrably natural in her laugh, that I declare it absolutely discomposes my nerves. How came she into our house!— (*Calls.*) Jenny!

(*Enter* JENNY.)

JESSAMY   Prythee, Jenny, don't spoil your fine face with laughing.

JENNY   Why, mustn't I laugh, Mr. Jessamy?

JESSAMY   You may smile; but, as my lord says, nothing can authorise a laugh.

JENNY   Well, but I can't help laughing— Have you seen him. Mr. Jessamy? Ha, ha, ha!

JESSAMY   Seen whom?—

JENNY   Why, Jonathan, the New-England colonel's servant. Do you know he was at the play last night, and the stupid creature don't know where he has been. He would not go to a play for the world; he thinks it was a show, as he calls it.

JESSAMY   As ignorant and unpolished as he is, do you know, Miss Jenny, that I propose to introduce him to the honour of your acquaintance.

JENNY   Introduce him to me! for what?

JESSAMY   Why, my lovely girl, that you may take him under your protection, as Madam Rambouliet, did young Stanhope; that you may, by your plastic hand, mould this uncouth cub into a gentleman. He is to make love to you

JENNY   Make love to me!—

JESSAMY   Yes, Mistress Jenny, make love to you; and, I doubt not, when he shall become domesticated in your kitchen, that this boor, under your auspices, will soon become *un aimable petit Jonathan*.

JENNY   I must say, Mr. Jessamy, if he copies after me, he will be vastly monstrously polite.

JESSAMY   Stay here one moment, and I will call him.—Jonathan!—Mr. Jonathan!—   (*Calls.*)

JONATHAN (*Within.*)   Holla! there.— (*Enters.*) You promise to stand by me—six bows you say.   (*Bows.*)

JESSAMY   Mrs. Jenny, I have the honour of presenting Mr. Jonathan, Colonel Manly's waiter, to you. I am extremely happy that I have it in my power to make two worthy people acquainted with each other's merit.

JENNY So, Mr. Jonathan, I hear you were at the play last night.

JONATHAN At the play! why, did you think I went to the devil's drawing-room!

JENNY The devil's drawing-room!

JONATHAN Yes; why an't cards and dice the devil's device; and the play-house the shop where the devil hangs out the vanities of the world, upon the tenterhooks of temptation. I believe you have not heard how they were acting the old boy one night, and the wicked one came among them sure enough; and went right off in a storm, and carried one quarter of the play-house with him. Oh! no, no, no! you won't catch me at a play-house, I warrant you.

JENNY Well, Mr. Jonathan, though I don't scruple your veracity, I have some reasons for believing you were there; pray, where were you about six o'clock?

JONATHAN Why, I went to see one Mr. Morrison, the *hocus pocus* man; they said as how he could eat a case knife.

JENNY Well, and how did you find the place?

JONATHAN As I was going about here and there, to and again, to find it, I saw a great croud of folks going into a long entry, that had lanterns over the door; so I asked a man, whether that was not the place where they played *hocus pocus?* He was a very civil kind man, though he did speak like the Hessians; he lifted up his eyes and said—"they play *hocus pocus* tricks enough there, Got knows, mine friend."

JENNY Well—

JONATHAN So I went right in, and they shewed me away clean up to the garret, just like a meeting-house gallery. And so I saw a power of topping folks, all sitting round in little cabins, just like father's corn-cribs;—and then there was such a squeaking with the fiddles, and such a tarnal blaze with the lights, my head was near turned. At last the people that sat near me set up such a hissing—hiss—like so many mad cats; and then they went thump, thump, thump, just like our Peleg threshing wheat, and stampt away, just like the nation; and called out for one Mr. Langolee,—I suppose he helps act the tricks.

JENNY Well, and what did you do all this time?

JONATHAN Gor, I—I liked the fun, and so I thumpt away, and hiss'd as lustily as the best of 'em. One sailor-looking man that sat by me, seeing me stamp, and knowing I was a cute fellow, because I could make a roaring noise, clapt me on the shoulder and said, you are a d——d hearty cock, smite my timbers! I told him so I was, but I thought he need not swear so, and make use of such naughty words.

JESSAMY The savage!—Well, and did you see the man with his tricks?

JONATHAN Why, I vow, as I was looking out for him, they lifted up a great green cloth, and let us look right into the next neighbour's house. Have you a good many houses in New York made so in that 'ere way?

JENNY Not many: but did you see the family?

JONATHAN Yes, swamp it; I see'd the family.

JENNY Well, and how did you like them?

JONATHAN Why, I vow they were pretty much like other families;—there was a poor, good natured, curse of a husband, and a sad rantipole of a wife.

JENNY But did you see no other folks?

JONATHAN Yes. There was one youngster, they called him Mr. Joseph; he talked as sober and as pious as a minister; but like some ministers that I know, he was a sly tike in his heart for all that: He was going to ask a young woman to spark it with him, and—the Lord have mercy on my soul!—she was another man's wife.

JESSAMY The Wabash!

JENNY And did you see any more folks?

JONATHAN Why they came on as thick as mustard. For my part, I thought the house was haunted. There was a soldier fellow, who talked about his row de dow dow, and courted a young woman: but of all the cute folk I saw, I liked one little fellow—

JENNY Aye! who was he?

JONATHAN Why, he had red hair, and a little round plump face like mine, only not altogether so handsome. His name was Darby:—that was his baptizing name, his other name I forgot. Oh! it was, Wig—Wag—Wag-all, Darby Wag-all;—pray, do you know him?—I should like to take a sling with him, or a drap of cyder with a pepper-pod in it, to make it warm and comfortable.

JENNY I can't say I have that pleasure.

JONATHAN I wish you did, he is a cute fellow. But there was one thing I didn't like in that Mr. Darby; and that was, he was afraid of some of them 'ere shooting irons, such as your troopers wear on training days. Now, I'm a true born Yankee American son of liberty, and I never was afraid of a gun yet in all my life.

JENNY Well, Mr. Jonathan, you were certainly at the play-house.

JONATHAN I at the play-house!—Why didn't I see the play then?

JENNY Why, the people you saw were players.

JONATHAN Mercy on my soul! did I see the wicked players?—Mayhap that 'ere Darby that I liked so, was the old serpent himself, and had his cloven foot in his pocket. Why, I vow, now I come to think on 't, the candles seemed to burn blue, and I am sure where I sat it smelt tarnally of brimstone.

JESSAMY Well, Mr. Jonathan, from your account, which I confess is very accurate, you must have been at the play-house.

JONATHAN Why, I vow I began to smell a rat. When I came away, I went to the man for my money again: you want your money, says he; yes, says I; for what, says he; why,, says I, no man shall jocky me out of my money; I paid my money to see sights, and the dogs a bit of a sight have I seen, unless you call listening to people's private business a sight. Why, says he, it is the School for Scandalization.—The School for Scandalization!—Oh, ho! no wonder you New York folks are so cute at it, when you go to school to learn it: and so I jogged off.

JESSAMY My dear Jenny, my master's business drags me from

you; would to heaven I knew no other servitude than to your charms.

JONATHAN Well, but don't go; you won't leave me so.—

JESSAMY Excuse me.—Remember the cash.

(*Aside to him, and—Exit.*)

JENNY Mr. Jonathan, won't you please to sit down. Mr. Jessamy tells me you wanted to have some conversation with me.

(*Having brought forward two chairs, they sit.*)

JONATHAN Ma'am!—

JENNY Sir!—

JONATHAN Ma'am!—

JENNY Pray, how do you like the city, Sir?

JONATHAN Ma'am!—

JENNY I say, Sir, how do you like New York?

JONATHAN Ma'am!—

JENNY The stupid creature! but I must pass some little time with him, if it is only to endeavour to learn, whether it was his master that made such an abrupt entrance into our house, and my young mistress's heart, this morning. (*Aside.*) As you don't seem to like to talk, Mr. Jonathan—do you sing?

JONATHAN Gor, I—I am glad she asked that, for I forgot what Mr. Jessamy bid me say, and I dare as well be hanged as act what he bid me do, I'm so ashamed. (*Aside.*) Yes, Ma'am, I can sing—I can sing Mear, Old Hundred, and Bangor.

JENNY Oh! I don't mean psalm tunes. Have you no little song to please the ladies; such as Roslin Castle, or the Maid of the Mill?

JONATHAN Why, all my tunes go to meeting tunes, save one, and I count you won't altogether like that 'ere.

JENNY What is it called?

JONATHAN I am sure you have heard folks talk about it, it is called Yankee Doodle.

JENNY Oh! it is the tune I am fond of; and, if I know anything of my mistress, she would be glad to dance to it. Pray, sing?

JONATHAN (*Sings.*)

>Father and I went up to camp,
>Along with Captain Goodwin;
>And there we saw the men and boys,
>As thick as hasty pudding.
>>Yankee Doodle do, etc.

>And there we saw a swamping gun,
>Big as log of maple,
>On a little deuced cart,
>A load for father's cattle.
>>Yankee Doodle do, etc.

>And every time they fired it off,
>It took a horn of powder,
>It made a noise—like father's gun,
>Only a nation louder.
>>Yankee Doodle do, etc.

>There was a man in our town,
>His name——

No, no, that won't do. Now, if I was with Tabitha Wymen and Jemima Cawley, down at father Chase's, I shouldn't mind singing this all out before them—you would be affronted if I was to sing that, though that's a lucky thought; if you should be affronted, I have something dang'd cute, which Jessamy told me to say to you.

JENNY Is that all! I assure you I like it of all things.

JONATHAN No, no; I can sing more, some other time, when you and I are better acquainted, I'll sing the whole of it—no, no—that's a fib—I can't sing but a hundred and ninety verses: our Tabitha at home can sing it all.— (*Sings.*)

> Marblehead's a rocky place,
> And Cape-Cod is sandy;
> Charleston is burnt down,
> Boston is the dandy.
>   Yankee Doodle do, etc.

I vow, my own town song has put me into such topping spirits, that I believe I'll begin to do a little, as Jessamy says we must when we go a courting—(*Runs and kisses her.*) Burning rivers! cooling flames! red hot roses! pig-nuts! hasty-pudding and ambrosia!

JENNY What means this freedom! you insulting wretch.

(*Strikes him.*)

JONATHAN Are you affronted?

JENNY Affronted! with what looks shall I express my anger?

JONATHAN Looks! why, as to the matter of looks, you look as cross as a witch.

JENNY Have you no feeling for the delicacy of my sex?

JONATHAN Feeling! Gor, I—I feel the delicacy of your sex pretty smartly (*rubbing his cheek*), though, I vow, I thought when you city ladies courted and married, and all that, you put feeling out of the question. But I want to know whether you are really affronted, or only pretend to be so? 'Cause, if you are certainly right down affronted, I am at the end of my tether;—Jessamy didn't tell me what to say to you.

JENNY Pretend to be affronted!

JONATHAN Aye, aye, if you only pretend, you shall hear how I'll go to work to make cherubim consequences.

(*Runs up to her.*)

JENNY Begone, you brute!

JONATHAN That looks like mad; but I won't lose my speech. My dearest Jenny—your name is Jenny, I think? My dearest Jenny, though I have the highest esteem for the sweet favours you have just now granted me—Gor, that's a fib though, but Jessamy says it is not wicked to tell lies to the women. (*Aside.*) I say, though I have the highest esteem for the favours you have just now granted me, yet, you will consider, that as soon as the dissolvable knot is tied, they will no longer be favours, but only matters of duty, and matters of course.

JENNY Marry you! you audacious monster! get out of my sight, or rather let me fly from you.   (*Exit hastily.*)

JONATHAN Gor! she's gone off in a swinging passion, before I had time to think of consequences. If this is the way with your city ladies, give me the twenty acres of rock, the bible, the cow, and Tabitha, and a little peaceable bundling.

SCENE 2. *The Mall.*

(*Enter* MANLY.)

It must be so, Montague! and it is not all the tribe of Mandevilles shall convince me, that a nation, to become great, must first become dissipated. Luxury is surely the bane of a nation: Luxury! which enervates both soul and body, by opening a thousand new sources of enjoyment, opens, also, a thousand new sources of contention and want: Luxury! which renders a people weak at home, and accessible to bribery, corruption, and force from abroad. When the Grecian states knew no other tools than the axe and the saw, the Grecians were a great, a free, and a happy people. The kings of Greece devoted their lives to the service of their country, and her senators knew no other superiority over their fellow-citizens than a glorious pre-eminence in danger and virtue. They exhibited to the world a noble spectacle, —a number of independent states united by a similarity of language, sentiment, manners, common interest, and common consent, in one grand mutual league of protection.—And, thus united, long might they have continued the cherishers of arts and sciences, the protectors of the oppressed, the scourge of tyrants, and the safe asylum of liberty: But when foreign gold, and still more pernicious, foreign luxury, had crept among them, they sapped the vitals of their virtue. The virtues of their ancestors were only found in their writings. Envy and suspicion, the vices of little minds, possessed them. The various states engendered jealousies of each other; and, more unfortunately, growing jealous of their great federal council, the Amphictyons, they forgot that their common safety had existed, and would exist, in giving them an honourable extensive prerogative. The common good was lost in the pursuit of private interest; and that people, who, by uniting, might have stood against the world in arms, by dividing, crumbled into ruin;—their name is now only known in the page of the historian, and what they once were, is all we have left to admire. Oh! that America! Oh! that my country, would in this her day, learn the things which belong to her peace!

(*Enter* DIMPLE.)

DIMPLE You are Colonel Manly, I presume?

MANLY At your service, Sir.

DIMPLE My name is Dimple, Sir. I have the honour to be a lodger in the same house with you, and hearing you were in the Mall, came hither to take the liberty of joining you.

MANLY You are very obliging, Sir.

DIMPLE As I understand you are a stranger here, Sir, I have taken the liberty to introduce myself to your acquaintance, as possibly I may have it in my power to point out some things in this city worthy your notice.

MANLY An attention to strangers is worthy a liberal mind, and must ever be gratefully received. But to a soldier, who has no fixed abode, such attentions are particularly pleasing.

DIMPLE Sir, there is no character so respectable as that of a soldier. And, indeed, when we reflect how much we owe to those brave men who have suffered so much in the service of their country, and secured to us those inestimable blessings that we now enjoy, our liberty and independence, they demand every attention which gratitude can pay. For my own part, I never meet an officer, but I embrace him as my friend, nor a private in distress, but I insensibly extend my charity to him.—I have hit the Bumkin off very tolerably. (*Aside.*)

MANLY Give me your hand, Sir! I do not proffer this hand to everybody; but you steal into my heart. I hope I am as insensible to flattery as most men; but I declare (it may be my weak side), that I never hear the name of soldier mentioned with respect, but I experience a thrill of pleasure, which I never feel on any other occasion.

DIMPLE Will you give me leave, my dear colonel, to confer an obligation on myself, by shewing you some civilities during your stay here, and giving a similar opportunity to some of my friends?

MANLY Sir, I thank you; but I believe my stay in this city will be very short.

DIMPLE I can introduce you to some men of excellent sense, in whose company you will esteem yourself happy; and, by way of amusement, to some fine girls, who will listen to your soft things with pleasure.

MANLY Sir, I should be proud of the honour of being acquainted with those gentlemen;—but, as for the ladies, I don't understand you.

DIMPLE Why, Sir, I need not tell you, that when a young gentleman is alone with a young lady, he must say some soft things to her fair cheek—indeed the lady will expect it. To be sure, there is not much pleasure, when a man of the world and a finished coquet meet, who perfectly know each other; but how delicious is it to excite the emotions of joy, hope, expectation, and delight, in the bosom of a lovely girl, who believes every tittle of what you say to be serious.

MANLY Serious, Sir! In my opinion, the man, who, under pretensions of marriage, can plant thorns in the bosom of an innocent, unsuspecting girl, is more detestable than a common robber, in the same proportion, as private violence is more despicable than open force, and money of less value than happiness.

DIMPLE How he awes me by the superiority of his sentiments. (*Aside.*) As you say, Sir, a gentleman should be cautious how he mentions marriage.

MANLY Cautious, Sir! No person more approves of an intercourse between the sexes than I do. Female conversation softens our manners, whilst our discourse, from the superiority of our literary advantages, improves their minds. But, in our young country, where there is no such thing as gallantry, when a gentleman speaks of love to a lady, whether he mentions marriage, or not, she ought to conclude, either that he meant to insult her, or, that his intentions are the most serious and honourable. How mean, how cruel, is it, by a thousand tender assiduities, to win the affections of an amiable girl, and though you leave her virtue unspotted, to betray her into the appearance of so many tender partialities, that every man of delicacy would suppress his inclination towards her, by supposing her heart engaged! Can any man, for the trivial gratification of his leisure hours, affect the happiness of a whole life! His not having spoken of marriage, may add to his perfidy, but can be no excuse for his conduct.

DIMPLE Sir, I admire your sentiments;—they are mine. The light observations that fell from me, were only a principle of the tongue; they came not from the heart—my practice has ever disapproved these principles.

MANLY I believe you, Sir. I should with reluctance suppose that those pernicious sentiments could find admittance into the heart of a gentleman.

DIMPLE I am now, Sir, going to visit a family, where, if you please, I will have the honour of introducing you. Mr. Manly's ward, Miss Letitia, is a young lady of immense fortune; and his niece, Miss Charlotte Manly, is a young lady of great sprightliness and beauty.

MANLY That gentleman, Sir, is my uncle, and Miss Manly my sister.

DIMPLE The devil she is! (*Aside.*) Miss Manly your sister, Sir? I rejoice to hear it, and feel a double pleasure in being known to you.—Plague on him! I wish he was at Boston again with all my soul. (*Aside.*)

MANLY Come, Sir, will you go?

DIMPLE I will follow you in a moment, Sir. (*Exit* MANLY.) Plague on it! this is unlucky. A fighting brother is a cursed appendage to a fine girl. Egad! I just stopped in time; had he not discovered himself, in two minutes more I should have told him how well I was with his sister.—Indeed, I cannot see the satisfaction of an intrigue, if one can't have the pleasure of communicating it to our friends. (*Exit.*)

END OF THE THIRD ACT.

ACT FOURTH

SCENE I. CHARLOTTE's *Apartment.* CHARLOTTE *leading in* MARIA.

CHARLOTTE This is so kind, my sweet friend, to come to see me at this moment, I declare, if I were going to be married in a few days, as you are, I should scarce have found time to visit my friends.

MARIA Do you think then that there is an impropriety in it?—How should you dispose of your time?

CHARLOTTE Why, I should be shut up in my chamber; and my head would so run upon—upon—upon the solemn ceremony that I was to pass through—I declare it would take me above two hours merely to learn that little monosyllable—*Yes.* Ah! my dear, your sentimental imagination does not conceive what that little tiny word implies.

MARIA Spare me your raillery, my sweet friend; I should love your agreeable vivacity at any other time.

CHARLOTTE Why this is the very time to amuse you. You grieve me to see you look so unhappy.

MARIA Have I not reason to look so?

CHARLOTTE What new grief distresses you?

MARIA Oh! how sweet it is, when the heart is borne down with misfortune, to recline and repose on the bosom of friendship! Heaven knows, that, although it is improper for a young lady to praise a gentleman, yet I have ever concealed Mr. Dimple's foibles, and spoke of him as of one whose reputation I expected would be linked with mine: but his late conduct towards me, has turned my coolness into contempt. He behaves as if he meant to insult and disgust me; whilst my father, in the last conversation on the subject of our marriage, spoke of it as a matter which laid near his heart, and in which he would not bear contradiction.

CHARLOTTE This works well: oh! the generous Dimple. I'll endeavour to excite her to discharge him. (*Aside.*) But, my dear friend, your happiness depends on yourself:—Why don't you discard him? Though the match has been of long standing, I would not be forced to make myself miserable: no parent in the world should oblige me to marry the man I did not like.

MARIA Oh! my dear, you never lived with your parents, and do not know what influence a father's frowns have upon a daughter's heart. Besides, what have I to allege against Mr. Dimple, to justify myself to the world? He carries himself so smoothly, that every one would impute the blame to me, and call me capricious.

CHARLOTTE And call her capricious! Did ever such an objection start into the heart of woman? For my part, I wish I had fifty lovers to discard, for no other reason, than because I did not fancy them. My dear Maria, you will forgive me; I know your candour and confidence in me; but I have at times, I confess, been led to suppose, that some other gentleman was the cause of your aversion to Mr. Dimple.

MARIA No, my sweet friend, you may be assured, that though I have seen many gentlemen I could prefer to Mr. Dimple, yet I never saw one that I thought I could give my hand to, until this morning.

CHARLOTTE This morning!

MARIA Yes;—one of the strangest accidents in the world. The odious Dimple, after disgusting me with his conversation, had just left me, when a gentleman, who, it seems, boards in the same house with him, saw him coming out of our door, and the houses looking very much alike, he came into our house instead of his lodgings; nor did he discover his mistake until he got into the parlour, where I was: he then bowed so gracefully; made such a genteel apology, and looked so manly and noble!—

CHARLOTTE I see some folks, though it is so great an impropriety, can praise a gentleman, when he happens to be the man of their fancy. (*Aside.*)

MARIA I don't know how it was,—I hope he did not think me indelicate—but I asked him, I believe, to sit down, or pointed to a chair. He sat down, and instead of having recourse to observations upon the weather, or hackneyed criticisms upon the theatre, he entered readily into a conversation worthy a man of sense to speak, and a lady of delicacy and sentiment to hear. He was not strictly handsome, but he spoke the language of sentiment, and his eyes looked tenderness and honour.

CHARLOTTE Oh! (*eagerly*) you sentimental grave girls, when your hearts are once touched, beat us rattles a bar's length. And so, you are quite in love with this he-angel?

MARIA In love with him! How can you rattle so, Charlotte? am I not going to be miserable? (*Sighs.*) In love with a gentleman I never saw but one hour in my life, and don't know his name!—No: I only wished that the man I shall marry, may look, and talk, and act, just like him. Besides, my dear, he is a married man.

CHARLOTTE Why, that was good natured.—He told you so, I suppose, in mere charity, to prevent your falling in love with him?

MARIA He didn't tell me so (*peevishly*); he looked as if he was married.

CHARLOTTE How, my dear, did he look sheepish?

MARIA I am sure he has a susceptible heart, and the ladies of his acquaintance must be very stupid not to—

CHARLOTTE Hush! I hear some person coming.

(*Enter* LETITIA.)

LETITIA My dear Maria, I am happy to see you. Lud! what a pity it is that you have purchased your wedding clothes.

MARIA I think so. (*Sighing.*)

LETITIA Why, my dear, there is the sweetest parcel of silks come over you ever saw. Nancy Brilliant has a full suit come; she sent over her measure, and it fits her to a hair; it is immensely dressy, and made for a court-hoop. I thought they said the large hoops were going out of fashion.

CHARLOTTE Did you see the hat?—Is it a fact, that the deep laces round the border is still the fashion?

DIMPLE (*Within.*) Upon my honour, Sir!

MARIA Ha! Dimple's voice! My dear, I must take leave of you. There are some things necessary to be done at our house.—Can't I go through the other room?

(*Enter* DIMPLE *and* MANLY.)

DIMPLE Ladies, your most obedient.

CHARLOTTE Miss Van Rough, shall I present my brother Henry to you? Colonel Manly, Maria,—Miss Van Rough, brother.

MARIA Her brother! (*Turns and sees* MANLY.) Oh! my heart! The very gentleman I have been praising.

MANLY The same amiable girl I saw this morning!

CHARLOTTE Why, you look as if you were acquainted.

MANLY I unintentionally intruded into this lady's presence this morning, for which she was so good as to promise me her forgiveness.

CHARLOTTE Oh! ho! is that the case! Have these two penserosos been together? Were they Henry's eyes that looked so tenderly? (*Aside.*) And so you promised to pardon him? and could you be so good natured?—have you really forgiven him? I beg you would do it for my sake. (*Whispering loud to* MARIA.) But, my dear, as you are in such haste, it would be cruel to detain you: I can show you the way through the other room.

MARIA Spare me, my sprightly friend.

MANLY The lady does not, I hope, intend to deprive us of the pleasure of her company so soon.

CHARLOTTE She has only a mantuamaker who waits for her at home. But, as I am to give my opinion of the dress, I think she cannot go yet. We were talking of the fashions when you came in; but I suppose the subject must be changed to something of more importance now.—Mr. Dimple, will you favour us with an account of the public entertainments?

DIMPLE Why, really, Miss Manly, you could not have asked me a question more *mal-apropos*. For my part, I must confess, that to a man who has travelled, there is nothing that is worthy the name of amusement to be found in this city.

CHARLOTTE Except visiting the ladies.

DIMPLE Pardon me, Madam; that is the advocation of a man of taste. But, for amusement, I positively know of nothing that can be called so, unless you dignify with that title the hopping once a fortnight to the sound of two or three squeaking fiddles, and the clattering of the old tavern windows, or sitting to see the miserable mummers, whom you call actors, murder comedy, and make a farce of tragedy.

MANLY Do you never attend the theatre, Sir?

DIMPLE I was tortured there once.

CHARLOTTE Pray, Mr. Dimple, was it a tragedy or a comedy?

DIMPLE Faith, Madam, I cannot tell; for I sat with my back to the stage all the time, admiring a much better actress than any there;—a lady who played the fine woman to perfection;—though, by the laugh of the horrid creatures around me, I suppose it was comedy. Yet, on second thoughts, it might be some hero in a tragedy, dying so comically as to set the whole house in an uproar.—Colonel, I presume you have been in Europe?

MANLY Indeed, Sir, I was never ten leagues from the continent.

DIMPLE Believe me, Colonel, you have an immense pleasure to come; and when you shall have seen the brilliant exhibitions of Europe, you will learn to despise the amusements of this country as much as I do.

MANLY Therefore I do not wish to see them; for I can never esteem that knowledge valuable, which tends to give me a distaste for my native country.

DIMPLE Well, Colonel, though you have not travelled, you have read.

MANLY I have, a little: and by it have discovered that there is a laudable partiality, which ignorant, untravelled men entertain for everything that belongs to their native country. I call it laudable;—it injures no one; adds to their own happiness; and, when extended, becomes the noble principle of patriotism. Travelled gentlemen rise superior, in their own opinion, to this: but, if the contempt which they contract for their country is the most valuable acquisition of their travels, I am far from thinking that their time and money are well spent.

MARIA What noble sentiments!

CHARLOTTE Let my brother set out from where he will in the fields of conversation, he is sure to end his tour in the temple of gravity.

MANLY Forgive me, my sister. I love my country; it has its foibles undoubtedly;—some foreigners will with pleasure remark them—but such remarks fall very ungracefully from the lips of her citizens.

DIMPLE You are perfectly in the right, Colonel—America has her faults.

MANLY Yes, Sir; and we, her children, should blush for them in private, and endeavour, as individuals, to reform them. But, if our country has its errors in common with other countries, I am proud to say America, I mean the United States, have displayed virtues and achievements which modern nations may admire, but of which they have seldom set us the example.

CHARLOTTE But, brother, we must introduce you to some of our gay folks, and let you see the city, such as it is. Mr. Dimple is known to almost every family in town;—he will doubtless take a pleasure in introducing you.

DIMPLE I shall esteem every service I can render your brother an honour.

MANLY I fear the business I am upon will take up all my time, and my family will be anxious to hear from me.

MARIA His family! But what is it to me that he is married! (*Aside.*) Pray, how did you leave your lady, Sir?

CHARLOTTE My brother is not married (*observing her anxiety*); it is only an odd way he has of expressing himself.—Pray, brother, is this business, which you make your continual excuse, a secret?

MANLY No, sister: I came hither to solicit the honourable Congress that a number of my brave old soldiers may be put upon the pension-list, who were, at first, not judged to be so materially wounded as to need the public assistance.—My sister says true: (*To* MARIA.) I call my late soldiers my family.—Those who were not in the field in the late glorious contest, and those who were, have their respective merits; but, I confess, my old brother-soldiers are dearer to me than the former description. Friendships made in adversity are lasting; our countrymen may forget us; but that is no reason why we should forget one another. But I must leave you; my time of engagement approaches.

CHARLOTTE   Well, but brother, if you will go, will you please to conduct my fair friend home? You live in the same street;— I was to have gone with her myself— (*Aside.*) A lucky thought.

MARIA   I am obliged to your sister, Sir, and was just intending to go.   (*Going.*)

MANLY   I shall attend her with pleasure.

(*Exit with* MARIA, *followed by* DIMPLE *and* CHARLOTTE)

MARIA   Now, pray don't betray me to your brother.

CHARLOTTE (*Just as she sees him make a motion to take his leave.*) One word with you, brother, if you please.

(*Follows them out.*)

(*Manent* DIMPLE *and* LETITIA.)

DIMPLE   You received the billet I sent you, I presume?
LETITIA   Hush!—Yes.
DIMPLE   When shall I pay my respects to you?
LETITIA   At eight I shall be unengaged.

(*Re-enter* CHARLOTTE.)

DIMPLE   Did my lovely angel receive my billet? (*To* CHARLOTTE.)
CHARLOTTE   Yes.
DIMPLE   What hour shall I expect with impatience?
CHARLOTTE   At eight I shall be at home, unengaged.
DIMPLE   Unfortunate! I have a horrid engagement of business at that hour.—Can't you finish your visit earlier, and let six be the happy hour?
CHARLOTTE   You know your influence over me.

(*Exeunt severally.*)

SCENE 2. VAN ROUGH's *House.*

(VAN ROUGH, *alone.*)

It cannot possibly be true! The son of my old friend can't have acted so unadvisedly. Seventeen thousand pounds! in bills! —Mr. Transfer must have been mistaken. He always appeared so prudent, and talked so well upon money-matters, and even assured me that he intended to change his dress for a suit of clothes which would not cost so much, and look more substantial, as soon as he married. No, no, no! it can't be; it cannot be.—But, however, I must look out sharp. I did not care what his principles or his actions were, so long as he minded the main chance. Seventeen thousand pounds!—If he had lost it in trade, why the best men may have ill-luck; but to game it away, as Transfer says—why, at this rate, his whole estate may go in one night, and, what is ten times worse, mine into the bargain. No, no; Mary is right. Leave women to look out in these matters; for all they look as if they didn't know a journal from a ledger, when their interest is concerned, they know what's what; they mind the main chance as well as the best of us.—I wonder Mary did not tell me she knew of his spending his money so foolishly. Seventeen thousand pounds! Why, if my daughter was standing up to be married, I would forbid the banns, if I found it was to a man who did not mind the main chance.— Hush! I hear somebody coming. 'T is Mary's voice: a man with her too! I shouldn't be surprized if this should be the other string to her bow.—Aye, aye, let them alone; women understand the main chance.—Though, i' faith, I'll listen a little.

(*Retires into a closet.*)

(MANLY *leading in* MARIA.)

MANLY I hope you will excuse my speaking upon so important a subject, so abruptly; but the moment I entered your room, you struck me as the lady whom I had long loved in imagination, and never hoped to see.

MARIA Indeed, Sir, I have been led to hear more upon this subject than I ought.

MANLY Do you then disapprove my suit, Madam, or the abruptness of my introducing it? If the latter, my peculiar situation, being obliged to leave the city in a few days, will, I hope, be my excuse; if the former, I will retire: for I am sure I would not give a moment's inquietude to her, whom I could devote my life to please. I am not so indelicate as to seek your immediate approbation; permit me only to be near you, and by a thousand tender assiduities to endeavour to excite a grateful return.

MARIA I have a father, whom I would die to make happy—he will disapprove—

MANLY Do you think me so ungenerous as to seek a place in your esteem without his consent? You must—you ever ought to consider that man as unworthy of you, who seeks an interest in your heart, contrary to a father's approbation. A young lady should reflect, that the loss of a lover may be supplied, but nothing can compensate for the loss of a parent's affection. Yet, why do you suppose your father would disapprove? In our country, the affections are not sacrificed to riches, or family aggrandizement:—should you approve, my family is decent, and my rank honourable.

MARIA You distress me, Sir.

MANLY Then I will sincerely beg your excuse for obtruding so disagreeable a subject and retire. (*Going.*)

MARIA Stay, Sir! your generosity and good opinion of me deserve a return; but why must I declare what, for these few hours, I have scarce suffered myself to think?—I am—

MANLY What?—

MARIA Engaged, Sir;—and, in a few days, to be married to the gentleman you saw at your sister's.

MANLY Engaged to be married! And have I been basely invading the rights of another? Why have you permitted this? —Is this the return for the partiality I declared for you?

MARIA You distress me, Sir. What would you have me say? You are too generous to wish the truth: ought I to say that I dared not suffer myself to think of my engagement, and that I am going to give my hand without my heart?—Would you have me confess a partiality for you? If so, your triumph is complete; and can be only more so, when days of misery, with the man I cannot love, will make me think of him whom I could prefer.

MANLY (*After a pause.*) We are both unhappy; but it is your duty to obey your parent,—mine to obey my honour. Let us, therefore, both follow the path of rectitude; and of this we may be assured, that if we are not happy, we shall, at least, deserve to be so. Adieu! I dare not trust myself longer with you.

(*Exeunt severally.*)

END OF THE FOURTH ACT.

ACT FIFTH

SCENE I. DIMPLE'S *Lodgings.* JESSAMY *meeting* JONATHAN.

JESSAMY Well, Mr. Jonathan, what success with the fair?

JONATHAN Why, such a tarnal cross tike you never saw!—You would have counted she had lived upon crab-apples and vinegar for a fortnight. But what the rattle makes you look so tarnation glum?

JESSAMY I was thinking, Mr. Jonathan, what could be the reason of her carrying herself so coolly to you.

JONATHAN Coolly, do you call it? Why, I vow, she was fire-hot angry: may be it was because I buss'd her.

JESSAMY No, no, Mr. Jonathan; there must be some other cause: I never yet knew a lady angry at being kissed.

JONATHAN Well, if it is not the young woman's bashfulness, I vow I can't conceive why she shouldn't like me.

JESSAMY May be it is because you have not the Graces, Mr. Jonathan.

JONATHAN Grace! Why, does the young woman expect I must be converted before I court her?

JESSAMY I mean graces of person; for instance, my lord tells us that we must cut off our nails even at top, in small segments of circles;—though you won't understand that—In the next place, you must regulate your laugh.

JONATHAN Maple-log seize it! don't I laugh natural?

JESSAMY That's the very fault, Mr. Jonathan. Besides, you absolutely misplace it. I was told by a friend of mine that you laughed outright at the play the other night, when you ought only to have tittered.

JONATHAN Gor! I—what does one go to see fun for if they can't laugh?

JESSAMY You may laugh;—but you must laugh by rule.

JONATHAN Swamp it—laugh by rule! Well, I should like that tarnally.

JESSAMY Why you know, Mr. Jonathan, that to dance, a lady to play with her fan, or a gentleman with his cane, and all other natural motions, are regulated by art. My master has composed an immensely pretty gamut, by which any lady, or gentleman, with a few years' close application, may learn to laugh as gracefully as if they were born and bred to it.

JONATHAN Mercy on my soul! A gamut for laughing—just like fa, la, sol?

JESSAMY Yes. It comprises every possible display of jocularity, form an *affettuoso* smile to a *piano* titter, or full chorus *fortissimo* ha, ha, ha! My master employs his leisure-hours in marking out the plays, like a cathedral chanting-book, that the ignorant may know where to laugh; and that pit, box, and gallery may keep time together, and not have a snigger in one part of the house, a broad grin in the other, and a d——d grum look in the third. How delightful to see the audience all smile together, then look on their books, then twist their mouths into an agreeable simper, then altogether shake the house with a general ha, ha, ha! loud as a full chorus of Handel's, at an Abbey-commemoration.

JONATHAN Ha, ha, ha! that's dang'd cute, I swear.

JESSAMY The gentlemen, you see, will laugh the tenor; the ladies will play the counter-tenor; the beaux will squeak the treble; and our jolly friends in the gallery a thorough bass, ho, ho, ho!

JONATHAN Well, can't you let me see that gamut?

JESSAMY Oh! yes, Mr. Jonathan; here it is. (*Takes out a book.*)

Oh! no, this is only a titter with its variations. Ah, here it is. (*Takes out another.*) Now you must know, Mr. Jonathan, this is a piece written by Ben Jonson, which I have set to my master's gamut. The places where you must smile, look grave, or laugh outright, are marked below the line. Now look over me.—"There was a certain man"—now you must smile.

JONATHAN Well, read it again; I warrant I'll mind my eye.

JESSAMY "There was a certain man, who had a sad scolding wife,"—now you must laugh.

JONATHAN Tarnation! That's no laughing matter, though.

JESSAMY "And she lay sick a-dying;"—now you must titter.

JONATHAN What, snigger when the good woman's a-dying! Gor, I—

JESSAMY Yes; the notes say you must—"And she asked her husband leave to make a will,"—now you must begin to look grave;—"and her husband said"—

JONATHAN Ay, what did her husband say?—Something dang'd cute, I reckon.

JESSAMY "And her husband said, you have had your will all your life time, and would you have it after you are dead too?"

JONATHAN Ho, ho, ho! There the old man was even with her; he was up to the notch—ha, ha, ha!

JESSAMY But, Mr. Jonathan, you must not laugh so. Why, you ought to have tittered *piano,* and you have laughed *fortissimo.* Look here; you see these marks, A. B. C. and so on; these are the references to the other part of the book. Let us turn to it, and you will see the directions how to manage the muscles. This (*turns over*) was note D you blundered at.—"You must purse the mouth into a smile, then titter, discovering the lower part of the three front upper teeth."

JONATHAN How! read it again.

JESSAMY "There was a certain man"—very well!—"who had a sad scolding wife,"—why don't you laugh?

JONATHAN Now, that scolding wife sticks in my gizzard so pluckily, that I can't laugh for the blood and nowns of me. Let me look grave here, and I'll laugh your belly full where the old creature's a-dying.—

JESSAMY "And she asked her husband"—(*Bell rings.*) My master's bell! he's returned, I fear—Here, Mr. Jonathan, take this gamut; and, I make no doubt but with a few years' close application you may be able to smile gracefully.

(*Exeunt severally.*)

SCENE 2. CHARLOTTE'S *Apartment.*

(*Enter* MANLY.)

MANLY What, no one at home? How unfortunate to meet the only lady my heart was ever moved by, to find her engaged to another, and confessing her partiality for me! Yet engaged to a man, who, by her intimation, and his libertine conversation with me, I fear, does not merit her. Aye! there's the sting; for, were I assured that Maria was happy, my heart is not so selfish, but that it would dilate in knowing it, even though it were with another.—But to know she is unhappy!—I must drive these thoughts from me. Charlotte has some books; and this is what I believe she calls her little library. (*Enters a closet.*)

(*Enter* DIMPLE *leading* LETITIA.)

LETITIA And will you pretend to say, now, Mr. Dimple, that you propose to break with Maria? Are not the banns published? Are not the clothes purchased? Are not the friends invited? In short, is it not a done affair?

DIMPLE Believe me, my dear Letitia, I would not marry her.

LETITIA Why have you not broke with her before this, as you all along deluded me by saying you would?

DIMPLE Because I was in hopes she would ere this have broke with me.

LETITIA You could not expect it.

DIMPLE Nay, but be calm a moment; 't was from my regard to you that I did not discard her.

LETITIA Regard to me!

DIMPLE Yes; I have done everything in my power to break with her, but the foolish girl is so fond of me, that nothing can accomplish it. Besides, how can I offer her my hand, when my heart is indissolubly engaged to you?—

LETITIA There may be reason in this; but why so attentive to Miss Manly?

DIMPLE Attentive to Miss Manly! For heaven's sake, if you have no better opinion of my constancy, pay not so ill a compliment to my taste.

LETITIA Did I not see you whisper her to-day?

DIMPLE Possibly I might—but something of so very trifling a nature, that I have already forgot what it was.

LETITIA I believe, she has not forgot it.

DIMPLE My dear creature, how can you for a moment suppose I should have any serious thoughts of that trifling, gay, flighty coquette, that disagreeable—

(*Enter* CHARLOTTE.)

DIMPLE My dear Miss Manly, I rejoice to see you; there is a charm in your conversation that always marks your entrance into company as fortunate.

LETITIA Where have you been, my dear?

CHARLOTTE Why, I have been about to twenty shops, turning over pretty things, and so have left twenty visits unpaid. I wish you would step into the carriage and whisk round, make my apology, and leave my cards where our friends are not at home; that you know will serve as a visit. Come, do go.

LETITIA So anxious to get me out! but I'll watch you. (*Aside.*) Oh! yes, I'll go; I want a little exercise.—Positively (DIMPLE *offering to accompany her*), Mr. Dimple, you shall not go, why, half my visits are cake and caudle visits; it won't do, you know, for you to go.—

(*Exit, but returns to the door in the back scene and listens.*)

DIMPLE This attachment of your brother to Maria is fortunate.

CHARLOTTE How did you come to the knowledge of it?

DIMPLE I read it in their eyes.

CHARLOTTE   And I had it from her mouth. It would have amused you to have seen her! She that thought it so great an impropriety to praise a gentleman, that she could not bring out one word in your favour, found a redundancy to praise him.

DIMPLE   I have done everything in my power to assist his passion there: your delicacy, my dearest girl, would be shocked at half the instances of neglect and misbehaviour.

CHARLOTTE   I don't know how I should bear neglect; but Mr. Dimple must misbehave himself indeed, to forfeit my good opinion.

DIMPLE   Your good opinion, my angel, is the pride and pleasure of my heart; and if the most respectful tenderness for you and and utter indifference for all your sex besides, can make me worthy of your esteem, I shall richly merit it.

CHARLOTTE   All my sex besides, Mr. Dimple—you forgot your tête-à-tête with Letitia.

DIMPLE   How can you, my lovely angel, cast a thought on that insipid, wry-mouthed, ugly creature!

CHARLOTTE   But her fortune may have charms?

DIMPLE   Not to a heart like mine. The man who has been blessed with the good opinion of my Charlotte, must despise the allurements of fortune.

CHARLOTTE   I am satisfied.

DIMPLE   Let us think no more on the odious subject, but devote the present hour to happiness.

CHARLOTTE   Can I be happy, when I see the man I prefer going to be married to another?

DIMPLE   Have I not already satisfied my charming angel that I can never think of marrying the puling Maria. But, even if it were so, could that be any bar to our happiness; for, as the poet sings—

"Love, free as air, at sight of human ties,
"Spreads his light wings, and in a moment flies."

Come then, my charming angel! why delay our bliss! The present moment is ours; the next is in the hand of fate. (*Kissing her.*)

CHARLOTTE Begone, Sir! By your delusions you had almost lulled my honour asleep.

DIMPLE Let me lull the demon to sleep again with kisses.

(*He struggles with her; she screams.*)

(*Enter* MANLY.)

MANLY Turn, villain! and defend yourself.—

(*Draws.* VAN ROUGH *enters and beats down their swords.*)

VAN ROUGH Is the devil in you? are you going to murder one another? (*Holding* DIMPLE.)

DIMPLE Hold him, hold him,—I can command my passion.

(*Enter* JONATHAN.)

JONATHAN What the rattle ails you? Is the old one in you? Let the colonel alone, can't you? I feel chock full of fight,—do you want to kill the colonel?—

MANLY Be still, Jonathan; the gentleman does not want to hurt me.

JONATHAN Gor! I—I wish he did; I'd shew him Yankee boys play, pretty quick—Don't you see you have frightened the young woman into *hystrikes*?

VAN ROUGH Pray, some of you explain this; what has been the occasion of all this racket?

MANLY That gentleman can explain it to you; it will be a very diverting story for an intended father-in-law to hear.

VAN ROUGH How was this matter, Mr. Van Dumpling?

DIMPLE Sir,—upon my honour—all I know is, that I was talking to this young lady, and this gentleman broke in on us, in a very extraordinary manner.

VAN ROUGH Why, all this is nothing to the purpose: can you explain it, Miss? (*To* CHARLOTTE.)

(*Enter* LETITIA *through the back scene.*)

LETITIA I can explain it to that gentleman's confusion. Though long betrothed to your daughter (*to* VAN ROUGH), yet allured by my fortune, it seems (with shame do I speak it), he has privately paid his addresses to me. I was drawn in to listen to him by his assuring me that the match was made by his father without his consent, and that he proposed to break with Maria, whether he married me or not. But whatever were his intentions respecting your daughter, Sir, even to me he was false; for he has repeated the same story, with some cruel reflections upon my person, to Miss Manly.

JONATHAN What a tarnal curse!

LETITIA Nor is this all, Miss Manly. When he was with me this very morning, he made the same ungenerous reflections upon the weakness of your mind as he has so recently done upon the defects of my person.

JONATHAN What a tarnal curse and damn too!

DIMPLE Ha! since I have lost Letitia, I believe I had as good make it up with Maria—Mr. Van Rough, at present I cannot enter into particulars; but, I believe I can explain everything to your satisfaction in private.

VAN ROUGH There is another matter, Mr. Van Dumpling, which I would have you explain:—pray, Sir, have Messrs. Van Cash and Co. presented you those bills for acceptance?

DIMPLE The deuce! Has he heard of those bills! Nay, then, all's up with Maria, too; but an affair of this sort can never prejudice me among the ladies; they will rather long to know what the dear creature possesses to make him so agreeable. (*Aside.*) Sir, you'll hear from me. (*To* MANLY.)

MANLY And you from me, Sir.—

DIMPLE Sir, you wear a sword.—

MANLY Yes, Sir:—This sword was presented to me by that brave Gallic hero, the Marquis De La Fayette. I have drawn it in the service of my country, and in private life, on the only occasion where a man is justified in drawing his sword, in defence of a lady's honour. I have fought too many battles in the service of my country to dread the imputation of cowardice.—Death from a man of honour would be a glory you do not merit; you shall live to bear the insult of man, and the contempt of that sex, whose general smiles afforded you all your happiness.

DIMPLE You won't meet me, Sir?—Then I'll post you for a coward.

MANLY I'll venture that, Sir.—The reputation of my life does not depend upon the breath of a Mr. Dimple. I would have you to know, however, Sir, that I have a cane to chastise the insolence of a scoundrel, and a sword and the good laws of my country, to protect me from the attempts of an assassin.—

DIMPLE Mighty well! Very fine, indeed!—ladies and gentlemen, I take my leave, and you will please to observe, in the case of my deportment, the contrast between a gentleman, who has read Chesterfield and received the polish of Europe, and an unpolished, untravelled American. (*Exit.*)

(*Enter* MARIA.)

MARIA Is he indeed gone?—

LETITIA I hope never to return.

VAN ROUGH I am glad I heard of those bills; though it's plaguy unlucky: I hoped to see Mary married before I died.

MANLY Will you permit a gentleman, Sir, to offer himself as a suitor to your daughter? Though a stranger to you, he is not altogether so to her, or unknown in this city. You may find a son-in-law of more fortune, but you can never meet with one who is richer in love for her, or respect for you.

VAN ROUGH Why, Mary, you have not let this gentleman make love to you without my leave?

MANLY I did not say, Sir—

MARIA Say, Sir!—I—the gentleman, to be sure, met me accidentally.

VAN ROUGH Ha, ha, ha! Mark me, Mary; young folks think old folks to be fools; but old folks know young folks to be fools. —Why, I knew all about this affair:—This was only a cunning way I had to bring it about—Hark ye! I was in the closet when you and he were at our house. (*Turns to the company.*) I heard that little baggage say she loved her old father, and would die to make him happy! Oh! how I loved the little baggage!—And you talked very prudently, young man. I have inquired into your character, and find you to be a man of punctuality and mind the main chance. And so, as you love Mary, and Mary loves you, you shall have my consent immediately to be married. I'll settle my fortune on you, and go and live with you the remainder of my life.

MANLY Sir, I hope—

VAN ROUGH Come, come, no fine speeches; mind the main chance, young man, and you and I shall always agree.

LETITIA I sincerely wish you joy (*advancing to* MARIA); and hope your pardon for my conduct.

MARIA I thank you for your congratulations, and hope we shall at once forget the wretch who has given us so much disquiet, and the trouble that he has occasioned.

CHARLOTTE And I, my dear Maria,—how shall I look up to you for forgiveness? I, who, in the practice of the meanest arts, have violated the most sacred rights of friendship? I can never forgive myself, or hope charity from the world, but I confess I have much to hope from such a brother; and I am happy that I may soon say, such a sister.—

MARIA My dear, you distress me; you have all my love.

MANLY And mine.

CHARLOTTE If repentance can entitle me to forgiveness, I have already much merit; for I despise the littleness of my past conduct. I now find, that the heart of any worthy man cannot be gained by invidious attacks upon the rights and characters of others;—by countenancing the addresses of a thousand;—or that the finest assemblage of features, the greatest taste in dress, the genteelest address, or the most brilliant wit, cannot eventually secure a coquette from contempt and ridicule.

MANLY And I have learned that probity, virtue, honour, though they should not have received the polish of Europe, will secure to an honest American the good graces of his fair countrywoman, and, I hope, the applause of THE PUBLIC.

THE END.

LITERARY CRITICISM

Partly a matter of the theory of literature, both for creator and critic, and partly a question of the judgment of literary values, criticism was naturally of fundamental importance in the years when American literature was finding itself. While American reactions to the Tory Dr. Johnson were mixed, the traditions of neo-classical decorum, limpidity, respect for the rules of genre, and satiric warfare à la Pope, lived on well into the nineteenth century. The two selections which follow reflect both the older tradition and the reaction against it. Brackenridge's critical digression, following Cervantes' example, is a good illustration of neo-classical survivals. But at the same time the Scottish common sense tradition of Kames and Blair was emerging as the mediating tradition between neo-classicism and what, by the end of our period, would be romantic ideas. Dwight's defense of modernity and the rights of genius in *The Friend,* no. IV, is couched in Scottish terms and supplies an excellent rationale for the persistent call for a national literature.

Bibliography: William Charvat, *The Origins of American Critical Thought, 1810-1835;* Oliver Larkin, *Art and Life in America,* New York, 1949. I must also acknowledge my indebtedness to the as yet unpublished work on American criticism, 1741-1820, by Mr. Arthur E. Jones of Brothers College, Drew University.

I H. H. BRACKENRIDGE
(1748-1816)

from MODERN CHIVALRY

TEXT: CLAUDE NEWLIN, ED., *Modern Chivalry,* NEW YORK, 1937.

VOLUME III

INTRODUCTION

Proceeding with my object; the giving an example of a perfect stile in writing, I come now to the third volume of the work. I well know, that it will not all at once, and by all persons, be thought to be the model of a perfect stile, for it is only the perfectly instructed, and delicately discerning that can discover its beauties: and perhaps none will be more apt to pass them by than the learned of the academies, versed in grammar rules of writing, for there is a greenness in the judgment of the school critics with respect to what is simple and natural in composition.

To illustrate this by analogy. Let a dancing master pass his judgment on the movements of the best bred man in life; and not finding in his position and attitudes, an evident conformity to the lessons of the saltatory art, he will conclude that he has not been taught to move with propriety. He does not know that it is this very circumstance that constitutes the excellence of the movements of the easy and perfectly genteel man; to wit, that when you observe him, it will never once come into your mind that he thinks of his attitudes or positions in the least; but that every movement is just as it happens, and without any intention on his part. Ars est celare artem. To wit; It is the secret of good taste and perfection in behavior to conceal that you ever think of it at all. So it is the most perfect proof of a good stile, that when you read the composition, you think of nothing but the sense; and are never struck with the idea that it is otherwise expressed than every body would express it.

That stile, is not good, where it appears that you have not dared to use a word without thinking a long time whether you ought to use it; that, in the disposition of words, you have carefully studied which ought to go first and which last; and, that your sentence has a cadence which could not come by chance; but is the effect of design and art.

I acknowledge that no man will ever possess a good stile that has not well studied, and exercised himself in writing, selecting with a most perfect delicacy, in all cases; the proper term; but he must go beyond this, and be able to deceive the world, and, never let it come into their heads that he has spent a thought on the subject. But it is not one in five hundred that is born with such sensibility of nerve as to be able to attain with the help of great instruction and practice, a perfect judgment in the use of words. It is for this reason that I am ambitious of the praise of writing well so far as respects language. For it requires no uncommon structure of nerves, or organization of the brain to produce good sense; the mass of mankind is equal to this.

Language, as it is the peculiar gift, so it is the highest glory of our species; and the philologist is to be considered as cultivating the most useful and ornamental of all arts. Pursuing therefore solely the use of words, I do not descend professedly to think of sense; nevertheless, if at any time there should be found ideas that have some consistency and meaning, they may deserve attention, as much as if it was the primary object of my work to express them; for it is not their fault if I set little store by them, and think more of the dress that I put upon them than I do of themselves.

I am happy to find that in the review of this publication, given in Young's magazine, my ideas of the merit of the stile, is recognized, and fully justified. And as my work may be well supposed, to have a much more extensive circulation, and to live longer than that miscellaneous performance, I have thought it not amiss, for the honor of the critics to extract some part of the observations which have been made by them, and which are as follows:

"The author of the work before us, is H. H. Brackenridge, well known in the literary world for his treatise on the oeconomy of Rats, a satirical composition, in which under the veil of allegory, he designates the measures of the federal government; as also for his history of Weazels, in which the same strokes are given to those at the helm of our affairs, in a different fable, and narration. In the present work which he entitles Modern Chivalry, he disowns the idea of any moral or sentiment whatsoever, and proposes stile only as the object of the composition. And to this object, in our opinion, he scrupulously adheres; for though on some occasions, there would seem to be a semblance of idea, yet this we must attribute to the imagination of the reader, just as in looking upon a plaistered wall, attentively for a long time, you will conceive the inequality of the surface, or accidental scratchings, to be the shape of birds and beasts, or the letters of the alphabet. Yet as reason in this case will correct the fancy, and bring to mind that there is really no character or image there, there being none intended; so on a perusal of the work in question, looking a long time for sense, you may at last conceive that you observe some glimmerings of it, yet when you recollect that you have it from the author himself that he means none, you will be sensible that it is nothing more than the accidental combination of words which has given this picture to the mind.

Stile, then, which is his object, must also be ours, in our view of the publication. For, to give a simile; if a manufacturer of cloth, or a taylor that forms it into vestments, should come forward, and produce each his work, to be considered merely as to the manufacture, or making up, without regard to the materials of the woof and warp in the one case, or the wearing in the other, it would be absurd to enquire of these when nothing was proposed to you respecting them, by the artists themselves.

Confining ourselves therefore to the stile of this performance, we observe, that it has what is the first characteristic of excellence; viz. Simplicity. This consists in the choice of the plainest and most familiar words, and in the arrangement of the words in their natural order. There is a great difference between a vulgar term, or phrase, and that which is common, and comes first upon the tongue, in easy and familiar conversation. It is the mistake of this distinction which leads some writers to avoid the phrase that any one would use, and seek out what is uncommon. Hence there appears a variation in the words they put upon paper, from those which they themselves would use in conversation. And why this? Ought not language to be precisely the same whether spoken or written.

Perspicuity is the natural result of simplicity, and needs not to be laid down as a different characteristic. For can there be obscurity in that composition where the most familiar word is used, and that word put in its proper place. This brings to mind the definition of stile by Swift; "proper words in proper places."

There can be nothing more easy than the composition of our author. His writing savours of the skill of an artificer who after many years exercitation in his art, acquires a power of accomplishing his work by a habit of the fingers, independent of any application of the mind. So that while in the stile of others there is an appearance of exertion, here there is what a superficial observer would call carelessness, but which the sound critic will discover to be the result of a perfect mastery of all that relates to language.

It is pretty generally believed that our stile has been constantly degenerating from the time of queen Anne, in whose reign flourished those immortal penmen, Swift, Addison, Arbuthnot, Tillotson, Bolinbroke, &c. If the stile of this author is examined, and compared with those models, it will be found to be in the same pure, simple attic taste. We shall therefore not hestitate to recommend it as a restorer of all that is correct and beautiful in writing." So far the reviewers.

I have said that I was happy to find that these have had the good taste to find out what I myself had thought of the composition. But as I wish at all times to let the reader, into a knowledge of my real sentiments, I will confess that these are merely words of course with me, and that I was not happy to find my work praised in any respect; because I wished to have a quarrel with the critics; and this not because I love war, abstractedly considered; but because in this case I should have had an opportunity of shewing my polemic talents. Nay, expecting an attack, I had prepared a number of good thoughts in my mind, to be used in my contest with them. What is more I had actually written a copy of verses in the Hudibrastic rhyme and manner, for their use, in which I considered them as muskitoes, or flies of some kind, that were troublesome to men; and though the occasion fails, yet there can be no impropriety in giving to the public those strokes of satire which lay dormant in my mind as these would apply more particularly to an attack upon me; yet the essay being in general terms, it may appear without a particular circumstance to call it forth; merely as a specimen of what I could do had there been occasion for it. And the insertion will be excuseable, when it is considered how painful it is to be frustrated in what we propose as our pleasure. I have known a good man wish to have bad news true, merely because he had related them: and we may conceive a saint vexed at not finding a man dead, when he had digested a funeral sermon in his mind, and was ready to bury him. On this principle, therefore, and in spite of critics, I will have my verses published: they are as follows:

> The critic first possess'd the earth,
> And by his rules gave authors birth.
> You may be ancient: critic, hark!
> Were you with Noah in the ark?
> In what compartment were you seen?
> 'Mongst creatures clean, or the unclean?
> The critic, sir's, the natural father
> Of every snifling, snufling author;
> And when you nod or snore or sleep,
> We slily on posteriors creep,
> And rouse you to a bright exertion,
> Of all your faculties; you whoreson.
> How can there be idea of beauties,
> Unless the critic genius shew't-us?
> The angle of the sight obtuse,
> Can see no more than doth a goose,
> Whilst we with microscopic eye,
> Examine as you would a fly,
> See through the crevices of fancy,
> As far as human eyesight can see,
> Tell where there is or is not Grammar;
> What phraseology wants hammer—
> Or file to make the verse run smoother,
> Where sound is harsh, or term uncouther.
> I grant you see defects and errors,
> Of those in genius your superiors:
> The skin however smoothly curried,
> To a flea's eye is deep and furrowed.
> His optics may perceive a wart,
> That grows upon the unseen part,
> But for the beauty of the frame,
> It is above the ken of them—
> Thus critics tell that bard divine

Has a rough word in such a line,
Or that the sacred poem scarce,
Can bear the trot of such a verse,
That feeble author in such sentence
Has not the vis, the spirit intense,
That Pegasus was lame when he rode,
Over this or that dull period:
They tell, but never felt the force,
Of genius in his rapid course.

  What? did not Quintilian fully,
Develop all the praise of Tully?
And 'mongst the Greeks, the great Longinus,
Who may be justly stil'd his highness,
With critic judgment join the fire,
Of Heaven itself? Who can go higher?
From your vile accusation who's safe?
Not even the elder scaliger Joseph,
Who had a mind as big's a mountain,
Could all defects, and beauties contain,
And shew'd that Homer was inferior,
And Virgil but perfection nearer,
Have you the assurance sir to speak,
Against the Roman worth and Greek?

  So much we hear I believe that no man's
Tongue is still of Greeks and Romans;
For if dispute should rise past curing,
Which way 'tis best to make our urine,
And each should argue stiffly his way,
All must give up, the Greeks piss'd this way.

  But there in modern times is Bently,
Who sung of Richard Blackmore daint'ly,

  I grant it, critic, there's a thousand;
The list beginning has nor knows end.
They swarm in millions from the flood—
The Hebrew critics first drew blood;
And this is what is meant by Babel

Where all were critics that were able.
The Rabbin and the Talmudist,
Fought hand to hand, and fist to fist,
About the pentateuch of Moses;
Their tales, the wildest stuff, God knows is.
  If there has been some Grecian critic,
Above the offspring of a seed tic;
Yet where is one in modern days
Who can deserve that share of praise.
For metamorphos'd down to vermin,
Who can the various shapes determine.
And small and great are prone to mischief,
And every clan and sect has his chief.
They swarm like Caledonian cluster,
When the MacNeils and Camrons muster;
Or as when house wife spreads her sugar,
With water mix'd, each insect bugar,
Relinquishes pots, tubs and pails,
And for the booty spreads his sails
Thus all the race of critics gather,
Around the footsteps of an author,
Bite through his overalls and stocking,
And biting shins, you know's no joking.
Who now a days sits down to write
Uninterrupted by a bite?
Unless he takes good care and puts on,
A pair of leggins, or has boots on.
  They say of Reynard who loves geese,
That when oppress'd with swarm of fleas
He takes in's mouth a lock of wool,
And gradually retires to pool;
The fleas by secret instinct led,
Fly from the tail and trunk to head,
With speed each mother's son of them goes
To seek the promontory of nose,
And when no more remains abaft,

> Fox shakes his head and leaves the raft.
>   Who could find out by book or sermon,
> An equal way t'allude the vermin
> Would merit a rich premium more,
> Than vers'd in philosophic lore,
> The member who dissects a glow-worm,
> To see if 'tis a beast and no worm,
>   I wish some virtuoso wou'd,
> Who natural history understood,
> Dissect a critic, shew his jaw teeth,
> Whether they are quite smooth or saw-teeth,
> Resembling butterfly or asp,
> Or sharp and pointed like a wasp;
> And by the grinders edge determine,
> Corn-eating or carnivrous vermin.
> I'd give, myself, a golden medal,
> To know if 't has a brown or red tail,
> And whether when it moves goes on
> An hundred feet or half a dozen;
> But many glasses must be ground out,
> Before these mysteries can be found out.
> I leave it to some great Linaeus,
> Who may by this be fam'd as he was.

The reviewers in Young's Magazine may see from hence how well it was for them, though unfortunate for me, that they have dealt in approbation solely. The prettiest part of the history of any author, is his war with the critics; and as that prince's reign, seems uninteresting where we are not amused with sieges and battles, so the life of an author is dull and monotonous where we hear of no litigations with a Bavius, or Maevius, a Dennis or a Colly Cibber.

II TIMOTHY DWIGHT
(*1752-1817*)

from THE FRIEND, NO. IV
TEXT: *The American Museum,* V, PHILADELPHIA, 1789

Among the prejudices which are entertained by the mind, none has a more powerful influence, than reverence for the opinions and practices of those who have lived before us. This prejudice reaches all classes of men, and extends its dominion over every method of thinking and acting. Great men observe, and laugh at it, in the conduct of little ones; every sect perceives it in every other sect; and every individual, in the conduct of every other. In agriculture, at least in this country, it decides every practice; in the mechanical arts, in the liberal arts, and even in science, it has a very extensive influence. Thus the nature of the subject to be considered, or pursued, is little attended to, the force of arguments, pleaded in vain; and men live not by reason, but by precedent. This folly has been often exploded by philosophy, and caricatured by satire; yet its power, either in extent or degree, is little abated. The reason is obvious: every man sees the defect in another, but not in himself; and while he wonders that his neighbours are so deaf to reasoning, and so slow of reformation, never reflects that himself is equally diseased, and equally needs the benefit of the cure.

The man, who, upon his shoulders, carried weekly to the mill, a stone of sufficient weight to balance a bushel of wheat, and who refused to rid himself of the burden, because his father and grandfather had carried the same stone, forty years, before him; was, in the eye of reason, a less ridiculous object than the person, who is voluntarily burdened with a load of errors and follies, because others, who have preceded him, chose to carry them. Yet we daily see multitudes, whose shoulders are humped higher than their heads, laughing heartily at the aukward figure, their fellow Hudibrasses make around them.

Homer, some thousand years since, with great force and beauty, formed the Iliad, an epic, or narrative poem. It was the first poem of the kind, and written with the first degree of human abilities. Accordingly, the pleasure it gave mankind was very great, and the praises they heaped upon it were without measure. Aristotle, a shrewd and curious investigator, examined the structure of this poem, and the Odyssey, and having satisfied himself what were the means of the pleasure they afforded, ventured to form, from the practice of Homer, general rules for the conduct of the epic poem. From the tragedies of Sophocles and Euripides, regarded by their countrymen with similar applause, he formed other rules for the conduct of tragedy. This code of criticism has partly escaped the depredations of time, and is now a law less disputed, even by most persons of taste, than either of the two fundamental rules of moral rectitude. Had these three poets been moderns—had Milton written Paradise Lost, when the Iliad was written, and the best tragedies of Shakespeare been exhibited on the Athenian stage, Aristotle would doubtless have consulted their writings, for the source of the pleasure derived from them, and formed his maxims of criticism on their authority. How different a system would these events have produced; and how many rules would have then been received, with the same implicit faith, with which every age has now swallowed their opposites? Many of Aristotle's present laws would then have been considered as the lunacies of Zoilus. All epic poems must have had an unfortunate issue; all tragedies five acts; and the inferior parts been written in prose. A chorus would have been railed at as a modern absurdity; simplicity of plot been deemed the effusion of dullness; and a new cluster of great ancients moved down the tide of ages, with undisputed glory and perfection. The dispute would then have been, whether the Iliad and Æneid were entitled to the name of epic poems; and whether their fortunate issues were not such a trespass on the established rules of criticism, as to preclude them from a rank in this high class of productions. Homer's machinery would have been the grossest of all absurdities; and the wonder of all men of taste would have been excited, at the groveling relish of such persons as were capable of enduring in dignified peformances, the heathen mythology. Thus the face of the critical world would have been essentially altered, and the propriety of every maxim would have been as questionless as of those, at present adopted.

To those persons who never questioned the authority of the received system of criticism, these remarks will appear ill founded; for the prejudice above mentioned, which produced their implicit faith in it, will prevent them from discerning their propriety. In the view of candour, the justice of them will scarcely be doubted. Yet how much of the common reverence for Aristotle, for all the ancients, and for many of the moderns, will the acknowledgment of them destroy?

I would not here be understood to condemn the generality of precepts in the present critical code, or to think disrespectfully of its author. Aristotle was an excellent, a wonderful critic, for the advantages he possessed; and many of the acknowledged critical maxims are undoubtedly just. But Aristotle's ideas of criticism were taken from a few performances: and had he lived in the present age, with the same independence of mind, he would have altered many of them for the better. As criticism, like the science of healing, forms all its precepts from facts, the more numerous the collection of facts is, the fairer opportunity is furnished for reducing it to the standard of truth. Milton and Shakespeare have added, every original genius adds, to the stock of critical ideas, and exhibits means of pleasure, the knowledge of which is true criticism. Hence criticism will advance towards a higher perfection, as the varieties of the human mind open new views of poetical objects, and peculiarity of genius furnishes new springs and meanderings of delight. The stock of poetical images is as infinite, as the diversities of infinite workmanship, in the natural and moral creation; and the modes of exhibiting them as various, as the endlessly various modes of perception in intelligent beings. All these constitute the field of criticism, and concerning them all just and valuable remarks in the progress of things will probably be made.

A few specimens of the influence of the above prejudice, on this branch of human knowledge may perhaps be advantageously subjoined to these observations.

The question, whether Paradise Lost, the Jerusalem Delivered, and various other poems, are epic poems, has often agitated the critical world. To decide this question with propriety, or even at all, one would naturally imagine it necessary to have previously decided the nature of the epic poem. Yet this article is hitherto totally undecided. It has indeed been often defined, but that definition has been as often contested. It would be not a little surprising—if any human folly were surprising—to see grave and learned men seriously and warmly debate, whether a poem belongs to a certain class, before they have agreed upon the characteristics of that class.

The word epic signifies merely narrative, and according to its plain meaning, every narrative poem is epic. But the phrase epic poem has been appropriated to such narrative poems, as concerned a dignified subject, were written in an elevated style, and contained noble images, and interesting sentiments. In this sense, also, the poems referred to are as truly epic, as any hitherto written. But if an epic poem must be exactly like the Iliad, Odyssey, or Æneid, or if it must rehearse the actions of a warrior, Paradise Lost will be excluded from the number.

The truth is, such is the reverence for Homer and Virgil, and such the submission to Aristotle's idea of this subject, that in deciding this question, we recur to Aristotle's ideas of that example, and not to the nature of the subject at large, nor to any definite principles of our own. Thus a single specimen is, by this prejudice, erected into a class, and while we make that a species, as a logician would say, which is no more than an individual of that species, in endeavouring to reduce other individuals of the species to the exact characteristic of that individual, an article necessarily impossible—we debate much with ourselves, and with others, where a little freedom of mind would at once dispel the cause of our doubts.

Indeed the general applause given to Paradise Lost, has almost forced the reluctant critics of the present age to silence, on this subject: but it has been long and warmly contested by eminent writers, and is even now scarcely reduced to a certainty.

Pastoral poetry has also suffered from this prejudice, in the highest degree. Theocritus, a Sicilian, wrote a number of pastoral poems of a particular character. Virgil copied after him, with less nature, and more art. From their examples, pastoral poetry has been defined; and to their modes of writing, succeeding pastoral writers have been limited. Hence a poem, however abounding in rural images and ideas, and however unadorned in its style, is denied the name, because it is not copied from Virgil, or Theocritus, as if all the scenes of rural life were not pastoral subjects, and all the pleasing modes of exhibiting them to the mind in verse, did not belong to this species of poetry.

The misfortunes of this mode of judging are great. Writers are fettered by it within such limits, as to prevent every genuine adventure of genius, and degraded to the humble character of copyers; and readers are precluded from that diversity of pleasure rationally to be expected from the perpetually variegated rovings of imagination. Poems, by the manner of forming them, are necessitated to be stale and trite, and innumerable beauties of nature are locked up from the enjoyment of mankind. From this prejudice arose most of that sterility and tastelessness, complained of in the pastorals of Pope, pardonable in a youth of sixteen, but foolishly defended by the author when grown to manhood, and more foolishly praised by doctor Warburton.

In our own happy state of society, disjointed from the customs and systems of Europe, commencing a new system of science and politics, it is to be ardently hoped, that so much independence of mind will be assumed by us, as to induce us to shake off these rusty shackles, examine things on the plan of nature and evidence, and laugh at the grey-bearded decisions of doting authority. There is ever a propensity in the mind, when forming a class, species, or genus, to form it from the knowledge of a few individuals. Hence it is of necessity imperfectly formed, and all conclusions based upon it, must be erroneous. This is the great imperfection of theories and systems, and the chief cause of their failure in a practical application; classes ought never to be erected but from the knowledge of many individuals belonging to them, and to be accurately just from the knowledge of all. Perhaps even with this knowledge, they would be constituted with difficulty in the poetical world. Most poems are of such a nature as to blend and harmonize, in several characteristics, with the kinds bordering on them; and can be no more exactly limited or separated than the hues of the rainbow.

For these reasons every definition intended to be just on this subject, ought to be general and liberal; nature ought to be consulted in preference to Aristotle; and other approved writers, as well as Homer and Virgil, Sophocles and Theocritus. On this plan, the wings of genius would be no longer clipped, and its flight, taking the natural direction, and using the natural strength of opinion, would be free and elevated; on this plan, the writer who produced pleasing selections of images and sentiments from the widely extended and endlessly diversified paradise of nature, would be assured of regaling the taste of his readers; and on this plan, Goldsmith's Deserted Village would hold the first rank in pastoral poetry, and Paradise Lost be clearly seen to be superior to every other epic production.

III NOAH WEBSTER
(1758-1843)

It is most improbable that Noah Webster accidentally chose to date his defense of Timothy Dwight on the Fourth of July, 1788. None of the innumerable workers for American cultural independence was more tireless than Webster. He made his name a household word with the dictionary by which he tried to stimulate the growth of an American language and with the school-books meant to educate Americans up toward his hopes for them. The militancy of Webster's attack on Dwight's detractor, the pedantry of his rhetoric-chopping, and the almost desperate effort to keep a balance between a national defense of America and the temptation to praise the native writer only because he is native, are all typical of nationalistic criticism in the period.

Bibliography: William B. Cairns, *British Criticisms of American Writings,* 1783-1815, Madison, 1918. Harry Warfel, *Noah Webster: Schoolmaster to America,* New York, 1936.

Text: *The American Magazine,* New York, October, 1788.

A DEFENCE OF AMERICAN LETTERS

TO THE AUTHORS OF THE LONDON REVIEW

Gentlemen,

In the *European Magazine* for February, March and April, I observe your *criticisms* on the Conquest of Canaan, a Poem in eleven books, by the Rev. Dr. Dwight. As I have the honor of some acquaintance with that gentleman, and with some circumstances respecting his Poem of which you appear to be ignorant, I presume to call in question the justness of some of your remarks, notwithstanding they are published under the authority of the *Philological Society* in London.

You introduce your critique with the following reflections:

"Every liberal mind must be pleased to see Genius, and that great humaniser of nations, polite Literature, expanding themselves in the infant States of America. However inferior to a Homer or a Milton; or however but little superior to a Blackmore; yet the attempt to cultivate the Muses in a new-formed

Commonwealth, and a decent and promising attempt the Poem before us undoubtedly is, such an attempt has a claim to more than ordinary candor, has a claim to liberal indulgence, and such due commendations as may cherish the lisping Muse. The critic who is the genuine friend of the interests of literature, where he perceives a total barrenness of genius, will admonish the unhappy author to desist; and will even add ridicule and severity, as the case may require. But where taste and merit are discernible, and capable of improvement, he will point out the blemishes and faults with tenderness, and in a manner calculated to promote the Author's future amendment. Such we intend to be the rule of our conduct in our animadversions on the American Epic Poem, the CONQUEST OF CANAAN."

Did these remarks, gentlemen, proceed from *liberal minds, which are pleased to see genius and polite literature, expanding themselves in the Infant States* of America? Or were they dictated by prejudice, in minds soured by political disappointment? Let the *liberal mind* determine.

As your remarks on the preface of Dr. Dwight's Poem are the least exceptionable, I pass them without notice.

Having given the argument of the first book at large, you subjoin the following remarks. "Here America is obviously placed before us under the allegory of the Israelites having left Egypt, which means the British government, and about to settle themselves by force of arms.[1] *Hanniel,* who advises to return to Egypt, and the *difficulties* he foretells, *represents*[2] the loyalists, and Joshua's reply sums up the arguments of the American patriots. But this allegory is not regularly carried through the work."

Here, Gentlemen, your opinions are *obviously* erroneous. It is your misfortune to forget the character you profess, and instead

---

[1] *What a curious construction of a sentence!—"the Israelites* having *left Egypt, and (having) about to settle themselves by force of arms." This language is like the criticisms, worthy of the celebrated English Philological Society.*

[2] *"Hanniel and the difficulties he foretells, represents."—is possibly another specimen of the grammatical accuracy of the Philological Society of London. But the writer is candid enough to believe, it may be a typographical error.*

of candid criticism, indulge yourselves in the malevolent reflections of peevish politicians. The separation of America from Great Britain wounds the narrow hearts of splenetic English politicians, and the mortifications they have suffered by that event have disordered their minds. They see every thing thro' the medium of prejudice, and their distempered imaginations convert the most natural appearances into hobgoblins and "Chimeras dire."

But, gentlemen, what have political subjects to do with an Epic Poem? On what authority did you assert that the Conquest of Canaan contains an allegory,——that the *Americans* are described under the character of the *Israelites,*—that Egypt is meant to represent the British government—and Hanniel, the loyalists? Is it any where asserted in the Poem, the preface, or any where else? Have you been informed of it by Dr. Dwight's friends, or by newspaper paragraphs? Gentlemen, your suppositions are without foundation: and to show how utterly you have mistaken the design of the author, I will lay before you an extract of a letter written by the author himself, on hearing that the London Reviewers had criticised his Poem on the idea that it is allegorical. He wrote to his informant in these words:

To ——, Sir,

"The idea of those gentlemen, that the Poem is allegorical, is so far from having a foundation, that until I received your letter, it never entered into my mind, that such an apprehension could be entertained by a man of common sense. Singular jealousy of American resentment, and perhaps a strong consciousness that the oppressive measures of Britain wore a striking similarity to the Egyptian abuse, must have originated their view of the Poem. In several particular incidents referred to, especially in the colloquy of the first book, there is, I confess, a considerable resemblance between the case of the Israelites and that of the Americans; and the feelings of the writer may have naturally colored a resemblance still nearer. But I presume the Reviewers must have thought the writer destitute of every critical idea, to imagine the *Conquest* of a country a proper event, under which to allegorize the *defence* of another country.

"That Gen. Washington should be supposed to resemble Joshua is not strange. They are both great and good characters, acting at the head of armies, and regulating the chief interests of their countrymen. Between such men, in such circumstances a resemblance is almost necessary.

"The truth is, the Poem was begun in the year 1771, and written out, several times before the year 1775:——all the essential parts were finished, before the war was begun, and the Poem advertised for the press, during the first year of the war. From these facts, Sir, you will perceive the impossibility of any foundation for the conjecture of the Reviewers.

> I am, dear Sir,
> Your very obliged and
> most obedient servant,
> TIMOTHY DWIGHT."

Greenfield, July 6, 1788.

To these facts, as stated by the author, many of his friends can bear witness; and the public can testify that proposals for printing the Poem were issued about the commencement of hostilities between Great Britain and America; and the execution of the design was suspended by reason of the war. So little foundation is there for the supposition that the Poem is an allegory. A few passages were introduced after the Poem was supposed to be finished and during the war. Among these, was the passage in which Captain HALE is mentioned.

"Thus while fond virtue wish'd in vain to save,
  HALE, bright and generous, found a hapless grave."

On this passage, you are pleased to remark, that "the verb *found* seems to want its nominative. We would ask Mr. Dwight,

Is it *fond virtue,* or are *Hale, bright* and *generous*[3] personifications that found a hapless grave? To say that the natural construction applies to *Aram,* is to break *Priscian's* head with a vengeance. Nor would we have been so particular on this fault, which might pass for inattention, did not similar instances abound in our author; and however he may dread that America should inbibe the vices and corruptions of Great-Britain, we would advise him and his brother poets, either to study the English language with more care, or to write their Poems in the tongue of their *great* and *good allies,* those *zealous* and *disinterested* defenders of the liberties of mankind, the *French."*

What a mixture of *ignorance* and *political spleen!* Is it impossible that an English Critic should view the smallest literary production in America, thro' any medium but that of *national prejudice?* Must every thing have a reference to the late separation of America from Great Britain, and Frenchmen be lugged into a decision of the merits of an American Poem? Is this the candor and impartiality of a *critic*—of an *English critics?*—Is this the boasted liberality of your nation?

But your inattention, gentlemen, is astonishing. You do not understand the passage on which you have bestowed so many severe remarks. "The verb *found* seems to want its nominative." No, gentlemen, there is no *seeming* in the passage. *Hale,* a Captain in the American service, a native of Connecticut, a man of noble heart and amiable character, the *Andre* of our army, and who suffered in New-York, the same fate that Andre did in the Highlands, *"found* a hapless grave." If you were ignorant of this historical fact, you ought at least to have supposed *Hale* to be the *name of a person,* especially as Dr. Dwight has informed you in a note on the passage, which you have recited, that "the comparisons of this kind were annexed to the Poem, to indulge the authors own *emotions of regard to the persons named in them."* As you "advise the American Poets to study the English language with more care," permit me, gentlemen, to advise the

---

[3] We have heard King William in this manner called, "Old Glorious."

London Reviewers to *understand the works they review,* before they indulge so much ridicule and severity, or decide with peremptory assurance, on the merit of the writings.

In your subsequent remarks you select for criticism such passages of the Poem, as you suppose carry on the *allegory,* which offends the pride of your nation. On such passages you freely indulge the rancor of your hearts.

But as the allegory is the work of your own invention, you are welcome to attack it with all the earnestness of a *Quixote,* engaged with a windmill.

Many of Dr. Dwight's friends will however acknowledge the propriety of the following criticisms—"That in some passages there is a strange confusion of ideas and language—that in others, there is a want of perspicuity—that there is too much bustling and killing—that the descriptions are too long, and often abound with repetitions of the same imagery."—To these faults or others must we ascribe the fatigue of reading the Poem, which is generally complained of in America. You suppose indeed that the *allegory* of the Poem, which is designed to describe the late revolution, will make it interesting to Americans. I can assure you, gentlemen, that the Americans never suspected such an allegory to exist; nor do they take any uncommon interest in the Poem. They think it has much merit—but they see and censure its faults. They do not indeed expect to realize all the happiness anticipated in the tenth book of the Poem; but they cannot think with you that the fictions of a Poet's fancy are subjects of derision. They may at times indulge a political enthusiasm—all nations do the same—it is the spring of heroic actions—it is laudable—but they are philosophic enough to expect that the real greatness and happiness of America will resemble those of other free countries. Nor do they really expect that the eastern continent will be doomed to the most deplorable slavery and misery—on the contrary, they predict that liberty and happiness will increase, in proportion to the progressive improvements in science and commerce.

With an ardent wish that a more *liberal spirit may breathe* thro' the English nation, and thro' your future criticisms on American writings, I am, Gentlemen, your very humble servant,

AN AMERICAN.

New York, July 4, 1788.

IV JOSEPH DENNIE
(1768-1812)

The leading literary center during the period of the early republic was Philadelphia. And the most distinguished organ of literary expression in America was Joseph Dennie's Philadelphia *Port Folio*. One of the few young literary lawyers who dared to make the plunge into a literary career, Dennie was inclined to think that deism and democracy, abhorred by good Federalists anyway, were responsible for the scanty response to elegant literary endeavors. He sometimes yearned for the return of monarchy to America so that he might shine at court like some of his transatlantic idols. The feelings and methods stimulated by such reflections are apparent in his treatment of Franklin.

Nevertheless, Dennie was sensitive and able, and he was one of the few really serious critics then working in America. The balance and clarity of his mind, and his debts to the neo-classical past may be seen in his light handling of the fashionable Gothicism. His very early recognition of Wordsworth and his ability to give sympathetic treatment of Freneau in spite of politics are monuments to his acumen and maturity.

Bibliography: Milton Ellis, *Joseph Dennie and His Circle*, Austin, 1915; Charvat, *op. cit*.

ON GOTHICISM [1]

THE LAY PREACHER

AND SAD VISIONS APPEARED UNTO THEM WITH HEAVY COUNTENANCES

With the punctuality of a merchant, I shall now perform the promise made in my last speculation. I then took occasion to review and to reprove the fantastic romances of the eighteenth century. To shew some of their operations upon nervous, timid, and, indeed, upon all exquisitely organized systems, shall be the business of this sermon. In my digressive manner, a few topics, slightly connected with the main design, will be started; and may possibly add to the amusement of the reader, though they will hardly improve his logic.

---

[1] Text: *The Port Folio*, Philadelphia, III, 1803.

If, as the farmers say, 'my memory serves me,' Dr. Beattie has somewhere cautioned youthful readers of sensibility to beware of immoderately indulging in the perusal of such works as the Night Thoughts of Young. This judicious Scotchman assigns an excellent reason for his rule. For he adds that books, which present sometimes false, and always gloomy views of life, and which wear out the mind by a constant succession of horrors, must ultimately prove pernicious. For terrific and mournful images are, from their very nature, striking; and, to men of strong fancy, easily adherent. Hence, in times of grief and sickness, and even amid the common calamities and cares of life, such images will rise, and, in a 'long, unbroken, funeral train,' will continually pass before our distracted eyes. One of the most useful and necessary of our virtues is Fortitude; a companion, in the season of distress, absolutely necessary to enable the fretful impatience of our nature to tolerate its woes. But, when, from our habits of reading and thinking, spectres, demons, Melancholy, Sorrow, black cares, and 'sights unholy,' are present with us, Fortitude flies away. We mistake the phantoms of Imagination for the ills of life. The poison of Romance tips every arrow from the quiver of Fate; and we fall victims, not so much to the fever in our veins, or to the poverty of our coffers, as to the despondency of our thoughts, and to the 'giant of Despair.'

In the works of Mrs. Radcliff, and of all her imitators, mournfull or horrible description predominates. The authors go out of the walks of Nature, to find some dreadful incident. Appalling noises must be created. Ghosts must be manufactured by dozens. A door is good for nothing, in the opinion of a romance writer, unless it creak. The value of a room is much enhanced by a few dismal groans. A chest full of human bones is twice as valuable as a casket of diamonds. Every grove must have its quiet disturbed, by the devil, in some shape or other. Not a bit of tapestry but must conceal a corpse; not an oak can grow, without sheltering banditti. Now, in real life, examined in any age, or in any country, we cannot find such a series, such a combination of horrible events, as the romance writers display in almost every page. All their knights are 'knights of the Doleful Countenance.' Fortunately for mortals, though there is much misfortune, and much evil here, yet every object is not covered with a pall. There are objects less sable to our eyes than the coffin. It is a misrepresentation to state that the whole world resembles Bunyan's valley of the shadow of death. It is mischievous to exhibit such a false picture. It enfeebles the mind. It induces a habit of melancholy; it strengthens frantic fear, a passion remarkable, according to COLLINS, for beholding 'appalled the unreal scene.' Instead of thus wantonly weakening the mind, by directing its attention to ghastly illusions, to 'horrible shadows, and unreal mockery,' we should adopt the discipline of the Poet,

> That superstition mayn't create
> And club its ills with those of fate,
> I many a notion take to task,
> Made by dreadful its vizor mask,
> Since optic Reason shews me plain,
> I dreaded spectres of the brain.

If I had a friend of exquisite sensibility, whose irritable nerves vibrated like the chords of music, I would lock up Mrs. Radcliff's novels from his morbid curiosity. I would not suffer him to turn pale at the thoughts of any of her ghosts. He should 'laugh and shake in Rabelais' easy chair.' He should not walk in any of her galleries, nor abide in any of her courts. I would address him then in words of the sensible Green.

> Love not so much the doleful knell,
> And news the boding night birds tell;
> Nor in imprest remembrance keep
> Grim tap'stry figures wrought in sleep;
> Nor rise to see, in antique hall,
> The moonlight monsters on the wall;
> And shadowy spectres darkly pass,
> Trailing their sables o'er the grass.

A hypochondriac would be as much injured by the perusal of the woeful romance, as by a denial of air and exercise. He would fancy, like Don Quixote, that his sick chamber was a castle. He would mistake his nurse for a witch; and call his apothecary 'Montoni.' He would convert his phails into 'vials of wrath' and poison, and insist that his pill box was made of 'gloomy pine or black larch wood.'

ON FRANKLIN

AN AUTHOR'S EVENINGS

From The Shop of Messrs. Colon and Spondee

———"For you
I tame my youth to philosophic cares,
And grow still paler by the midnight lamps."
                                    DR. ARMSTRONG.

I remember, when I was a boy, somebody put into my hand the life and essays of Dr. Franklin. At the time this man lived, and particularly when his *philosophy,* and his newspaper ethics and economics were diffused over the continent, it was the fashion for Vanity to "rejoice and be exceeding glad" in the possession of such a treasure. I have heard somewhere of a book, for the use of apprentices, servant maids, &c. entitled, "The *Only* Sure Guide to Love and Esteem." In like manner it was thought that there was no other road to the temple of Riches, except that which run through—Dr. Franklin's works; and that, as quacks boast of an infallible cure for the itch, the doctor could communicate a nostrum for the preservation of prudence, and the cure of poverty. Every miser read his precepts with rapture, and Franklin was pronounced not only wise, and good, and *patriotic,* and all that—but an *original writer!* Such a strange opinion as the last never could have been entertained, except in a country, from its newness, paucity of literary information, and the imperfection of its systems of education, puzzled to distinguish an original from a copy. For, the fact is, that "our Benjamin" was no more distinquished for the *originality* of his conceptions, than for the purity of his life, or the soundness of his religious doctrine. As a writer, he plundered his thoughts and his phrases from others—and as a deist, he supported his religion with the *arts* of infidelity; with the rank garbage of Mandeville, Tindal, and Chubb; with the *crumbs* which fell from those *poor* men's tables. It may be recollected, that among other things which appear in his "Essays," there is a scheme for an "air bath," and hints for procuring quiet sleep, by rising in the night, and beating up your bed, and walking about your chamber, &c. This profound discovery was ushered into the world with the greatest pomp, copied into innumerable newspapers, and praised as a most ingenious invention. Every American, who had read or spelt through two or three almanacs, or two or three papers in the Spectator, talked of the doctor's genius, and *philosophy,* and simplicity in writing. Ignorance and unskilfulness, as they are wont, naturally wondered at what bore the semblance of specious novelty. Like those children, described in *Shenstone's* School-mistress,

"They in gaping wonderment abound,
And think he was the greatest wight on ground."

Unfortunately for the doctor's philosophy and invention, as they respect the discovery of the above opiate, both of them are as baseless as his reputation. If a man, whose brain is labouring with thought, or agitated by the spells of hypochondria, or fired with the rays of Fancy, should rise from a sleepless couch, and patrol his chamber like a sentinel, and then return to bed, he may still ask in vain for the poppies of Morpheus. For the experience of almost every sedentary scholar will prove that there are moments, nay hours, when the billows of the brain will not, at bidding, subside. The soul of a man of genius is, often, broad awake at midnight hours, and to attempt to stupefy it into sleep, by the above and similar tricks, is worthy of Franklin, and of

Frenchmen, and of their philosophy. It becomes all three to treat the mind as they would a bit of wax or a lump of dough, and presumptuously strive to mould it into any and every fantastic shape. But this occasional *vigilance* of our mental faculties is an ordinance of the CREATOR OF MIND, and wisely intended as a hint, as a goad to the sluggishness of our grosser powers to arise to action. When sleeplessness is experienced, let a man leave his bed, and light his lamp, and read or write, or meditate, as was the custom of Mr. POPE, and tire the body in that way, and not stalk about like the ghost of Banquo, or stand at open windows, to terrify the owls, and to "make night hideous." This trick of Benjamin has been repeatedly tried, and he, who made the experiment, has a right to declare it fallacious. Strolling about one's chamber will not close the mental eye: all such schemes are a bubble, and it is a risible proof of the emptiness of modern philosophy, that its vain followers imagine mind may be managed upon mechanical principles, and, as an ingenious friend once expressed it, that we can throw off speculation from the soul, as a miller throws a sack of corn from his shoulder.

Thus much for the *truth* and *utility* of Franklin's scheme, to sleep at will. Now, "mark how a plain tale shall put down" all the glory of the *invention*. Americans are so little in the habit of literary research and so arrogantly confident ours "is the first and most enlightened country in the world," that, without examination, they eulogize extravagantly every thing that is their own; as Dr. Benjamin has the double honour to be born in Boston, and print in Philadelphia, therefore he must be an Addison in stile, and a Bacon in philosophy. I have heard and read encomiums by dozens, on the intention of the above scheme to cheat the senses into a slumber. But, even this receipt to procure drowsiness, though childish, trivial, and false, is not *new*. The doctor *stole* it from an old and obscure writer; and,

> As *saints* themselves will sometimes be
> Of gifts, that cost them nothing, free,

he bountifully imparted it to the American world, and this same world, so liberally *"free"* to give and so thoroughly "enlightened" to discern, discovered that he was a philosopher, who *could beat up a bed,* and walk about in his shirt, and stand at the window without catching cold, and then fall a sleep, and snore till morning. The proof of plagiarism may be found in AUBREY, a writer nearly obsolete. He published "Miscellanies," which, like the Noctes of Atticæ of Aulus Gellius, are quoted frequently by the learned, more for the quaint and curious than for the true and useful. He is speaking, in his loose and rambling way, of Dr. HARVEY, the celebrated discoverer of the circulation of the blood. "He was very hotheaded, and his thoughts, working much, would oft times keep him from sleeping. His way was to rise out of his bed, and walk about his chamber, in his shirt, till he began to have a horror or shivering, and then return to bed, and sleep very comfortably." Here is the grand discovery, described in the words of an old, weak, and credulous writer, and what is curious, Franklin's boasted essay is almost a literal transcript of Aubrey's anecdote.

It is proposed to devote some future speculations to the subject of Dr. FRANKLIN. Something shall be said of his stile, his economics, politics, philosophy, &c. As his stile has been compared to Addison's, as his electricity is boasted of as his sole invention, as his strings of proverbs have been called wit, and his beggarly maxims, humour, it is time to have these things diligently scrutinized. The inquiry shall be fairly, but faithfully pursued. From a diligent review of his character, conduct, and writings, the author of this article has acquired the right to affirm, that this pseudo philosopher has been a mischief to his country. He was the founder of that Grubstreet sect, who have professedly attempted to degrade literature to the level of vulgar capacities, and debase the polished and current language of books, by the vile alloy of provincial idioms, and colloquial barbarism, the shame of grammar, and akin to any language, rather than English. He was one of our first jacobins, the first to lay his head in the lap of French harlotry; and prostrate the Christianity and honour of his country to the deism and democracies of Paris. Above all he was the author of that pitiful system of Economics, the adoption of which has degraded our national character. Far, very far, be it from the writer of this article, to attempt to vilify that clear sighted prudence, which at once discerns the remotest possibility of penury, and wisely guards itself against the evil. But there is a low and scoundrel appetite for small sums, acquired by base and pitiful means; and, whoever planted or cherished it, is worthy of no better title than the foul disgrace of the country.

Of economy there are two kinds, the liberal and the sordid. The first is perfectly consistent with the habits and generosity of a gentleman and a cavalier; it legitimates every expense, and is the lord high treasurer of every real delight, and the natural and necessary ally of tranquility, honour, and independence. I believe this species of economy was well understood by many of the *ancient gentlemen* of France, and that it is at home among the high minded Castilians, the munificent, punctual, upright and fair dealing merchants of England, and many of the high and honourable among our own countrymen. Whether Dr. Franklin, his associates, or his *disciples* understood, or practised this last species of economy is not a question, among men of "long views," of *"prisca* fides," [2] and of habitual liberality.

FRENEAU'S POEMS [3]

There is nothing with which the inhabitants of the United States have been so much reproached, as the little encouragement given by them to the Belles Lettres. No traveller, or Journalist, can mention us without making this charge; and even they who kindly endeavour to apologize for our defects, for the most part find our excuse in a poverty of genius, or negation of intellect with which nature has cursed our unhappy land; and for which, they think, as her operations were beyond our control, we should rather be excused than condemned.

---

[2] "Ancient faith."
[3] Text: Philadelphia *Port Folio,* October, 1807.

If foreigners, however, would take the trouble to view the scenes which we present to their observation, they could not avoid seeing, at a glance, why the works of fancy or imagination are less attended to than the crudest political theories, or the dryest details of mercantile calculation.

In this country, though, perhaps, a moderate competency is more general than in any other part of the world, large fortunes are rare, and the youth released from college, immediately applies himself to some business or profession, to which he finds it necessary to devote an assiduous attention in order to obtain a proper rank in society; and thus a period of life is passed in close application to business, in which, otherwise, a taste for polite literature would have been either formed or fixed; and the lustre of that eye is extinguished, which else, perhaps, had rolled "in a fine frenzy" of poetick inspiration. Youthful leisure, which *alat formetque poetam,* is almost unknown to us. How many of the English poets have felt—I might, indeed, ask, how few have not felt the *res augusta domi?* [4] And when the poverty of their bards is so common as even to be proverbial, in a nation, the birthright of whose numerous nobility and gentry it should be to foster the Muses; shall we be reproached if, as fortune here is within the reach of every man of talents, he forsake the barren steeps of Parnassus for the rich lowlands of domestick comfort and independence? In popular governments, eloquence has justly been called the road to wealth and power, and our foes themselves will not deny that in the United States it is a well beaten one, and that some of our oratours might safely challenge a comparison with the most exalted names which Europe could oppose to them. The literature encouraged by us is solid and useful, and although it may not have the fragrance of the flower-garden, it assuredly has the fruitfulness of the harvest field.

Among the few in this country who have wandered from "the main road of business" to stray in the paths of poesy, is PHILIP FRENEAU, who, as I have been informed, was born in New-Jersey,

---

[4] "Nourishes and moulds poets."

educated at Princeton College, and, with a singular versatility of character, has been alternately a commander of a ship, and an editor of a newspaper. A volume of this gentleman's poems, "printed at the press of the authour," is now before me, and as I think it much deserving of attention, I shall devote some pages to an examination of it.

The poet, as well as the oratour, is to be encouraged in his race *clamore plausuque;* our authour, however, if we may judge from the following lines, appears to have anticipated very little of either: [EDITOR'S NOTE: Here follow 28 lines from "To an Author" (*q.v.*)].

Freneau's habits of life lead to an acquaintance with Nature, and he did not pass by her with a regardless eye. The measures of his poetry, like the subjects of his *Muse,* are various and desultory. The following lines, on an Indian burying-ground, are extremely beautiful: the two last stanzas are in the sweetest style of Collins: [EDITOR'S NOTE: "The Indian Burying Ground" (*q.v.*)].

Many a volume has been written on the comparative advantages of the civilized and savage life; and the expansion of intellect and personal comforts of the one have been opposed by the few wants, and proud feeling of independence of the other.

"What happier natures shrink from with affright,
The hard inhabitant contends is right."

It is a difficult subject to give an opinion on, for to do so impartially, it would be necessary that we should add the mental improvement of the one to the hardihood of body of the other. Sitting in our study, surrounded by books, and fenced from the least inclemency of air, we shudder at the thoughts of the difficulties to which the life of the savage is exposed; while he, whose body is hardened almost beyond the sensation of pain, would view with sovereign contempt a man employing his life in turning over page after page, or scrawling black marks on paper. Notwithstanding all that has been said in favour of the civilized state, it is very certain that the Indians who have been educated at our seminaries of learning, have sighed for their former mode of life, and on returning to their tribes, immediately assumed their old habits. The following little poem very beautifully describes what may be supposed to have been the feelings of an Indian lad, who, separated from his companions, had been some time immured in a New-England College.

THE INDIAN STUDENT

From Susquehanna's western springs,
    Where savage tribes pursue their game,
His blanket tied with yellow strings,
    A native of the forest came.

Not long before, a wandering priest
    Exprest his wish, with visage sad;
"Ah why," he cried, "in Satan's waste,
    "Ah why detain so fine a lad?

"In *Yankee land* there stands a town,
    "*Where learning may be purchased low:*
"Exchange his blanket for a gown,
    "And let the lad to college go."

From long debate the council rose,
    And viewing Shallum's tricks with joy,
To *Harvard Hall,* o'er wastes of snows,
    They sent the copper-coloured boy.

One generous chief a bow supplied,
    This gave a sheaf, and that a skin;
The feathers, in vermillion dy'd,
    Himself did from a turkey win.

Thus dress'd so gay, he took his way
    O'er barren hills, alone, alone!

His guide a star, he wander'd far,
  His pillow ev'ry night a stone.

At last he came, with foot so lame,
  Where learned men talk heathen Greek,
And Hebrew lore is gabbled o'er,
  To please the Muses, twice a week.

Awhile he writ, awhile he read,
  Awhile he conn'd their grammar rules—
An Indian savage so well bred,
  Great credit promis'd to the schools.

Some thought he would in *law* excel,
  Some said in *physick* he would shine;
And one, who knew him passing well,
  Beheld, in him, a sound divine.

But those of more discerning eye,
  Even then could other prospects show,
And saw him lay his *Virgil* by
  To wander with his dearer *bow*.

The tedious hours of study spent,
  The heavy-moulded lecture done,
He to the woods a hunting went,
  Through lonely wastes he'd walk, he'd run.

No mystick wonders fir'd his mind;
  He sought to gain no learn'd degree,
But only sense enough to find
  The squirrel in the hollow tree.

The shady bank, the purling stream,
  The woody wild his heart possess'd;

The dewy lawn his morning dream
  In Fancy's gayest colours dress'd.

"And why (he cry'd) did I forsake
  "My native woods for gloomy walls!
"The silver brook, the limpid lake,
  "For musty books and college halls!

"A little could my wants supply:
  "Can wealth and honour give me more?
"Or will the sylvan god deny
  "The humble treat he gave before?

"Let seraphs gain the bright abode,
  "And Heaven's sublimest mansions see;
"I only bow to NATURE's GOD,
  "The land of shades will do for me.

"These dreadful secrets of the sky
  "Alarm my soul with chilling fear—
"Do planets in their orbits fly?
  "And is the earth, indeed, a sphere?

"Let planets still their *course* pursue,
  "And comets to the CENTRE run;
"In him my faithful friend I view,
  "The image of my God—the SUN.

"Where Nature's ancient forests grow,
  "And mingled laurel never fades,
"My heart is fix'd;—and I must go
  "To die among my native shades."

He spoke, and to the western springs,
  (His gown discharg'd, his money spent,

> His blanket tied with yellow strings)
> The native of the forest went.

Freneau very seldom attuned his lyre to love, and in his works we find none of those "fabled tortures, quaint and tame," so common in the writings of the amatory poets. The following stanzas conclude an address, in a seaman's phrase, to a "scornful lady;" and although the threat of Time punishing the fair one for her cruelty is very common, yet the introduction of this personage in the last line is certainly very uncommon:

> Ah, Celia, what a strange mistake,
>   To ruin thus for ruin's sake;
> Thus to delude us, in distress,
>   And quit the prize you should possess.
>
> Years may advance with silent pace,
>   And rob that form of ev'ry grace;
> And all your conquests be repaid
>   By—Teague O'Murphy, and his spade.

In many passages he evinces a capacity for the pathetick; but in general passes rapidly to other sensations. The following lines are not unlike some written by Cowper on seeing a favourite grove of trees cut down:

> Inspir'd at the sound, while the *name* she repeats,
> Wild fancy conveys me to Hudson's retreats—
> At sweet recollection of juvenile dreams,
> In the groves and the forests that skirted his streams!
> How often with rapture those streams were survey'd,
> When, sick of city, I flew to the shade!
> How often the bard and the peasant shall mourn
> Ere those groves shall revive, and those shades shall return!

And again, with a happy allusion to one of the emblems of Time:

> But days such as these were too happy to last;
> The *sand of felicity settled too fast!*

The lines to his dog are an affectionate recollection of that faithful animal, and all who read them will remember the days of their boyhood.

> How oft in the year shall I visit your grave,
> Amid the lone forest that shadows the wave!
> How often lament, when the day's at its close,
> That a mile from my cot is your place of repose!
>
> Ah here (I will say) in this path he has run;
> And there stands a tree where a squirrel he won;
> And here, in this spot where the willow trees grow,
> He dragg'd out a rabbit that lurk'd in the snow.

Speaking of the battle of Eutaw springs, his language is both pathetick and forcible, and the epitaph on those who were slain in the action, is, at once, beautifully simple and comprehensive:

> Ah! had our friends that led the fray
> Surviv'd the ruins of that day,
> We should not mix our joy with pain,
> Nor, sympathizing, now complain.
>
> Strange! that of those who nobly dare
> Death always claims so large a share!
> That those of virtues most refin'd,
> Are soonest to the grave consign'd!
>
> But fame is theirs—and future days
> On pillar'd brass shall tell their praise;
> Shall tell—when cold neglect is dead—
> *"These"* for their country fought and bled."

JOSEPH DENNIE

Freneau has given several translations and imitations from the Latin and French. The conclusion of the sixteenth ode of the second book of Horace,

> On me a poor and small domain,
> With something of a poet's vein,
> Kind fate bestow'd—*and share of pride*
> *To spurn a scoundrel from my side,*

is extremely indignant, and expresses the very sensations of the Prince of lyrick poets:

> ———Mihi parva rura, et
> Spiritum Graiæ tenuem camenæ
> Parca non mendax dedit, et malignum
>   Spernere vulgus.

The address to a Jug of Rum is very much in the manner of Swift, who with all his power of condensing his expression, could not afford us a better example of the multum in parvo than the following:

> Here only by a cork control'd,
> And slender walls of earthen mould,
> In all the pomp of death repose
> The seeds of many a bloody nose;
> The chattering tongue, the horrid oath,
> The fist for fighting nothing loth,
> The passion which no words can tame,
> That bursts, like sulphur, into flame;
> The nose carbuncled, glowing red,
> The bloated eye, the broken head;
> The true that bears the deadly fruit
> Of murder, maiming, and dispute;
> Assault that Innocence assails,

The images of gloomy jails,
The giddy thought, on mischief bent,
The midnight hour in riot spent:
All these within this jug appear,
And Jack, the hangman, in the rear!

Falconer, Captain Thompson, and Freneau have shown that the Muses may be induced to accommodate themselves to the boisterous habits of a sailor's life, and sing as melodiously on board a ship, as on Parnassus. Æschylus was, at the same time, a poet and a sailor. Homer, Virgil, Appolonius Rhodius, and others, with the maritime adventures of their respective heroes, describe the vessels on board of which they were embarked: these, however, with little rigging, and of simple structure required no great art to introduce, with a description of all their parts, into poetry, in comparison with the complex machinery of modern navigation. When, a soldier was at once, by a mandate of his officer, transformed into a sailor, and a general, upon stepping on board a galley, became an admiral: now, years are necessary to acquire a requisite knowledge of the science of directing a ship, as well as of the language spoken on board it, which is perfectly unintelligible to a landsman; and which some of our best writers have in vain endeavoured to use. Shakspeare's "Lay her a-hold!" and Dryden's "Veer starboard sea and land," would be understood neither at sea nor on shore. Falconer first wrote a nautical poem in nautical language, and his work may justly be termed classical in a new department of poetry.

Sannazarius, stepping out of the beaten path of pastoral, wrote his Piscatory Idylls; but this required little invention, and although they talked of mullets, tunnies, oysters, &c. the language and sentiments of his fishermen, and the language and sentiments of the shepherds of the pastoral bards, who have all servilely imitated each other in committing so great an outrage on nature, as to cause rivers to weep and rocks to groan whenever some country wench was supposed to be in an ill humour.

The following lines describe the building, sailing, and capture of the Aurora with great beauty. [EDITOR'S NOTE: Here follow 172 lines of a long narrative poem describing a sea-fight.]

Too many criticks judge of the excellence of a poet by the length of his pieces. Freneau, measured by this scale, would not rank high; for he never detains his reader long on one subject. He, in too many places, shows a disrespect for the pulpit, which deserves to be highly censured; but although we touch, with much reverence, in whatever is connected with that guardian of our happiness both here and hereafter, we cannot avoid smiling at the odd association in the stanzas on the crew of a certain vessel several of whom happened to be of the same name with celebrated clergymen.

> In life's unsettled, odd career
> What changes every day appear
>   To please, or plague the eye;
> A goodly brotherhood of priests
> Are here transformed to swearing beasts
>   That heaven and hell defy.
>
> Here Bonner, bruised with many a knock,
> Has chang'd his surplice for a frock;
>   Old Erskine swabs the decks:
> And Watts, that once such pleasure took
> In writing hymns, here turn'd a cook,
>   No more shall sinners vex.
>
> Here Burnet, Tillotson, and Blair,
> With Jemmy Hervey, curse and swear;
>   Here Cudworth mixes grog;
> Pearson the crew to dinner hails,
> A graceless Serlock trims the sails,
>   And Bunyan heaves the log.

Our authour has, in a very desultory manner, rambled from subject to subject, but satire appears to be his favourite one. Here, however, we cannot, in general, praise him. He is far from being elegant in the choice of his language, which is, for the most part, downright railing: and this we do not think sufficiently justified by the examples of the ancient satyrists, the vulgarity of whose expressions affords no favourable ideas of their own manners. His subjects also, which are local, have lost much of their interest; and we are unwilling to recall the recollection of feuds long past. In the phrase of the aborigines, the tomahawk is buried, and we wish not to dig it up. It is the more to be regretted, that Freneau wasted so much of his time in this manner, as he has convinced us that he is capable of better things. As a proof of that kind of satire, which can

"Tickle, while it gently probes the wound."

we select the following lines from The Life of Hugh Gaine, which we are disposed to mention with much encomium. [EDITOR'S NOTE: Here follows 155 lines of anti-Tory satire.]

Having thus rambled through Freneau's Poems, with a spirit of no illiberal criticism, it may not be amiss to mention our regret at the authour, in several places giving us cause to censure him for principles, which in this country, are rarely in union with genius. Providence, while she permits the pest of Jacobinism to range at large among us, has kindly shown her in her foulest colours; she displays no elegance of form, no fascination of manners, no persuasion of eloquence, but rude and deformed, is equally disgusting to the spirit of philosophy and to the eye of taste.

We have mentioned some causes of the little encouragement given to our bards; but we confidently look forward to a time not distant, when we may say, in the words of Cicero: *Rudem enin esse omnino in nostris poetis, aut inertissimæ signitiæ est, aut fastidii delicatissimi. Mihi quidem nulli satis eruditi videntur, quibus nostra ignota sunt.*[5]

---

[5] "To be completely ignorant of our own poets is typical either of the most inert sloth or of the most exquisite overfastidiousness. Indeed, to me no one seems sufficiently learned to whom our own writings are unknown."

Should another edition of these poems be published, we recommend, that the 455 closely printed pages of the present one be diminished to less than half that number, by the omission of a large part of its contents, and give the following as a table of all that is worthy of preservation.

The Deserted Farm-House
The New-England Sabbath-day-Chace
The Wish of Diogenes
Epitaph on a man killed by a pretented Physician
Humanity and Ingratitude
The Desolate Academy
Advice to a Friend
The Vernal Ague
The Market Girl
The Jug of Rum
The Indian Student
The Oratour of the Woods
On the Sleep of Plants
The Prisoner
Quintilian to Lycidas
The Indian Burying-ground
The Almanack-maker
The Scornful Lady
The Vanity of Human Existence
The Drunkard's Apology
On Tobacco
The Bay Islet
The Man of Ninety
Santa Cruz
On the Death of Captain Biddle, of the Randolph
The Seaman's Invitation
On several of the crew of a certain Ship of War, that happened to have a name similar to those of celebrated foreign Clergymen.
The British Prison Ship as far as we have quoted

Amanda's Complaint
Stanzas addressed to an Old Man
On the Ruins of a Country Inn
The Political Balance, or the fate of Britain and America compared, 1782
Sir Henry Clinton's Invitation to the Refugees
On General Arnold's Departure from America
Prophecy of the Indian King, Tammany
Political Biography; or the life of H. Gaine
On the Departure of the British forces from Charleston
On General Washington's retirement from publick life, after having, with a patriotick army, established the Independence of The United States of America
The Triumphal Arch, occasioned by rejoicings in Philadelphia on the acknowledgment of the National Independence
Pewter-Platter Alley, in Philadelphia
The Hurricane
On the New-Year's Festival
On the Vicissitudes of Things
Devastations in a Bookseller's Library
Sketches of North American History
To Lydia, a young Quaker Lady
Log-town Tavern
Hatteras
The Newsmonger
The Wintry Prospect
The Invalid
The Drunken Soldier
Carribeana
An Authour, on Authourship
Slender's Journey
The Wanderer
St. Catherine's Island
Marcella in a consumption
Addressed to a Deceased Dog
To the Memory of a Lady

To a Dog, occasioned, &c.
To Clarissa, a handsome shop-keeper
To Cynthia
Balloons
Federal-Hall
Neversink, or the Heights near Sandy-Hook
To Zoilus, a severe Critick
To Cracovius Putridus
To My Lord Snake, a title hunter
To Misfortune
Epistle supposed to be written by Dr. Franklin, deceased, in answer to certain silly effusions of poetical panegyrists
The COUNTRY PRINTER
To Mr. Churchman, on the failure of his Petition, &c.
The Pyramid of the Fifteen American States

Ibsen, THREE PLAYS: Ghosts, Enemy of the People, Wild Duck 4
Irving, Washington, SELECTED PROSE 41
James, Henry, THE AMBASSADORS 104
James, Henry, THE AMERICAN 16
James, Henry, SELECTED SHORT STORIES 31
Johnson, Samuel, RASSELAS, POEMS, & SELECTED PROSE 57
Keats, John, SELECTED POETRY AND LETTERS 50
Lincoln, Abraham, SELECTED SPEECHES, MESSAGES, AND LETTERS 82
LITERATURE OF THE EARLY REPUBLIC 44
London, Jack, MARTIN EDEN 80
MASTERPIECES OF THE SPANISH GOLDEN AGE 93
Melville, Herman, MOBY DICK 6
Melville, Herman, SELECTED TALES AND POEMS 36
Milton, John, PARADISE LOST AND SELECTED POETRY AND PROSE 35
MODERN AMERICAN LITERATURE 53
Newman, John Henry, THE IDEA OF A UNIVERSITY 102
Norris, Frank, MC TEAGUE 40
Parkman, Francis, THE DISCOVERY OF THE GREAT WEST: LA SALLE 77
PLUTARCH—EIGHT GREAT LIVES 105
Poe, Edgar Allan, SELECTED PROSE AND POETRY, Rev. 42
POETRY OF THE NEW ENGLAND RENAISSANCE, 1790–1890 38
Pope, Alexander, SELECTED POETRY AND PROSE 46
THE RINEHART BOOK OF SHORT STORIES 59
THE RINEHART BOOK OF VERSE 58
Robinson, E. A., SEL. EARLY POEMS AND LETTERS 107
Roosevelt, F. D., SPEECHES, MESSAGES, PRESS CONFERENCES, & LETTERS 83
Scott, Sir Walter, THE HEART OF MIDLOTHIAN 14
SELECTED AMERICAN PROSE, 1841–1900 94
SELECTIONS FROM GREEK AND ROMAN HISTORIANS 88
Shakespeare, FIVE PLAYS: Hamlet; King Lear; Henry IV, Part I; Much Ado about Nothing; The Tempest 51
Shakespeare, AS YOU LIKE IT, JULIUS CAESAR, MACBETH 91
Shakespeare, TWELFTH NIGHT, OTHELLO 92
Shaw, Bernard, SELECTED PLAYS AND OTHER WRITINGS 81
Shelley, Percy Bysshe, SELECTED POETRY AND PROSE 49
SIR GAWAIN AND THE GREEN KNIGHT 97
Smollett, Tobias, HUMPHRY CLINKER 48
SOUTHERN STORIES 106
Spenser, Edmund, SELECTED POETRY 73
Sterne, Laurence, TRISTRAM SHANDY 37
Stevenson, Robert Louis, MASTER OF BALLANTRAE 67
Swift, Jonathan, GULLIVER'S TRAVELS 10
Swift, Jonathan, SELECTED PROSE AND POETRY 78
Tennyson, Alfred, SELECTED POETRY 69
Thackeray, William Makepeace, VANITY FAIR 76
Thoreau, Henry David, WALDEN, ON THE DUTY OF CIVIL DISOBEDIENCE 8
Trollope, Anthony, BARCHESTER TOWERS 21
Turgenev, Ivan, FATHERS AND CHILDREN 17
Twain, Mark, THE ADVENTURES OF HUCKLEBERRY FINN 11
Twain, Mark, ROUGHING IT 61
Vergil, THE AENEID 63
VICTORIAN POETRY: Clough to Kipling 96
Whitman, Walt, LEAVES OF GRASS AND SELECTED PROSE 28
Wordsworth, THE PRELUDE, SEL'D SONNETS & MINOR POEMS, Rev. & Enl. 3

Addison and Steele, SEL. FROM THE TATLER & THE SPECTATOR 87
AMERICAN THOUGHT: CIVIL WAR TO WORLD WAR I 70
ANTHOLOGY OF ENGLISH DRAMA BEFORE SHAKESPEARE 45
ANTHOLOGY OF GREEK DRAMA: FIRST SERIES 29
ANTHOLOGY OF GREEK DRAMA: SECOND SERIES 68
ANTHOLOGY OF ROMAN DRAMA 101
Arnold, Matthew, SELECTED POETRY AND PROSE 62
Austen, Jane, PRIDE AND PREJUDICE 22
Balzac, Honoré de, PÈRE GORIOT 18
Benét, S. V., SELECTED POETRY & PROSE 100
THE BIBLE: SEL. FROM OLD & NEW TESTAMENTS 56
Brontë, Charlotte, JANE EYRE 24
Brontë, Emily, WUTHERING HEIGHTS 23
Browning, Robert, SELECTED POETRY 71
Bunyan, John, THE PILGRIM'S PROGRESS 27
Burke, Edmund, REFLECTIONS ON THE REVOLUTION IN FRANCE 84
Butler, Samuel, THE WAY OF ALL FLESH 7
Byron, George Gordon, Lord, SELECTED POETRY AND LETTERS 54
Chaucer, Geoffrey, THE CANTERBURY TALES 65
Coleridge, Samuel Taylor, SELECTED POETRY AND PROSE 55
COLONIAL AMERICAN WRITING 43
Conrad, Joseph, LORD JIM 85
Cooper, James Fenimore, THE PIONEERS 99
Cooper, James Fenimore, THE PRAIRIE 26
Crane, Stephen, RED BADGE OF COURAGE, SEL'D PROSE & POETRY 47
Dante, THE DIVINE COMEDY 72
Defoe, Daniel, MOLL FLANDERS 25
De Forest, John William, MISS RAVENEL'S CONVERSION 74
Dickens, Charles, GREAT EXPECTATIONS 20
Dickens, Charles, HARD TIMES 95
Dreiser, Theodore, SISTER CARRIE 86
Dryden, John, SELECTED WORKS 60
Eliot, George, ADAM BEDE 32
ELIZABETHAN FICTION 64
Emerson, Ralph Waldo, SELECTED PROSE AND POETRY 30
Fielding, Henry, JOSEPH ANDREWS 15
FIFTEEN MODERN AMERICAN POETS 79
Flaubert, Gustav, MADAME BOVARY 2
FOUR MODERN PLAYS: Ibsen, Shaw, O'Neill, Miller 90
Franklin, Benjamin, AUTOBIOGRAPHY AND SELECTED WRITINGS 12
Garland, Hamlin, MAIN-TRAVELLED ROADS 66
Godwin, William, CALEB WILLIAMS 103
Goethe, Johann Wolfgang von, FAUST: PART I 75
Goethe, SORROWS OF YOUNG WERTHER, NEW MELUSINA, NOVELLE 13
Gogol, Nikolai, DEAD SOULS 5
GREAT ENGLISH AND AMERICAN ESSAYS 34
Hardy, Thomas, FAR FROM THE MADDING CROWD 98
Hardy, Thomas, THE MAYOR OF CASTERBRIDGE 9
Hardy, Thomas, THE RETURN OF THE NATIVE 39
Hauptmann, THREE PLAYS: The Weavers, Hannele, The Beaver Coat 52
Hawthorne, Nathaniel, THE HOUSE OF THE SEVEN GABLES 89
Hawthorne, Nathaniel, THE SCARLET LETTER 1
Hawthorne, Nathaniel, SELECTED TALES AND SKETCHES 33
Howells, William Dean, THE RISE OF SILAS LAPHAM 19

Rinehart Editions